WOMANIST INTERPRETATIONS
OF THE BIBLE

SEMEIA STUDIES

Steed V. Davidson, General Editor

Editorial Board:
Pablo R. Andiñach
Fiona Black
Denise K. Buell
Gay L. Byron
Masiiwa Ragies Gunda
Monica Jyotsna Melanchthon
Yak-Hwee Tan

Number 85

WOMANIST INTERPRETATIONS OF THE BIBLE

Expanding the Discourse

Edited by
Gay L. Byron and Vanessa Lovelace

 **PRESS**

Atlanta

Copyright © 2016 by SBL Press

All rights reserved. No part of this work may be reproduced or transmitted in any form or by any means, electronic or mechanical, including photocopying and recording, or by means of any information storage or retrieval system, except as may be expressly permitted by the 1976 Copyright Act or in writing from the publisher. Requests for permission should be addressed in writing to the Rights and Permissions Office, SBL Press, 825 Houston Mill Road, Atlanta, GA 30329 USA.

Library of Congress Cataloging-in-Publication Data

Names: Byron, Gay L., editor. | Lovelace, Vanessa, editor.
Title: Womanist interpretations of the Bible : expanding the discourse / edited by Gay L. Byron and Vanessa Lovelace.
Description: Atlanta : SBL Press, [2016] | Series: Semeia studies ; number 85 | Includes bibliographical references and index.
Identifiers: LCCN 2016040615 (print) | LCCN 2016040794 (ebook) | ISBN 9781628371529 (pbk. : alk. paper) | ISBN 9780884141853 (hardcover) | ISBN 9780884141846 (ebook)
Subjects: LCSH: Bible—Feminist criticism.
Classification: LCC BS521.4 .W66 2016 (print) | LCC BS521.4 (ebook) | DDC 220.6082—dc23
LC record available at https://lccn.loc.gov/2016040615

Printed on acid-free paper.

Contents

Acknowledgments ix
Abbreviations xi

Introduction: Methods and the Making of Womanist Biblical
    Hermeneutics
    Gay L. Byron and Vanessa Lovelace... 1

Part 1: Gender and Sexuality

The Invisible Women: Numbers 30 and the Politics of Singleness
    in Africana Communities
    Stacy Davis 21

A Womanist Midrash of Delilah: Don't Hate the Playa Hate the Game
    Wil Gafney 49

The Song of Songs: Redeeming Gender Constructions in the Age
    of AIDS
    Cheryl B. Anderson 73

Part 2: Agency and Advocacy

Race, Gender, and the Politics of "Sass": Reading Mark 7:24–30
    through a Womanist Lens of Intersectionality and
    Inter(con)textuality
    Mitzi J. Smith 95

Antitypes, Stereotypes, and Antetypes: Jezebel, the Sun Woman,
    and Contemporary Black Women
    Love L. Sechrest...113

One More Time with Assata on My Mind: A Womanist Rereading
of the Escape to Egypt (Matt 2:13–23) in Dialogue with an
African American Woman Fugitive Narrative
Shively T. J. Smith 139

"Battered Love": Exposing Abuse in the Book of Job
Marlene Underwood 165

Part 3: Foregrounding Women on the Margins

Black Collectors and Keepers of Tradition: Resources for a Womanist
Biblical Ethic of (Re)Interpretation
Gay L. Byron 187

Flowing from Breast to Breast: An Examination of Dis/placed
Motherhood in African American and Indian Wet Nurses
Sharon Jacob and Jennifer T. Kaalund..209

"We Don't Give Birth to Thugs": Family Values, Respectability
Politics, and Jephthah's Mother
Vanessa Lovelace 239

Part 4: Illuminating Biblical Children/Childhood

Outrageous, Audacious, Courageous, Willful: Reading the
Enslaved Girl of Acts 12
Margaret Aymer..265

"Nobody's Free until Everybody's Free": Exploring Gender and
Class Injustice in a Story about Children (Luke 18:15–17)
Bridgett A. Green 291

"I Will Make Boys Their Princes": A Womanist Reading of
Children in the Book of Isaiah
Valerie Bridgeman...311

Part 5: In Response

Miracles and Gifts: A Womanist Reading of John 14:12–14 and
Ephesians 4:11–16
    Layli Maparyan...331

Looking Forward from the Horizon: A Response in Africana
Sisterhood and Solidarity
    Althea Spencer-Miller..339

Challenged and Changed
    Katharine Doob Sakenfeld 349

The Road We Are Traveling
    Emilie M. Townes..359

Contributors...369
Ancient Sources Index...375
Subject Index...384

Acknowledgments

We are honored that so many of our colleagues responded enthusiastically to our invitation to contribute to this volume. For their commitment and willingness to press the boundaries of womanist hermeneutics, we are grateful. We are also honored that this volume includes responses by some of the leading scholars who have embraced womanist theory and praxis and who value the spirit of collaboration this volume represents.

We stand on the shoulders of womanist theologians, ethicists, religious scholars, cultural critics, and biblical interpreters who dared to read their way through the struggle and to offer rich trajectories and paths for our own explorations. Indeed, "if it wasn't for the(se) women," to borrow a phrase from Cheryl Townsend Gilkes, this volume would have never emerged from its dark womb of knowing. In particular we are grateful for Renita J. Weems and Clarice J. Martin, who have inspired our efforts and much of the scholarship reflected in this volume and continue to remind us that we are "just a sister away." We are also grateful for the early support of Cheryl Kirk-Duggan and Bridgett Green, who embraced the idea of a womanist volume when we first conceived of it. Cheryl suggested an outline and Bridgett offered to contact potential editors, including Gay Byron who was serving on the Semeia Studies editorial board. Although the initial outline did not come to fruition, we are appreciative of Cheryl's support and encouragement in pursuing this project.

We thank the Semeia Studies Editorial Board for their acceptance of these essays for publication and the very constructive feedback offered during the early phase of conceptualizing the volume. In particular, general editor Gerald West, offered great encouragement and sound advice. Steed Davidson, who succeeded Gerald as general editor, offered timely and keen editorial support as the volume progressed toward publication. We also express our gratitude to the entire staff of SBL Press, especially Bob Buller and Nicole Tilford, for their expert assistance throughout the publication process. In addition, we acknowledge Barbara Fears,

Jonathan McPhee, and Rickdrieka Sanders for their assistance with this volume.

We are grateful for our families and other networks of support—especially Wilfred Bentley, patient spouse to Vanessa, who endured our many conference calls. Finally, we dedicate this volume to our children: Christopher, Shauna, Khalil, Lloyd, and PJ—who constantly remind us why such a volume on expanding the discourse about womanist biblical interpretation is not an optional academic exercise but a necessary life-affirming reflection of our commitment to wholeness of our entire community and peace throughout the world.

Gay L. Byron, Washington, DC
Vanessa Lovelace, Atlanta, GA

Abbreviations

Primary Sources

Ag. Ap.	Josephus, *Against Apion*
Ant.	Josephus, *Jewish Antiquities*
b.	Bablyonian Talmud
B. Bat.	Baba Batra
Ber.	Berakhot
B.J.	Josephus, *Bellum judaicum*
Cels.	Origen, *Contra Celsum*
Embassy	Philo, *On the Embassy to Gaius*
Ep. Tra.	Pliny the Younger, *Epistulae ad Trajanum*
'Erub.	Eruvin
Flaccus	Philo, *Against Flaccus*
Gen. Rab.	Genesis Rabbah
Geogr.	Strabo, *Geography*
Gos. Mary	Gospel of Mary
Gub. Dei	Salvian, *The Governance of God*
Hist.	Rufinus, *Eusebii Historia ecclesiastica a Rufino translata et continuata*
Hist.	Rufinus, *Eusebii Historia ecclesiastica a Rufino translata et continuata*; Tacitus, *Historiae*
Hist. rom.	Dio Cassius, *Historiae romanae*
Let. Aris.	Letter of Aristeas
Leuc. Clit.	Achilles Tatius, *Leucippe et Clitophon*
Ling.	Varro, *De lingua latina*
Naz.	Nazir
Num. Rab.	Numbers Rabbah
Physiogn.	Pseudo-Aristotle, *Physiognomonica*
Poet.	Aristotle, *Poetics*
Pol.	Aristotle, *Politics*

Šabb.	Shabbat
Sanh.	Sanhedrin
Sat.	Juvenal, *Satires*

Secondary Resources

AARCCS	American Academy of Religion Cultural Criticism Series
AB	Anchor Bible
AIL	Ancient Israel and Its Literature
AJSR	*Association for Jewish Studies Review*
ASOR	American Schools of Oriental Research
ASV	American Standard Version
ATLA	American Theological Library Association
BAGD	Bauer, Walter, William F. Arndt, F. Wilbur Gingrich, and Frederick W. Danker. *Greek-English Lexicon of the New Testament and Other Early Christian Literature*. 2nd ed. Chicago: University of Chicago Press, 1979.
BASOR	*Bulletin of the American Schools of Oriental Research*
BDAG	Danker, Frederick W., Walter Bauer, William F. Arndt, and F. Wilbur Gingrich. *Greek-English Lexicon of the New Testament and Other Early Christian Literature*. 3rd ed. Chicago: University of Chicago Press, 2000.
BDB	Brown, Francis, S. R. Driver, and Charles A. Briggs. *A Hebrew and English Lexicon of the Old Testament*. Peabody, MA: Hendrickson, 1996.
BECNT	Baker Exegetical Commentary on the New Testament
BibInt	*Biblical Interpretation*
BJS	Brown Judaic Studies
BSac	*Bibliotheca Sacra*
CBQ	*Catholic Biblical Quarterly*
CDC	Centers for Disease Control
CET	Common English Translation
CJ	*The Classical Journal*
CurTM	*Currents in Theology and Mission*
DBI	*Dictionary of Biblical Interpretation*. Edited by John Hays. 2 vols. Nashville: Abingdon, 1999.
EDB	*Eerdmans Dictionary of the Bible*. Edited by David Noel Freedman. Grand Rapids: Eerdmans, 2000.
ExpTim	*Expository Times*

FCB	Feminist Companion to the Bible
FCNTECW	Feminist Companion to the New Testament and Early Christian Writings
GR	*Greece and Rome*
GSS	General Social Survey
HALOT	Koehler, Ludwig, and Walter Baumgartner. *The Hebrew and Aramaic Lexicon of the Old Testament*. Translated and edited by Mervyn E. J. Richardson. Study ed. 2 vols. Leiden: Brill, 2001.
HAR	*Hebrew Annual Review*
HBM	Hebrew Bible Monographs
Historia	*Historia: Zeitschrift für alte Geschichte*
HMML	Hill Museum and Manuscript Library
HTR	*Harvard Theological Review*
HUSD	Howard University School of Divinity
IBC	Interpretation: A Bible Commentary for Teaching and Preaching
IEJ	*Israel Exploration Journal*
JAH	*Journal of American History*
JAOS	*Journal of the American Oriental Society*
JBL	*Journal of Biblical Literature*
JBQ	*Jewish Bible Quarterly*
JFA	*Journal of Field Archaeology*
JFSR	*Journal of Feminist Studies in Religion*
JITC	*Journal of the Interdenominational Theological Center*
JNE	*The Journal of Negro Education*
JNH	*Journal of Negro History*
JPS	*Tanakh: A New Translation of the Holy Scriptures according to the Traditional Hebrew Text*. Philadelphia: Jewish Publication Society, 1985.
JRA	*Journal of Religion in Africa*
JRS	*Journal of Roman Studies*
JRT	*Journal of Religious Thought*
JSB	*Jewish Study Bible*. Edited by Adele Berlin, Marc Zvi Brettler, and Michael Fishbane. Oxford: Oxford University Press, 2004.
JSOT	*Journal for the Study of the Old Testament*
JSOTSup	Journal for the Study of the Old Testament Supplement Series

JSNT	*Journal for the Study of the New Testament*
JWJ MSS	James Weldon Johnson Manuscripts
KJV	King James Version
LCL	Loeb Classical Library
LXX	Septuagint
MT	Masoretic Text
NA[28]	*Novum Testamentum Graece*, Nestle-Aland, 28th ed.
Neot	*Neotestamentica*
NET	New English Translation
NIB	*The New Interpreter's Bible*. Edited by Leander E. Keck. 12 vols. Nashville: Abingdon, 1994–2004.
NICNT	New International Commentary on the New Testament
NIGTC	New International Greek Testament Commentary
NIV	New International Version
NRSV	New Revised Standard Version
NTL	New Testament Library
NTS	*New Testament Studies*
NWPC	National Women's Political Caucus
OTL	Old Testament Library
PACS	Philo of Alexandria Commentary Series
PEPFAR	President's Emergency Plan for AIDS Relief
PL	Patrologia Latina
PTMS	Princeton Theological Monograph Series
Pneuma	*Pneuma: Journal for the Society of Pentecostal Studies*
SemeiaSt	Semeia Studies
SHBC	Smyth & Helwys Bible Commentary
SNCC	Student Nonviolent Coordinating Committee
SNTSMS	Society for New Testament Studies Monograph Series
SP	Sacra Pagina
Spectrum	*Spectrum: A Journal on Black Men*
SymS	Symposium Series
TTR	*Teaching Theology & Religion*
UNESCO	United Nations Educational, Scientific, and Cultural Organization
VT	*Vetus Testamentum*
WBC	Word Biblical Commentary

Introduction:
Methods and the Making of Womanist Biblical Hermeneutics

Gay L. Byron and Vanessa Lovelace

Womanist Interpretations of the Bible: Expanding the Discourse is a long-awaited collection of original essays that features bold new womanist approaches to biblical hermeneutics. We first conceived of this volume through a series of conversations, which first began at the 2011 Annual Meeting of the Society of Biblical Literature in San Francisco. At that time, Vanessa Lovelace shared with a group of colleagues her desire to publish a volume of womanist interpretations of the Bible to honor the trailblazing scholarship of Renita J. Weems and Clarice Martin. Around the same time, Gay L. Byron was serving on the Semeia Studies editorial board and having conversations with board members and other colleagues about editing a volume showcasing womanist readings of the Bible. Our mutual friend and editor, Bridgett Green, was privy to both of these conversations and connected us together. Once we realized that we shared the same idea and a commitment to womanist biblical scholarship, it seemed natural for the two of us to collaborate and serve as coeditors of this volume.

We both have generated various essays and articles using gender criticism, critical race theory, and other theories and methods dealing with the interlocking oppressions of black women. Though in some cases not explicitly identifying a womanist hermeneutic, we have been greatly influenced by the writings of author, poet, and activist Alice Walker. She is often credited with coining the term *womanist*, which she first used in her essay "Coming Apart" published in the 1979 anthology *Take Back the Night*. In this essay, Walker wrote that a "'womanist' is a feminist, only more common." She elaborated in a footnote:

> "Womanist" encompasses "feminist" as it is defined in Webster's, but also means instinctively pro-woman. It is not in the dictionary at all. Nonetheless, it has a strong root in black women's culture. It comes (to me) from the word "womanish," a word our mothers used to describe, and attempt to inhibit, strong, outrageous or outspoken behavior when we were children: "You're acting womanish!" A labeling that failed, for the most part to keep us from acting "womanish" whenever we could, that is to say, like our mothers themselves, and like other women we admired. (Walker 1979, 100)[1]

Walker refined her description of womanist in her classic four-part poetic definition of the term in the preface to her 1983 book *In Search of Our Mothers' Gardens*:

> 1. From womanish. (Opp. of "girlish," i.e., frivolous, irresponsible, not serious.) A black feminist of color. From the black folk expression of mothers to female children, "You acting womanish," i.e., like a woman. Usually referring to outrageous, audacious, courageous or willful behavior. Wanting to know more and in greater depth than is considered "good" for one. Interested in grown-up doings. Acting grown up. Being grown up. Interchangeable with another black folk expression: 'You trying to be grown.' Responsible. In charge. Serious. 2. *Also:* A woman who loves other women, sexually and/or nonsexually. Appreciates and prefers women's culture, women's emotional flexibility (values tears as natural counterbalance of laughter), and women's strength. Sometimes loves individual men, sexually and/or nonsexually. Committed to survival and wholeness of entire people, male *and* female. Not a separatist, except periodically, for health. Traditionally a universalist, as in: "Mama, why are we brown, pink, and yellow, and our cousins are white, beige, and black?" Ans. "Well, you know the colored race is just like a flower garden, with every color flower represented." Traditionally capable, as in: "Mama, I'm walking to Canada and I'm taking you and a bunch of other slaves with me." Reply: "It wouldn't be the first time." 3. Loves music. Loves dance. Loves the moon. *Loves* the Spirit. Loves love and food and roundness. Loves struggle. *Loves* the Folk. Loves herself. *Regardless.* 4. Womanist is to feminist as purple is to lavender. (Walker 1983, xi)

---

1. Two lesser-known progenitors of the notion and terminology of *womanism*, independent of Walker, are Chikwenye Okonjo Ogunyemi (1985) and Clenora Hudson-Weems (1998). See Layli Phillips 2006.

Shortly after the publication of *In Search of Our Mothers' Gardens*, the term *womanist* began to appear in the discipline of religious studies. A group of black female theological students at Union Theological Seminary in the City of New York studying with Dr. James Cone were the first to begin to express new black liberationist theology that was also inclusive of their particular experiences of sexism and racism in the academy and the church, perpetuated even by their own black male colleagues. The group consisted of doctoral students Jacquelyn Grant and Katie Geneva Cannon and Master of Divinity students Delores Williams and Kelly Brown Douglas. They began to raise critical questions regarding the absence of black women's voices in black and feminist theological discourses. It was their exploration of black women's tridimensional oppression of gender, race, and class that led them to embrace the term womanist to identify their religious thought.

Womanist theological discourse expanded in 1985 when a number of black women members of the American Academy of Religion and the Society of Biblical Literature gathered at the first session of Womanist Approaches to Religion and Society, convened by Cheryl Townsend Gilkes. This was the beginning of womanist theological, ethical, and biblical interpretation in the academy. That same year Cannon (1985) published the formative essay "Black Feminist Consciousness," in which she used the terms *black womanist* and *womanist* to speak of black women's biblical interpretive tradition to confront racism and other forms of oppression. This was followed by Williams's (1987) seminal essay on "Womanist Theology," which identified the sources and methods for this new area of theological inquiry.[2]

Also among this budding group of womanist religious scholars was Martin, who earned her doctorate in New Testament (Christian Scriptures) in 1985 and Weems, who earned her doctorate in Old Testament (Hebrew Bible) in 1989.[3] Weems published the monograph *Just a Sister Away: A*

---

2. We recognize that nineteenth-century black women such as Jarena Lee, Sojourner Truth, and Maria Stewart have a documented history of engaging in biblical interpretation in their social activism. Moreover, contemporary womanist religious scholars such as Grant, Cannon, and Williams use the Bible in their ethical and theological formulations. However, unlike Grant, Cannon, and Williams, the former would not be considered womanists since the term postdates them.

3. It is not evident from their dissertation titles whether Martin and Weems refer to a black woman's or womanist perspective: "The Function of Acts 8:26–40 within the

Womanist Vision of Women's Relationships in the Bible in 1988. Weems combined feminist biblical criticism with African American oral tradition to construct a womanist interpretation of stories of biblical women, such as Sarah and Hagar (Gen 16 and 21) and Mary and Martha (Luke 10), and their relationships with one another. Her other writings include "Reading *Her* Way through the Struggle: African American Women and the Bible" (1991), which addresses the significance of the Bible for African American female readers despite its patriarchy and use in racial and gender oppression, and "Womanist Reflections on Biblical Hermeneutics" (1993), where Weems gives her critique of the shortcomings of historical critical and feminist biblical criticism and offers womanist biblical criticism as an alternative for African American women biblical scholars.[4]

Martin's essays included "Womanist Interpretations of the New Testament: The Quest for Holistic and Inclusive Translation and Interpretation" (1990), where she placed the interpretive interests of women of color in general and black women in particular at the forefront; "The *Haustafeln* (Household Codes) in African American Biblical Interpretation" (1991), which advocated for African American women and men to adopt more liberative biblical traditions in response to the traditionally hierarchical approaches to the enslaved-woman regulation in the *Haustafeln*; and "Biblical Theodicy and Black Women's Spiritual Autobiography" (1993), which appears in *A Troubling in My Soul: Womanist Perspectives on Evil and Suffering*, edited by Emilie Townes (1993).[5] In addition Martin provided the first comprehensive working definition of womanist biblical interpretation, which consists of four tasks:

> 1) the recovery of women's history in the Judeo-Christian tradition by expanding on earlier works and using appropriate methods of recovery, analysis, and reconstruction of the biblical texts and their worlds; 2) reclamation of neglected histories and stories of the presence and func-

---

Narrative Structure of the Book of Acts: The Significance of the Eunuch's Provenance for Acts 1:8c" and "Sexual Violence as an Image for Divine Retribution in the Prophetic Writings," respectively.

4. Weems does not use an explicitly womanist approach in her monograph *Battered Love* (1995). For further review of this book, see Underwood's essay in this volume.

5. Townes was also among the group of first-generation womanists to attend the inaugural consultation of the American Academy of Religion and the Society of Biblical Literature in 1985.

tion of black peoples within divergent biblical traditions; 3) critique the persistent and still normative narrowness of vision of feminist theologians and biblical interpreters on the subject of race; 4) retrieval and documentary analysis of the effective history of the Bible in Western culture in general and on peoples of African descent in Black diasporic communities in particular. (1999, 655)

Other black women slowly began to pursue doctoral degrees in biblical studies. However, by the end of the 1990s, there were still only eleven who had completed their studies and earned degrees (Bailey 2000, 696, 707).

Nearly thirty years have now passed since Martin and Weems introduced readers to womanist biblical hermeneutics—biblical interpretation that incorporated African American women's lived experiences; and yet the appearance of womanist biblical interpretation in books and articles have been few and far between, despite the new addition of black women earning terminal degrees in Hebrew Bible/Old Testament and New Testament/Early Christianity. This was due in part, as Nyasha Junior outlined in an essay on womanist biblical interpretation, to a number of circumstances. For one, while there are several works of womanist biblical interpretation, Junior noted that the preponderance has been by scholars outside the field of biblical studies, such as Williams (1993), Cannon (1995), and Cheryl Kirk-Duggan (1997). Moreover, biblical criticism by self-identified womanist scholars has not always reflected an explicitly womanist methodological approach (Byron 2002; Anderson 2004). Finally, and probably the greatest factor, is that while black women continue to join the growing ranks of blacks and women of color in biblical studies, black women biblical scholars are still underrepresented (Junior 2006, 40–41, 43).[6] Even with the increasing numbers, all black women scholars, as Junior herself noted, do not choose to identify as a womanist or feminist.

Despite the circumstances and challenges noted above, recent African American commentaries such as *True to our Native Land* (Blount et al. 2007) and *The Africana Bible* (Page 2010) and feminist commentaries such as *The Women's Bible Commentary* (Newsom, Ringe, Lapsey 2012) and A Feminist Companion to the Bible series have included contributions by womanist and other black women scholars. There has also been a growing number of articles, essays, and books by black women using a

---

6. Society of Biblical Literature US members of African descent are only 3.8 percent, which means that black women are even fewer (Society of Biblical Literature 2015).

womanist hermeneutic. *When Momma Speaks: The Bible and Motherhood from a Womanist Perspective* (2016) by Stephanie Buckhanon Crowder engages a womanist reading of biblical mothers, including Rizpah, Hagar, Bathsheba, Mary, the Canaanite woman, and Zebedee's wife, to argue that their stories can be beneficial to contemporary women who are seeking models for self-identification and empowerment. In addition, Wil Gafney's forthcoming *Womanist Midrash: A Reintroduction to the Women of the Torah and The Throne* uses a midrashic interpretation rooted in African American preaching traditions and imagination to bring to life both familiar and often overlooked female characters in the Hebrew Bible. Other recent publications include Mitzi J. Smith's *I Found God in Me: A Womanist Reader* (2015), Nyasha Junior's *An Introduction to Womanist Biblical Interpretation* (2015), and Shanell Smith's *The Woman Babylon and the Marks of Empire: Reading Revelation with a Postcolonial Womanist Hermeneutics of Ambiveilence* (2014), the first womanist monograph since Raquel St. Clair's *Call and Consequences: A Womanist Reading of Mark* (2008).

Mitzi Smith and Junior's recent works deserve a little more attention in relation to our volume. Both scholars expressed that a motivating factor for writing their respective books was the lack of a textbook on womanist biblical scholarship when they were seminary students. Smith's (2015) edited volume provides the reader with a brief introduction to the development of womanist biblical interpretation and its growth from the pioneering works of Martin and Weems, to subsequent groups or "generations" of womanist biblical scholars, such as the second-generation scholars Gay Byron, Cheryl Anderson, and Valerie Bridgeman, third-generation scholars Margaret Aymer, Wil Gafney, and Love L. Sechrest, and fourth- and recent-generation scholars Shanell Smith and Bridgett Green (M. Smith 2015, 5–7).[7] The remainder of Mitzi Smith's volume is divided into two parts: reprinted essays of significance for an introduction to womanist biblical interpretation and womanist readings of biblical texts, both reprints and original essays.

---

7. Historians usually speak of the feminist movement in terms of "waves" to define the different periods in the movement: first wave (nineteenth to early twentieth century), second wave (1960s to 1980s), third wave (1990s to present). For more on the differences between feminists' use of waves and womanists' use of generations, see Stacey Floyd-Thomas (2006) and Monica Coleman (2013).

Junior's (2015) book is intended as an introductory-level resource on womanist biblical interpretation for graduate students. It traces the trajectory of womanist biblical interpretation from its early roots in US black women's activism and biblical interpretation around issues of race and gender by both nonprofessionals and professionals, its development independent of feminist biblical interpretation, and its emphasis on womanist reading strategies by scholars outside of biblical studies. Junior's monograph offers the reader a comparative analysis of feminist and womanist biblical interpretation. In particular, the book devotes several chapters to analyzing the different waves of feminism, feminist forerunners, and feminist biblical interpretation.[8] The novice reader should understand that Junior's book is an introduction to both the use of feminist and womanist approaches across disciplines rather than a generative example of womanist biblical interpretation.

Diverse Range of Interpretations: Expanding the Discourse

Given the growing body of literature, this volume expands on the recent publications on womanist biblical criticism in the following ways. First, it is intentional in naming themes and interpretive trajectories that characterize womanist hermeneutics. In this regard, our purpose is to build upon the scholarship that has already been generated and extend the conversations and interpretive frameworks among biblical critics and all interested readers concerned with contemporary injustices perpetrated against African American and other people of color throughout the world. Second, it offers a comprehensive, global, and interdisciplinary compilation of essays from the Hebrew Bible, New Testament, and extracanonical sources, including books that have never been treated to a womanist interpretation, as these readings interface with the experiences of black and other women of color. These essays feature a range of methodological approaches such as postcolonial, sociological, psychological, gender and race theory, literary and rhetorical theories, and the like. Third, the range of contributors is indicative of the wide breadth of scholars who

---

8. See chapter 5, "Feminist Biblical Interpretation" (76–94), in which several contemporary feminist biblical critics and their methodologies are provided. For example, scholars such as Mary Ann Tolbert, Elisabeth Schüssler Fiorenza, and Katharine Doob Sakenfeld have outlined different tasks and forms of engagement for feminist biblical criticism.

are now applying womanist theories to their interpretations of the Bible. Thus, included in this volume are emerging scholars (including those in their early years of teaching or completing their dissertations), independent scholar-activists, and those along various stages of their academic careers who are teaching in theological schools and departments of religion across the United States.

It is not our intention to offer an all-inclusive survey of womanist biblical scholarship. We are featuring broad methodological, geographical, and ideological approaches to womanist criticism. We also choose to include women who do not self-identify as womanist but who foreground black and other women of color's experiences in their interpretive process. Therefore, we have Stacy Davis who in her article self-identifies as a black feminist, Margaret Aymer reading from her particularity as a black "Caribbean, naturalized, economic migrant" woman in America, and Sharon Jacob's interpretation of sacred Hindu texts as an Indian immigrant living in the United States.

We contend with scholars such as Layli Phillips (2006, xxii, xxxvi) that womanism is an ethnically and culturally situated but not bounded perspective that allows room for black and other women of color who self-identify as womanist. For example, Sarojini Nadar (2001), a South African Indian who uses a womanist approach to her biblical interpretation, is explicit in acknowledging her ethnic and cultural location. Nevertheless, we maintain that although womanists and black feminists share a common cultural and historical heritage and certain political concerns, womanism and black feminism are not interchangeable; indeed, marking the distinctions between the two is an ongoing debate among feminist and womanist critics (West 2006). They "favor" each other, to use a family metaphor (Phillips 2006); but in contrast to womanism, feminism is still generally regarded as the "universal" experience of white women, which invariably leads to inequitable power dynamics that are often too difficult to overcome and best expressed in the classic text on black women's studies by Gloria T. Hull, Patricia Bell Scott, and Barbara Smith: *All the Women Are White, All the Blacks Are Men, But Some of Us Are Brave* (1982).

In light of this, we believe that what makes these essays womanist is, first, the intentionality with which the contributors in this volume bring into sharp focus the multilayered and interlocking systems of oppression and microaggressions that keep all women of color, locally and globally, stymied in racialized pits of poverty, violence, and despair. Second is the way in which these contributors draw upon sources from black cultural traditions such as the activism of Fannie Lou Hamer or Assata Shakur, the hip hop lyrics of Beyoncé or Rihanna, and the courageous women of the Civil Rights or #BlackLivesMatter movements. They recognize that, without a womanist hermeneutic, the mothers, children, infants, single women, power brokers, bibliophiles, activists, moral agents, landowners, strategists, and other carriers of life and hope would remain invisible, ignored, and marginalized in biblical narratives. Third, is the commitment with which these contributors bring their experiences as black and brown women to name and work towards ending the multidimensional oppression faced by women of color that limit the progress of all humanity. Thus, our goal in pulling together this volume is to provide a sample of essays that represent some of the best in womanist scholarship using interdisciplinary approaches for reading biblical texts. In this regard, we seek to expand the discourse among womanist biblical scholars and invite other interested interpreters to the table.

The book is organized into four parts that reflect some of the overarching themes of womanist biblical interpretation. This organizational schema does not account for the myriad themes and commitments that are evident among the contributors. For example, the themes of respectability politics, sexual independence, and political and social activism appear, to some degree, in all of the essays. Yet, we have identified the following key subheadings that have emerged from the content of the various essays: (1) Gender and Sexuality; (2) Agency and Advocacy; (3) Foregrounding Women on the Margins; and (4) Illuminating Biblical Children/Childhood. The final section includes the responses to the essays from four leading womanist and feminist scholars.

Part 1: Gender and Sexuality

In several ways the articles by Davis, Gafney, and Anderson each examine issues of race, gender, and sexuality especially around the theme of independent women, sexuality, and the need by some interpreters to use the Bible both to celebrate black women's independence and to police their sexuality, especially if they are unmarried.

Davis takes on the biblical anomaly of the unmarried woman in her article, "The Invisible Women: Numbers 30 and the Politics of Singleness in African American Communities." She reads the passage about women's vows in Num 30 to show how women typically are defined by one of four categories in the biblical text: wife, minor daughter, widow, or divorcée. However, missing is the adult daughter who has never married. Davis approaches the passage from the perspective of a never-married African American woman, using womanist theory, masculinity studies, and queer theory to highlight the ways unmarried biblical women and contemporary women, especially black women are discriminated against.

Gafney applies her distinctive womanist midrash to the biblical figure Delilah (Judg 16) in her essay, "A Womanist Midrash of Delilah: Don't Hate the Playa Hate the Game." Gafney combines a womanist biblical hermeneutic informed by hip hop lyrics and rhetoric and the rabbinic midrash tradition of filling in what the text omitted to paint a portrait of Delilah as a subject of her own story, who makes her own choices about her body and life, while besting the men in the story. Gafney exposes heteropatriarchal interpretations of Delilah as a "playa hata" seeking to bring down the valiant Samson to reveal the truth of the story—that Samson engages in a twisted game of bloodsport that is lethal to the women in his life.

Anderson proposes a different biblical gender and sexuality paradigm for the African American church to confront the transmission of HIV in her article, "The Song of Songs: Redeeming Gender Constructions in the Age of AIDS." Anderson contends that leadership on this issue has been lagging in the African American church due to an emphasis on race as its primary concern and its reluctance to address sexuality and sexual expression. She argues that the church's teaching on sex is limited to traditional hierarchical gender and sexuality constructions based on Gen 2–3 that are undermining African American well-being in the age of AIDS. Anderson offers the mutuality paradigm in the Song of Songs as an alternative to help prevent new HIV infections in the African American community.

Part 2: Agency and Advocacy

A few of the articles express a solidarity with or indirect reference to the #BlackLivesMatter social justice movement, begun after the acquittal of George Zimmerman, neighborhood watch volunteer, who shot and killed black teenager Trayvon Martin. Each article in this section emphasizes some form of agency, in which the biblical characters or contemporary activists express the ability to transform their social circumstances.

Mitzi Smith approaches her article, "Race, Gender, and the Politics of 'Sass': Reading Mark 7:24–30 through a Womanist Lens of Intersectionality and Inter(con)textuality," from the womanist hermeneutic of "sass/talk back." She engages the story of Sandra Bland, the black female motorist whose arrest led to her shocking death in jail. Smith puts Bland in dialog with the Greek Syro-Phoenician woman in this Markan text. She also combines sass and Mikhail Bakhtin's *heteroglossia* to give resistance speech to the Syro-Phoenician woman and contemporary women of color who would dare to raise their consciousness by talking back to those in authority at the risk of condemnation or death.

Sechrest's article, "Antitypes, Stereotypes, and Antetypes: Jezebel, the Sun Woman, and Contemporary Black Women," examines the role of women's agency in the book of Revelation by comparing and contrasting the figures Jezebel and the Sun Woman in Rev 2 and 12, respectively, with contemporary black women activists in the Civil Rights and #BlackLivesMatter movements. Sechrest explores how John, the writer of Revelation's use of stereotypes about "good" and "bad" women in the public square to describe Jezebel and the Sun Woman, obscures the reader's vision of feminine agency in the text. Similarly, she argues that such stereotypes associated with the imagery and language in Revelation are used to shape and constrain women of color's agency today.

We affirm the new generation of black women religious scholars who have adopted the #BlackLivesMatter's call to action against antiblack racism without regard to the respectability politics revolving around sexual orientation. The #BlackLivesMatter was founded by three queer black women activists who decried the violence against black people saying, "Our lives matter, black lives matter."[9] This is, ironically, in contrast to the earlier rejection of womanism by some black women Christian ethicists and theologians because Walker's poetic definition included "loves other women sexually and/or nonsexually." Although the articles in this section do not explicitly address LGBTQ perspectives, this omission was not intentional. The contributors in this volume focused more on their own sociopolitical location. Nevertheless, we acknowledge the importance of the women loving women aspect of Walker's definition.

We also affirm the historical precursors that are referenced in the #BlackLivesMatter movement. Cofounder Alicia Garza wrote, "When Black people get free, everybody gets free," a paraphrase of the famous line by civil rights activist Hamer. Garza also draws inspiration from black

---

9. Black Lives Matter was founded by Alicia Garza, Patrisse Cullors, and Opal Tometi ("A Herstory of the #BlackLivesMatter Movement," n.d.)

liberation and Black Panther activist Shakur in her own activism against antiblack racism, whom she quotes: "It is our duty to fight for our freedom, it is our duty to win. We must love each other and support each other. We have nothing to lose but our chains."[10] Shakur is the subject of Shively T. J. Smith's article.

Shivley Smith's "One More Time with Assata on My Mind: A Womanist Rereading of the Escape to Egypt (Matt 2:13–23) in Dialogue with an African American Woman Fugitive Narrative" examines how Shakur's account of her transition and assimilation from life in the United States to life in Cuba, issues related to the reasons for political flight, changing territorial relations, and the challenges of cultural adaptation. These themes resonate with the biblical story of the flight of Jesus's family from Judea to Egypt in Matt 2:13–23. Smith argues that using Shakur's story to read Matt 2 afresh expands the breadth of African American women's experiences and history that womanist biblical readings engage in its interpretative work.

Finally, Marlene Underwood's essay, "'Battered Love': Exposing Abuse in the Book of Job," engages the social cycle theory developed by psychologist Lenore Walker called "cycle of abuse." Contrasting the retributive justice implied in YHWH's punishment of Israel in the marriage metaphor with the unmerited suffering of Job, Underwood exposes the abuse perpetrated by YHWH against Job as a form of domestic violence. After taking the reader through Job's various cycles of abuse at the hand of YHWH (tension building, acute battering incident, loving-contrition), she highlights Job's agency throughout his trials, including maintaining his innocence despite his friends' protests and his calls for justice.

Part 3: Foregrounding Women on the Margins

Most womanist interpretations have focused on Hebrew Bible and New Testament canonical sources. Although feminist and womanist interpreters have called for an expansion of texts, there still remains a significant gap in the scholarship. Byron's essay, "Black Collectors and Keepers of Tradition: Resources for a Womanist Biblical Ethic of (Re)Interpretation," illuminates the rich tradition of black bibliophiles and collectors such as

---

10. Assata Shakur, Unisex, Liberation Ink (quoted on "Get Involved in the Fight for Black Lives," n.d.).

Dorothy Porter Wesley, Mayme Clayton, Arthur Schomburg, and others who have amassed archival artifacts and sources that offer a new world of source material for the biblical critic. In particular, she discusses Dr. André Reynolds Tweed, who amassed during his lifetime one of the largest collections of Ethiopic manuscripts and artifacts in the United States. She theorizes how "living sources" such as the experiences of these virtually overlooked black bibliophiles and the often-ignored experiences of black women in biblical and other early Christian sources open a more critical and expansive lens for understanding early Christianity.

Byron is not the only contributor foregrounding women on the margins. Two essays call attention to the marginalized roles of mothers, in particular the deleterious impact of their social status on their children's lives and the displaced (surrogate) nature of their maternal contributions to society. Sharon Jacob and Jennifer T. Kaalund's essay "Flowing from Breast to Breast: An Examination of Dis/placed Motherhood in African American and Indian Wet Nurses" uses the Sun Woman in the book of Revelation in conversation with the Hindu text Linga Purana to explore the phenomenon of black and Indian women being forced to nurture empire with their breasts in the contexts of antebellum slavery in the United States and the British colonization of India. Jacob and Kaalund demonstrate how the wet nurse illuminates not only the violent nature of surrogate motherhood in hegemonic systems, but also the role that class, or socioeconomic status, plays in the displacement of motherhood.

Lovelace critiques interpreters of Judg 11 who maintain that Jephthah is doomed to fail because he is the son of an unmarried woman. In her essay " 'We Don't Give Birth to Thugs': Family Values, Respectability Politics, and Jephthah's Mother," she approaches the text from a functionalist perspective on the family with a womanist hermeneutic, which asserts that commentaries on Jephthah and his mother depict them as lacking traditional family values. This sounds much like the functionalist argument that children born to single mothers become juvenile delinquents and create social instability. This rhetoric, targeted mostly at black children, is the same language used to describe Jephthah, which in turn functions to racialize Jephthah and his mother as black.

Part 4: Illuminating Biblical Children/Childhood

The next section of this volume illuminates the experiences of children in biblical narratives and adds to the ongoing dialogues among biblical scholars who are highlighting the multilayered dimensions of children in the biblical world. The essays in this section challenge some of the assumptions contemporary readers have about children, such as their youth, innocence, and vulnerability.

In "Outrageous, Audacious, Courageous, Willful: Reading the Enslaved Girl of Acts 12," Margaret Aymer examines the enslaved girl Rhoda in Luke's narrative and reads her story intersectionally, darkly, and ambi*veil*ently (using Shanell Smith's term) to allow the subaltern to speak. Aymer's womanist reading of Rhoda attends to the issues of trauma arising from the darkness of the intersectional oppression based on racism/ethnocentrism, sexism, classism, and ageism considering Rhoda's youth. She also raises questions about the ancient text and modern forced migration and human trafficking. Aymer challenges the early church's idealized narrative that Luke's Gospel is sympathetic to women while listening for Rhoda's silenced cry for liberation.

Valerie Bridgeman likewise examines the plight of children in her essay, "'I Will Make Boys Their Princes': A Womanist Reading of Children in the Book of Isaiah." She adds to the growing body of literature on children in the world of the Bible with her piece on how the book of Isaiah contributes to the ways the writer symbolically portrays Israel as a wayward child that needs punishment for correction. Bridgeman lifts up the danger of a literal reading of the text that may lead the contemporary reader to conclude that the Bible condones child abuse.

Bridgett Green focuses on children (more specifically, infants) in the Gospel of Luke. Her article, "'Nobody's Free until Everybody's Free': Exploring Gender and Class Injustice in a Story about Children (Luke 18:15–17)," interprets the story of Jesus blessing the children through civil rights' activist Hamer's gender, class, and race analysis of power dynamics that legitimated interlocking systems of oppression. Using Hamer's speech "Nobody's Free until Everybody's Free" delivered at the founding meeting of the National Women's Political Caucus as a hermeneutical guide, Green reads Luke's version of the blessing of the children for a liberative thrust that empowers the marginalized and admonishes the privileged.

Part 5: In Response

The final part of the book offers responses from four leading womanist and feminist scholars who each bring a unique perspective for setting in context the diverse essays included in this volume: Layli Maparyan, Katharine Doob Sakenfeld, Townes, and Althea Spencer-Miller. Their insights highlight the theoretical, interdisciplinary, global, pedagogical, and practical implications of the different essays and articulate new horizons for womanist biblical interpretation.

Concluding Thoughts

As we developed this volume through our own dialogues and through conversations with the contributors, we realized that collaboration and sharing is at the heart of womanist doings and ways of being in the world. We recognize that interpreting sacred texts cannot be done independent of the communities with whom we read and to whom we are accountable. All of the essays demonstrate that our black bodies and our black lives cannot be left outside of the interpretive process. Likewise, the bodies and lives of all interpreters are integral in the interpretive process.

Furthermore, we acknowledge that injustices and challenges in our contemporary world are an indispensible component of womanist hermeneutics and not matters to be left solely for theologians, ethicists, policy analysts, or other scholars committed to social justice. The contributors to this volume have consistently emphasized their responsibility to speak out against the deep, systemic nature of the interlocking systems of oppression related to race, ethnicity, class, gender, sexuality, et cetera that cannot be ignored by biblical interpreters—not just black women biblical interpreters. All interpreters of sacred texts are responsible for exposing and analyzing the power dynamics in both the ancient texts and the interpretations of the texts that have been used to further injustices and global systemic challenges.

The question of where we go from here was raised in regard to the insights in these womanist ways of reading the Bible and other sacred texts. One of the desirable outcomes from this volume would be that readers come away with a new understanding of womanist readings of sacred texts that highlight the myriad perspectives that black and other women of color bring to interpreting these texts. In addition, that more interpreters (including those outside the discipline of biblical studies) would be emboldened to read the texts from their own social location and be empowered to take action and work toward building new relationships and coalitions that can transform the injustices in our society and across the globe. Finally, we hope that this volume will lead to further collaborative efforts and conversations that will keep the interests of black women and other women of color at the forefront of interpretations of biblical and extrabiblical sources.

Works Cited

Anderson, Cheryl B. 2004. *Women, Ideology, and Violence: Critical Theory and the Construction of Gender in the Book of the Covenant and the Deuteronomic Law.* JSOTSup 394. New York: T&T Clark.

Bailey, Randall C. 2000. "Academic Biblical Interpretation among African Americans in the United States." Pages 696–711 in *African Americans and the Bible: Sacred Texts and Social Textures.* Edited by Vincent L. Wimbush. New York: Continuum.

Blount, Brian K., Cain Hope Felder, Clarice J. Martin, and Emerson B. Powery, eds. 2007. *True to Our Native Land: An African American New Testament Commentary.* Minneapolis: Fortress.

Byron, Gay L. 2002. *Symbolic Blackness and Ethnic Difference in Early Christian Literature.* London: Routledge.

Cannon, Katie G. 1985. "The Emergence of Black Feminist Consciousness." Pages 30–40 in *Feminist Interpretation of the Bible.* Edited by Letty M. Russell. Philadelphia: Westminster.

———. 1995. *Katie's Canon: Womanism and the Soul of the Black Community.* New York: Continuum.

Coleman, Monica. 2013. *Ain't I a Womanist Too? Third-Wave Womanist Religious Thought.* Minneapolis: Fortress.

Crowder, Stephanie Buckhanon. 2016. *When Momma Speaks: The Bible and Motherhood from a Womanist Perspective.* Louisville: Westminster John Knox.

Floyd-Thomas, Stacey. 2006. *Deeper Shades of Purple: Womanism in Religion and Society.* New York: New York University Press.

Gafney, Wilda. Forthcoming. *Womanist Midrash: A Reintroduction to the Women of the Torah and Throne.* Louisville: Westminster John Knox.

"Get Involved in the Fight for Black Lives." n.d. #BlackLivesMatter. http://tinyurl.com/SBL0688v2.

"A Herstory of the #BlackLivesMatter Movement." n.d. #BlackLivesMatter. http://tinyurl.com/SBL0688u2.

Hudson-Weems, Clenora. 1993. *Africana Womanism: Reclaiming Ourselves.* Troy, MI: Bedford Publishers.

Hull, Gloria T., Patricia Bell Scott, and Barbara Smith. 1982. *All the Women*

Are White, All the Blacks Are Men, But Some of Us Are Brave. Old Westbury, NY: Feminist Press.

Junior, Nyasha. 2006. "Womanist Biblical Interpretation." Pages 37–46 in *Engaging the Bible in a Gendered World: An Introduction to Feminist Biblical Interpretation in Honor of Katharine Doob Sakenfeld*. Louisville: Westminster John Knox.

———. 2015. *An Introduction to Womanist Biblical Interpretation*. Louisville: Westminster John Knox.

Kirk-Duggan, Cheryl. 1997. *Exercising Evil: A Womanist Perspective on the Spirituals*. Maryknoll, NY: Orbis Books.

Martin, Clarice J. 1985. "The Function of Acts 8:26–40 within the Narrative Structure of the Book of Acts: The Significance of the Eunuch's Provenance for Acts 1:8c." PhD diss. Duke University.

———. 1990. "Womanist Interpretations of the New Testament: The Quest for Holistic and Inclusive Translation and Interpretation." *JFSR* 6.2:41–61.

———. 1991. "The *Haustafeln* (Household Codes) in African American Biblical Interpretation." Pages 206–31 in *Stony the Road We Trod*. Edited by Cain Hope Felder. Minneapolis: Augsburg Fortress.

———. 1993. "Biblical Theodicy and Black Women's Spiritual Autobiography: The Miry Bog, the Desolate Pit, and a New Song in My Mouth." Pages 13–36 in *A Troubling in My Soul: Womanist Perspectives on Evil and Suffering*. Edited by Emilie M. Townes. Maryknoll, NY: Orbis Books.

———. 1999. "Womanist Biblical Interpretation." *DBI* 2:655–58.

Nadar, Sarojini. 2001. "A South African Indian Womanist Reading of the Character of Ruth." Pages 159–75 in *Other Ways of Reading: African Women and the Bible*. Edited by Musa W. Dube. Atlanta: Society of Biblical Literature.

Newsom, Carol A., Sharon H. Ringe, and Jacqueline E. Lapsley, eds. 2012. *Women's Bible Commentary*. 3rd ed. Twentieth-Anniversary ed. Louisville: Westminster John Knox.

Ogunyemi, Chikwenye Okonjo. 1985. "Womanism: The Dynamics of the Contemporary Black Female Novel in English." *Signs* 11:63–80.

Page, Hugh R., Jr., and Randall C. Bailey, eds. 2010. *The Africana Bible: Reading Israel's Scriptures from Africa and the African Diaspora*. Minneapolis: Fortress.

Phillips, Layli, ed. 2006. *The Womanist Reader*. New York: Routledge.

Smith, Mitzi J. 2015. *I Found God in Me: A Womanist Biblical Hermeneutics Reader.* Eugene, OR: Cascade.

Smith, Shanell. 2014. *The Woman Babylon and the Marks of Empire: Reading Revelation with a Postcolonial Womanist Hermeneutics of Ambiveilence.* Minneapolis: Fortress.

Society of Biblical Literature. 2015. *Society Report.* http://tinyurl.com/SBL0688t2.

St. Clair, Raquel. 2008. *Call and Consequences: A Womanist Reading of Mark.* Minneapolis: Fortress.

Townes, Emilie M., ed. 1993. *A Troubling in My Soul: Womanist Perspectives on Evil and Suffering.* Maryknoll, NY: Orbis Books.

Walker, Alice. 1979. "Coming Apart." Pages 95–104 in *Take Back the Night: Women on Pornography.* Edited by Laura Lederer. New York: Morrow.

———. 1983. *In Search of Our Mothers' Gardens.* San Diego: Harcourt Brace Jovanovich.

Weems, Renita J. 1988. *Just a Sister Away: A Womanist Vision of Women's Relationships in the Bible.* San Diego, CA: LauraMedia.

———. 1989. "Sexual Violence as an Image for Divine Retribution in the Prophetic Writings." PhD diss., Princeton Theological Seminary.

———. 1991. "Reading *Her* Way through the Struggle: African American Women and the Bible." Pages 57–77 in *Stony the Road We Trod: African American Biblical Interpretation.* Edited by Cain Hope Felder. Minneapolis: Fortress.

———. 1993. "Womanist Reflections on Biblical Hermeneutics." Pages 216–24 in *Black Theology: A Documentary History.* Edited by James H. Cone and Gayraud Wilmore. 2 vols. Maryknoll, NY: Orbis Books.

———. 1995. *Battered Love: Marriage, Sex, and Violence in the Hebrew Prophets.* Minneapolis: Fortress.

West, Traci C. 2006. "Is a Womanist a Black Feminist? Marking the Distinctions and Defying Them: A Black Feminist Response." Pages 291–95 in *Deeper Shades of Purple.* Edited by Stacey M. Floyd-Thomas. New York: New York University Press.

Williams, Delores S. 1987. "Womanist Theology: Black Women's Voices." *Christianity and Crisis* 47:66–70.

———. 1993. *Sisters in the Wilderness: The Challenge of Womanist God-Talk.* Maryknoll, NY: Orbis Books.

Part 1
Gender and Sexuality

The Invisible Women: Numbers 30 and the Politics of Singleness in Africana Communities

Stacy Davis

The invitation to write an essay for this collection arrived as I was finishing a seminar on Leviticus and Numbers. I had just taught a class on Num 30, which discusses women's vows. According to the text, fathers may annul the vows of young women living at home; husbands may annul their wives' vows. Widows and divorced women may make and keep their own vows without any man's approval. When I asked my students which group of women the text excludes, they gave me puzzled looks, until I laughed and pointed to myself—a never-married adult (and specifically middle-aged) woman. We then spent some time talking about why I had been left out. As biblical scholar Carol Meyers (2013, 120) notes, in the ancient Israelite world, "Rather than being an autonomous entity, a woman was someone's daughter, mother, wife, and so forth." In this world, which Num 30 describes, I and those like me are invisible, if not the biblical equivalent of unicorns.

What does such ancient invisibility signify in a modern Christian context?[1] I wrestle with this question by utilizing several different perspectives: womanism, which calls for reading strategies that foreground black women's experiences; masculinity studies, which argues that definitions of manhood often reinforce male dominance over women; and queer theory, which challenges the cultural assumption of heterosexuality. Intersectionality, the recognition that identity categories such as gender, race, class,

---

1. While the essay includes data about Muslim women and analysis of the Hebrew Bible, the analysis focuses primarily upon Africana Christian women.

and sexuality overlap and shape individuals and their social interactions and locations, holds these perspectives together.[2]

Reading Num 30 as a never-married African American feminist theorist, I suggest that the passage reinforces hegemonic masculinity (a man can override the promises that the women in his household make) and heteronormativity and does not fit the contemporary reality of black single women's lived experiences. The text describes an ideal whose time has passed. Women no longer transition strictly and inevitably from virgin daughters to chaste wives, although that presumed transition continues to shape contemporary Christian discourses about gender. The ancient insistence upon female chastity functioned to guarantee the protection and transmission of male property rights, but puberty is no longer the universal marriage age for women, and the invisible women of Num 30 now make up a significant demographic. Historically, black women have been both hypervisible, with stereotypes about our sexuality and identity as overexposed as our bodies have often been in the dominant culture, and invisible, as antiracist movements often called for a reinforcement of patriarchal ideas about women's "proper" place. A Christian womanist ethic of singleness therefore resists hypervisibility and invisibility, affirming sexual expression and not simply the absence of sexual activity.

Using a text that excludes single[3] women as a starting point for a conversation about womanist ethics may seem unusual but need not be. Womanist theologian Diana L. Hayes (1995, 30) writes, "And so today we [black women] continue to speak out of our own contexts, from within our own lived experiences, confronting and challenging the silences which have kept us chained and bound to definitions of womanhood not of our own making." Examining and questioning patriarchal and limited gender

---

2. I cannot use the term *intersectionality* without giving credit to Kimberlé Crenshaw, who coined it in 1989 as a way to describe the marginalization of black women in gender and race discrimination lawsuits (Cho, Crenshaw, and McCall 2013, 787–92). Today, women's, gender, and sexuality studies programs consider the concept foundational (Shaw and Lee 2015, 7, 51–60).

3. *Single* is defined as "unmarried or not in a romantic relationship" ("Single," Dictionary.com) or "when you are currently not in a relationship with a significant other" ("Single," Urban Dictionary). Later in this essay, the word *single* focuses specifically on the never-married, who in Christian circles are presumed to be abstinent and/or virgins; the divorced and widowed are often separate census categories and presumably have already had sexual experiences.

constructions counts as a womanist enterprise, if it takes seriously the call to free all people, regardless of gender, race, and class, insists that one must work for one's own emancipation and envisions a church "that lifts up the gifts and talents of all—female and male, adult and child, married, single, divorced—rather than those of just a few" (59; see also 33, 53). Carol B. Duncan's (2006, 31) analysis of womanism and girlhood notes that Alice Walker, who coined the term womanism, praises a concept that often leads to adult criticism of black girls for forgetting their proper place of obedient silence. Womanist thought, however, is not "girlish" but "contemplative, responsible, and serious" (34). A thoughtful examination of the absence of single women as a biblical or theological subject, written from my context as a black single woman, challenges the disingenuous idea of objectivity that historically established white male subjects as the normative standard in scholarly discourse.

While rejecting that standard, womanism creates a clear methodology. Foregrounding black women's lived experience makes space for storytelling as evidence. As Katie G. Cannon (2006, 21) argues, "Anecdotal evidence does a lot to reveal the truth as to how oppressed people live with integrity, especially when we are repeatedly unheard but not unvoiced, unseen but not invisible." Cannon highlights three elements of a womanist methodology: "power analyses," or questioning the traditions that often go unquestioned; "biotextual specificity," or talking about one's context and life; and "embodied mediated knowledge," or rejecting claims of objectivity while not engaging in deconstruction simply for its own sake (23–26). Cannon concludes, "Those of us who are serious about not wanting partial and false generalizations about Black women in religion to persist, we have decided to remedy the situation by bringing our best embodied reasoning to the academic venue of scholarly inquiry and publication" (26–27). Ideally, sound womanist scholarship combines clear academic sources with clear personal experience.

At this point, the task becomes complicated. Trained methodologically as a historian, I rejected the idea of objectivity decades ago, and "why" has been my favorite word since I was four years old. Bringing my personal identities into an academic project, however, even as a scholar trained in feminist theory and African American biblical hermeneutics, has been difficult. Extremely introverted, I prefer to speak using a text's voice as opposed to my own, rushing through the expected identification of social location and context as quickly and with as little revealing information as possible. Why (my favorite word again) in this case did I pick a topic so terribly close to home? I think part of the answer may be the strange silences surrounding straight single women's sexuality.

After you reach a particular age, and I think forty-one is that age, one's feminist and/or secular friends and companions assume that you are not a virgin; one's traditional and/or nonfeminist Christian friends assume that you are a virgin. Both assumptions are reasonable but complicated. A 2011 study by the National Campaign to Prevent Teen and Unplanned Pregnancy indicated that 80 percent of single evangelicals (ages eighteen to twenty-nine) have had sex, as opposed to 88 percent of singles in that age bracket (Charles 2012). According to the 2008 GSS survey, only 14–30 percent of Catholics state that premarital sex is "always wrong" ("Replicate Before You Speculate Too Much" 2010).[4] Thinking that any response to the "Is she or isn't she?" question will shock and disappoint at least one group of people I dearly love, "silence is my only option" (Blackburn 2004, xii). It also may be my only option here, in order to avoid my later arguments being summarily dismissed either as a justification for allegedly sinful behavior, on the one hand, or a hypothetical construct, on the other. At best, it is the option I choose, finding it less socially and professionally awkward to leave the contradictory assumptions intact. As I struggle with the ethic of honesty and the ethic of self-preservation,[5] I nevertheless hope that I will, in Cannon's words (2006, 27), "bring my best embodied reasoning" to this project.

Not only do I fail in the task of personal self-disclosure, I also use womanist theory while personally identifying as a feminist and feminist theorist. I have been a feminist since seventh grade, four years after Alice Walker's groundbreaking work on womanism and decades before I encountered it. The idea that women were equal to men (or should be)

---

4. The range depends upon whether the respondent attends mass weekly. The 2006 CARA Catholic Poll, cited in the same article, reached a similar conclusion, with only 19 percent of those surveyed agreeing that premarital sex is wrong between a committed couple. Incidentally, one need not limit the data to Christians. A 2001 national college survey indicates that 54 percent of Muslim college students, 48 percent of them women, have had sex (Ahmed, Abu-Ras, and Arfken 2014).

5. I fully recognize that my silence perpetuates the problem of silence about sexuality. As Evelyn Hammonds notes, "Historically, Black women have reacted to the repressive force of the hegemonic discourse on race and sex and this image [Black women as empty space] with silence, secrecy, and a partially self-chosen invisibility" (1997, 171; quoted in Springer 2002, 1074). While this makes me a bad feminist, to use Roxane Gay's phrase, I am also an aware feminist.

made perfect sense to my twelve-year-old brain, struggling at the time between my church's prolife position and my nagging sense that an adult woman (which I hoped to become) should not be compelled into a life-altering decision. As I aged, it never occurred to me to substitute womanist for feminist, and I take comfort in Traci C. West's (2006, 292) conclusion: "Frankly, specifying the boundaries between feminism and womanism in my work is of little significance to me, unless it furthers some form of woman-affirming shift toward a more just and compassionate world." West notes that womanism's intellectual foundation rests in the "exclusively black community-based tradition of intellectual work" (292). Raised as an Air Force brat, I experienced racism but did not live in black communities, and I wonder if that has shaped my language. Even if it has, West questions the assumption of some that black women are or should be womanist and not feminists (294), arguing that such an assumption "problematically [erases] the contribution of a generation of black feminist foremothers" (295). West's arguments confirm that practice matters less than label, but in this case, I call feminist. If my attempts at utilizing womanist theory fail miserably, womanists at least do not have to claim me.

Like womanism, black feminism is alive and well. While recognizing that feminist theory and the wave model often exclude women of color's experiences, Kimberly Springer argues that black women continue to do feminist work. She writes, "The recuperation of the self in a racist and sexist society is a political enterprise and a Black feminist one that reprioritizes generational differences in the interest of historical, activist continuity" (Springer 2002, 1060–61). For example, feminist writers such as Joan Morgan and Veronica Chambers offer a critique of the strongblackwoman syndrome, which can be mentally and physically damaging (1069–72). Springer notes, however, that more attention should be paid to sexuality, heterosexism, and heteronormativity in black feminist work (1073–74), a point that West (2006, 294) also makes about womanist work.

In response to Springer's article, Beverly Guy-Sheftall and Sheila Radford-Hill affirm black feminism and question the feminists. Guy-Sheftall (2002, 1093) wonders if "young Black feminists are carrying on the legacy left by nineteenth century abolitionists, antilynching crusaders, club women, Civil Rights organizers, Black nationalist revolutionaries, and 1970s Black feminists."[6] Radford-Hill (2002, 1089–90) recognizes

---

6. The 1970s feminists had a rough road. As John P. Bowles (2007, 621) notes,

that the strongblackwoman allowed black women to participate in antiracist and antisexist movements, without challenging black male sexism,[7] and gave them an identity besides the hyper-sexual stereotype. Perhaps no one articulated the lack of challenge better than Michele Wallace in her *Black Macho and the Myth of the Superwoman* (1978). As a survival mechanism, however, mothers taught their daughters "our version of the SBW [Strongblackwoman].... Attitude—Don't take abuse. Call the question. Altitude—Don't settle. Have lofty aspirations. Image—Look good. The worse you feel, the better you need to look. Have style. Faith—Never give up. Love yourself, your people, and your community" (Radford-Hill 2002, 1086). Even while critiquing current black feminist discourse, Radford-Hill acknowledges the discourse (1089).

So, what does a feminist's womanist interpretation of Num 30 look like? Textually, it looks thin, because women fit into only two categories, daughters and wives (or former wives).[8] According to Num 30, a woman's

---

"Audre Lorde and other black lesbian theorists have described how outspoken black women found themselves derided as traitors by both white feminists and black men, as if they were somehow neither women nor black." One response was Adrian Piper's public persona as the Mythic Being, allowing her to "act in ways that, as a black woman, she was expected not to" (Bowles 2007, 621; 624, 627, 629–30, 638); specifically, those ways were sexual, "confronting society with an image of what it fears most—the sexually liberated black woman" (639).

7. The Black Power movement, for example, linked racial uplift to ideals of patriarchal masculinity, or benevolent sexism (Matlin 2006, 93–94, 98). Daniel Matlin notes that Amiri Baraka's arguments for patriarchal gender complementarity fit the mainstream Civil Rights argument "that greater patriarchal authority would assist race progress.... In the black nationalist magazine *The Liberator*, black women vowed to 'reject the insidious, castrating feminist concept' and reclaim the 'softness and femininity' that American society had denied them" (100). Complementary gender roles and glorification of marriage complemented Baraka's ideals of and programs for racial uplift (106–11, 116). Sheila Radford-Hill (2002, 1088) notes "that black men and women share conservative patriarchal notions of black families. Feminist organizing has not changed these attitudes."

8. The text assumes that heterosexual activity or the lack thereof separates one category of women from the other. The Hebrew words, however, are more complicated. נערה, translated "daughter," means a girl, usually unmarried and of marriageable age (BDB s.v.). While the huge assumption is that the girl has not had vaginal intercourse (all unmarried women are presumed to be virgins), נערה is not usually translated as virgin. The Hebrew word for virgin is בתולה. Both words, however, suggest that vaginal intercourse makes a girl a wife (אשה), or a nonvirgin. A passage in Deuteronomy suggests that the evidence of virginity in a contested situation was

relationship to a man literally may define her relationship to God. If a father rejects a young daughter's vow as soon as he hears of it, he annuls the vow. God releases the daughter, "[living] in her father's house, in her youth," from her vow, "because her father had expressed to her his disapproval" (Num 30:3, 5).[9] The Hebrew reinforces both gender and age hierarchies. The woman (אשה, from איש, man) living with her father as a minor child (נערה, girl) remains subject to his authority. A husband may overturn his wife's vow on the day he hears of it; if he waits, then the vow cannot be annulled unless he accepts the consequences of the broken promise (Num 30:8, 11–15).[10] The chapter concludes, "These are the statutes that the LORD commanded Moses concerning a husband and his wife [בין איש לאשתו] and a father and his daughter while she is still young [בנעריה] and in her father's house" (Num 30:16). In the middle of the chapter, however, Num 30:9 appears in parentheses.[11]

A widow (אלמנה) or divorced woman (גרושה) may keep her vows without interference (Kawashima 2011, 8, 9, 10 n. 33), but the Hebrew words for widows and the divorced ooze negativity. Widow's etymology may come from the Arabic *'armal*, "helpless," and possibly the Hebrew אלם, "dumb," since "widows [are] often bound to silence" (*HALOT* s.v.). Divorce derives from גרש, "to cast out" (BDB s.v.). A woman separated from male authority may keep her own vows, but she is a tragic figure, due to "the unenviable event" (Kawashima 2011, 19). Widows in particular lived on the social margins, with divorced women right on their heels, unless they remarried or found some way to support themselves. The divorced "woman must be sent from one house (the husband's) to another house (presumably the father's), in which she would have an opportunity for life" (Berquist 2000, 351).[12] Widows theoretically had the same opportunity, but "given that landed property in ancient Israel was normally

---

a bloodstained sheet, displayed the morning after a wedding; the sheet would confirm that the girl's hymen was broken as the result of her first sexual experience that included vaginal penetration (Deut 23:13–21).

9. All translations, unless otherwise stated, come from the NRSV.

10. As Robert Kawashima (2011, 10) notes, "The law, in other words, enables the husband to receive a bride who is free of legal liabilities, a 'clean slate,' as it were—*not unlike the ideal of virginity itself*" (emphasis added).

11. While Hebrew does not contain such grammatical marks, the NRSV separates the verse with parentheses.

12. Berquist does not define this "opportunity for life." Is it a second marriage (Deut 24:2)? Additionally, such opportunities, if they exist, come out of a context of

passed down from father to son(s), a widow who had no son to inherit patrilineal property was in an economically precarious and socially vulnerable situation" (Day 2000, 1377). For all four groups of women, interaction with a man, or lack thereof, defines them—wife, minor daughter, widow, or divorcée.

Where, however, is the never-married adult woman? In this text, nowhere. Robert S. Kawashima (2011, 2–3) argues that women had no legal standing in biblical Israel, except within their household connections: "conversely, 'confirmed bachelors' and 'spinsters' have left few if any traces in the Bible, since they effectively constituted structural impossibilities, it being well nigh unthinkable that a boy or girl should not marry at the proper age and thus assume his or her rightful place within a house" (6). Elizabeth Goldstein (2008, 993) writes that the young adult daughters in Num 30 probably have no land, but "the law does not explicitly account for an unmarried woman who is neither 'youthful,' widowed, or divorced."[13] While Rashi suggests that "an adult woman is not under her father's legal control, even if she is still living at home, and her father cannot annul her vows" (Weisberg 2008, 1007), one could debate the extent of this medieval woman's freedom, particularly since moving out of the parental home was and is one marker of adulthood. Jacqueline Koch Ellenson (2008, 1008) concludes that in order to guarantee fulfillment of her vow, a woman had to make it silently and secretly.

If vows are secret, then adult single women are as well. The Hebrew Bible offers few examples of such women. In the cases of Dinah and Tamar, they are rape victims; Tamar lives as "a desolate [שממה] woman in her brother Absalom's house" (2 Sam 13:20),[14] and Dinah's fate remains unknown after her brothers remove her from her rapist's home (Gen 34:26). At least the prostitute [זנה] Rahab has her own house (Josh 2:1). Generally, single women are a textual and social aberration. As Meyers (2013, 112) notes, "Except in truly urban settings in which goods could be obtained in a market and in which subsistence could be procured by means other than agriculture, people could survive only by being part

---

abandonment; only a man can initiate a divorce, and he may do so almost at will (Deut 24:1–3).

13. There also is no space for same-sex love or attraction, as the text and the culture presume opposite-sex marriage.

14. No longer able to marry, Tamar still "[remains] attached to a specific house," under a man's authority (Kawashima 2011, 6 n. 20).

of a household. That is, there was virtually no such thing as individual existence."¹⁵ She then offers what sounds like a defense of historical reality:

> Israelite women lived in a world utterly lacking the focus on achievement and self-fulfillment that characterizes individual development in much of today's world. Thus they must not be judged by the same criteria we would apply today; they cannot be considered the victims of sexism or gender bias because they (like their spouses) could neither choose their own life paths nor even conceive of choosing them. (121)

Choice is not the issue here; the Hebrew Bible literally does not have the equivalent of a single women's (or men's) census category. Excluding death or divorce, all people should be in a male-headed household.

Simply put, however, the world of the Bible does not match the world of today. Single women exist publicly and privately, neither as invisible nor as mythical creatures somehow bound to a patriarch. In spite of that reality, singletons often struggle against social and economic structures that privilege and presume coupling and patriarchy, with singletons of color facing the additional challenge of white privilege. In her analysis of the recent US housing crisis, Amy Castro Baker (2014, 59, 81–82) argues that, "single women represented the fastest-growing group of homeowners in the United States, but they also experienced higher rates of risky lending than their male peers, even when controlling for financial profile." Risky lending increases the likelihood of default and foreclosure, and it includes subprime mortgages,¹⁶ which are more likely to be offered to single women of color; African American women, for example, are five times "more likely to have a subprime mortgage than a white man with the same financial profile" (62; see also 60, 79–80). Women who default on their mortgages risk not finding affordable housing and becoming homeless or significantly damaging their finances for years to come (63–65).

Single women of color have faced discrimination in the housing market for decades. Baker notes that the Home Owners Loan Act of 1933 initially excluded single women and all women of color from federal housing benefits. While the 1968 Fair Housing Act prohibited racial

---

15. Meyers (2013, 118) later states that "the concept of the individual as a separate and independent entity was not part of the ancient Hebraic mindset."

16. Such mortgages, linked to the stock market, have higher interest rates, fluctuating interest rates, and higher initial costs (Baker 2014, 60).

discrimination, women did not receive protection until 1974, and the act still did not guarantee access to housing loans. Women of color and single women in the early 1970s received the least amount of credit (Baker 2014, 66–69), and "regardless of age or income, lenders required single women to secure their own mortgages with a man's signature" (70). Milllennia after Num 30, adult single women remained legal dependents. The 1974 Equal Credit Opportunity Act did not eliminate the discrimination because of the use of the subprime market, which encouraged brokers to increase their profits by pushing subprime loans, "even if a borrower qualifies for a safer prime loan" (77; see also 71–76).[17] Such loans receive no federal regulation or scrutiny, and with "never-married women [possessing] just 6 cents in wealth for each dollar in wealth held by never-married men" (81; see also 78), the consequences of defaulting on an already risky loan proved devastating. The subprime mortgage bubble burst (84), but the damage remains, and single women of color disproportionately suffered, in part because of lenders' perception of them as an exploitable population.

Obstacles aside, single women have become independent property owners, and they also have become independent sexual agents. Just as in ancient times, virginity is assumed to be the lack of heterosexual vaginal intercourse. Such a definition, however, precludes multiple forms of sexual expression and different types of intercourse ("Virginity," Planned Parenthood). Medical dictionary definitions of *virginity* are vague at best, as Merriam-Webster, the Free Dictionary, and MediLexicon confirm; the most common is the unhelpful "the virgin state." In some cultures today, a broken hymen still functions as proof of virginity. The problem is that not all women have hymens by the time of their first experience of vaginal intercourse. As Melissa A. Fabello (2013) concludes, "There is no medical or biological definition of virginity. None. Nothing.... Virginity as a concept was invented as an attempt to control (female) sexuality. It's just an idea. And ideas can change." Because the idea still shapes political and theological discourse, I use the words virginity and virgin in this essay, while being fully aware of the constructed, contingent, and gendered nature of both words.[18]

---

17. These loans have fixed interest rates (Baker 2014, 72).
18. See Therese Schecter's documentary, *How to Lose Your Virginity* (2013).

In the United States, virginity until marriage is now a minority state of being, in spite of religious preaching and abstinence-only government funding.[19] According to the 2002 National Survey of Family Growth, "thirty-six percent of women aged 20–44 are single, and nine in 10 single women are sexually experienced. Seventy percent of the latter women are currently sexually active" (Lindberg and Singh 2008, 27). The need for sexually transmitted infection and pregnancy prevention education, therefore, has increased (32). Additionally, single black women are more sexually experienced and more sexually active than their white and Latina counterparts (29, 30)[20] and statistically marry at lower rates, placing greater strain on any public policy goal of promoting "abstinence until marriage" (32). Laura Duberstein Lindberg and Susheela Singh conclude that:

> Government policies aimed at encouraging adult women to have sex only within marriage appear out of touch with the reality of the sexual behavior of single women.... And with the median age at first marriage now around 25, and with single adult women reporting high levels of sexual activity, the behavioral changes required for current efforts to promote abstinence until marriage to succeed would have to be phenomenal. (27, 33)

Yet, religious rhetoric and beliefs continue to hold up this ideal in the face of reality, even though self-identified single religious women may be having sex at similarly high rates as nonreligious women. *Relevant Magazine*, written for "twenty-and thirty-something Christians" ("The Relevant Story," n.d.) suggests "giving the abstinence message a makeover," reinforcing the importance of marriage, and encouraging "renewed abstinence" for single Christians who have had premarital sex (Charles 2012). The Center for Applied Research in the Apostolate (CARA) concludes that "young

---

19. While the Office of Population Affairs had a goal of promoting abstinence in 2003 ("For adolescents and unmarried individuals, the message is 'A' for abstinence" [Lindberg and Singh 2008, 27]), 2014 guidelines focus on artificial contraception as part of reproductive health outcomes (Office of Population Affairs 2014 and Family Planning National Training Center 2014).

20. Nearly 94 percent of single black women are sexually experienced, and 75 percent of single black women are sexually active, in comparison with 88 percent and 68 percent of single white women and 87 percent and 68 percent of single Latina women. The survey defines sexually active as having "had vaginal intercourse in the past three months" (Lindberg and Singh 2008, 29).

Catholics are often sent off to college from homes where the parents do not have attitudes regarding this issue that are consistent with Catholic teachings" ("Replicate Before You Speculate Too Much" 2010). The conclusion suggests that if people simply aligned themselves with the abstinence message, then the "problem" of premarital sex would be "solved."[21] The abstinence message itself, however, remains uninterrogated.

The social expectation that women will marry and the individual desire for marriage further complicate the abstinence ideal. Which women will win the marriage lottery? Analyzing 1990s data from the National Survey of Family Growth and the National Longitudinal Survey of Youth, Daniel T. Lichter, Christie D. Batson, and J. Brian Brown (2004, 2; also 7–9, 14) conclude that "a majority of unmarried women, including disadvantaged single and cohabiting mothers, value marriage as a personal goal. Among disadvantaged women, single mothers, and racial minority women, systematic differences point to subgroups with lower marital expectations. However, our results also indicate that marital desires do not easily translate into marriage." The desire for marriage cuts across race, class, and age, but all influence the likelihood of getting married (3–5, 10). Perhaps because older women think the prospect of marriage has become less likely, they are less likely to state that they want to marry (8, 10). Single mothers also express less confidence that they will marry (11), and so do poorer women, possibly due to "objective marriage market opportunities (e.g., few marriageable men) than with any lack of receptivity toward marriage" (13; see also 8, 12, 16). Regardless of race, the desire for marriage is high, and it also increases with higher levels of education (15). So, if single women want to marry, why did 80 percent of them remain unmarried four years after the survey (17)? The authors do not know but suggest that in the case of black women, "marital desires ... may be affected by characteristics of the potential male partners available in the marriage market" (19) or what contemporary media discourse calls the black male shortage.

Although the scholarly analysis notes that "black women have a substantially lower *risk* of marrying than white women" (Lichter, Batson, and Brown 2004, 19, emphasis added), the language still may be kinder than the mainstream media's. In a 2011 blog post, Bené Viera expresses weariness about continued discussion of black women's marriage rates and

---

21. Notably, women of other faiths are addressing up front the tension between the ideal of abstinence and the reality of premarital sexual activity. See Katsman 2015 and "How Do Muslim Girls Deal with Their Natural Sexual Desires?" 2014–2015.

eligible marriage partners. The proximate cause of the complaint is Ralph Richard Banks's *Is Marriage For White People?* (2011), which argues that black women should consider nonwhite spouses.[22] Viera (2011) protests that "black women's singleness has become a spectacle. For starters, this story has been covered … since 2009." Well, not quite. Remember that Lichter, Batson, and Brown write in 2004, using data from 1994–1998. So, the story predates Banks by nearly a generation. Viera (2011) continues, "It is beyond problematic that authors, journalists, researchers, social commentators and mainstream media find that black women's singleness is a crisis, and that the solution is to marry white men." The white scholarly conclusion that black educated women also want to marry sounds patronizing,[23] but it cannot be more patronizing than *Essence Magazine*'s near total erasure of single black women, for example, except to show their engagement stories or give dating tips on "10 Behaviors that Keep You Single" (Brunson n.d.).[24]

The social-scientific focus on women's sexuality and singleness, however, also assumes heteronormativity. Women struggling to marry and having sex during the struggle are heterosexual, although with same sex marriage now legal in all fifty states, the discourse will likely change. Perhaps not surprisingly, the one sociological study I did find about black lesbians analyzes couples and family formation. Mignon R. Moore (2012, 36) notes that, "in an intragroup (within-race) analysis, Black heterosexuality becomes normative while Black homosexuality remains deviant." Black lesbians with children "offer a manifestation of respectability that is simultaneous with an active expression of Black women's sexual autonomy and freedom" (37). Such freedom, however, presumes a partner, so single lesbians may be even less visible than their opposite sex loving sisters. Respectability presumes coupling, but the presumption makes sense, because a lingering and destructive stereotype of LGBTQ communities is promiscuity.

---

22. Banks, a black man, married a black woman, so his wife did not follow his book's thesis.

23. "Such data are clearly inconsistent with the commonplace argument that more education encourages women's economic independence from men, transforms gender role orientations, and reduces the likelihood of marriage" (Lichter, Batson, and Brown 2004, 15).

24. I analyzed the website for a March 2014 presentation. The contents of the site has not been updated since then.

The presumption of and emphasis upon heterosexuality not only masks the reality of sexual diversity in African American (and indeed all) communities but also creates masculine norms that further complicate single women's lives. Black women often receive blame for black men's failures. As single mothers, "Black women are held responsible in some academic literature and in the popular press for Black males' maladaptive characteristics and behaviors" (Bush 2004, 381). Trying to reverse this image, V. Lawson Bush concludes that black women can and do raise successful men, but the definition of masculinity may be essentialist. He argues that "what these Black mothers have constructed is neither traditional masculinity nor femininity" and lies between white ideals of both (384), yet the table of masculine characteristics suggests otherwise. Black mothers want their sons to be "financially independent, reliable, responsible, responsible to his community, [and] strong in his mind and strong in his heart" (383); however, this sounds similar to the common white masculine ideals described by scholars such as Michael Kimmel and R.W. Connell. The characteristics of "[believing] that there is a God, Christian, *married*, and religious" (383, emphasis added) sound positive but also limiting. What are the consequences of mothers holding up these ideals to their sons? What about nonreligious boys, or boys who may not want to marry? Does the ideal of Christianity presume the ideal of heterosexuality?

The last question assumes the previous two, and the answer may be yes. Just as black women's heterosexuality is normative, so is black men's. Those who are gay may find themselves struggling to exist within their communities as black gay men. Terrell L. Strayhorn and Derrick L. Tillman-Kelly (2013, 83) find three primary constructions of masculinity in black gay male college students—(1) "accepting, adhering to, and performing traditionally masculine norms," (2) "intentionally, or subconsciously, challenging hegemonic notions of Black masculinity through their behaviors and self-beliefs," and (3) "recognizing that their masculine identity(-ies) are influenced by other social factors and locations." Because black masculinity presumes independence, spirituality, and "sex with multiple female partners," or compulsive heterosexuality, not fitting in with the third category can lead to teasing when younger and violence when older (88; see also 89–90). To avoid both, a majority of the research subjects stated masculine ideals of strength, fatherhood, and presumed heterosexuality (96–98), with *"religion ... identified as a major determinant of masculine beliefs"* (100, emphasis added). The authors utilized "a constructivist qualitative approach" because of "its congruent positioning with our own ethics and values as researchers in terms of how invisible and voiceless people can be seen and heard without doing damage or 'violence' to their authentic voice" (91, 92). Single women are not the only invisible community members.

The recent glorification of single women, or at least the acceptance of singleness as a viable life choice, personified by Kate Bolick, assumes both a class and race position that may exclude black women. Bolick grabbed headlines with her 2011 *The Atlantic* article, "All the Single Ladies," and expanded her thesis that women need not be defined by marriage in her 2015 book, *Spinster: Making a Life of One's Own*. While Bolick uses Beyoncé's hook in her shorter piece (and quite well), the nonwhite reader searches in vain for role models in the book. All of Bolick's "awakeners" are white,[25] and her acknowledgement of this is dismissive:

> Not until I was driving through my blindingly white hometown did I realize that the only characteristics all five had in common were a highly ambivalent relationship to the institution of marriage, the opportunity to articulate this ambivalence, and whiteness—each of which, arguably, was inextricable from the rest. During the period I was drawn to—primarily, the turn of the last century—vanishingly few women of color were given the privilege to write and publish, and, therefore, speak across the decades. And then thinking ceased and muscle memory took over. (2015, 9)

This will not do. Women like Ida B. Wells Barnett and Mary McLeod Bethune, Harlem Renaissance authors like Zora Neale Hurston and Nella Larsen, and any woman published in *The Crisis* can be easily accessed.[26]

---

25. All also married at some point.

26. I thank Jennifer Tomscha, a white woman who reviewed *Spinster* on apracticalwedding.com, which "supports laid-back feminist weddings" ("About APW" n.d) for being my awakener. Tomscha's subtitle, "In which, once again, the white woman is still the Everywoman," gave me a critical lens with which to read Bolick's work, since I read her review first before deciding to purchase the book. Tomscha praises Bolick for challenging the ubiquitous presumption of marriage, which "keeps popping up like an obnoxious photobomber," but calls her to task for white privilege: "Autopilot for her and for other Americans of privilege is when the very fact of that privilege recedes. White America is America, right?... It's 2015, and in publishing, whiteness is still rendered as the universal experience, that from which all people can draw inspiration. The white, heterosexual woman reigns as the Everywoman" (Tomscha 2015).

Bolick's general ignorance of race and class frequently shapes her narrative of single women. Her discussion of the history of women's work does not mention that these women are white, and she describes them as "we" (the assumed reader must be white as well?), yet she rejects a comparison of (white) Maeve Brennan and Billie Holiday because "the political, social, and economic forces that shape the African-American single experience is an entire book unto itself" (Bolick 2015, 177). Single woman equals white woman. While recognizing that social class shaped a woman's life chances, whiteness again remains the default identity—the turn of the century Bachelor Girl, the New Woman, the respectable bachelorette, the Barbican girl, and the Grande Dame are all white (82, 91–92, 174–75, 187). The only acknowledgement of alternative ethnic universes comes in her utilization of possible selves, which she borrows from white social psychologist Hazel Markus, who borrows it from black and Latino civil rights movements; "all of it was premised on the idea that you should claim and reimagine your category," and single women should do the same (65–66). Bolick's cover photo of herself, in a dress and heels, complete with teacup and saucer in one hand, downcast eyes, and demure smile, displays a particular form of singleness;[27] although she insists upon the intentionality of her singleness (138, 154), she also claims that "as a woman, I wasn't required to take care of myself—ever.... I could create personal meaning and social validation through getting married and having children" (72). This option, however, ignores both race and class. As noted earlier, poor women and women of color cannot assume this escape hatch exists for them. Work equals survival and not simply another life choice. The option also tacitly accepts the invisibility of Num 30, where a woman's identity only exists in relation to a man's.

Simply offering singleness as an option and acceptable identity marker and alternative to marriage overlooks the complexity and reality of intersectionality—race and religion matter. Laura Kipnis (2015) criticizes Bolick for answering an already outdated question: "Is marriage really the *basis* of female ontology in 2015?... It's depressing that women seem to

---

27. Laura Kipnis (2015) humorously and seriously critiques the photo, writing, "Clearly she's [Bolick's] a spinster by choice! She could be married in a heartbeat! Message received. It's a message that doesn't exactly allay the anxieties the book claims to be militating against—namely that we spinsters aren't choosing our fates, we're just losers in the marriage market.... The reality is that for every decade older or 10 pounds heavier or number of hours outside of New York, the social prospects get dimmer."

keep forgetting that basically *we can do whatever we want*. And thus the master's house keeps getting dismantled, then reconstructed, then dismantled all over again, one dreary brick at a time." Kipnis' italicized sentence, however, may fall into the same essentialist trap as Bolick's work—choices are neither inevitable, universal, nor equally created. If single black women do not exist in Num 30 or the new spinster model, our fit in black communities, religious or secular, is often a poor one as well.

Part of the poor fit comes from the admirable goal of resisting sexual stereotypes. In her study of Henriette Delille, who founded the Sisters of the Holy Family, womanist theologian M. Shawn Copeland (2009, 10; also 8) notes that Delille chose freedom and bodily agency by becoming a nun; she "challenged the dominant white cultural ideology about black women" by "[redefining] black women as chaste." In antebellum times, chastity, virtue, and obedience, code words for womanhood, belonged only to white women; "commodified, fungible, and labeled as lascivious, black women were made something less than human, but *not* persons" (44; see also 43). By starting a religious order for black women, Delille contributed to the work of restoring black women's humanity (47–78). I am reluctant to argue with the mission of a nun, particularly one rightly recognized as Venerable, and especially since the marginalization and vilification of black women and their bodies remains a real problem a century and a half after emancipation.[28] I will suggest, however, that chastity may be one method of resistance but not the only one; the way to full humanity may have multiple paths. Copeland knows this, arguing that in spite of stereotypes of black bodies as either invisible ("a 'peculiar' and 'perverted' form of presence that renders the individual black human person anonymous") or "promiscuous, loud, illiterate, diseased," free black women claimed their humanity, including sexuality, "denying neither sexual pleasure nor desire, resisting both coercion and intimidation" (2010, 16–17, 19, 50; see also 48).

Womanist use of postmodern theory recognizes multiple definitions of blackness and the influence of intersectionality on those definitions (Copeland 2010, 21). At the core, however, should be the ideal of full humanity, or *humanum*, a term that Copeland borrows from Edward

---

28. For one example, critiques of Serena Williams's physique and femininity continue, even as she establishes herself as one of the best tennis players ever. See Kendall 2015 and Freeman 2015.

Schillebeeckx.[29] The definitions include "a social being; unafraid of difference and interdependence; and willing to struggle daily against 'bad faith' and *ressentiment* for the survival, creation, and future of all life" (Copeland 2010, 92).[30] Bad faith, in anthropological and sociological terms, often means maintaining a position as unchangeable without acknowledging its contingency and/or constructedness,[31] for example, insisting that God ordained slavery because the Bible includes slavery, without taking seriously the contexts of the verses and the political and economic agendas of those who used them. Delille notwithstanding, the Christian insistence on virginity until marriage, and particularly the ways in which that affects women, exemplifies bad faith—the insistence holds up an ancient, androcentric concept that has outlived its original rationale (protect male property). If new rationales can be created by and for women, as Delille did, then fabulous. The current focus on virginity, however, ignores the statistics I mentioned earlier, insists upon the maintenance of one biblical sexual "norm" while others quietly go into retirement (a good number of marriages end in divorce for reasons besides sexual unfaithfulness; see Matt 19:9), and worst of all, glorifies marriage to the point of idolatry, reinforcing the Num 30 ideal of women as daughters or wives.

No sources make this argument more effectively than those written by Africana scholars about single women in the church. For the last thirty years, single women have been pressured to marry and tow the virginity line while waiting. Theologian Chipo M. Mtombeni, speaking in 1989, argued that many African societies view singleness as morally suspect. An unmarried woman over twenty-five must be either possessed, promiscuous, or too disagreeable to find a husband; "very few people sympathize with single women who have never attempted marriage" (Mtombeni 1990, 125). She notes, "Every young lady is expected to marry and settle down.

---

29. *Humanum* means "the vision of a full humanity that, while not antecedently given by God, presents itself as a goal to be achieved by justice" (Copeland 2010, 174 n. 25).

30. *Ressentiment* comes from Nietzsche and means the reliving of a situation of pain and shame by a person without power, which may lead to anger against those in power, along with toxic revenge fantasies (Copeland 2010, 163–64 n. 23).

31. Clifford Geertz (1973, 20 n. 4) states that anthropologists engage in bad faith when they ignore their own cultural contexts. Sociologist Peter Berger (1990, 85, 93) views bad faith as a type of alienation; if people forget that they make their own social worlds and conclude that only one world is open to them, then they act in bad faith, identifying with one social role to the exclusion of all other options.

If she fails to meet the expectations, society becomes negative" (129). Churches reinforce the expectation of marriage, looking favorably only upon nuns or single women in public ministry (126, 129). While Mtombeni concludes that women should be free to remain single, the church's response reinforces the idea that women's sexuality must be contained, either in marriage or religious service.

Even the latter may be an inferior state. Baptist minister Kate Coleman, a British Ghanaian, learned that her mother in Ghana was trying to find her a husband. Upon going home, a speaker introduced her as "a Baptist minister in London and *still* single" (Coleman 2000, 11; 10). Analyzing her situation, she remarks, "The Church may not call single people lepers but it often treats them as though they were unnatural and therefore incapable of serving God in key leadership positions.... It appears that the major, if not the single problem for people such as myself continues to be that of invisibility" (14, 15). Reverend Coleman struggles with this invisibility in spite of practicing and preaching the religious ideal of celibacy (20), but her language certainly is more positive than M. E. Baloyi's 2010 article, "Pastoral care and the *agony* of female singleness in the African Christian context" (emphasis added). He argues that "nothing is being done to address singleness and its related problems," including social shaming, inferiority, and loneliness (723; see also 725, 728–30, 731–32). Baloyi, however, criticizes those women who do not live as singles (i.e., celibate), suggesting that they use sex only for pleasure and "it no longer fulfills its aims and objectives clearly.... Therefore, many singles also have sexually transmitted diseases" (734; see also 730–31). He calls on the church to teach the equality of all people, but the unmarried must "live a Christian life"; singleness does not equal sinfulness, "but ... there are instances in which that person was not fortunate enough to be coupled" (737–38). Marriage remains the ideal; for those living out plan B, pastors must encourage them to "a life of pure singleness," meaning no sex outside of marriage, masturbation, or lesbianism (738). Again, churchwomen may be either virgins or wives, following a heteronormative ideal; not even pastoral theology challenges the binary, which Baloyi maintains as biblical. He does not utilize Num 30, but its gender roles remain.

In South African Pentecostal churches, the binary places single women in a difficult position. Maria Frahm-Arp's fieldwork in these churches leads her to the following thesis: women who want to remain virgins face social pressures from boyfriends and significant others; professional women may be viewed as undesirable marriage partners; and

"PCC [Pentecostal Charismatic Churches] tell these women that improving their economic status is their God-given vocation, but at the same time they preach that it is through marriage that women fulfill their Christian calling" (2012, 370). While the single woman professional offers an alternative social role to "celibate nun," the role should be an "interim stage" (371). The interim stage includes praying for a husband, sacrificing social opportunities for economic opportunities, and struggling to remain virgins. Women who have sexual relationships before marriage, particularly if children result, have more difficulty finding a spouse. Their churches, however, teach the women that hard work and chastity will lead to success, defined as economic stability and marriage (376–78). Once married, the women can then become homemakers (380). Frahm-Arp concludes that the "churches have been changing people's social relations and change social behavior, not by offering a different ideal to what the culture in general regards as an ideal but by offering an alternative way to achieve it" (380).[32]

In the United States, Pentecostal and evangelical churches promote a similar message. Monique Moultrie's (2011, 238–40, 44) "After the Thrill Is Gone: Married to the Holy Spirit but Still Sleeping Alone" analyzes ministries geared towards single black Christian women and concludes that such ministries emphasize marriage to God as a replacement for sexual longing and sexual activity. She writes, "This niche within faith-based ministries is very profitable because it relies on standard tropes of female sexuality to maintain social order, namely, controlled female sexual expression" (239). Sex is to be avoided for the sake of living the right way with Jesus, at least until the right man comes along (247, 249–50).

The virgin-wife binary may be old and religiously sanctioned, but older is not always better. Radford-Hill states that the strongblackwoman should "call the question." Regardless of strength, black women should call *this* question. Why are churches still holding onto a gendered binary that

---

32. Her final footnote is as follows: "It is important to note that for those women who do not conform to or fit into this family ideal, a conservative church can become a problematic place where the values and teachings fail to equip these members for dealing with the problems of divorce and singleness. In the research I conducted in 2006, one reason why some women left His People and Grace Bible churches was because the churches' pressure for an ideal marriage became too much for them, either because they were not married or because their marriages were less than ideal and they felt they would never attain the churches' standards" (Frahm-Arp 2012, 383 n. 5).

does not work for women? Hayes (1995, 25) writes that "mothering thus requires an ability and willingness to maintain traditions while reshaping them for future generations—discarding that which is not nurturing and upholding while incorporating that which is." The more I study and live, the more convinced I become that the narrow traditions around single women's sexuality need reshaping at best. Some of us are virgins; most of us are not. We are straight, lesbian, and bisexual. Some want marriage, for a variety of reasons, and some of us do not want spouses at all. Blaming and shaming sexually active single women for being sexually active and single runs contrary to the womanist ideal of freedom for all. The Christian emphasis on universal premarital celibacy places anyone outside of that state in a position of judgment and condemnation. Simply defaulting to the biblical texts that sanction premarital virginity begs the question I am calling. I go to church without a hat, have taught a mixed-gender Sunday school class, and wear a fabulous gold charm bracelet, all of which the New Testament frowns upon (1 Cor 11:2–16; 1 Tim 2:9–15), and all of which other Christian women do. So why is celibacy privileged over other biblical suggestions or prohibitions, and should it have such privilege?

These questions turn us back to womanist methodology, specifically power analyses and embodied-mediated knowledge. Africana demography gives the lie to the virgin-wife binary, and yet the traditional binary often goes unchallenged. Discussions about sexuality, crime rates, and socioeconomic challenges regularly devolve into shrill calls about the necessity of increasing marriage rates and decreasing single motherhood in black communities, as if the institution of marriage will automatically solve all structural problems. For economic reasons, the latter call matters a great deal. Behind the former call, however, lies a crushing combination of fear and respectability. It seems as if since the nineteenth century, the fear of black women's sexuality and the insistence upon controlling it has been the goal of white men, black nationalists, and Christians of all colors. Viera (2011) "[calls] patriarchy and white privilege." Bingo. The need to appear nonthreatening and above reproach has often outweighed the desire to be free. Roxane Gay (2014, 258, 260), in "The Politics of Respectability," notes that the idea of fitting nonwhite people into dominant cultural norms cannot be a solution to racism or a strategy to live with racism's consequences, in spite of some black men's claims to the contrary. Yet, the politics of respectability functioned then and now in precisely that way. If black people behaved soberly and modestly, they would disprove all negative stereotypes about their identity and sexuality. That has not happened yet. Instead, new stereotypes keep forming, including "the tragic single black woman meme," which "reinforces that black women are unlovable" (Viera 2011). Churches, instead of affirming black women, often reinforce the meme, but as Teresa Morgan (2005, 32) rightly notes, "If one can eat and work and be a Christian, there seems no obvious reasons to exclude sexual relationships."

Cannon (2006) warns against deconstruction for its own sake; however, any ideal that makes women feel like freaks if they have sex or failures if they have no spouse may be eligible for deconstruction. The dual emphases on chastity and marriage reinforce a particular patriarchal worldview and benefit those with the most to gain from its perpetuation—men and women who value the ideal and live it out. For those who cannot or will not do so, there is no one size fits all model for sexuality and identity. West (2006, 293) advises womanists not to essentialize black women; resisting Christian essentialist notions of women as wives or wives-to-be may be one way to take her advice. I do not use Facebook, but its twelve relationship options and fifty-eight gender categories point to a diverse world that could not even have been glimpsed 2,500 years ago, when Num 30 perhaps reached its final form. As a Bible scholar who cannot personally go a day without the Psalms, it pains me to see the Bible being used potentially to make people feel worse about the people with whom they voluntarily or consensually sleep. The Bible's call for helping the poor may well be timeless, as poverty seems to be built into human social structures. Sexuality, however, is much more fluid. Instead of placing people in a narrow box, expanding the box seems like a more reasonable and compassionate response.

Compassion matters. Gay (2014, 300) beautifully writes, in response to those who do not think certain deaths worthy of lamentation, "I have never considered compassion a finite resource." Singleness is not death, and it should be viewed neither as a social tragedy nor a temporary phase for black women; it is one identity marker among many. Womanist ideology and theology calls for a love of humanity, all of it. Playing with the call and response communication style so common in black churches, Gay concludes, "Compassion. Response. Compassion. Response" (300). After the shooting at Emanuel AME Church, Solange Knowles tweeted, "Where can we be black?" (Maule n.d.). The question fundamentally asks, where and with whom can we be ourselves? Where and with whom can we be seen? Katha Pollitt's definition of feminism offers one possible answer, and I close this essay with it as a prayer:

For me, to be a feminist is to answer the question "Are women human?" with a yes. It is not about whether women are better than, worse than or identical with me. And it's certainly not about trading personal liberty—abortion, divorce, sexual self-expression—for social protection as wives and mothers.... It's about justice, fairness and access to the broad range of human experience. It's about women consulting their own well-being and being judged as individuals rather than as members of a class with one personality, one social function, one road to happiness. It's about women having intrinsic value as persons rather than contingent value as a means to an end for others. (1994, xiii)

Amen.

Works Cited

"About APW." n.d. A Practical Wedding. http://tinyurl.com/SBL0688s.
Ahmed, Sameera, Wahiba Abu-Ras, and Cynthia L. Arfken. 2014. "Prevalence of Risk Behaviors among U.S. Muslim College Students." *Journal of Muslim Mental Health* 8: 5–19. http://dx.doi.org/10.3998/jmmh.10381607.0008.101.
Baker, Amy Castro. 2014. "Eroding the Wealth of Women: Gender and the Subprime Foreclosure Crisis." *Social Service Review* 88:59–91.
Baloyi, M. E. 2010. "Pastoral Care and the Agony of Female Singleness in the African Christian Context." *In die Skriflig* 44:723–42.
Banks, Ralph Richard. 2011. *Is Marriage for White People? How the African American Marriage Decline Affects Everyone.* Dutton Adult.
Berger, Peter L. 1990. *The Sacred Canopy: Elements of a Sociological Theory of Religion.* New York: Anchor Books.
Berquist, Jon L. 2000. "Divorce." *EDB* 351.
Blackburn, Simon. 2004. *Lust.* New York: Oxford University Press.
Bolick, Kate. 2011. "All the Single Ladies." *The Atlantic.* http://tinyurl.com/SBL0688p.
Bolick, Kate. 2015. *Spinster: Making a Life of One's Own.* New York: Crown.
Bowles, John P. 2007. "'Acting Like a Man': Adrian Piper's Mythic Being and Black Feminism in the 1970s." *Signs* 32:621–47.
Brunson, Paul Carrick. n.d. "Modern Day Matchmaker: 10 Behaviors that Keep you Single." *Essence Magazine.* http://tinyurl.com/SBL0688o.

Bush, V. Lawson. 2004. "How Black Mothers Participate in the Development of Manhood and Masculinity: What Do We Know about Black Mothers and Their Sons?" *JNE* 73:381–91.

Cannon, Katie G. 2006. "Structured Academic Amnesia: As If This True Womanist Story Never Happened." Pages 19–28 in *Deeper Shades of Purple: Womanism in Religion and Society*. Edited by Stacey M. Floyd-Thomas. New York: New York University Press.

Charles, Tyler. 2012. "The Secret Sexual Revolution." *Relevant Magazine*. http://tinyurl.com/SBL0688a.

Cho, Sumi, Crenshaw, Kimberlé Williams, and Leslie McCall. 2013. "Toward a Field of Intersectionality Studies: Theory, Application, and Praxis." *Signs* 38:785–810.

Coleman, Kate. 2000. "Woman, Single, Christian." Pages 10–23 in *Sisters with Power*. Edited by Bishop Joe Aldred. London: Continuum.

Copeland, M. Shawn. 2009. *The Subversive Power of Love: The Vision of Henriette Delille*. New York: Paulist.

———. 2010. *Enfleshing Freedom: Body, Race, and Being*. Minneapolis: Fortress.

Day, Peggy L. 2000. "Widow." *EDB* 1377–78.

Duncan, Carol B. 2006. "From 'Force-Ripe' to 'Womanish/ist': Black Girlhood and African Diasporan Feminist Consciousness." Pages 29–37 in *Deeper Shades of Purple: Womanism in Religion and Society*. Edited by Stacey M. Floyd-Thomas. New York: New York University Press.

Ellenson, Jacqueline Koch. 2008. "Contemporary Reflection." Pages 1008–9 in *The Torah: A Women's Commentary*. Edited by Tamara Cohn Eskenazi and Andrea L. Weiss. New York: URJ Press.

Fabello, Melissa A. 2013. "4 Myths about Virginity." Everyday Feminism. http://tinyurl.com/SBL0688b.

Family Planning National Training Center. 2014. "New Federal Recommendations to Improve the Quality of Family Planning Services." US Department of Health and Human Services. http://tinyurl.com/SBL0688d.

Frahm-Arp, Maria. 2012. "Singleness, Sexuality, and the Dream of Marriage." *JRA* 42:369–83.

Freeman, Hadley. 2015. "It's Still Harder for Black People to Win Respect. Even Serena Williams." http://tinyurl.com/SBL0688u.

Gay, Roxane. 2014. *Bad Feminist: Essays*. New York: Harper Perennial.

Geertz, Clifford. 1973. *The Interpretation of Cultures*. New York: Basic Books.

Goldstein, Elizabeth. 2008. "Vows and Vengeance." Pages 989–1005 in *The Torah: A Women's Commentary*. Edited by Tamara Cohn Eskenazi and Andrea L. Weiss. New York: URJ Press.
Guy-Sheftall, Beverly. 2002. "Response from a 'Second Waver' to Kimberly Springer's 'Third Wave Black Feminism?'" *Signs* 27:1091–94.
Hammonds, Evelynn M. 1997. "Toward a Genealogy of Black Female Sexuality: The Problematic of Silence." Pages 170–182 in *Feminst Genealogies, Colonial Legacies, Democratic Futures*. Edited by M. Jacqui Alexander and Chandra Talpade Mohanty. Routledge.
Hayes, Diana L. 1995. *Hagar's Daughters: Womanist Ways of Being in the World*. New York: Paulist.
"How Do Muslim Girls Deal with Their Natural Sexual Desires?" 2014–2015. The Student Room. http://tinyurl.com/SBL0688r.
Katsman, Hannah. 2015. "What Happens to Sexually Active Orthodox Singles?" The Sisterhood. http://tinyurl.com/SBL0688q.
Kawashima, Robert S. 2011. "Could a Woman Say 'No' in Biblical Israel: On the Genealogy of Legal Status in Biblical Law and Literature. *AJSR* 35:1–22.
Kendall, Erika Nicole. 2015. "Female Athletes Often Face the Femininity Police—Especially Serena Williams." http://tinyurl.com/SBL0688t.
Kipnis, Laura. 2015. "Marry by 30." Slate Book Review. http://tinyurl.com/SBL0688c.
Lichter, Daniel T., Christie D. Batson, and J. Brian Brown. 2004. "Welfare Reform and Marriage Promotion: The Marital Expectations and Desires of Single and Cohabiting Mothers." *Social Service Review* 78:2–25.
Lindberg, Laura Duberstein, and Susheela Singh. 2008. "Sexual Behavior of Single Adult American Women." *Perspectives on Sexual and Reproductive Health* 40:27–33.
Matlin, Daniel. 2006. "'Lift up Yr Self!' Reinterpreting Amiri Baraka (LeRoi Jones), Black Power, and the Uplift Tradition." *JAH* 93:91–116.
Maule, Alicia. "Pop Singer Solange Voices National Angst: 'Where Can We Be Black?'" MSNBC. http://tinyurl.com/SBL0688v.
Meyers, Carol. 2013. *Rediscovering Eve: Ancient Israelite Women in Context*. New York: Oxford University Press.
Moore, Mignon R. 2012. "Intersectionality and the Study of Black, Sexual Minority Women." *Gender and Society* 26:33–39.
Morgan, Teresa. 2005. "Bridget Jones's Theology: Reflections on Involuntary Singleness." *Theology* 108:32–39.

Moultrie, Monique. 2011. "After the Thrill Is Gone: Married to the Holy Spirit but Still Sleeping Alone." *Pneuma* 33:237–53.

Mtombeni, Chipo M. 1990. "Attitude towards Single Women in Africa." Pages 125–30 in *Talitha, qumi!: Proceedings of The Convocation of African Women Theologians, Trinity College, Logon-Accra, September 24–October 2, 1989*. Edited by Mercy Amba Oduyoye and Musimbi Kanyoro. Ibadan: Daystar.

Office of Population Affairs. 2014. "Providing Quality Family Planning Services Recommendations for Primary Care Providers." US Department of Health and Human Services. http://tinyurl.com/SBL0688e.

Pollitt, Katha. 1994. *Reasonable Creatures: Essays on Women and Feminism*. New York: Knopf.

Radford-Hill, Sheila. 2002. "Keepin' It Real: A Generational Commentary on Kimberly Springer's 'Third Wave Black Feminism?'" *Signs* 27:1083–89.

"The Relevant Story." n.d. *Relevant Magazine*. http://tinyurl.com/SBL0688f.

"Replicate Before You Speculate Too Much." 2010. Nineteensixty-four. http://tinyurl.com/SBL0688g.

Schechter, Therese, dir. 2013. *How to Lose Your Virginity*. Trixie Films.

Shaw, Susan M., and Janet Lee. 2015. *Women's Voices, Feminist Visions: Classic and Contemporary Readings*. 6th ed. New York: McGraw Hill Education

"Single." Dictionary.com. http://tinyurl.com/SBL0688h.

"Single." Urban Dictionary. http://tinyurl.com/SBL0688i.

Springer, Kimberly. 2002. "Third Wave Black Feminism?" *Signs* 27:1059–82.

Strayhorn, Terrell L., and Derrick L. Tillman-Kelly. 2013. "Queering Masculinity: Manhood and Black Gay Men in College." *Spectrum* 1:83–110.

Tomscha, Jennifer. 2015. "Kate Bolick's 'Spinster': In Which, Once Again, the White Woman Is Still the Everywoman." A Practical Wedding. http://tinyurl.com/SBL0688j.

Viera, Bené. 2011. "Single Black Women Are Tired of Being a Spectacle." Huffington Post. http://tinyurl.com/SBL0688k.

"Virginity." n.d. The Free Dictionary. http://tinyurl.com/SBL0688w2.

"Virginity." n.d. mediLexicon. http://tinyurl.com/SBL0688l.

"Virginity." n.d. Merriam Webster. http://tinyurl.com/SBL0688n.

"Virginity." n.d. Planned Parenthood. http://tinyurl.com/SBL0688m.

Wallace, Michele. 1978. *Black Macho and the Myth of Superwoman*. New York: Dial Press.
Weisberg, Dvora E. 2008. "Post-biblical Interpretations." Pages 1006–7 in *The Torah: A Women's Commentary*. Edited by Tamara Cohn Eskenazi and Andrea L. Weiss. New York: URJ Press.
West, Traci C. 2006. "Is A Womanist a Black Feminist? Marking the Distinctions and Defying Them: A Black Feminist Response." Pages 291–95 in *Deeper Shades of Purple: Womanism in Religion and Society*. Edited by Stacey M. Floyd-Thomas. New York: New York University Press.

A Womanist Midrash of Delilah:
Don't Hate the Playa Hate the Game*

Wil Gafney

So it happened after [the Philistine woman and sex-worker in Gaza] that Shimson [Samson] loved a woman in the valley of Sorek, whose name was Delilah.[1] (Judg 16:4)

A diva is a female version of a hustler
...best believe her, you see her, she getting paid
She ain't calling him to greet her, don't need him her bed's made. ("Diva")[2]

Delilah is a "true playa for real" (Williams and Hugo 2001). While the term *playa* has its origin in hypermasculine performativity in rap and hip-hop music, videos, and associated media and promotional materials, the term and certain aspects of the performance have been claimed by some women performers and fans. Whether they adopt the playa role or not, women performers in hip-hop are almost all by default occupying and transforming a male role (Perry 2004, 156). Within that schema, the hypermasculine male playa exists in a fictively rigidly binary world; however, the world around them is not a polarized binary. The notion of a woman like Delilah or Nicki Minaj as a playa is not so much a blurring of lines or transgression of boundaries as it is evidence of the fluidity of gender roles and perfor-

---

* Editors' note: Gafney defines her womanist midrash as an exegetical approach to the Hebrew Scriptures grounded in her "womanist, black feminist identity and experience" and her "knowledge and love" of classical and contemporary Jewish interpretation of Torah and other parts of Scripture (Gafney 2007, 134).

1. Translations of the biblical text are mine unless otherwise noted. In those translations, I use the Hebrew names of characters from which the more familiar traditional names often vary significantly.

2. Crawford, Garrett, and Knowles 2008.

mativity. Female MCs and hip-hop artists often signal their playa status through highly sexualized lyrics that focus on their own gratification and a display of wealth and material culture comparable to male artists; some notable examples include Lil Kim, Trina, Foxy Brown, Suga, and Missy Elliott.[3] Even so women's sexuality is "the most brazenly commodified representation of gender in hip-hop" (Bradley 2015, 181) and, arguably, in the biblical text. In both hip-hop and the biblical text, gender portrayals and performances are highly nuanced, occasionally subversive, and transgressive. I argue here that Delilah is one such character.[4]

As a womanist I am interested in Delilah apart from masculinist constructions, even those in sacred texts. I see in the biblical text structural elements of another portrait, one in which Delilah is the subject of her own story. Using the typology of Imani Perry (2004, 156–59, 167),[5] I view Delilah as a "bad woman" who uses her sexuality to her own benefit within the overarching androcentric and patriarchal power systems. In a womanist reading Delilah is her own woman, making her own choices with her body and her life and, surprisingly, ends off better than one might imagine in the androcentric scriptures of Israel.[6] She plays the game the men in and behind the text have devised for her, and she bests them at it. "Play on playa, play on" (Broadus 2006).

The story of Delilah is submerged in the story of Shimson (Samson) where she is positioned as ancillary.[7] It is probably the intent of the canon-shapers that Delilah be reviled. Her name or the one given her is most likely preserved for this reason. Phonetically, her name sounds like "she

---

3. Many thanks to Earl Fisher, PhD student (Rhetoric and Communication), University of Memphis, for helping me think through these issues.

4. Bradley (2015, 184) offers "the queerness of Frank Ocean" and "the consistently fluctuating performances of gender donned by rapper Nicki Minaj" as exemplars.

5. Perry initially uses the term *female badmen* then transitions to *badwomen* and *badasses*.

6. I am framing Delilah's story in hip-hop lyrics that have taken on axiomatic qualities apart from their original lyrical settings, which can be sexist, misogynist, homophobic, and glorifying of violence. Their use in conversation and in this essay does not affirm their original contextual usage. I count myself among those womanists who embrace hip-hop music and culture and, at the same time, critique those aspects that do not represent my values as a womanist.

7. The Samson story takes up four chapters consisting of Judg 13–16, some ninety-six verses. Delilah's story in Judg 16:4–31 makes up nearly 30 percent of Samson's story.

is of the night" in Hebrew, may stem from the verb *d-l-l*, "to lay low [the glory of another]," and has an Arabic cognate evoking seductive behavior on the part of women (BDB s.v.).

Delilah is one of a series of women whose literary existence is dependent on Samson and his story. His story is one of twisted games, riddles, and blood sport. It is lethal to other women in his life, but Delilah survives it and him. Pious readings of the saga focus on Samson, his strength, and the rise and fall of his fortunes. In those readings women are pawns in his story with Delilah both pawn and villain. A heteropatriarchal reading of Samson valorizes him as a playa, a "player," because of his series of sexual liaisons, in the same way David is often venerated. Samson's "game" is love/sex/life/death. Indeed, I have heard more than one sermon in which Delilah is presented as a playa-hata, constructing her as vengeful, envious, spiteful and or hateful, determined to take down Samson because of her own character deficiencies. Women who object to normative readings of the saga might well be told, "Don't hate the playa, hate the game" (Marrow and Ascencio 1999). Since the game is biblical, hating or challenging the game has theological implications—since the game is presented as God-ordained. However, womanist biblical interpretation is womanish, drawing from Alice Walker's (1983) definition, and does not hesitate to talk back to the Bible or its God.[8]

Delilah's Textual 'Hood

There are women and girls in the backgrounds of stories without whose presence the book of Judges could not exist as Scripture: the indigenous women and girls of Canaan (including Jerusalem) whose presence in their own land gave rise to so much biblical angst and fear of intimate relations, the women and girls of Israel who lived with cycles of Canaanite oppression and war, the women and girls of the former Israelite tribe Meroz (apparently cursed out of existence according to a fascinating snippet of

---

8. "From womanish. (Opposite of 'girlish,' i.e., frivolous, irresponsible, not serious.) A black feminist or feminist of color. From the black folk expression of mothers to female children, 'You acting womanish,' i.e., like a woman. Usually referring to outrageous, audacious, courageous, or willful behavior. Wanting to know more and in greater depth than is considered 'good' for one. Interested in grown-up doings. Acting grown up. Being grown up. Interchangeable with another black folk expression: 'You trying to be grown.' Responsible. In charge. Serious" (Walker 1983, xi).

text),[9] the women and girls of Midian who lived in subjugation to the women and men of Israel (Judg 8:28), the women of Shechem—hundreds of whom were burned alive by Avimelek (Abimelech, the first king of Israel who has been all but forgotten),[10] the thirty daughters and thirty more daughters-in-law of Izban of Bethlehem (Judg 12:9), the women and girls of Benjamin who were slaughtered by fellow Israelites (Judg 20:48) in retaliation for not handing over the rape-mob that attacked the Levite's low-status wife in Gibeon in Judg 19, the women of Jabesh-Gilead who were slaughtered by fellow Israelites because their men did not participate in the decimation of Benjamin, the girls of Jabesh-Gilead who watched their Israelite kin butcher their entire families yet saving them to be raped into marriage to repopulate the decimated tribe of Benjamin (Judg 21:10–14), and lastly, the girls of Shiloh abducted from what should have been the safety of sacred space by their Israelite kin, forced into rape-marriages to breed more Benjaminites (Judg 21:20–23).

There are more than a dozen active individual female characters in the book of Judges, and they are much more active than many of their sisters in the Scriptures. A number of them kill: Ya'el (Jael) and the woman who killed Avimelek with their own hands and Devorah (Deborah) who killed by command and likely with her own hands on the field of battle. There are women whose names have been preserved for us: Achsah bat Kalev (Caleb's daughter), Anath Em Shamgar (the mother of Shamgar the judge), Devorah, Ya'el, and Delilah. There are women whose names have been erased: the mother of Sisera and the women of the Canaanite court with her, the woman who killed Avimelek, Gideon's sex-and marriage partners, Gilead's sex- and marriage partners, the daughter of Yiftach (Jephthah) and her girlfriends, Samson's mother, sex- and marriage partners with the notable exception of Delilah, and Samson's one-time sister-in-law, Micah's mother, the Levite's low-status wife, and the young Gibeonite woman whose father offered her up to be raped. Delilah's story is in the company of a collection of women's stories from what may be regarded as the "Wild West" of Israel's saga, a time of pioneering settlement expansion on hostile inhabited frontiers.

---

9. In Judg 5:23, Devorah (Deborah) calls for the cursing of the women, children, and men of Meroz, and they are never seen or heard from again.

10. According to Judg 9:22, Abimelech ruled over Israel for three years. To put his reign in perspective, Abimelech ruled longer than Zechariah, Shallum, and Pekaiah of the Northern Kingdom and Amon, Jehoahaz, and Jehoiachin of Judah.

Delilah's story is part of Samson's epic, which is in turn a part of the stories of the judges of Israel, the women[11] and men who served as leaders of tribal coalitions, governed and ruled, waged war, and made and kept the peace in the days when Israel was in Canaan but without a monarchy of its own. The entire book reads as promonarchical propaganda illustrated by its famous refrain: "in those days, there was no king in Israel and each person did what was right in their own eyes" (see Judg 17:6; 18:1; 19:1; 21:25). In spite of the extraordinary military victories of Devorah (and Ya'el), the superhuman strength of Samson, and the accomplishments of the judges before, between, and after, Israel is imperiled by the bad behavior of its own people as much as by the aggression of its neighbors. Delilah and Samson are props in that neoimperial drama.

Hip-hop has its own monarchical narrative with many artists portraying themselves as monarchs in their lyrics and videos. In the canons of hip-hop as in the canon of Scripture, misogyny and monarchy are intertwined, and at the same time there are powerful women who own their bodies and in turn are critiqued for their self-assertion. The images of Biggie Smalls, Tupac Shakur, and Jay-Z as monarchical and in some cases divine figures share space with Queen Latifah, MC Lyte, Yo-Yo, Lauryn Hill, and Nicki Minaj, who offer alternate constructions of power, agency, and female sexuality.

As agitprop, Judges has some of the most striking images of women in the Scriptures, from the warrior prophet Devorah to women raped on an industrial scale, including women butchered like meat—one as an offering to God and one possibly alive when the carving began. The horrific violence in Judges is rendered partially sensible by its promonarchy framing, at least the biblical authors and editors condemn the wanton— "extravagant" in Phyllis Trible's (1984) classic *Texts of Terror*—violence. However, their perceived remedy, establishment of a monarchy, leaves much to be desired for many contemporary readers, particularly in postcolonial settings that have dispatched their previous monarchical powers in which many womanists work and live.

---

11. Devorah is the only woman presented as governing Israel and commanding its armies; however, she is not presented as the only female judge or trial leader. In addition, the leadership of women like the sages of Tekoa (2 Sam 14:1–20) and Abel Beth Maacah (2 Sam 20:14–22) mitigates against presuming Devorah is unique rather than prominent or suited for narrative purposes.

'Round the Way Girls

Delilah is one of a series of women whose stories permeate the Samson story in a way that evokes the story of Moses; indeed hers is the longest. These women include the mother of Samson, the woman who weds Samson and her sister, a sex-worker, and Delilah. That only her name is preserved among the constellation of women in Samson's life (contra the many named women in Exod 1–3) points to her import in and the design of the narrative, building towards her contribution to the dramatic conclusion. The acts for which Delilah becomes infamous can only be properly understood in their narrative context, the tales of the women who precede her in Samson's life as she is the last woman in his life. In addition, Delilah and Samson's family live in the same place, along the Sorek River. Her home is in the river valley; theirs is in town overlooking the river, a mile away. I contend that Delilah would have been aware of the notorious Samson and the stories of the women in Samson's life so much so that her choices may be informed by their outcomes.

The first woman in Samson's life is his mother who is not afforded the dignity of having her name remembered by the tradents of the Hebrew Scriptures. She is identified as "the woman," "his woman,"[12] and "his mother." However in the narrative God accorded her a high dignity: God (or God's divine messenger) appeared to her, repeatedly, intentionally choosing times when she was not encumbered by her man (Judg 13:3, 10). The visitation is significant and revealing. The celestial messenger, a *mal'ak Yah*, regularly translated as an "angel of the LORD," is often a sort of disguise from which YHWH can interact with human beings veiled from their eyes.[13] The divine disguise is frequently revealed when the character transitions from third person speech *about* God to first person speech *as* God. In other words, it is God in drag. In this episode the heavenly visitor

---

12. Biblical Hebrew uses a single word for all women without respect to conjugal status. English-speaking translators regularly supply "wife," which changes the rhythm of the text; the combination of "the wife" and "his wife" does not make sense, and "the woman" and "his wife" lack the same level lexical fidelity. The corollary holds for "man" and "husband." I use the word "wife" sparingly, only in places in which "woman" is not sensible in the syntax.

13. As a general rule, I resist translating YHWH with the traditional *qere* reading, "the Lord," in hermeneutical and homiletical work owing to its male human gender and hierarchy corollaries. I translate using a variety of terms influenced by the choices of Joel Rosenberg in the *Kol HaNeshamah* siddur (Teutsch 2002).

is also called a "messenger," which can be either human or angelic, but she describes him/it as "man of God," which in virtually every other case describes a prophet.[14] While the being does not speak as God, the visitor accepts their offering, and they both understand that they have indeed seen God, Judg 13:22–23.

The divine visitation was also an annunciation. This anonymized woman follows Hagar and Sarah in receiving a divine promise of progeny (Hannah, Mary, and Elizabeth will follow her). She joins a smaller list of barren women—Sarah, Hannah, and Elizabeth—whose barrenness God dramatically reverses. Curiously, only this woman has her name stripped from her. Yet she does not fade easily into to background. She continues in the story beyond minimal announcements of conception and birth that have become the biblical standard for so many nameless women.

The traditional way to name her as the subject of her own story in the larger story is to call her by name. Naming is a fundamental womanist practice from remembering the dead in Africana liturgies with the refrain, "Ashé, we call your name" to the current "Say her name" commitment of the #BlackLivesMatter movement to keep the names of black women who have been killed at the center of the conversation. There is also Destiny's Child's iconic single, "Say My Name" (Jerkins et al. 1999). The naming formulae most readily available, *'Em Shimson* (Samson's mother) or *Eshet Manoah* (Manoah's woman) make her naming dependent on the men in her life and is the antithesis of much of womanist and feminist practice. While classical Jewish biblical interpretation cannot be said to be feminist by design, it (like the biblical text) can and does lend itself to feminist exegesis. One practice of rabbinic hermeneutics that has passed into feminist and womanist biblical scholarship is the practice of providing names for (some) women not given names in the canon. In Num. Rab. 10:5, R. Judan declaims in the name of R. Simeon that from the moment of her visitation she was called Zlelponi, having turned her *ponah* (face) toward the *zal* (shadow)-messenger. She was also called Hazlel, the double L denoting that she has seen the divine messenger twice. In so doing, they identify her with Hazlelponi bat Yehudah, Judah's daughter in 1 Chr 4:3. Zlelponith, as she is called in b. B. Bat. 91a, is also the mother of a daughter, Nashyan, who would be Samson's sister. The rabbis explain that their names along

---

14. Deut 33:1; Josh 14:6; 1 Sam 2:27; 1 Kgs 12:22; 13:1; Ezra 3:2; Jer 35:4; et al., though Nehemiah uses the expression to refer solely to David who is not known as a prophet in the canon, Neh 12:24, 36. It is not clear what Nehemiah means by this.

with that of David's mother were intentionally kept from the biblical text and passed down only in oral tradition because of "heretics," *minim*, "separatists," that is, Christians.[15]

Zlelponith's story sets the stage for Samson's entry into the world. The divine being initiated her into the disciplines of the nazirites. She will be a nazarite so that Samson will be a nazirite "from the belly, *min-habeten*."[16] Her ritually prepared body is the medium through which Samson enters the world. She also mediates between her man and the one who speaks the will of heaven on earth. Mediating between humanity and divinity is the primary definition of prophecy (Gafney 2007, 23). This does not sit well with her man, and he prays for a visitation that includes him. Surprisingly, the divine being snubs him and appears to her again, when he is not present. In a strange turn of events, Zlelponith leaves the emissary alone in a field so she could go get her man. Finally, he too sees and hears the supernatural being and hears the exact same message that she had previously relayed to him. She is proved a faithful prophet; he is proved faithless and foolish.[17]

Zlelponith's last words in the narrative are womanist wisdom. When the Holy One consumes their offering with fire from heaven, her man cries aloud in fear that God will kill them because they have seen God. Zlelponith teaches her man her womanist theology: God has accepted their offerings. Therefore, God will not destroy them. She is articulating a relational understanding of God. She also reflects on the power of God, who could have certainly killed them before her man had time to be afraid. Perhaps she knew Hagar's story and therefore knew better. Samson is the son of this thinking woman and this somewhat clueless man. By the end of his life, he will draw on the strength his mother has implanted in him

---

15. "The mother of David was named Nizbeth the daughter of Adael. The mother of Samson [was named] Zlelponith, and his sister, Nashyan. In what [respect] do [these names] matter? In respect of a reply to the heretics" (b. B. Bat. 91a [Epstein 1948]).

16. I find it worth noting that Samson's nazirite observances are contrived to start at his birth, when he emerges from the womb rather than in it, *babeten*, as the text is written. His mother's preparations are geared towards his first day of life reckoned from birth, not prenatally.

17. That God gives her a message for him (arguably) and for the child she will bear meets the minimum criteria of prophethood. He is regularly characterized as "ignorant," "uneducated," and "one of the poor of the land"—that is, of low class with low expectations—in the Talmud, b. Ber. 61a, b. ʿErub. 18b; Zohar A 7a. Gen. Rab. 45:7 contrasts the faith of Hagar with that of Manoah.

from her womb. He will also display his father's lack of understanding of the things that matter regularly before then. Delilah will demonstrate a strength evoking that of his mother, Zlelponith, perhaps rooted in the strength of the women who settled and survived the settlement-cum-colonization of that land.

The second woman whose story frames that of Samson's is that of his wife, also nameless in the text. I argue this woman's story in particular impacts the choices Delilah makes. Samson will be famous, infamous; this woman's story is part of that infamy, a cautionary tale from which Delilah learns. I call her Yashirah from the characteristic that drew Samson to her. She is *yasherah*, "smooth," "straight," and "right" in his sight (Judg 14:3). He saw something in her, something he wanted, and he set out to get it and her. That characteristic whether beauty, shapeliness, sexiness, or indescribable attractiveness was just right in his sight. Her appeal whether it is beauty or something else, is hers, but her parents negotiate it and her away to Samson. In the narrative her fate is her fault: she is one of those (foreign) women from that (foreign) place out in public looking like that. Writing in a time when too many men use what they think or feel about a woman's looks to catcall or solicit her and some when rebuffed feel so entitled and defrauded that they strike out with physical, even lethal violence shaped the way I see Yashirah and her desirability.

But Yashirah is not "right" in the eyes of the larger narrative; she is a Philistine; she is other. As a womanist I feel compelled to read from her position. She and her people were regarded as "other" by those who were regarded as chosen and by many contemporary readers. Because of this her body and those of her people will be available for indiscriminate violence. Everything about her culture and peoplehood was regarded as inferior. The text and Samson's parents are biased against her because of who she is, who her people are. In spite of the fact that she is in her home, in her town, among her people, she is a foreign woman and is on the bottom of the Bible's hierarchies. She occupies a position in the story that Delilah would seem to share on the surface: To the men of her people she is a thing, a possession, a provocation, a bargaining chip. To the narrator she is a plot twist. They see neither the divine image nor subjectivity in her, and the (religious) reader was expected to read only from the perspective of Samson.

Samson's father accompanied by his mother (who is submerged in her man's masculine singular verb) objects to his son marrying a Philistine woman: "Are there no daughters among your kin, or among my people a single woman that you go to take a woman from the uncircumcised Philistines?!" (Judg 14:3). Samson tells his father "the woman looks good to me," *she is yasherah in my sight*, and he demands using the imperative command form that his father get her for him as his wife-woman. His parents yield, not knowing God is orchestrating a larger plan according to the narrator.

Samson and his parents engage in the culturally appropriate conjugal rituals; they travel to Yashirah's Philistine town Timnah to form the union. Samson's mother is present, silent, but not invisible; she continues in the story for a while longer. But she is no longer the woman who interpreted the ways of God to her man. She is following him as he follows Samson who is following his physical desires. Along the way Samson gets ahead of his parents. He runs into a lion and rips it apart, shredding it, *vayeshasse'hu*, with his bare hands, "just like one tears a young goat apart." The image brings to mind a goat cooked to perfection in Afro-Caribbean cuisine, so tender its flesh is falling off of the bone, such as he might shortly feast on in celebration of his nuptials. It is a hint of Samson's supernatural strength that will be increasingly revealed. It is also part of a macabre humor that winds through these chapters.

Yashirah's family agreed to the union with Samson. The woman's feelings, like her own name, are irrelevant to the story; she is a character, perhaps even a prop. Samson makes three, possibly four trips to Timnah giving the sense of ongoing courting, reflecting his eagerness and desire: he meets her on the first (14:1), arranges the marriage on the second (14:5), "goes down" to talk with her (14:7), and married her (14:8, these last two may be part of the same trip). There is an investment of time and resources in this union.

These trips provide more opportunities for Samson to demonstrate his strength. The space between his second and last trips is long enough for the shredded lion's body to decay, *miyammim* in 14:8, "days-(upon-days)," could mean any number of days. Samson sees the lion's carcass has been colonized by a swarm of bees, reaches into the lion and takes some honey, finds his mother—silent again—and his father, and shares it with them. He does not tell them where he got it.

Now Zlelponith, Samson's mother, disappears from the story. She has accompanied her son and her man to Timnah and shared in the honey, but now she fades away. She serves no further purpose. Samson's father goes seemingly alone to the woman with whom Samson is smitten. With the marriage Samson's father disappears from the story. Virtually alone among strangers, Samson celebrates his marriage, throwing the traditional wedding feast. The people of Timnah provide the wedding party; they assign thirty men to accompany him in this rite of passage. Why did Samson not have his own wedding party? The distance was not too great to travel as Zorah and Timnah[18] were less than five miles apart. Did he have no other family or friends to celebrate with him? Or was his marriage to a Philistine woman rejected by his kin? As the celebration progresses, he offers what would seem to be a harmless wager on a riddle. That riddle will lead to the brutal deaths of thirty innocent men and later the bride and her father followed by an untold number of Philistine people in addition to their crops and the tortuous deaths of wild foxes burned alive.

Samson's wife has one sorrowful bit of agency in the account of her wedding; she cried every day of the seven-day wedding feast (Judg 14:17). Many readers construe her tears as a ploy to wheedle the solution to the riddle out of Samson in spite of the fact that she started weeping on the first day, three days before she was told to get the solution or die horribly with her family on the fourth day of the feast (Judg 14:15). On that fourth day of conjugal celebration, the shadow of death entered the life of the woman once called *yasherah*. Her people, her own folk, most likely her kinfolk and extended family, promised to kill her. They promised to burn her alive. They promised to burn her sister. They promised to burn her father. They promised to burn everyone who lived in her father's household; that would include untold numbers of servant and animals and perhaps her mother who is otherwise missing from the narrative.

The history of violence against women in particular and folk in general, in the Scriptures, in the world of the Scriptures, makes clear that this was no empty threat. Pulling back the layers of anti-Philistine propaganda in the story and reading with Yashirah finds she knew the men celebrating her marriage today would be willing to kill her tomorrow. If she and her family were going to survive her wedding, she would have to get the solution to that riddle out of the husband she did not choose for herself. She had one resource; he was besotted with her. They told her to seduce, *p-t-h*, the solution out of him; instead she pressed him, *tz-v-q*. She pressed him to the point of oppressing him. She pressed her way to her own deliverance.[19]

---

18. Philistine Timnah was in the Shephelah; Timnah between Sinai and the Arabian Peninsula is not the referent here.

19. The notion of "pressing one's way" stems from Phil 3:14: "I press towards the mark of the high calling of God in Christ Jesus." The language of "pressing" denoting the struggle to live faithfully is prominent in Africana expressions of Christianity.

Yet translators who hold no regard for her life and death struggle say she "nagged" him. She made him tell her the solution so that she could save her life and the lives of her family. Interpreters seem to disregard or lose track of her motivation.

For his part, Samson seems to understand that his wife was forced into this position. He displays no anger towards her but no longer sees her as *yasherah* in his sight; now she is a cow, an *eglah*, a heifer. In 14:18 Samson accuses the Philistine men of "plowing *in*" her (not "with," as in NRSV), a double entendre and veiled accusation of adultery or perhaps rape. Samson goes to war against the men who put her in that position, sort of; he kills thirty men at random in another Philistine town, Ashkelon, plunders their corpses, and uses their goods to pay the lost wager. Then Samson comes back for his woman.

When he seeks to claim his neglected bride, her father has given her to one of the wedding companions and offers her sister instead. But she is his, and he wants her. The episode is suspiciously similar to the later Merab-David-Michal triangle.[20] Samson's revenge is vicious: announcing he is not to blame for the evil he is about to do, he sets foxes on fire and uses them to set the Philistine crops on fire. As a womanist, I cannot ignore this wanton act of cruelty or its uncritical acceptance in the many sermons and Sunday school lessons I have heard on this text. I am also watching Delilah watching these events learning about the man with whom she would one day be intimate. I contend this knowledge shapes her subsequent decision-making process.

The story of Samson's Philistine bride ends with her being burned alive along with her father in retribution for Samson's actions. In another cycle of retaliation, Samson "smites them [the Philistines] hip and thigh a great smiting."[21] The complete death toll from Samson's marriage is unknown but includes thirty random men, an unknown number of foxes, the bride and her father, and an untold number of slaughtered men. Samson's wedding feast turned into more than thirty funeral feasts.

Before moving to Samson's next woman or on to Delilah, I must pause in womanist solidarity with Yashirah, mark and mourn her passing. I do

---

The notion has found its way into womanist discourse informed by but not tied to its Christian origins.

20. See 1 Sam 18:17–19:17; 25:44; 2 Sam 3:13–16.

21. I remain convinced that the somewhat antiquated "smite" remains the best translation for *n-k-h*.

not know the name her mother called her. I call her Yashirah, good and pleasing in herself, to herself, not dependent on the approval of any man. According to the narrator, Yashirah and her entire family were murdered because God was spoiling for a fight and using the nameless woman and her people as props towards that end, declaring in 14:4: "all this came from God-Whose-Name-is-Holy, who was seeking grounds for a quarrel with the Philistines." As a womanist I wrestle with the god in the text who is only the god of the Israelites, who does not appear to see or value the divine image in the people of Timnah, Ashkelon, or anywhere in Philistia.

As new stories of Samson's strength and penchant for slaughter unfold in the text and throughout the region, he turns to a sex-worker in Judg 16:1 who is also a Philistine woman. As a foreign sex-worker, she is on the bottom of all the power curves that matter to the curators of Israel's Scriptures. Not surprisingly, no name has been preserved for her. Given the Semitic, Phoenician, origin of many extant Philistine cities (Shai 2009) and personal names, I have chosen the name Arishat for her, attested from a funerary inscription; its consonants also mean "desire" in Hebrew, *areshet* (Kempinski 1987). The circumstances surrounding sex-work in the narrative and her culture it reflects are difficult to determine. I cannot say with any degree of certainty that the unnamed Philistine sex-worker chose her life and controls her own sexuality, though that is a possibility. It is also possible that her sex-work is survival work. In the narrative she is a mid-point between a proper marriage and Samson's relationship with a woman who is neither wife nor sex-worker.

One might imagine that Samson has demonstrated sufficient feats of strength for the narrative to move to the main event. Yet the editors feel we must know about this brief episode of monetized sex, failed attack, and Samson's swaggering escape from the failed ambush set by the men of her city which he easily avoids, carrying off the gates of the town as a trophy. Arishat apparently survives her encounter with Samson and the consequences of his escape. Using my sanctified imagination,[22] I believe Delilah heard all of these stories and knew exactly who and what Samson was when he walked in her door, a threat to her life and the lives of anyone she cared about or was related to, maybe even her entire town.

---

22. The sanctified imagination is the fertile creative space where the preacher-interpreter enters the text, particularly the spaces in the text, and fills them out in many black preaching traditions. I have experienced it as a type of African American indigenous midrash.

It is in this context, with the frustrated Philistines still hungry for vengeance, that the text turns to Delilah, much maligned in the interpretative tradition, and her relationship with Samson. In my reading, Delilah enters the narrative knowing who Samson is, what he has done, what has happened with the women in his life before her, and, most importantly, that the Philistines want him badly enough to kill their own and have done so. She must know as does everyone around her his own history of slaughtering the Philistines. She knows this because Samson and Delilah are from the same place; his ancestral town Tzorah is also in the valley of Sorek where Delilah lives. At no point in the valley (less than twenty miles from where the Shephelah abuts the central highlands to the shore of the Mediterranean) would he be more than a few miles from the place of his birth or the place of his eventual death (Eshta'ol).[23] Their geographical proximity raises a number of questions: Does she know his parents? How far do they live from each other? For that matter, what might Samson's now-invisible mother think of his relationship pattern?

Delilah's name rhymes with the Hebrew word for night, *laylah*, leading some to suggest she is a "lady of the night," a sex-worker. She is not identified as such, and the biblical text is not interested in protecting her. Her name may be derived from or intended to suggest both "being brought low" from the root *d-l-l* (I; BDB s.v.) and "hair that hangs down/low," *d-l-l* (II; *HALOT* s.v.), punning on her cutting off Samson's hair. Another double root, *d-l-h* may also be the source of her name: (I) "hang low" (BDB s.v.) and (II) "hair" or "threads" (in a loom) (BDB s.v.). With any of these derivations, Delilah's name likely signals that the story turns on the fate of Samson's hair and says nothing about her occupation.

In the pews where I have heard Delilah's story preached, I was taught that Delilah was either a professional sex-worker or a promiscuous woman; in either case she was a whore. A close reading of the passage does not sustain that reading. Were she a sex-worker, the text would not hold that information back. Her unexplained life is presented to evoke suspicion; it also begs many questions. What does she do? How did she get that house? Who are her people? Where are they? Why are neither people nor place named as part of her naming formula? What is Delilah's side of the story?

---

23. Tzorah and Eshta'ol are set up as the geographical parameters in which Samson's life and the "stirring" or "disturbing" of God's spirit in his life are set in Judg 13:25.

It is possible, even likely, that Delilah or at least one of her parents is an Israelite, which would explain her residence in Israelite territory of Dan. Israelites reckoned identity paternally; if her father were Israelite, she would be Israelite. The text's omission of her identity mitigates towards obscuring an Israelite, not a foreign one. If Delilah's father were Philistine, Canaanite, or any other non-Israelite, she would be Philistine or Canaanite, certainly foreign. It is hard to imagine that the framers of the narrative would not trumpet her foreign origin, especially given the larger hostility towards foreign women in Judges (cf. 3:1–6) and the larger Tanak. That the Philistines have easy access to her might indicate that one of her parents is also Philistine. It is most likely Delilah has an Israelite father and a Philistine (or Canaanite) mother.

Delilah enters the text as the object of Samson's love. Unlike the previous women Samson has desired, pursued, and used, Delilah is beloved though no love story is told. Samson's feelings are simply presented as fact in 16:4. It is important to note that the love articulated in the passage is expressed as a one-sided love. He loves her. The text is silent on her feelings for him. This is not uncommon, with the exception of Michal, Saul's daughter who loves David, women in the Hebrew Scriptures do not love men.[24] They are loved. Men love women (and men). The agency and subjectivity of love is gendered and unidirectional. The text does not describe how he came to love her, what he saw in her that pleased him. He simply loves her.[25]

The text is not interested in Delilah's motives. Why is she with Samson? Does she love him? Does his rep, his reputation, provide the otherwise unattached woman in an androcentric regularly patriarchal society a measure of protection? There is nothing in the account that would indicate Delilah did not consent to this relationship, whatever its form. The

---

24. Isaac loves Rebekah (Gen 24:67); Jacob loved Rachel more than Leah (Gen 29:30); Elkanah loved Hannah in spite of her barrenness (1 Sam 1:5); Jonathan and David love each other (1 Sam 18:3; 20:17; 2 Sam 1:26); Solomon loved many foreign women (1 Kgs 11:1); the Persian king loved Esther more than his other women (Est 2:17). Leah yearns for Jacobs's love but is not said to love him in Gen 29:32. The rapists Shechem and Amnon are said to love their victims, Dinah and Tamar, who neither love nor want them in Gen 34:3 and 2 Sam 13:1. Finally, Solomon's son Rehovoam loves Absalom's daughter Maacah more than his other eighteen primary and sixty secondary wives in 2 Chr 11:21.

25. The expression "fall in love" is a modern one; it is not used in the Hebrew text in spite of being in NRSV and JPS translations.

narrative says nothing of how they met or whether they formalized their relationship (the Talmud presumes they are married, b. Naz. 4a). Given the text does not hesitate to acknowledge Samson's previous (inter)marriage, there is no reason for it to obscure another as it lists his sexual partners. I contend Delilah and Samson are not married. This would make Delilah a rare nonmarried[26] woman of marriageable age in the canon. Beyond the question of her conjugal status, Delilah is peculiarly unattached; she is not identified in relationship to father or family, craft or profession. She has no mother and only one lover. What is the reader supposed to infer about her lack of any relationships apart from Samson? Did their cohabitation mean that they were de facto in a socially recognized conjugal relationship? It seems the text cannot honestly present her as a promiscuous woman with a damaged reputation so it relies on innuendo.

I have heard few sermons critique or even address Samson's sexual choices. All of these stand in opposition to the conjugal monogamy many understand as a normative biblical value and would render a woman promiscuous if not a whore in the biblical idiom: Only one of Samson's sex partners is his wife. His subsequent two partners are outside of the patriarchal marriage structure that dominates the Hebrew (and Christian) Scriptures. Samson also chose non-Israelite women preferentially, which is condemned in Judges and in the wider canon, though actually common among leading male characters.[27] The text does not judge Samson for his series of relationships because Samson's conduct illustrates the wide latitude men enjoyed for sexual gratification in Israelite society within the bounds of normative interpretation of the Torah. Men in Israel had legitimate sexual access to a variety of partners without censure including foreign women,

---

26. The other context in which women do not marry with some regularity is among women prophets: Miriam, Devorah (Deborah), the woman with whom Isaiah fathers at least one child, and Noadiah are all unmarried. Devorah's description, *eshet lappidoth*, "woman of flames," i.e. "fiery woman" is regularly mistranslated (See Gafney 2007, 90, 140–41). On the politics of singleness in the Hebrew Bible, see Davis's earlier essay in this volume.

27. Patriarchs Judah and Simeon both marry and father children with Canaanite women. Joseph marries and fathers children with an African woman, Asenath the Egyptian. Their sons become the ancestors of the half-tribes of Ephraim and Manasseh. Moses marries and fathers children with a Midianite woman, Zipporah, before marrying an African (Nubian) woman. David's Moabite heritage from his great-grandmother Ruth violates the ban in Deut 23:3 on anyone with Moabite heritage for ten generations being admitted to the divine assembly.

prostitutes, and slaves. This was true for married and single men.[28] Within his story Samson remains as uncriticized for his sexual exploits as for his acts of violence. In a contemporary Africana reading in which womanism is flavored with hip-hop, Samson's series of sex partners would seem to mark him as a playa, but the hip-hop oral tradition declares: you can't play a playa. Since Delilah will play him like a fiddle, Delilah is the playa, and Samson is the one being played. Yet the text does not pass any judgment on Delilah for her sexual arrangement with Samson.

The story takes place in Delilah's home. She is, in womanist terms, "grown." More than an adult in mere chronological terms, she is physically, sexually, and emotionally mature and self-sufficient. She is *ntozake*, "she who comes into her own things," the Xhosa word from which poet and playwright Ntozake Shange drew her own name. That Delilah is an apparently single and independent woman, financially secure with no ties to a man before her union with Samson, is an unresolved puzzle in the text. Samson and the Philistines come to her indicating she has her own home though residence is never described in the text. Moreover, it appears that Samson is living with Delilah in her house. Can she say of her house like Destiny's Child, "I bought it" (Barnes et al. 2000)? With what funds? From where? How does she support herself? Delilah is a hustla,[29] but her hustle is not explained in the text.[30] One way or another Delilah has had to hustle, or better, grind[31] to support herself. Reading from Delilah's perspective means we cannot knock her hustle.[32] An independent woman with her own resources is dangerous, particularly to patriarchy. Yet Delilah suffers violence only in interpretation and not in the text.

Contemporary interpreters supply the condemnation of Delilah readily. She is included in sermons, conferences, and workshops, particularly for women as "one of the bad girls of the Bible" based on Liz Curtis Higgs's (1999) influential text of the same name, in which Delilah receives

---

28. A married or engaged woman was guilty of adultery for having sex with anyone other than her husband. A married man was only guilty of adultery if he has sex with a married or engaged woman.

29. While there is no single authoritative lexicon for contemporary cultural terminology, in contemporary womanist and hip-hop parlance the term *hustla*, derived from *hustler*, is generally used to characterize someone who pursues money at any cost.

30. As a noun, *hustle* is any money making enterprise without regard to legality, ethics, or social or moral norms.

31. In the biblical text, *grinding* also has a sexual connotation (see Job 31:10).

32. Paraphrased from Jay-Z's "Can't Knock the Hustle" (Miller et al. 1996).

the most severe judgment, "bad to the bone" as opposed to lighter judgments, "bad for a moment" or "bad for a season, but not forever," of the "bad girls"—not even "women."[33] Bradley Crowell (2013, 7), who lumps Delilah in with the Philistine women, is representative of the male-stream scholarship and masculinist hermeneutics with which I have most often heard Delilah interpreted: "They are highly seductive but deceitful foreign women who use their beauty to mislead and ultimately destroy the Israelite Samson … foreign women, despite their allure, seek to destroy the righteous Israelite. Allowing these women to have power with influential men would contribute to the lawlessness experienced in the subsequent chapters when "no king ruled in Israel."

Delilah and Samson's wife are linked through the command of the Philistines to seduce, *p-t-h*, Samson. Samson's wife was threatened with the gruesome death of being burnt alive with her family. In contrast, Delilah was offered a queen's ransom for betraying Samson. In both contexts the Philistines dictate their demands. They do not ask the women; they issue instructions and the consequences associated with those instructions. What accounts for the difference in treatment? Did Delilah lack family to use as leverage? I think not. If Delilah's father was Israelite as I propose, then to attack her family was to attack Israel and start an unsanctioned war. The Philistines could slaughter their own people with little consequence, but starting an international incident was an entirely different matter. Samson, on the other hand, was a combatant and known antagonist.

The Philistine conspirators each offer to pay her 1,100 pieces of silver; assuming that group represents the five lords of the Philistine pentapolis, Delilah would receive 5,500 pieces of silver. Identifying each silver piece as a shekel, the *Jewish Study Bible* (*JSB*), reckons an Israelite shekel at 11.42 grams, meaning that the Philistine nobles offered Delilah some 62,810 grams—roughly 138.5 pounds—of silver. At $15.88 per ounce (the price I found while preparing this manuscript in the fall of 2015), a contemporary value for their offer would be $35,190.08. In the Middle Bronze Era setting of this text, that might be a million or perhaps even a billion rhetorical dollars, more than she would need for the rest of her life, more than enough to grant her security as an independent woman in an androcentric and patriarchal world. I prefer to think of it as Delilah being offered more than her weight in silver. The amount is astronomical and was likely understood as

---

33. See the table of contents in Higgs 1999.

such; at one level it demonstrates the extremes to which the Philistines are willing to go to capture and kill Samson. The payment may have also been so large so as to compensate Delilah for betraying a fellow Israelite. The Philistine track record with Samson's wife and her family made it unlikely that Delilah had a choice whether to cooperate with the Philistines. With the windfall or without it, Delilah was going to betray Samson.

Often overlooked in the Philistine directive to Delilah is what it reveals about their intent: "how we may (go) against him that we might bind him in order to hurt him." The Philistines use the verb '-n-h, "oppress" or "afflict," which I translate as "hurt" in 16:5. It broadly refers to physical violence and regularly refers to rape. Notably it describes Sarah's physical (and I argue, sexual)[34] abuse of Hagar in Gen 16:6 and the Egyptian abuse of the Israelites in Exod 1:11. If this level of violence is what they have planned for Samson, what would they do to her if she did not comply? Once the terms have been set, Delilah does not shrink from the real but unarticulated threat. Entering into the relationship with a man she does not love and using his love for her to achieve her goals also characterizes Delilah as a playa. Her willingness to handle her business at the cost of another's life also marks Delilah as a gangsta.[35]

I posit Delilah is not playing Samson for sport or money; she is playing for her life and therefore willing to take a life or, in this case, hand over a life. Interpretations that portray Delilah negatively often posit greed as her motivation, or they position her in opposition to God and God's man, Samson, making her betrayal a religious or theological choice rather than a matter of survival. In the text Delilah does not know that Samson's strength is a matter of religious observance. She is not intentionally setting herself against Samson or his God. She is a pragmatist trying to save her life because she knows that death follows in Samson's wake, at his hands and those of the Philistines—even if the sex-worker he used did survive all of them.

---

34. The text and culture from which it emerges presume Sarah has the right to unfettered access to and the right to dispose of Hagar's body as she sees fit. Nevertheless, the passage uses a verb with resonances of both physical and sexual violence to describe her treatment of Hagar. See also Shechem's rape of Dinah, Gen 34:2; the Gibeonite rape of the Levite's woman, Judg 20:5; and Amnon's rape of Tamar, 2 Sam 13:14.

35. *The Godfather* (movie and saga) functions as an OG, "original ganster/gangsta" canon in much of hip-hop culture. In the original film (Coppola 1972), Al Pacino's character Michael Corleone utters an iconic line that characterizes a true gangsta, "It's not personal, Sonny; it's strictly business."

Delilah does have a choice as to how she would comply with the Philistine demands, how she would conduct herself with them and with Samson. She will not cry or beg, him or them. She will not use his love for her against him as did his wife. She will not weep, either honestly or manipulatively. She will not lose her dignity. She will not stoop to using sex as a weapon. In the interpretive tradition, Delilah's character has been hypersexualized though it is Samson who sleeps his way through Israel and Philistia. Delilah uses her wit and her will to best him, and she uses Samson's arrogance against him. In agreeing to provide the Philistines a way to capture and do violence to Samson, Delilah becomes a partner to their conspiracy, willing to see the man who loves her beaten, tortured, or killed for an exorbitant sum of money. But Delilah is not on their side; the only side Delilah is on is her own because, arguably, no one else is.

By presenting her as a woman without family or tribe, the text presents Delilah without safety net or social security. Delilah must hustle to survive; she is a "bonafide hustla" (Brown et al. 2004). Delilah knows the reason the lords of the Philistines want to know the secret of his strength, to counteract it, is so that they can capture and hurt him. It's her or him. That's an easy calculation. However, in the Bible and in the world in which the Bible is Scripture, women are not supposed to choose themselves over men. They are supposed to sacrifice themselves, lay down their lives and offer up their bodies to protect men and male interests. Delilah is not having any of that. She will hand Samson over to what she has every reason to believe will be a tortuous death, and she will benefit from it.

Delilah gets straight to the point. First she simply asks Samson how he could be bound so that he could be hurt in 16:7. She uses the same verb, *'-n-h*, meaning "oppress," "afflict," and "violate," as the Philistines in their demand of her. Her question is almost conversational: "In what is your strength, and in what (by what means) can you be bound?" It is as though she is just getting to know him better like lovers do. Samson tells her the first of several lies in verse 8. He is playing her. She is playing him, but only one of them will get played because you can't play a playa.[36]

Samson's response, "If they bind me ..." indicates that he knows the Philistines are after him and using her. Delilah follows his instructions using fresh bowstring, likely fresh tendons or sinews from a recently slaughtered animal, and binds him herself in verse 8. The story skips over

---

36. A nearly ubiquitous contemporary proverb.

her preparation, a trip to the market and butcher. Is she buying the supplies out of her own pocket? If so it is a small investment, which will yield a great return. Delilah arranges for men to hide nearby yet does not turn the bound Samson over to them; instead she tests him by calling out an alarm in verse 9. By testing Samson herself, Delilah does not call for the Philistines prematurely and protects her future income. He breaks the bonds, and the Philistines never reveal themselves. Delilah maintains the fiction that neither of them believes; she is just trying to figure out the source of his strength, and Samson continues to play along, getting played.

They play again. Samson lies again. Now he claims that if they bind him with new ropes he would become weak. His response is formulaic, repeating his line from verse 7 in verse 11. Again Delilah tests him herself and does not prematurely declare victory. She is patient. They play a third round. This time, in verses 13–16, Samson says it is not so much what he is bound with but how, saying that the seven locks of his hair must be woven into a web and secured to a loom. That his hair is styled into seven locks evokes dreadlocks for many readers. Seven braids, twists, or curls would require regular repeated maintenance and styling to avoid becoming locked and, between killing and sex, Samson does not appear to have or take the time to style his hair. Further, given the secret locked into his hair, it is extremely unlikely that he would risk having someone else style it. Samson has slipped up; he has given Delilah a piece of the truth. In the streets that birthed hip-hop, slipping is a precursor of death. If someone catches you slipping they can kill you, and you deserve to get killed. Samson knows he slipped up. Does Delilah? Can she sense it? I think so.

This time the text is careful to mention that Delilah waits until Samson is asleep to secure him. That he might have been awake during the previous attempts makes them sound like love play. They are playing but not at love, in spite of Samson's love for her. It is not clear if the Philistines are hidden nearby again; there is no mention of them. They may be tiring of the game. Delilah is not giving up. She is working her plan day and night. Now she forgoes sleep, waiting for Samson to sleep so she can bind him. Samson wakes and frees himself again. That night or the next day—the passage of time is uncertain—Delilah calls Samson out on lying to her.

Delilah prepares to up her game. Delilah moves from simply asking Samson to tell her his secret to pressing him, *tz-w-q*, wearing him down to the point of oppressing him in 16:5. I find the old King James translation to be useful here: "she pressed him ... so that his soul was vexed to death." This is much more precise than the "nagging ... until he was tired/wearied" preferred by the NRSV and JPS translators and not dependent on sexist stereotypes. As Delilah interrogated him like a police officer trying to get a confession, Samson stays with her, in her home. Why does he not leave? Does he think that she will not break him? He underestimates her.

Delilah spent time wearing him down, literally, "all the days" in verse 16. The whole episode could have taken place within a week, or it could have been stretched out over several weeks, perhaps even months. When Samson finally tells Delilah "his whole heart," she knows he has told her the truth. In Judg 16:17, she tells the Philistines to come before she has shaved him or had him shaved. She is confident; her confidence will not prove to be false as will his. Delilah does not discuss the money since they have already agreed to terms, and she has kept up her end; she will not beg for what is hers. Using my sanctified imagination, I hear Delilah singing "Bitch Better Have My Money" by Rihanna (Pierre et al. 2015),[37] a song described as the "freedom song for freelancers everywhere" (Ajayi 2015).

Once again Delilah exercises caution, secreting the Philistines while she immobilizes Samson and tests him. She seems particularly ruthless[38] here, lulling him to sleep on her lap while arranging for a man to come at her signal and barber him without waking him. Having weakened him in order that the Philistines might hurt him in verse 19, she cries out the alarm that she has raised three times before. This time he is powerless.

As the Philistines begin to hurt him in earnest, Delilah disappears from the text. But did she disappear from the scene? Did she watch as they put out his eyes? Was Delilah's the last face Samson saw? Did she take her money and run? Did she live out her days in comfort and ease? Did she feel remorse for her actions? (And why would she?) The Philistines take Samson to Gaza in verse 21 where he will die but not without killing more than three thousand Philistine women and men along with him, verses 27–30. There is no reason for Delilah to follow the Philistines to Gaza; she has her money. She may well have left her home in the territory of Dan where his family lives; they retrieved his body and buried him there. Delilah and her fortune disappear.

Delilah got paid. Delilah appears to be the rare woman who has escaped biblical patriarchy with her body weight in bling, silver, to boot. (Compare her to the sex-worker in 16:1 who leaves with her life and pre-

---

37. The song has been immortalized with the Twitter hashtag #BBHMM.
38. I assign no negative value to that characteristic; here it is a mark of efficiency.

sumably her regular wages.) She is not punished in the text for her role in Samson's death. She is not subjected to the authority of any man. She leaves the text, wealthy and free. In a text with so much grotesque violence against women, including in the larger Samson story, it is all the more amazing that Delilah escapes untouched. Delilah joins a long line of biblical men whose ethical standards are at some variance from contemporary readers but are perfectly appropriate in the world of the text.

Delilah is an independent woman, a characterization which is a polarized identity for some Africana women. On the one hand, independent black women are lionized; on the other hand, they are castigated for not being appropriately dependent on men in a patriarchal framework. Delilah works within the patriarchal strictures imposed on her and secures her liberation. She is a pawn in Samson's destruction, which is laid at his own feet primarily and those of the Philistines secondarily. In terms of the book's theology, Delilah can be read as an agent of God. Delilah is not tamed by her text. She is not rewarded with marriage or children. She does not need them. She can support herself. Delilah is free. She exits the text on her own terms. Like a boss.

Works Cited

Ajayi, Luvvie. 2015. "Rihanna's 'Bitch Better Have My Money Is the Freelancer's Freedom Anthem." *AwesomelyLuvvie* blog. http://tinyurl.com/SBL0688w.

Barnes, Samuel, Jean Olivier, Beyoncé Knowles, Mark Rooney, Rapture D. Stewart, and Eric L. Seats. 2000. "Independent Women." *Independent Women*. Columbia Records. 44K-79493. Compact disc.

Bradley, Regina N. 2015. "Barbz and Kings: Explorations of Gender and Sexuality in Hip-Hop." Pages 181–91 in *The Cambridge Companion to Hip-Hop*. Edited by Justin A. Williams. Cambridge: Cambridge University Press.

Broadus, Calvin Cordazor [Snoop Dogg]. 2006. "Play On Playa." *Hip Hop Is Dead*. Performed by Nas and Snoop Dogg. The Island Def Jam Music Group and Columbia Records. B0007229-01. Compact disc.

Brown, David, Homer Banks, Marvin Bernard, Raymond Jackson, Carl Hampton, and Curtis Jackson. 2004. "Bonafide Hustler." *Straight Outta Cashville*. Performed by Young Buck, 50 Cent, and Tony Yayo. G-Unit and Interscope Records. B0002972-01. Compact disc.

Coppola, Francis Ford, dir. 1972. *The Godfather*. Paramount Pictures.

Crawford, Shondrae, Sean Garrett, and Beyoncé Knowles. 2008. "Diva." *I Am ... Sasha Fierce*. Sony Music. 88697-19492-2. Compact disc.

Crowell, Bradley L. 2013. "Good Girl, Bad Girl: Foreign Women of the Deuteronomistic History in Postcolonial Perspective." *BibInt* 21:1–18.

Epstein, Isidore. *The Babylonian Talmud*. London: Soncino, 1948

Gafney, Wilda C. 2007. *Daughters of Miriam: Women Prophets in Ancient Israel*. Minneapolis: Fortress.

Higgs, Liz Curtis. 1999. *Bad Girls of the Bible: And What We Can Learn from Them*. Colorado Springs: WaterBrook Press.

Jerkins, Rodney, Fred Jerkins III, LaShawn Daniels, Beyoncé Knowles, LeToya Luckett, Kelendria Rowland, and LaTavia Robertson. 1999. "Say My Name." *Say My Name*. Columbia Records. 44K-79346. Compact disc.

Kempinski, Aharon. 1987. "Some Philistine Names from the Kingdom of Gaza." *IEJ* 37:20–24.

Marrow, Tracy Lauren [Ice-T], and Richard Ascencio [DJ Ace]. 1999. "Don't Hate the Playa." *The Seventh Deadly Sin*. Atomic Pop.

Miller, Marcus, Melisa Morgan, Melvin Bradford, Jerome Foster, Andre Young, Lesette Wilson, and Shawn Carter. 1996. "Can't Knock the Hustle." *Reasonable Doubt*. Performed by Jay-Z and Mary J. Blige. Roc-A-Fella Records. P1-50592. Compact disc.

Perry, Imani. 2004. *Prophets of the Hood: Politics and Poetics in Hip Hop*. Durham: Duke University Press.

Pierre, Jamille, Badrilla Bourelly, Robyn Fenty, and Travis Scott. 2015. "Bitch Better Have My Money." *Roc Nation*. AAC.

Shai, Itzhaq. 2009. "Understanding Philistine Migration: City Names and Their Implications." *BASOR* 354:15–27.

Teutsch, David. 2002. *Kol Haneshamah: Shabbat Vehagim (Hebrew and English Edition)*. Translated by Joel Rosenberg. Elkins Park: Reconstructionist Press.

Trible, Phyllis. 1984. *Texts of Terror: Literary-Feminist Readings of Biblical Narratives*. Philadelphia: Fortress.

Walker, Alice. 1983. *In Search of Our Mothers' Gardens: Womanist Prose*. San Diego: Harcourt Brace Jovanovich.

Williams, Pharrell, and Chad Hugo. 2001. "U Don't Have To Call." *8701*. Performed by Usher. Arista Records. 74321-87471-2. Compact disc.

The Song of Songs: Redeeming Gender Constructions in the Age of AIDS

Cheryl B. Anderson

Introduction

The statistics concerning HIV infections in the African American community are shocking. As a report on the Centers for Disease Control (CDC) website reveals (CDC 2016, 1–2), African Americans, who are only 12 percent of the population in the United States, represent 44 percent of all new cases annually, and we are nearly half of all persons currently living with HIV in the United States. In 2010, about 70 percent of new infections in the black community were found in men who were gay or bisexual, and black women, infected primarily through heterosexual transmission, were close to 30 percent of those with new infections.

To help us understand these statistics, some comparisons are helpful. Young African American gay and bisexual men between the ages of thirteen and twenty-four accounted for more than twice as many new infections as either young white or Hispanic/Latino gay and bisexual men. Similarly, young black females between the ages of thirteen and twenty-four have infection rates that are five times as high as that of young Hispanic females and twenty times that of young white females. At these rates, the CDC projects that, unless the course of the epidemic changes, one in sixteen black males and one in thirty-two black females will be diagnosed with HIV infection at some point in their lifetimes.

African Americans are overwhelmingly Christian, deeply committed to their faith, and our churches have historically taken strong social and political stances to improve the well-being of the community. Since well-being is undermined by the spread of HIV, why have black churches failed to take such stances to prevent new infections in our community? To be clear, I am not arguing that black churches have been inactive. To the contrary, black churches have initiated testing programs in their communities and supported those who are HIV positive in multiple ways. Instead, my concern focuses on prevention. After more than thirty years of the global pandemic of HIV and AIDS, we know that it is possible to prevent new infections. The issue is whether black churches can have the conversations and do the advocacy needed to get to zero new infections. Without such actions, there will continue to be about 50,000 new infections each year, and we know that almost half of them will be in the African American community.

African American scholars have identified two main reasons for the relative lack of leadership by black churches concerning the pandemic. First, black leadership has tended to focus on race as its primary concern and, in effect, has only addressed the interests of the black middle class. Since those African Americans who were disproportionately affected by HIV tended to be poor, there was less motivation to advance their cause (Cohen 1999). Second, the virus is primarily spread through sexual contact, whether heterosexual or homosexual, and sexual expression is a taboo topic in black churches. That taboo is based in large part on the traditional readings of the Bible concerning gender and sexuality that these churches uphold (Douglas 1999). From such traditional readings, Gen 2–3 becomes the basis on which homosexuality is condemned ("God created Adam and Eve, not Adam and Steve"), women are to be subordinate to men ("he shall rule over you"), and, correspondingly, sex should be within marriage and primarily for reproduction. As will be shown in later sections, this hierarchical gender construction with its emphasis on heterosexuality and procreation are deeply problematic in the context of HIV and AIDS.

As a womanist biblical scholar who seeks the well-being of the whole African American community, my purpose in writing this essay is to suggest that a different gender and sexuality paradigm can be found in the Bible. As a result, African American Christians can continue to use the Bible as a source of inspiration and direction in our lives, but we must choose alternative biblical paradigms that will enhance rather than undermine our well-being. My starting point for finding alternative paradigms is the work of Phyllis Trible. In her groundbreaking book based on feminist hermeneutics, *God and the Rhetoric of Sexuality*, Trible contrasts the gender constructions described in Gen 2–3 with that in the Song of Songs. Comparing the two texts, she finds that the hierarchical gender construction of Gen 2-3 presents "love lyrics lost" but that the mutuality reported in the Song of Songs represents "love lyrics redeemed" (Trible 1978).

Using Trible's work as a starting point and employing a womanist hermeneutic, this inquiry explains why the Gen 2-3 gender paradigm is especially harmful in the context of HIV and AIDS generally and in the African American community specifically. This brief study then details why the Song of Songs, focusing on 3:1-4, offers an alternative that can indeed "redeem" traditional gender and sexuality constructions. If used in black churches, such redeemed paradigms could help reduce the rate of new HIV infections in the African American community.

Trible on Love Lyrics Lost and Then Redeemed

Before proposing her own reading of Gen 2-3, Trible summarizes well the traditional understanding of this narrative as the story of "Adam and Eve." As she notes, the story is usually thought to "proclaim male superiority and female inferiority as the will of God" and "(to portray) woman as a 'temptress' and troublemaker who is dependent upon and dominated by her husband" (1978, 73). Yet there are even more problematic implications, just a few of which are included here: "a male God creates first man (2:7) and last woman (2:22), [and] first means superior and last means inferior or subordinate"; since, "taken out of man (2:23), woman has a derivative, not an autonomous, existence"; and "woman's desire for man (3:16) is God's way of keeping her faithful and submissive to her husband" (Trible 1978, 73).

Trible counters these traditional understandings of Gen 2-3 in two ways. First, she offers a close reading of the text that undermines the usual assumptions. For example, she argues that God created, not Adam, but "the earth creature (*ha-adam*) who is made from the ground (*ha-adamah*)," and it is "sexually undifferentiated (neither male nor female nor a combination of both)." According to Trible's reading, that "earth creature," that human, is transformed into Adam, a male, only when the female (Eve) appears (1978, 77, 98). Such a reading counters notions that Eve is derivative or subordinate. Similarly, Trible finds that the Hebrew word '*ezer*, which is translated in English as "helper" and "suggests an assistant, a subordinate," has "no such connotation" in the Hebrew. In fact, she notes that elsewhere in the Hebrew Scriptures the word "often describes God as the superior who creates and saves Israel" and, with the addition of the term *kenegdo*, indicates that this connotation of superiority is tempered "to specify identity, mutuality, and equality" (90). Finally, Trible reminds us that the enmity, the hierarchical relationship that results between males and females in the text, is the result of "shared disobedience" and not God's intent: "(male) supremacy is neither a divine right nor a male prerogative," and (female) "subordination is neither a divine decree nor the female destiny" (128).

Second, after her rereading of Gen 2–3, Trible turns her attention to the Song of Songs as a text that redeems the love lyrics lost through disobedience in the garden of Eden. Using Scripture to interpret Scripture, she finds that the mutual love that was lost in the garden of Eden is found in "the garden of Eros, the Song of Songs" (1978, 144). Like her discussion of Gen 2–3, her discussion of the Song of Songs is detailed. However, as in the previous section, I highlight only a few of her salient points. First, Trible finds that the male-female relationships described in the Song of Songs are not hierarchical but sensual and mutual: the woman invites, the man accepts the invitation, and issues of marriage and procreation are not addressed (53, 162). Then, Trible notices the lush variety of plants and flowers that "adorn this place of pleasure," but "no tree of disobedience grows (cf. Gen 2:16–17)" (154–55). Finally, in her fantasy, "'the cherubim and a flaming sword' appear to guard the entrance to the garden of the Song (cf. 3:24)," and they serve to "keep out those who lust, moralize, legislate, or exploit"—as well as those who are "literalists" (162). Trible ends her discussion of the Song of Songs with the observation, focusing on ch. 2:10–13, that this text "welcomes lovers to romp and roam in the joys of eroticism" (ibid.).

After providing this brief introduction, the next sections of this essay explore how Trible's groundbreaking work, published in 1978, has been developed by later scholars and reveal the significance all of this work has for reading the Bible as African American Christians in the context of HIV and AIDS. Specifically, we address three areas: the construction of gender, the issue of homosexuality, and the question of sexual desire.

Challenging Traditional Gender Paradigms

As Trible described, Gen 2–3 has been interpreted in ways that consider women to be "inferior" and suggest they should be "subordinate" to men. In other words, the traditional heteronormative gender paradigm is that men should be dominant and that women should be subordinate. Such a hierarchical understanding of masculine and feminine roles appears to be reinforced by highly selective readings of particular New Testament texts such as: "Wives, be subject to your husbands as you are to the Lord. For the husband is the head of the wife just as Jesus is the head of the church" (Eph 5:22–23), and "Women should be silent in the churches. For they are not permitted to speak, but should be subordinate, as the law also says" (1 Cor 14:34).[1] Taken together, these texts appear to "proclaim male superiority and female inferiority as the will of God," just as Trible contends. A fuller discussion—and fairer analysis—of these texts can be found elsewhere (Martin 2006; Williams 2004). For the purposes of this discussion, the focus lies on the harm caused by that male dominance/female subordination gender paradigm in the context of the AIDS pandemic.

Globally, more than two-thirds of all persons living with HIV are found in sub-Saharan Africa, and it is on this continent that women theologians and biblical scholars of different faiths have come together and published an extensive body of literature on the connection between traditional gender paradigms and the high rates of HIV infection in women (i.e., Dube and Kanyoro 2004; Phiri, Haddad, and Masenya 2003). For example, cultural patterns favor male privilege and condone husbands having access to women outside of marriage, yet the wife's subordinate status prevents her from negotiating safer sex practices when her husband is at home. As a result of these and other factors, there are more women than men who are HIV-positive in sub-Saharan Africa, and, globally, heterosexual marriage puts women at risk for contracting the virus.

Another significant harm associated with the traditional gender paradigm is gender-based violence. There is a connection between violence against women in all forms—including rape and intimate partner violence—and the male dominant gender paradigm. It simply stands to reason that if manhood is defined as control over women, violence will be used to maintain or reestablish control (Anderson 2004, 101–17). As Kelly Brown Douglas explains, black women are disproportionately impacted by intimate partner violence, yet black churches have often failed to address the issue. She finds that, in effect, black women are thought of as "temptresses," "blamed for the attack on their bodies," and consequently "black women are compelled to 'sit in silence' regarding their abuse, since they are very aware that they will not be fairly heard" (2012, 178).

---

1. Unless otherwise noted, biblical translations follow the NRSV.

Compared to that in Gen 2–3, the construction of gender in the Song of Songs is refreshing. As described by Trible (1978, 161), this is a redeemed male and female relationship where "there is no male dominance, no female subordination, and no stereotyping of either sex." Rather than requiring her silence, the Song of Songs offers "the only unmediated female voice in all of Scripture," and "unlike many women in the Bible, she is assertive, uninhibited, and unabashed about her sexual desires" (Weems 1997, 364). Many aspects of this nontraditional gender paradigm can be seen in just one pericope: Song 3:1–5.

> Upon my bed at night
>   I sought him whom my soul loves;
> I sought him, but found him not;
>   I called him, but he gave no answer.
> "I will rise now and go about the city,
>   in the streets and in the squares;
> I will seek him whom my soul loves."
>   I sought him, but found him not.
> The sentinels found me,
>   as they went about in the city.
> "Have you seen him whom my soul loves?"
> Scarcely had I passed them,
>   when I found him whom my soul loves.
> I held him, and would not let him go
>   until I brought him into my mother's house,
>   and into the chamber of her that conceived me.
> I adjure you, O daughters of Jerusalem,
>   by the gazelles or the wild does:
> do not stir up or awaken love
>   until it is ready! (Song 3:1–5)

In the woman's voice, this pericope shows her to be active rather than passive, and, since she is responding to her lover having sought her in 2:8–17, the mutuality of the relationship is shown. Furthermore, this search for her lover can be contrasted with that of the woman in Prov 7; whereas the woman is depicted as a "villain" in Prov 7, the woman in the Song of Songs is depicted as a "heroine." This difference, it may be argued, shows that "the Song offers an alternative image of a woman searching the city for her lover and insists on a more complex and spacious view of female desire than Proverbs offers" (Cox and Paulsell 2012, 219–22).

However, there are elements of the pericope that undermine this depiction of gender mutuality and female empowerment. The heroine peacefully encounters sentinels in chapter 3 but, in 5:6–7, sentinels find her, beat her, and leave her wounded (Ostriker 2000, 51–52). As J. Cheryl Exum (2005, 25) observes, a "literary work might challenge its culture's traditional gender roles and expectations, but it could hardly be expected to be free from its influences." Similarly, Stephen Moore and Virginia Burrus (2010, 252) question how feminists can see the text as one of mutuality when it remains implicitly heteronormative, and "heterosexuality is the eroticization of gender inequality." Then, both David Clines (1995) and Jack Sasson (1987) argue that the Song of Songs is a male fantasy that meets a need for erotica, that is, depictions of available females who seek out lovers. The impact of the male gaze on female bodies is especially important to consider in this discussion, because the effect of the white male gaze on black female bodies has been extremely damaging.

That harm can be illustrated by a more detailed analysis of Song 3:4, a text that refers to the female taking her lover to her "mother's house" (*bet 'em*)—an unusual reference since most biblical references are to the "father's house" (*bet 'ab*). Carol Meyers (2013, 113) has found that references to a "woman's household" indicates that texts focus on women and "that the prominence of women in household tasks meant that the household becomes identified with the senior female." It would appear that identifying a household with the senior female in the Song of Songs is a positive development in today's context. However, in a white supremacist culture, as Douglas (1999, 50–54) details, black females as heads of households are deemed defective and pathological ("welfare queens") and, ultimately, blamed for their children's and their community's failure to thrive in an oppressive system. Consequently, not all women would find the more sexually expressive depiction of the female lover in the Song of Songs to be liberating. For many African American women, this depiction would simply reinforce a racist stereotype.

Nevertheless, the Song of Songs calls us to find new ways of loving that go beyond our traditional boundaries and limitations. In her reflection on 3:1–5, Renita Weems (1997, 398) writes the following words: "Love encourages us to stretch beyond our boundaries, beyond our narrow self-interests, beyond our comfort zones. Love encourages us to take risks, to embrace other ways of thinking, other ways of being, and other ways of doing." Finding such new ways to love ourselves, each other, and our communities is imperative for African Americans in the context of the AIDS pandemic.

Going Beyond Heteronormativity: The Question of Homosexuality

Traditionally, churches have condemned homosexuality, affirming that heterosexuality is the only acceptable form of sexual expression for Christian believers, and black churches are no exception. Such positions are ostensibly based on biblical texts such as Lev 18:18 and Rom 1:26–27 that are deemed to be, as is often heard, "crystal clear." Since the AIDS pandemic in the United States disproportionately affects men who have sex with men (MSM), intravenous drug users (IDU), and those presumed to have engaged in sexual activity outside of a monogamous heterosexual marriage, HIV-positive status has sometimes been viewed as the consequence of bad behavior. Such an association may explain why black churches were initially reluctant to address the issue publicly. Some leaders may have thought that addressing the issue would be misconstrued as their "implicitly condoning behaviors that the Church considers immoral" (Harris 2010, 49).

In spite of vigorous vocal opposition to the greater acceptance of LGBTQ persons in the life of black churches, there has also been a growing recognition of their presence in and contributions to those same faith communities. As a result, a kind of theological compromise has developed in the form of "love the sinner but hate the sin." Such a statement permits homosexual expression to still be considered a sin, but it also allows traditional Christians to be more welcoming and to become more engaged with measures to combat the pandemic. However, the negative consequences of continuing the staunch opposition to the greater inclusion of LGBTQ persons remain profound.

One consequence is that the condemnation of homosexuality and the initial association of the pandemic with homosexual men have created a stigma, and that stigma can deter persons from getting tested or beginning treatment. Any activity concerning HIV diagnosis or treatment is feared because it could identify persons as "gay" or mark them as involved in questionable behavior. As a result, rates for HIV testing tend to be lower than they should be in the African American community, and individuals who have tested positive enter treatment later than they should.

In addition, the condemnation of homosexuality impacts black LGBTQ youth who are rendered homeless when they are forced out of their homes after disclosing their gender identity or sexual orientation to their parents. Alternatively, these youth leave because they would face abuse if they remained in the home. When these youth end up on the streets, they all too often have to use transactional sex to meet the basic human needs of food, clothing, and shelter—and those encounters put them at a higher risk of contracting the virus. Finally, there is a dynamic referred to in the popular media as the "down low," where men present themselves as heterosexuals, have girlfriends, or even marry a woman, but they also have sex with men. The common view is that these men prefer to appear to comply with traditional patriarchal norms rather than face the condemnation of the black community. Furthermore, men who identify as heterosexual may engage in same-sex activity while incarcerated. These forms of closeted behavior put the men, as well as the women with whom they are involved, at risk for infection. Because of the three negative consequences described here, it is not an exaggeration to conclude that the condemnation of homosexuality by black churches continues to put black persons—and the black community—at risk. Given the church's ability to shape the community's values, this exclusionary policy must end if we are to effectively prevent new HIV infections. It is noteworthy that the same black church tradition that was able to see beyond biblical mandates for "slaves to be obedient to their masters" fails to interrogate the biblical witness with respect to either women or homosexuals. In fact, some black scholars have actually questioned why heteronormativity is so strongly upheld. Douglas (1999, 67–68) posits that, because the white culture labeled black sexuality as deviant, the black community has sought to distance itself from any nonnormative behavior that would seem to justify imposed stereotypes. Others suggest that heterosexual privilege may be the only privilege that black men and women have, and to give up that privilege appears to be anathema (Harris 2010, 57–58).

In the final analysis, Christian believers claim that their opposition to homosexuality is solely based on the apparent biblical proscriptions. However, little to no attention is ever paid to the ancient cultural values that shaped those proscriptions. For example, the same traditional gender paradigm that requires males to be dominant and females to be subordinate undergirds, in part, the condemnation of homosexuality in both the Hebrew Bible and the New Testament. Since the male is to be dominant (the one who penetrates), the possibility of a male who is penetrated is unacceptable. Furthermore, in the Hebrew Bible, based on an ancient understanding of human biology, the male's seed was not to be wasted, and so male-to-male sexual relationships were suspect; but female-female relationships that did not involve male seed were not addressed (Fewell and Gunn 1993, 106–9).

My intention here is not to offer an exhaustive analysis of the well-known "clobber passages" that are usually cited to support the church's condemnation of homosexuality. That kind of analysis can be found elsewhere (Rogers 2009; Martin 2006). Instead, I simply point out that the biblical condemnation of same-sex relationships rests on two different ancient cultural assumptions: a hierarchical gender paradigm is required, and sex should only be for procreation since, based on an antiquated and inaccurate concept of the human reproductive process, male seed was not to be wasted. Since these underlying rationales are countered in the Song of Songs, it becomes a helpful resource to move us towards readings of the Bible that will help us prevent new HIV infections.

As mentioned in the previous section, the usual hierarchical gender paradigm is challenged in the Song of Songs: the female lover is active, not passive, and the relationship of the two lovers is mutual rather than one of dominance/submission. Yet these are not the only significant differences in the gender paradigm described in the Song of Songs. In addition, the lovers are not married, and procreation is not the purpose of their encounters. In fact, Athalya Brenner (1997, 88) writes that "quite a number of the plants repeatedly mentioned in the Song of Songs have been used as female contraceptives and abortifacients throughout the Mediterranean world, for quite literally, ages," and she includes pomegranates, dates, myrrh, cinnamon, and mixed wine, among others, as examples. More pointedly, she finds that, some of the exchanges between the lovers, thought to demonstrate their mutuality, also communicated messages about the availability of contraceptives, given the types of plants and liquids mentioned.

> In such a social context, it is imperative for a woman not to become illicitly pregnant…, not to seem to have lost her virginity. Therefore, for instance, a seductive male voice in 4:9–5:1 may be reassuring his lover through his recital of a list of aromatic plants which double as contraceptives that no consequences will have to be suffered. Or, a female invitation for a male lover to come to her mother's house, so that "I will let you drink mingled wine, pomegranate juice" (8:2b) might be read as a reminder of contraception, too—at least on a supplementary level. (Brenner 1997, 88)

Since the traditional patriarchal values concerning marriage and reproduction are not the main lesson to learn from the lovers' longings, another message can emerge in the Song of Songs. The text then becomes one in which the lovers are able to model "a genuine self-offering in which each belongs fully to the other" (King 2006, 364). In his queer analysis of the Song of Songs, Christopher King notes the reciprocity that occurs in 2:16 and 6:3: "My beloved is mine and I am his; he pastures his flock among the lilies" (2:16) and "I am my beloved's and my beloved is mine; he pastures his flock among the lilies" (6:3) (ibid.). He then argues that such mutual and full self-giving in erotic love requires the freedom to develop a true identity that, in turn, will allow persons to "follow where eros leads" without having to pledge "obedience to ironclad laws of natural morality." On this basis, King can assert that "it is this liberty to love as one wills that queer people of faith must finally claim as a fundamental principle of human well-being and, truly, of salvation itself" (364–65). For King, then, the Song of Songs is a text that "celebrates socially transgressive eros" (370). That eros is transgressive because it transcends biblical traditional norms—thought to require marriage before having sex and then limiting sex to procreation—and touches on a universal human need for deep connection. In this way, a queer analysis of the Song of Songs is helpful to all human beings and not just the LGBTQ community.

Learning to Affirm Sexual Desire and the Erotic

Whenever the topic of homosexuality and the African American faith community comes up in a conversation, a pattern emerges. If one person says that we have difficulty talking about homosexuality, the other person inevitably responds with "But we have difficulty talking about sex in general." In all honesty, these topics are probably addressed quite frequently in church circles, but we know what is said: "Women should be subordinate to men" (or stated in a different way: "Husbands should be heads of the household"), "Homosexuality is a sin," and "Sex should only be for procreation or, at the very least, within marriage." Clearly these are frequently heard messages that any traditional Christian would find both comfortable and definitive. The problem is that, in the context of HIV, these messages are counterproductive and contribute to the spread of the virus rather than its eradication. Here are some basic statistics:

- On average, American teens start having sex at age seventeen, but they do not marry until the middle to late twenties. As a result, there is almost a decade when they have sex before marriage—yet "abstinence-only" education programs in schools and churches may leave youth uninformed and more likely to contract sexually transmitted diseases and to have unplanned pregnancies ("American Teens' Sexual and Reproductive Health" 2016).
- About 40 percent of all babies born in the United States today are born to unwed women, and the rates for African American women are nearly twice as high. Obviously, then, women are having children before they get married, illustrating, once again, that more comprehensive and age-appropriate sex education is needed as a means of HIV prevention (Livingston and Brown 2014; "Births to Unmarried Women" 2015).
- As mentioned earlier, marriage is not even the "safe zone" in the AIDS pandemic that traditionalists want it to be. Marriage is a risk factor for HIV infections because, for example, infidelity can occur within marriage (some cultures may even expect the husband to have relationships outside of marriage). Then there are also the possibilities of hidden or previous intravenous drug use by a spouse or the phenomenon of apparently heterosexual men who are married but also have sex with men on the "down low."

In spite of these developments in the United States, the only approach to HIV prevention that has been acceptable to conservative Christians is "Abstain (until marriage), Be faithful in marriage, and, if necessary use a Condom ('ABC')." Such a program is consistent with the "abstinence-only" programs used in schools, and its use was a condition for funding under President George W. Bush's PEPFAR program (Zimmerman 2013, 137–45). Yet ABC is not an adequate prevention strategy in the United States—especially since it ignores same-sex partners who until recently were not able to marry and who constitute about 70 percent of new HIV infections among men in the African American community. However, my concern here is not the (in)effectiveness of ABC as a prevention strategy. Instead, my concern is that abstinence-only sex education programs in schools and ABC as a prevention strategy in the context of the AIDS pandemic reflect and are consistent with compulsory heterosexuality as already outlined: women should be subordinate to men, homosexuality is condemned, and sex should only be within marriage and, ideally, for procreation. Given the current realities of sexual expression in the United States, an effective HIV prevention program must be one that affirms (or at least acknowledges) sexual desire as part of human nature and that functions independently of marital status and procreation.

Once again, Trible's reading of the Song of Songs, identified as love lyrics redeemed, can be instructive. For her, the Song of Songs does not speak "to the issues of marriage and procreation.... Love for the sake of love is its message" (1978, 162). Another scholar writes that the Song of Songs, "perhaps more than any other biblical book, refuses to be limited by common notions of 'family values.' Instead, this book celebrates pleasure for pleasure's sake" (Knust 2011, 25). Still another scholar finds that the Song of Songs "depicts the joys of love unconnected with marriage or procreation" (Ostriker 2000, 44). In his book *A Lily among the Thorns: Imagining A New Christian Sexuality*, Miguel A. De La Torre refers to the Song of Songs as unique for two reasons. First, the text "vividly describes sexual yearning" and so refutes the "prevalent fear of sexual desire" that has featured so prominently in the development of Christianity. Second, he finds that the descriptions of sex go beyond references to a particular act "but encompass the pleasure and passion that build toward a final release" (2007, 59).

De La Torre, whose field is Christian ethics, uses the work of the biblical scholar, Carey Ellen Walsh, in his analysis of the Song of Songs. Walsh's book, *Exquisite Desire: Religion, The Erotic, and The Song of Songs*, manages to communicate in accessible language the metaphorical references that are difficult for contemporary readers to understand. Just a few examples of her analysis are warranted here and will have to suffice. Walsh writes that wine is associated with sexual pleasure as seen in "your love is better than wine" (1:2, 4:10), "let us be drunk with love" (5:1), and finally, "in the woman's imagined seduction with pomegranate wine" (8:2). According to Walsh, "wine and sexual pleasure are linked by their sweetness and by their intoxicating properties." Similarly, the predominance of fruit imagery in the text can be explained by the analogous properties of fruit to a woman: "it has taut, delicate skin, pulpy and yielding flesh, and pungent, fresh scents and tastes" (2000, 118–19).

Furthermore, Walsh (2000, 111–12) notes that there are also passages in the Song of Songs, such as 5:2–6, where no explanation is needed and the "poetry is palpably erotic."

> I slept, but my heart was awake.
> Listen, my lover is knocking,

> "Open to me, my sister, my love,
> for my head is wet with dew …"
> My lover thrust his hand into the hole,
> and my insides yearned for him,
> I arose to open to my lover,
> and my hands dripped with myrrh,
> my fingers with liquid myrrh,
> upon the handles of the lock.
> I opened to my lover,
> but he was gone. (5:2–6 [Walsh])

Such erotic poetry in the Song of Songs is important because it unequivocally describes and affirms sexual desire. According to James Nelson and Sandra Longfellow (1994, xiv), sexuality includes procreation but, more fundamentally, it is "the basic eros of our humanness that urges, invites, and lures us out of our loneliness into intimate communication and communion with God and our world." Consequently, erotic desire expressed in the Song of Songs is not limited to heterosexual couples—it reflects the humanity of any person, regardless of gender identity or sexual orientation.

David Carr, in his work on the Song of Songs, finds that the erotic, the desire for connectedness, enables us to bring spirituality and sexuality together. In his book, *The Erotic Word: Sexuality, Spirituality, and the Bible*, Carr points out that the Song of Songs provides us with three levels of understanding the erotic. One level describes "our attachments to loved ones, nature, and other things"; a second level focuses on "sensuous connection with another person, a poem, a piece of nature, the world"; and yet another level "opens us to experiencing God loving us in and through those things." For Carr, it is important to accept the fact that "God lies beyond even our best erotic connections"; otherwise, we may be tempted to "love those things as if they were God." As a Hebrew Bible scholar, Carr's analysis is grounded in the biblical witness—our having been made in "God's bodily image" (Gen 1:26–27) and that we are to love God *and* other human beings (Deut 6:5) (2003, 17, 148–49).

In bringing together our spirituality and our sexuality in this way, Carr is reminding us of our embodiment—and that God deems it "very good" (Gen 1:31) (2003, 148). However, as Douglas (2012, 169) contends, an anti-body narrative has had a particularly destructive effect on black bodies in a white supremacist culture that labels our bodies as "out of control."

In the white collective consciousness the black body represented all that had to be overcome, it was a body fueled with passions and desire—it was a body out of control. As we have seen, in an effort to escape the caricature of being an out-of-control body people, the black community fostered a body denying/body phobic narrative of civility to match that of white culture.

The "body denying/body phobic narrative" that Douglas describes helps us to understand why African American communities, in general, and our churches, in particular, have supported the ABC approach to HIV prevention, promoted by white, conservative evangelicals. In such a context, for African Americans to reject abstinence-based measures runs the risk of reinscribing white racist caricatures of our community. At the same time, in the context of the AIDS pandemic, adopting the ABC approach means the behaviors that put our people at risk are ignored and consequently not addressed sufficiently in any prevention efforts.

Rather than denying our bodies and the power of the erotic, we need to embrace our bodies and the power of the erotic within them. As Audre Lorde (1984, 53) has written, the power of the "erotic" "is a resource within each of us that lies in a deeply female and spiritual plane, firmly rooted in the power of our unexpressed or unrecognized feeling." Furthermore, she writes that the power of the erotic is the connection to the capacity to feel joy and that connection to the deep feeling of joy can help us to live our lives more authentically (56–57). According to Lorde, our sense of the erotic becomes the basis on which we can evaluate all dynamics in our lives.

> For once we begin to feel deeply all the aspects of our lives, we begin to demand from ourselves and from our life-pursuits that they feel in accordance with that joy which we know ourselves to be capable of. Our erotic knowledge empowers us, becomes a lens through which we scrutinize all aspects of our existence, forcing us to evaluate those aspects honestly in terms of their relative meaning within our lives. And this is a grave responsibility, projected from within each of us, not to settle for the convenient, the shoddy, the conventionally expected, nor the merely safe. (57)

Applying Lorde's analysis to the current context, it is undeniable that we in the African American community are settling for "the conventionally expected" and "the merely safe" when it comes to strategies for HIV prevention. If we are to end the pandemic, we must begin to embrace our bodies, our inherent need for connection and joy, and fashion prevention strategies that are consistent with our multifaceted realities.

Conclusions

More than thirty years of experience with the HIV/AIDS pandemic in the United States has taught us that infection rates tend to be high where gender inequities are prevalent, homosexuality is condemned, and the use of condoms is discouraged or questioned. In other words, effective prevention strategies call for greater social and financial equality for women, lowering the stigma against homosexuality, and encouraging the use of condoms. However, the traditional notions of gender often found in African American churches undermine such prevention strategies: women are to be subordinate to men, homosexuality is condemned, and condom use is not encouraged because sex should be primarily for procreation and not pleasure.

The purpose of this essay is to show that such concepts of gender, sexuality, and sexual expression, attributed to Gen 2–3, are not the only ones found in the Bible. To the contrary, as seen here, the Song of Songs presents a biblical model of gender that is mutual rather than hierarchical, where sexual expression is based on the human need for connection more than procreation, and so homosexuality does not have to be condemned. It is this relationship between the hierarchical construction of gender and the condemnation of homosexuality that warrants further discussion.

A hierarchical construction of gender means that the masculine and the feminine are not only different but that the masculine is superior to the feminine. Consequently, as Ken Stone (1996, 76) writes, "it is nearly always considered an insult to say that a man is acting like a woman." In this understanding of gender, male homosexual acts are suspect because, although one of the men remains the sexual subject, the other one takes on the role of sexual object, the one acted upon. It is this role of sexual object that traditionally has been the role specifically allotted to the female. As Stone explains, "the male who allows himself to be (or is unable to prevent himself from being) acted upon sexually shows himself to be the object of another man; he therefore becomes 'feminized'" (76). In this way, Stone concludes, the negative attitude toward homosexuality is a function of traditional concepts of gender differentiation and hierarchy (76). Furthermore, it is this hierarchical concept of gender that arguably influences what is "natural" in the ancient world—and not necessarily the possibility of procreation as we sometimes think today (Rogers 2009, 74). Sexual expression, then, could be deemed "unnatural" under a male dominant/female subordinate gender paradigm, if it involved a male who was acted upon and therefore was subordinate and, presumably, if it involved a female who took the dominant position (Rogers 2009, 75; Brownson 2013, 237).

Once a relationship between dominant/subordinate gender constructions and the condemnation of homosexuality is understood, the significance of Trible's reading of the Song of Songs can be appreciated more fully. According to her, the hierarchal understanding of Gen 2–3 is when "love lyrics were lost," but they are "redeemed" in the Song of Songs. Succinctly stated, whereas in Gen 2–3 the relationship between the male and the female became hierarchical, in the Song of Songs that relationship became mutual. A more mutual and nonhierarchical gender paradigm would help to eliminate the association between "female" as sexual object—rather than sexual subject—and being considered "less than" the dominant male. Ideally, helping to eliminate that traditional gender paradigm would mean also that same-sex relationships would not be viewed as "unnatural" for having violated that paradigm.

Furthermore, as argued in this essay, the Song of Songs allows us to imagine sexual expression that is not solely for the purposes of procreation, and, in this way, it alludes to the power of the erotic, as described by Lorde. Of course, a return to the era of "free love" is not sought here. Without a doubt, we need to address the related issues of intimacy, responsibility, and accountability in all relationships. My point is simply that we cannot get to those more substantive discussions about sexual expression if we cannot admit that we sometimes have sex without intending to get pregnant and that we sometimes have sex outside of marriage. To simply say to the African American community "Abstain until you get married" is not an effective prevention strategy in the age of AIDS.

This womanist analysis of the Song of Songs offers those of us who are black and Christian a way to remain biblically based, yet better able to address the realities in our lives. Since those realities are now unaddressed, effective prevention strategies such as comprehensive sex education are not fully utilized, and the well-being of our community remains in jeopardy. In contrast, a womanist reading of the Song of Songs could help us reclaim our bodies, address our realities, and ultimately lower the rate of new HIV infections in our community.

Works Cited

"American Teens' Sexual and Reproductive Health." 2016. Guttmacher Institute. http://tinyurl.com/SBL0688x.

Anderson, Cheryl B. 2004. *Women, Ideology, and Violence: Critical Theory and the Construction of Gender in the Book of the Covenant and Deuteronomic Law.* London: T&T Clark.

"Births to Unmarried Women." 2015. Child Trends DataBank. http://tinyurl.com/SBL0688z.

Brenner, Athalya. 1997. *The Intercourse of Knowledge: On Gendering Desire and 'Sexuality' in the Hebrew Bible.* Leiden: Brill.

Brownson, James V. 2013. *Bible, Gender, Sexuality: Reframing the Church's Debate on Same-Sex Relationships.* Grand Rapids: Eerdmans.

Carr, David M. 2003. *The Erotic Word: Sexuality, Spirituality, and the Bible.* New York: Oxford University Press.

Centers for Disease Control. 2016. "CDC Fact Sheet: HIV among African Americans." http://tinyurl.com/SBL0688fg.

Clines, David J. A. 1995. *Interested Parties: The Ideology of Writers and Readers in the Hebrew Bible.* Sheffield: Sheffield Academic.

Cohen, Cathy J. 1999. *The Boundaries of Blackness: AIDS and the Breakdown of Black Politics.* Chicago: University of Chicago Press.

Cox, Harvey, and Stephanie Paulsell. 2012. *Lamentations and the Song of Songs: A Theological Commentary on the Bible.* Louisville: Westminster.

De La Torre, Miguel A. 2007. *A Lily among the Thorns: Imagining a New Christian Sexuality.* San Francisco: Jossey-Bass.

Douglas, Kelly Brown. 1999. *Sexuality and the Black Church: A Womanist Perspective.* Maryknoll, NY: Orbis Books.

———. 2012. *Black Bodies and the Black Church: A Blues Slant.* New York: Palgrave Macmillan.

Dube, Musa W., and Musimbi Kanyoro. 2004. *Grant Me Justice! HIV/AIDS and Gender Readings of the Bible.* Maryknoll, NY: Orbis Books.

Exum, J. Cheryl. 2005. *Song of Songs: A Commentary.* OTL. Louisville: Westminster.

Fewell, Danna Nolan, and David M. Gunn. 1993. *Gender, Power and Promise: The Subject of the Bible's First Story.* Nashville: Abingdon.

Harris, Angelique. 2010. *AIDS, Sexuality, and the Black Church: Making the Wounded Whole.* New York: Lang.

King, Christopher. 2006. "Song of Songs." Pages 356–70 in *The Queer Bible*

Commentary. Edited by Deryn Guest, Robert E. Goss, Mona West, and Thomas Bohache. London: SCM.

Knust, Jennifer Wright. 2011. *Unprotected Texts: The Bible's Surprising Contradictions about Sex and Desire*. New York: HarperCollins.

Livingston, Gretchen, and Anna Brown. 2014. "Birth Rate for Unmarried Women Declining for First Time in Decades." Pew Research Center. http://tinyurl.com/SBL0688y.

Lorde, Audre. 1984. *Sister Outsider: Essays and Speeches*. Freedom, CA: Crossing.

Martin, Dale B. 2006. *Sex and the Single Savior: Gender and Sexuality in Biblical Interpretation*. Louisville: Westminster John Knox.

Meyers, Carol. 2013. *Rediscovering Eve: Ancient Israelite Women in Context*. New York: Oxford University Press.

Moore, Stephen D., and Virginia Burris. 2010. "Unsafe Sex: Feminism, Pornography, and the Song of Songs." Pages 247–72 in *The Bible in Theory: Critical and Postcritical Essays*. Edited by Stephen D. Moore. Atlanta: Society of Biblical Literature.

Nelson, James B., and Sandra P. Longfellow, eds. 1994. Introduction to *Sexuality and the Sacred: Sources for Theological Reflection*. Louisville: Westminster John Knox.

Ostriker, Alicia. 2000. "A Holy of Holies: The Song of Songs as Countertext." Pages 36–54 in *The Song of Songs: A Feminist Companion to the Bible*. Edited by Athalya Brenner and Carole R. Fontaine. FCB 2/6. Sheffield: Sheffield Academic.

Phiri, Isabel Apawo, Beverley Haddad, and Madipoane Masenya, eds. 2003. *African Women, HIV/AIDS and Faith Communities*. Pietermaritzburg, South Africa: Cluster Publications.

Rogers, Jack. 2009. *Jesus, the Bible, and Homosexuality: Explode the Myths, Heal the Church*. Rev. and exp. ed. Louisville: Westminster John Knox.

Sasson, Jack M. 1987. "A Major Contribution to Song of Songs Scholarship." *JAOS* 107:733–39.

Stone, Ken. 1996. *Sex, Honor, and Power in the Deuteronomistic History*. Sheffield: Sheffield Academic.

Trible, Phyllis. 1978. *God and the Rhetoric of Sexuality*. Philadelphia: Fortress.

Walsh, Carey Ellen. 2000. *Exquisite Desire: Religion, The Erotic, and The Song of Songs*. Minneapolis: Fortress.

Weems, Renita J. 1997. "Song of Songs." *NIB* 5:361–434.

Williams, Demetrius K. 2004. *An End To This Strife: The Politics of Gender in African American Churches*. Minneapolis: Fortress.

Zimmerman, Yvonne C. 2013. *Other Dreams of Freedom: Religion, Sex, and Human Trafficking*. New York: Oxford University Press.

Part 2
Agency and Advocacy

Race, Gender, and the Politics of "Sass": Reading Mark 7:24–30 through a Womanist Lens of Intersectionality and Inter(con)textuality

Mitzi J. Smith

Introduction

On July 10, 2015, Sandra Bland, a twenty-eight-year-old black female activist, was stopped by a Texas trooper for allegedly switching lanes without signaling. Three days after her controversial arrest, Texas authorities claimed that Bland hanged herself in her Waller County jail cell (Sanchez 2015). Not a few people on social media, across race, gender, and class, blamed Bland for her own death arguing that she had the audacity to sass or talk back to a police officer. For some people it is acceptable for people of color and black women in particular to be illegally detained, tried on the streets, and executed in our jails for sassing or talking back to a trooper or police officer. Therefore, black women's sass is viewed as a capital offense and of having no intrinsic value or meaning.

In this essay I read the story of the Syro-Phoenician woman (Mark 7:24–30; cf. Matt 15:21–28) through a womanist hermeneutical lens of sass (sometimes referred to as talk back).[1] I interpret a biblical text as a black woman who embodies sass. Womanist sass is a legitimate contextual language of resistance. It is a "mother tongue," a subversive, defiant, grown woman's speech (Stover 2003, 139). It is also what Mikhail Bakhtin (1981, 253) calls *heteroglossia* (a "social diversity of speech types"). I read with sass and embody sass as an African American womanist biblical scholar

---

1. I chose Mark's version of the story because it is the shorter, earlier version. It emphasizes the power of the Syro-Phoenician woman's word (*logos*) as opposed to Matthew, who explicitly emphasizes her faith in Jesus.

who, like other women of color and women generally, has been labeled as "argumentative" and sassy by men and women alike, simply for persistently expressing a desire to know more than is "good" for a black woman to know, seeking clarification, or refusing to be silenced and dismissed. As a sassy womanist biblical scholar, I construct dialogue inter(con)textually, critically engaging and sassing/talking back to the story of the Syro-Phoenician woman. I also construct a dialogue between my readings of the biblical text and talk back derived from the black community, including the talk back of Maya Angelou, Audre Lorde, bell hooks, Frantz Fanon, and Ta-Nehisi Coates.

A Womanist Lens: Black Womanish Sass

According to Alice Walker, a *womanist* is a woman of color who speaks and acts "womanish." She behaves and talks like a grown and capable woman who assumes responsibility for her own well-being, and she is "committed to the survival and wholeness of entire people, male *and* female" (1983, xi). A womanist's commitment is manifest in her audacious, vocal, and vociferous pursuit of justice and freedom from dis-ease and oppression. Silence in the face of injustice and oppression can be complicit in those forces and systems that diminish life and wholeness while giving the illusion of survival. A womanist understands her survival and freedom to be interconnected with the well-being of the community. Sassy women who talk back to systemic injustice and oppression know these truths. Like Harriet Tubman, Sojourner Truth, Shirley Chisholm, Angela Davis, and so many others before her, Bland embodied a black womanish sass; she spoke and acted womanish. Texas authorities called her "argumentative and uncooperative" (Sanchez 2015). Bland's mother believes Bland "should be remembered … as an 'activist, sassy, smart … she knew her rights'" (Silva 2015).

A womanist prioritizes and highly values black women's epistemology (ways of knowing), agency, experiences, lives, and artifacts, rather than accepting them as peripheral to white feminist thought. Womanism centers black women as forethought and not as a theoretical addendum or critically provoked afterthought of white women's and black men's collective political awakening, activism, and God-talk. Womanism is feminism's sister and not its child. Black women's protowomanism was seldom televised or legitimized, except, for example, in writing their autobiographies. Yet black women have always been improvising and creating as well as resisting slavery, lynching, disenfranchisement, racism, sexism, classism, sexual violence, and other oppressions inflicted upon black women, the black community, and others. Womanism, as a political movement, seeks to eradicate hegemonic interlocking systems of oppression, including sexism, classism, and racism, and their impact on the lives of black women and their communities.

For black women, talk back and/or sass has been and remains in some situations the only means of agency, of being heard and of combating an other-imposed invisibility; it is resistance language that children, women, people of color, and black women in particular, speak and embody, inside and outside black communities and institutions. *Sass* is often defined as mouthing off, talking back, back talking, attitude, a woman not backing down to a man, or a child determined to have the final word in response to a real or perceived injustice or wrong. A sassy person is said to be impudent and insolent and is regarded as one who fails to show another person, a presumed superior, the respect or submissive behavior he or she has been socialized to expect within patriarchal systems, normally served up with so-called "arrogance" and "rudeness." Wives, children, slaves, and others of inferior social or economic standing can be guilty of sassing their husbands or significant others, fathers, masters, patrons, or employers.

The term is usually applied to the behavior of persons considered inferior or subordinate, by race, gender, position, class, or age to the person toward whom the talk, back talk, gesture, and/or attitude is addressed. Black feminist scholar bell hooks (1989, 5) defines *back talk* or *talking back* as "speaking as an equal to an authority figure ... daring to disagree ... having an opinion." Sass or talk back can refer to verbal and nonverbal behaviors, like placing one's hands on one's hips, rolling one's eyes. A person can sass, be sassy, or talk back without saying a word, by simply doing the opposite of what is expected or asked of him or her and in an in-your-face sort of way.

I use sass or talking back interchangeably, since sass consists of verbal and nonverbal gestures of defiance and resistance. Sass is when the oppressed name, define, call out, and sometimes refuse to submit to oppressive systems and behaviors. More specifically, according to literary critic Johnnie Stover, it is black women's refusal to remain silent about, or in the face of, oppression and violence committed against black women's bodies and minds and their families and communities (Stover 2003).

During slavery, Jim Crow, and the disenfranchisement of black people, it was expected that black people and women would happily defer to all white people regardless of age, gender, and position. Some believe this societal norm should never have changed, that sass or being sassy is never appropriate behavior for black people when directed at white people, even if one holds the most powerful office in the world. For example, Ariana Dickey's (2014) comment about President Obama's appearance on the Internet talk show "Between Two Ferns" is at least reminiscent of a lingering mindset and its refusal to die: "and boy, did Obama *sass* Zach [Galifianakis] back."

Sass or talk back are unacceptable behavior when directed at men, particularly white men. The *Opie and Andy* radio talk show posted a video entitled "Sassy Fat Black Girl Witness at Trayvon Martin Trial" (2013) in which Gregg "Opie" Hughes and Anthony Cumia berated nineteen-year-old Haitian American Rachel Jeantel's hair, weight, physiognomy (lips, eyes), sexuality, "incoherent" speech (her *heteroglossia*), and her audacity (in their eyes) to become angry, frustrated, and finally to talk back to the prosecutor during her testimony. Apparently, Ms. Jeantel's race, class, and gender made her sass even more unpalatable and intolerable at best and a source of comedic humiliation at worst.

Sass is an Americanism; it is slang created in the context of a patriarchal, gendered, and racialized society. America has always been and remains a racialized, patriarchal society. Yet the black woman, as the subject of Maya Angelou's poem "Still I Rise," survives and thrives despite the history of lies and oppression that objectify and demonize her; her rising is a talking back and sass/sassy. The second verse of that poem begins with the first of a series of rhetorical questions: "Does my sassiness upset you? / why are you beset with gloom? / cause I walk like I've got oil wells / pumping in my living room" (1995, 7). Angelou's poem, dedicated to her mother, Vivian Baxter, is sass/talk back and testifies about the experience of many other sassy black women who preceded her and follow her. The poem's rhetorical questions imply that the black woman's oppressors would rather see her broken and submissive ("bowed head and lowered eyes") than sassy and haughty. She rises as "the dream and hope of the slave" abandoning the past, its terror and fear (8, 9).

In reading Mark's story of the Syro-Phoenician Woman (7:24–30; cf. Matt 15:21–28) through a womanist lens of sass, I examine her speech as *heteroglossia*. Bakhtin (1981, 263) defines *heteroglossia* as the broad range and possibilities of "social diversity of speech types" embedded in a narrative through the speech of characters, narrators, authorial voice, and genres. The Syro-Phoenician woman's speech represents a social diversity; it is a culturally determined and subversive improvisation. I read her speech as resistance language. It is a contextual, subversive mother tongue. I read as a sassy woman talking back to the text from a place of anger and pain at the senseless deaths of black women like Bland and Natasha McKenna who sassed and died.[2] I read in remembrance of the sassy black women who preceded Bland and McKenna. I read also with those oppressed women who could not muster the courage to be sassy, to talk back to their oppressors and oppressions. I also "read darkness," which is "viewing and experiencing the world in emergency mode, as through the individual and collective experience of trauma" (Wimbush 2003, 21). I stand in solidarity with Bland. I read because of her and other sassy womanists. Knowing Bland's story has changed me in the way that the murder of Ta-Nehisi Coate's friend Prince Jones, killed by a Prince George's County police officer, changed him: "The entire episode took me from fear to a rage that burned in me then, animates me now, and will likely leave me on fire for the rest of my days.... My response was, in this moment, to write" (2015, 82).

I read the story of the Syro-Phoenician woman intentionally as a black woman consciously aware of my solidarity with Bland, McKenna, and with black women before her who have experienced the same or a similar fate and those after her whose stories will be read similarly. I read knowing that my sisters, nieces, nephews, brothers, and adoptive child could face a fate similar to these black women. We might, at any time, resist our oppressor, our oppression as sassy black women, but we might not survive.

Border Crossings: Place, Race, and Gender

Before she died, Bland had relocated from Chicago to Texas, having accepted a position at her alma mater, Texas Prairie A&M. In Texas, Bland planned to continue her work as an activist in support of #BlackLivesMatter. Chicago is a city plagued by violence, but it was in Waller County, Texas, which is infamous for a different kind of violence, where Bland was so unfortunate to be stopped. Former Waller County Judge DeWayne Charleston describes Waller County as "the most racist county in the state of Texas which is probably one of the most racist states in the country" (Toh 2015). Hempstead, a city in Waller County, still has separate cemeteries for white and black residents. Between 1882 and 1968, Mississippi had the highest lynchings with 581, Georgia was second with 531, and Texas

---

2. Natasha McKenna was an African American woman diagnosed with schizophrenia who died in police custody after being shocked four times with a stun gun (Weil 2015).

was third with 493 (Chestnut 1999). Violence, racism, sexism, and other forms of oppression transcend boundaries.

Such boundaries are evident in how Jesus moves from place to place in his ministry in the Gospel of Mark. Although this is the first time in Mark's narrative that Jesus himself crosses over into Tyre (7:24), people from Tyre and Sidon had come to him in Galilee for healing (3:7–8). Once word traveled that Jesus was healing people of diverse illnesses and casting out demons or unclean spirits, the crowds seeking his help increase exponentially. The people whom Jesus healed from Tyre and Sidon likely went back home. Maybe it is in the home of someone whom Jesus previously healed that he finds refuge. This is the first time Jesus enters a house for the purpose of being alone. At other times Jesus sought relief and respite from the press of the crowds, but he never successfully avoided people or the crowds in anybody's house. Why should this house be any different just because it is in Tyre?

In this house in Tyre, Jesus's disciples are conspicuously absent from the narrative (cf. Matt 15:23, where the disciples are present in the house and aggressively oppose the Canaanite woman). Perhaps Jesus thought that by crossing the border into Tyre he could finally escape the crowds, that people would not be so needy. But people need help and deliverance from unclean spirits on both sides of the border. The human need for wholeness transcends borders; it transcends gender, race, and class. The reader has been prepared for the resolution of the tension created by Jesus's desire to escape notice.

What is different about this place is Jesus's encounter with a solitary woman who locates Jesus despite his desire to be left alone. The narrator does not think it significant to inform his readers how the woman gained entry into the house or whether she experienced resistance at the door. Mark does not say whether the master of the house is Jewish, gentile, part Jewish and part gentile (like Timothy, Acts 16:1), Godfearer, or what? Maybe it does not matter. Racial and gender biases are impactful, efficacious when practiced by people who have power and authority to limit or deny access to resources. We know that somehow the Syro-Phoenician woman gains an audience with Jesus, but we do not know whether the interaction takes place inside or outside of the house. But this place, Tyre, should be neutral and friendly territory for her. It is either home or close to home. But oppressions, like sexism, racism, and classism, transcend place and transgress borders because defiled, fallible human beings are carriers of oppression, and Jesus is no exception.

Mark's Jesus enters and exits houses, but each threshold tells a new story. The narrator explicitly informs his readers that the woman who finds Jesus is Greek ('Ελληνίς). Many Greeks in Palestine and southern Syria shared collective identities that distinguished them from Jewish people (and vice versa). Nathan Andrade (2010, 370) asserts that "despite their internal ethnic and cultural disparities, the citizen bodies of Iamnia, Caesarea, Scythopolis, and other such cities constituted Greek collectivities, to be distinguished from Jewish ones." Jewish people claimed certain civic states as their own based on the previous conquest of Greek cities, like Tyre under the Hasmonaeans, despite subsequent Roman colonization. Syria was annexed to Rome in 64 BCE and Judea the previous year in 63 BCE. Prior to Roman annexation, the Hasmonaeans had conquered both Syria and Phoenicia (Koester 1995, 208–10).

More precisely, the woman is racially a Syro-Phoenician; she is possibly mixed race. In the first century BCE and CE "the terms Greek and Syrian could be used to describe intersecting civic categories, not mutually exclusive ethnic ones" (Andrade 2010, 353). While the term *Greek* could describe the Syro-Phoenician woman's language, "it is just as possible that it framed her in civic terms as a gentile member of a Greek polity, whether she spoke Greek or a near Eastern language," such as Aramaic (254). "As a Tyrian, she belonged to what by [Mark's] lifetime were the regional *koinon* or *eparchaeia* of Phoenicia (or Tyre), the Syrian *ethnos*, and the Greek city-state of Tyre, which was of course Phoenician by origin" (354).

The woman is impure in relation to Jesus. Jesus is what she is not, a Jewish man. In the immediate narrative context (7:1–23), Jesus had previously taught his disciples at someone's house. He taught them it is not what goes into the body that defiles a person, but it is what comes out of him that defiles (7:14–23). Did this teaching only apply to hand washing and food, or does it apply to people as well (cf. Acts 10:28)?

The other thing that we are told about the woman is that she has a daughter with an unclean spirit. This Greek Syro-Phoenician woman bears a triple stigma because of her race, gender, and status as the mother of a demon-possessed daughter. Like African American women and other women of color she experiences racism, sexism, and classism as interlocking forms of oppression. All three forms of oppression are highlighted in the narrative, and they impact how Jesus responds to the woman.

In Mark, the diagnosis of being demon-possessed or having an unclean spirit seems to be a blanket category. An unclean spirit is a stubborn visitor that will not willingly leave the body it has called home; it will throw a temper tantrum when commanded to leave (3:26); unclean spirits recognize Jesus, and each calls him by a different name or title (Holy One of God, 1:24; Son of the Most High God, 5:7). Perhaps, the labeling of someone as demon possessed was a way of explaining behavior that was otherwise considered abnormal, objectionable, and threatening. For example, when Jesus went home to get a break from the overwhelming crowds, the crowds were so needy and intrusive that he could not even enjoy a meal with his family (3:19–20). Exhausted and unable to get a break from the overwhelming crowds, Jesus reacted in a human way; his family had to constrain him (3:21). Consequently, some wondered whether he had lost his mind, accusing Jesus of having an unclean spirit (ὅτι ἔλεγον πνεῦμα ἀκάθαρτον ἔχει, 3:30), a demon like the ones he had been exorcising from other folks (3:23). This Syro-Phoenician woman's daughter, like Jesus, has been diagnosed as having an unclean spirit. Impurity is socially constructed. What is constructed can be deconstructed.

Significantly, Jesus never touches people that are said to have unclean spirits; they are the untouchables. Jesus touches a leper who is considered unclean, but his uncleanliness is not viewed as demon possession (1:40–41). The only person with an unclean spirit that Jesus touches is the boy from whom the disciples failed to exorcise the demon; however, it is only after the unclean spirit is expelled that Jesus touches the corpse (9:14–29). Even a corpse is touchable, but not people with unclean spirits.

It is out of ignorance that people are labeled as having "unclean spirits," as demon possessed because society finds something about their behavior unacceptable, abnormal, distasteful, threatening; they are out of order and different. Mary Douglas (1984, 36) states: "where there is dirt there is system"; there is a normal way of being and behaving. We can respond to perceived anomalies in two ways. We can ignore them as if they do not exist, or we can acknowledge their existence and condemn them (39).

In relation to Jesus, the woman as a Syro-Phoenician experiences triple stigmatization even in her own neighborhood. She has no ontological existence outside of her colonized, racialized, and othered group identity. Frantz Fanon (1967, 109–10) wrote that "every ontology is made unattainable in a colonized and civilized society.... In the *Weltanschauung* of a colonized people there is an impurity, a flaw that outlaws any ontological explanation.... Ontology—once it is finally admitted as leaving existence by the wayside—does not permit us to understand the being of the black man [or woman].... The black man [or woman] has no ontological resistance in the eyes of [white people]."

The Politics and Power of Sass

The Syro-Phoenician woman bowed and begged for Jesus's attention and help. But Jesus responded to her deference, her submissiveness with these words: "Permit the children [τέκνα] to be fed first, for it is not good [καλός] to take the bread from the children [τέκνα] and to throw it to the dogs" (7:27; my translation). Jesus responded to her in a way that betrayed his Jewish male bias. As Emerson Powery states (2007, 136), Jesus has triply marginalized this woman: she is female, a Greek, non-Jewish foreigner, and she is, if implicitly, a dog. In Jesus's reasoning, to give bread to the dogs requires taking it from the children; to give to the "dogs" will result in short changing the children who deserve priority. In other words, "all lives matter," despite the fact that all people do not experience dis-ease and oppressions to the same degree as others. In this moment, the mother pleading the imminent, urgent case of her sick child should matter most. (The slogan "all lives matter" in response to "black lives matter" dismisses the impact of racism on people of color in a racialized society.)

The woman is likened to the "dogs" that have no place at the table. Generally, ancient Semitic peoples did not care for dogs as household pets (Lazenby 1949, 245; see Gosling 1935). If there happens to be any leftovers they will be thrown at her, like a dog in an alley. She must behave like a Greek, a Syro-Phoenician, and a woman in relation to this Jewish man. She is impure and subordinate to Jewish people, despite their shared geopolitical status as colonized peoples. Fanon (1967, 114) writes, "I was expected to behave like a black man—or at least like a nigger" while a man should behave like a man. Similarly, black women must be black women in relation to white men. In a racialized society, black women are not viewed and treated as women on equal footing with white women. Black women's skin color trumps their gender; they are seen and treated as black persons first and secondarily as flawed females inferior to white women. Sojourner Truth so poignantly responded to this racist ideology in her "Ain't I a Woman" speech at a Women's Rights Convention in Akron, Ohio, in 1851, disrupting with her sass and back talk the racist ideology that questioned her womanhood because of her race and her former enslavement. With thunderous voice, Truth asserted that nothing she experienced or that was withheld from her nullified or changed the fact of her identity as a woman.

Jesus's words signify a tradition and ideology of racial priority, an "unreasoned" reason, justifying his denial of the woman's request. The woman can either submit to her oppression, or she can challenge and resist affirming her own humanity. Colonization does not encourage unity among the colonized; it encourages them to guard the crumbs. The oppressed are expected to achieve wholeness on the crumbs, to be treated like dogs and yet remain civil and silent.

But the Syro-Phoenician woman will not be silenced; she will resist. She resists this triple marginalization with her logos, her word, her sass; she draws upon "inner resources" left to the reader's imagination (Powery 2007, 136). She resists as a woman, as a mother with a sick child. Jesus invoked a text, an oppressive text—oppressive for mother and child. So the woman resists with sass and talk back: "she answered and said to him, 'Master even the household table dogs [τά κυνάρια ὑποκάτω τῆς τραπέζης] eat from the crumbs of the children [παιδία]'" (7:28, my translation). I propose that the noun "crumbs" metonymically signifies the children's plates. In the woman's sass, the dogs do not have to wait until the children are fed first; the dogs are treated with compassion as beloved household pets. Ancient Greeks and Romans, unlike Semitic peoples generally, did not abhor animals like dogs but welcomed them into their houses. In fact, dogs and other animals were "dedicated to gods or goddesses" (Lazenby 1949, 245). Homer's *Iliad* mentions "dogs I raised in my halls to be at my table" and "nine dogs of the table that had belonged to the lord Patroklos" (22.69; 23.173 [Lattimore]). As early as 600 BCE, ancient vase paintings show dogs in houses under tables. Rich and poor alike loved their dogs. An ancient Gallic relief depicts "a boy reclining on a couch and giving his pet dog his plate to lick clean" (Lazenby 1949, 246).

Because of the woman's experiences, her context as a Greek, Syro-Phoenician woman, she embodies sass from her unique epistemological context. Her sass is *heteroglossia*. The woman resists with the only thing she has, her reason (logos), her sass; she was up against something unreasoned. "For a man whose only weapon is reason there is nothing more neurotic than contact with unreason" (Fanon 1967, 118). To be despised because of one's race (gender, sexuality, class) is to be "up against something unreasoned" (118).

The fact that we can seek liberation from one form of oppression while thoroughly entrenched in another is the beast of socialization absent conscientization. Surekha Nelavala (2006, 68) argues that the woman in her response to Jesus says yes but no; she plays it smart by "pretending she was accepting" Jesus's argument and used it to her own advantage and by not behaving as if Jesus insulted her. But the woman's deference to Jesus demonstrated by her addressing him as master would be typical behavior of most women socialized in a patriarchal society. Besides her initial genuflecting and pleading do not result in a positive outcome but an oppressive word.

The Syro-Phoenician woman did not let the differences in their ethnicity or status, Jesus's reputation as a healer, or any stigma associated with her having a daughter possessed by an unclean spirit hinder her from sassing or talking back to Jesus. She questioned Jesus and the authoritative tradition he quoted that could have stopped her in her tracks and denied her daughter the healing she sought and needed and which he had so freely bestowed upon others. Clearly, all lives do not matter equally. Jesus had no right to treat her as less than a dog in her hour of motherly desperation. Her life matters; her daughter's life matters—at least as much as the "dogs under the table." Syro-Phoenician lives matter! Syro-Phoenician women's lives matter!

The Syro-Phoenician woman went toe to toe with Jesus. The woman "uses his own argument" (Dewey 1998, 485). "More than anything else, the personal narratives that formerly enslaved black women wrote are products of their resistance to various oppressions, and each writer uses the language of the oppressor to express that resistance" (Stover 2003, 137). The woman counters Jesus's speech with her *heteroglossia*. She engages in subversion and improvisation: (1) she speaks from her own cultural context, recontextualizing and substituting Jesus's words with her sass. In her sass, τέκνα becomes παιδία. In her sass, her people sit at the table; (2) the παιδία, unlike the τέκνα demonstrate compassion for the table dogs, allowing them to eat crumbs off their plates; and (3) she eliminates the language of priority. "An African American vernacular has always been recognized as a black way of speaking, and like all vernaculars, it grew out of a need to speak subversively, to speak in a 'language' that was shared by other members of one's 'community' but that confounded those outside of it" (140).

Significantly, Jin Young Choi (2015, 93) argues that the Syro-Phoenician woman utilizes an "embodied tactic." However, I disagree with Choi's assertion that it is the "art of the weak." Rather, given this cultural linguistic shift, the Syro-Phoenician woman has flipped the script. It is *heteroglossia*. With παιδία, here is a mother's tongue or language for her people and her child. As Stover (2003, 139) argues, "African American forms of expression such as black folktales, signifying, playing the dozens, and an infinite variety of subversive use language—sass, invective, impudence, back talking, just to name a few—demonstrate Bakhtin's *heteroglossia* criteria, forming the base for … an African American 'mother tongue.'" As bell hooks (1989, 5) writes, in her community where she grew up in the south talking back was risky and daring and satisfied the craving (or need) to "have a voice, and not just any voice but one that could be identified as belonging to" her. The Syro-Phoenician woman improvises at the axis of her need and Jesus's denial, constructing her own *heteroglossia*, a language that resists oppression and claims her own humanity.

Jesus's consciousness is raised as a result of the woman's sass. Mark's Jesus uses the grammatically neuter Greek noun τέκνον (child) when he addressed the man-child whose friends lowered him through the roof so that Jesus might heal him (2:5). Mark's Jesus used τέκνον the second time in this conversation with the Syro-Phoenician woman to refer to the Jewish people (7:27). In between these two instances of τέκνον, we find one occurrence of the Greek noun παιδίον (child) referring to Jairus's fatally ill daughter (θυγάταριον) whom Jesus resurrects (5:39). Perhaps, when Mark's Jesus calls Jairus's daughter (θυγάταριον) a παιδίον, it signifies her putative subordinate status as a female. She is an outsider belonging to an insider (Jairus).

The Syro-Phoenician woman's sass mattered, tugging at, tapping into Jesus's humanity and compassion. She was an advocate and an activist for her child and for other mothers and their children who could be denied justice and wholeness based on biased traditions and Rabbis who have been socialized to value those traditions. The Syro-Phoenician mother challenged what Jesus labeled good or fair (καλός, 7:27). That is what sass does; it challenges those systems, traditions and people that are neither just nor moral, but deleterious and deadly to one's self, one's people, and to the human race. "Moving from silence into speech is for the oppressed, the colonized, the exploited, and those who stand and struggle side by side a gesture of defiance that heals, that makes new life and new growth possible. It is … the liberated voice" (hooks 1989, 9).

After Jesus's encounter with her, Mark's Jesus uses παιδίον as a more inclusive term. He embraces a παιδίον and admonishes that anyone who welcomes any παιδίον like this one welcomes him and God (9:36–37). Also after his encounter with the Syro-Phoenician woman, people bring their children (παιδίον) to him; it is such children (παιδίον) as these to whom the kingdom of God belongs (10:13–16). Jesus only reverts to τέκνον when speaking directly to his circle of disciples, referring to them as τέκνον (10:24, 28; cf. 12:18–21 where τέκνον is put into the mouths of Sadducees; 13:12).

It Is Because of Your Word (Logos)/Sass

In response to the woman's sass, Jesus acknowledges the power of her word (logos), her reasoning. Choi acknowledges that it is the woman's logos that engenders healing for her daughter, but she further asserts that the woman consumes the crumbs partaking of the mystery of Jesus's body (2015, 100). In Mark, when Jesus casts a demon or unclean spirit out of an individual, the language is clear that Jesus has cast out the demon/unclean spirit (1:21–28, 34; 3:21–28; 6:13; 9:25). These exorcisms are expressed with the Greek verb ἐξέρχομαι in the second aorist imperative (ἔξελθε) when Jesus is the agent (1:25; 5:8; 9:25), with the Greek verb ἐκβάλλω when the narrator or other characters refer to Jesus's exorcism activities in the third person (1:34; 3:22, 23); or when Jesus commissioned the twelve apostles to perform exorcisms, the present infinitive of ἐκβάλλω occurs (3:15; cf. 6:13), usually translated "cast out." In Caesarea Philippi, despite Jesus having given his apostles power over unclean spirits, they were unable to expel the spirit from a young boy (9:17–18), which suggests being one of Jesus's followers and being commissioned by him does not guarantee successful exorcisms. The twelve apostles were disturbed that in Capernaum somebody who was not one of them was casting out demons in Jesus's name (9:38–41; cf. Luke 9:49–50). Mark demonstrates that perceived others/outsiders can exorcise demons or unclean spirits; I argue that this Syro-Phoenician woman becomes one of them. When she seeks Jesus's help for her daughter, she does not know the power of her sass, but she is about too.

Here Jesus says, "on account of this word, go [home]; the demon has gone out of your daughter" (7:29, διὰ τοῦτον τὸν λόγον ὕπαγε, ἐξελήλυθεν ἐκ τῆς θυγατρός σου τὸ δαιμόνιον). He does not command the demon to leave but directs the sassy mother to go home. Jesus knows that the demon has left her child's body. Nelavala (2006, 68) argues that Jesus has been transformed, that this is "the miracle" when the oppressed can "persuade their oppressor for a change." The assertion that "without the oppressor's readiness to change, the voice of the oppressed is in vain" (66) contributes to a hopelessness that too many oppressed feel, a hopelessness that keeps too many away from the ballot box and assures complicity in their own oppression.

In his book *Between the World and Me*, Coates (2015, 97) advises his son about the intrinsic value of struggle and resistance against oppression: "you are called to struggle, not because it assures you victory but because it assures you an honorable sane life." Jesus simply affirms the power of this Greek Syro-Phoenician woman's sass. Her word, her sass has power. But Jesus casts no spell; there is no ἐκβάλλω. The Greek syntax differs from the other Markan exorcism episodes. Jesus gives his twelve disciples the authority to cast out demons, but they do not; instead, he affirms the authority embodied in this woman's sass. It is *her* word, *her* sass that brings restoration and relief to her child. Her daughter is no longer one of the untouchables.

Sass gushes up from a place of pain and anger, of being "sick and tired of being sick and tired" of living with "unclean spirits" that claim one's body, mind and soul. One might say, therefore, that it is truth-telling with an attitude and for good reason. Sass explodes on the scene, talking back to racism, sexism, classism, and other isms that persist and refuse to desist, that refuse to be expelled without leaving its mark on one's body, soul, and mind. The power of sass is the power of truth-telling, the power of breaking the silence that oppression inflicts upon its victims. Sass is often a woman's last resort. A sassy woman takes a risk, a possibly fatal risk, in confronting oppression. The last stanza in Audre Lorde's (1995, 32) poem "A Litany for Survival" reads: "and when we speak we are afraid/our words will not be heard / nor welcomed / but when we are silent / we are still afraid / so it is better to speak /remembering / we were never meant to survive." Women like Bland sass or talk back not because of the absence of fear, but because they know history and current events show that "we were never meant to survive." But we use our "mother tongues," our sass and talk back, for our children, at least hoping they will have a better life and not have to be constrained and demonized by the unclean spirits of racism, sexism, and classism.

Certainly sass and talk back can have fatal outcomes when the person to whom it is directed has more regard for unjust traditions or for his own ego and authority than for human freedom and life, as in the case of Bland and others. The biblical writers were selective regarding the stories they chose to preserve and narrate. Life is a lot messier and does not wrap up in tidy salubrious and felicitous denouements. The empire always strikes back. For unjust systems to fall, it takes a movement of women and men willing to sass and talk back, risking retaliation and even life. Unjust systems and the people who prosper from them do not just wake up one day and decide that they are tired of the benefits and implode. What we also know for sure is that the utter silence of the oppressed (and their supposed allies) will never topple the master's house.

Conclusion

The story of the Syro-Phoenician woman provides an antithesis to the silent submissive woman who dares not sass or talk back to male authority figures, regardless. This story can assist in constructing a more empowering and freeing theology of sass or talk back that demonstrates the impact and value of women's sass or talk back. The Syro-Phoenician woman stands in the tradition of biblical predecessors like Queen Vashti, Esther, and even Mary, the mother of Jesus, who orders the servants to assist Jesus, who turns water into wine (John 2:3–5). Bland stood that fatal day in the tradition of protowomanists like Ida Wells Barnett, Fannie Lou Hamer, Septima Clark, Rosa Parks, and other activists. However, she did not choose to be memorialized in a similar tragic fashion as Miriam Carey, Natasha McKenna, Yvette Smith, Tanisha Anderson, Rekia Boyd, Kindra Chapman, and so many others who were murdered by law enforcement officials because of their race. The abuse and illegal arrest of Bland and subsequent attempts by Trooper Encinia and his department to cover up the "truth" at the very least precipitated her untimely and unnecessary death and at most constitutes a modern-day lynching (allegedly with a plastic bag around her neck and a large quantity of marijuana while in custody). Bland would be alive today had Trooper Encinia not singled her out for harassment and escalated the situation because she dared to sass and talk back, to resist his oppressive ways.

Women continue to be taught that they are to be good "foot stools" for men. When a woman "acts up" or refuses to be that footstool, a "biblically" submissive woman, then she deserves any violence inflicted upon her. Too many women remain shackled to this type of thinking, and so they do all they can to be "good girls,"[3] always submissive to male authority and abuse. Sass or back talk (talk back) are certainly not the qualities of submission.

The story of the Syro-Phoenician woman shows that sass can call our attention to and challenge unjust, biased, and oppressive traditions, laws, and expectations. The power of sass can reveal and question the destructive forces at work in or against our communities. Too often when many women of color have sassed or talked back, confronting unfair practices, biased policies, and racist behaviors that they have witnessed or experience in church,

---

3. I even heard a female minister not long ago at a breast cancer event promoting the book she wrote about how women can be little girls again and thus become good marriage material.

society, or the academy, they have been labeled as trouble makers, castigated, marginalized, and ostracized by men as well as by their sister feminists and womanists. This practice of silencing the sass of women of color hinders womanism/feminism from being the political and self-critical movement it is meant to be. We need to celebrate sass and talk back in women of color as well as in white women as a legitimate form of agency and method of truth telling rather than punishing women for speaking truth boldly in the face of corrupt, biased, life-threatening, and denying authority. Sass and talk back are legitimate forms of resisting oppression and exploitation. It can be considered a language ("mother tongue") of black women seeking to expose their exploitation and to dismantle the master's house built from and on the sands of racism, class, sexism, and domination generally. We must celebrate sassy sisters and tell their stories.

I travel alone for long distances relatively often. I am black and female. On some days I am fed up, and I might just be courageous enough to assert my right to know, to be sassy, if I should be stopped by a cop. That cop might be like Trooper Encinia. He might refuse to tell me why I am being stopped and yet expect my full unmitigated compliance. Or I might comply but be bullied and provoked—everyone, most people, have a breaking point. Like other black women and men in this country, my life could be cut short by one trivial, unnecessary encounter with the wrong police officer. Black people's fears are real. Bland, Kindra Chapman, Tamir Rice, Freddie Gray, and many others who died as a result of interactions with the police, in marked and unmarked graves, were real people who are mourned and missed by family and friends. For some it will not be real, the fear, the facts, until it happens to them or to someone they know. But now is past time to name and oppose this insidious brutality of people of color, women and men and demand "never again." #SayHerName #BlackWomensLivesMatter.

Works Cited

Andrade, Nathanael. 2010. "Ambiguity, Violence, and Community in the Cities of Judea and Syria." *Historia* 59:343–70.

Angelou, Maya. 1995. "Still I Rise." Pages 7–9 in *Phenomenal Woman: Four Poems Celebrating Women*. New York: Random House.

Bakhtin, Mikhail M. 1981. "Discourse in the Novel." Pages 259–422 in *The Dialogic Imagination*. Edited by Michael Holquist. Translated by Caryl Emerson. Austin: University of Texas Press.

Chesnutt, Charles. 1999. "Lynching Statistics." Charles Chesnutt Digital Archives. http://tinyurl.com/SBL0688a1.

Choi, Jin Young. 2015. *Postcolonial Discipleship of Embodiment: An Asian and Asian American Feminist Reading of the Gospel of Mark*. New: Palgrave Macmillan.

Coates, Ta-Nehisi. 2015. *Between the World and Me*. New York: Spiegel & Grau.

Dewey, Joanna. 1998. "The Gospel of Mark." Pages 470–509 in *A Feminist Commentary*. Vol. 2 of *Searching the Scriptures*. Edited by Elisabeth Schüssler Fiorenza. New York: Crossroad.

Dickey, Ariana. 2014. "Obama 'Between Two Ferns,' Kevin Bacon, Baby Tigers and More Viral Videos." *The Daily Beast*. http://tinyurl.com/SBL0688c1.

Douglas, Mary. 1984. *Purity and Danger: An Analysis of the Concepts of Pollution and Taboo*. London: Routledge.

Fanon, Frantz. 1967. *Black Skins, White Masks*. New York: Grove.

Gosling, W. F. 1935. "Pets in Classical Times." *GR* 4:109–13.

Homer. 1951. *The Iliad*. Translated by Richmond Lattimore. Chicago: University of Chicago Press.

hooks, bell. 1989. *Talking Back*. Boston: South End.

Koester, Helmut. 1995. *History, Culture and Religion of the Hellenistic Age*. Vol. 1 of *Introduction to the New Testament*. 2nd ed. Berlin: de Gruyter.

Lazenby, Francis D. 1949. "Greek and Roman Household Pets." *CJ* 44:245–52.

Lorde, Audre. 1995. "A Litany for Survival." Pages 31–32 in *The Black Unicorn: Poems*. New York: Norton.

Nelavala, Surekha. 2006. "Smart Syrophoenician Woman: A Dalit Feminist Reading of Mark 7:24–31." *ExpTim* 118:64–69.

Opie and Andy. 2013. "Sassy Fat Black Girl Witness at Trayvon Martin Trial." http://tinyurl.com/SBL0688d1.

Powery, Emerson B. 2007. "The Gospel of Mark." Pages 121–57 in *True to Our Native Land: An African American New Testament Commentary*. Edited by Brian Blount. Minneapolis: Fortress.

Sanchez, Ray. 2015. "What We Know about the Controversy in Sandra Bland's Death." CNN. http://tinyurl.com/SBL0688e1.

Silva, Daniella. 2015. "Sandra Bland's Mother Speaks Out on Sandra Bland's Life, Investigation." NBC News. http://tinyurl.com/SBL0688f1.

Stover, Johnnie M. 2003. "Nineteenth-Century African American Women's Autobiography as Social Discourse: The Example of Harriet Ann Jacobs." *College English* 66:133–54.

Toh, Michelle. 2015. "Sandra Bland Death: Is Waller County the Most Racist County in Texas?" The Christian Science Monitor. http://tinyurl.com/SBL0688g1.

Walker, Alice. 1983. "Womanist." Pages xi–xii in *In Search of Our Mothers' Gardens: Womanist Prose*. San Diego: Harcourt Brace Jovanovich.

Weil, Martin. 2015. "Death of Woman Shocked by Stun Gun in Fairfax Jail is Ruled an Accident." *Washington Post*. http://tinyurl.com/SBL0688h1.

Wimbush, Vincent L. 2003. "Introduction: Reading Darkness, Reading Scriptures." Pages 1–43 in *African Americans and the Bible: Sacred Texts and Social Textures*. Edited by Vincent L. Wimbush. New York: Continuum.

Antitypes, Stereotypes, and Antetypes: Jezebel, the Sun Woman, and Contemporary Black Women

Love L. Sechrest

Introduction

It is possible to make the case that technological innovation was a necessary accompaniment of the Civil Rights movement in the 1960s. Without news broadcasts of scores of confrontations between nonviolent black civil rights protesters and angry uniformed and nonuniformed white protectors of the status quo, this nation might never have granted the sons and daughters of enslaved Africans the most basic rights of citizenship. Today's ubiquitous cell phone cameras and video recording devices operated by officers and civilians as well as journalists may similarly be stimulating a new era of Civil Rights protest. When this ever-present technology captures violent encounters between police and unarmed black men, women, and children, it plays no small part in moving a new generation of blacks to demonstrations and protests. Footage of Freddie Gray's arrest, Sandra Bland's traffic stop, and Tamir Rice's and Walter Scott's murders at the hands of the police sometimes makes all the difference when it comes to making the case regarding police misconduct in interactions with African Americans, even if it is still not enough to result in criminal charges and convictions against the officers. Media images even played a part in removing Confederate flags from state symbols and public spaces across the South in the wake of the 2015 Charleston massacre: Facebook images of Dylann Roof draped in a Confederate flag arguably helped unveil his racist motivation for the murders of nine blacks at prayer in an African

Methodist Episcopal church. In other words, images are powerful purveyors of values; they shape conduct, stimulate action, and frame meaning.

In the wake of powerful media images of law enforcement's over-militarized responses to protests of a police officer's shooting of an unarmed black teenager in the summer of 2015 in Ferguson, Missouri, another image fired my imagination: a photo of a T-shirt worn by a black female protestor proclaimed, "This Ain't Yo Mama's Civil Rights Movement." This statement was evocative and stimulating on a number of levels as it simultaneously honored the too-often overlooked contributions of black women in the Civil Rights movement of the 1960s while also proclaiming the advent of an updated, different, and perhaps edgier refrain in the struggle for black dignity in the #BlackLivesMatter movement.[1] Young women wearing that kind of T-shirt might be expected to be as devoted and bold in their confrontation with oppressive systems of law and order as were their mothers who marched with Martin Luther King Jr. But those who view the marches of those mothers through a romanticized patina of decorum might also be disappointed that such contemporary T-shirt wearing women are eschewing any politics of respectability that might have characterized their mothers' efforts. This slogan hints at the complicated nature of agency and the way that women's agency is transformed and transferred from generation to generation between mothers and daughters, parents and children.

Musings on the power of images can be as fruitful in the realm of biblical interpretation as it is in contemporary political critique. This essay explores two of the women in Revelation through the lens of a womanist hermeneutic by peeling away marginalizing ancient and contemporary stereotypes. I recover and analyze the agency displayed by two of the female characters depicted in Revelation and put this recovered agency into conversation with contemporary black women who have new and fresh ways of exhibiting perseverance and faithful witness.[2] The essay

---

1. The #BlackLivesMatter social movement was founded by three young black women, Alicia Garza, Patrisse Cullors, and Opal Tometi, in the aftermath of the exoneration of George Zimmerman in 2013. Zimmerman, a private citizen, had been arrested for killing Trayvon Martin, an unarmed black teenager who, during a visit, was walking in the Florida neighborhood where his father lived. For more on the movement, see the founders' website ("Who We Are," n.d.) and a different public account of the movement on *Wikipedia* ("Black Lives Matter," n.d.).

2. In this article I use a definition of *agency* developed by William H. Sewell. In an article that discusses the way that human agency and social structures mutually influence each other, Sewell (1992, 20–21) defines agency as the culturally determined

examines "Jezebel"[3] the "false" prophet in Rev 2:20-23 as well as a female character who may be her antitype,[4] the Sun Woman of Rev 12 (i.e., the woman clothed with the sun). In the first case John uses Jezebel imagery to thwart an influential leader in a particular church and to depict her and her associates as idolatrous, while in the second case he uses the Sun Woman as a composite symbol of the fidelity of God's people who suffer oppression and combat evil.

The essay also explores the way that stereotypes, ancient and modern, intersect with interpretations of feminine agency. It is likely that John used ancient stereotypes about "good" and "bad" women in describing Jezebel and the Sun Woman by playing on tropes about proper and improper feminine behavior in the public sphere in a way that obstructs our vision of feminine agency in Revelation. Today, Jezebel imagery like the one used in Rev 2 lies behind a common stereotype of the hypersexed uncontrollable foreign woman that disparages black, Latina, and Asian Pacific women. Similarly maternal stereotypes of black women, Latinas, and Asian Pacific women—mammies, maids, and dragon moms—also intersect with readings of the Sun Woman in Rev 12, and both of these characters' portraits have the power to shape and constrain ideas about

---

human capacity to exert "some degree of control over the social relations in which one is enmeshed, which in turn implies the ability to transform those social relations to some degree." According to Sewell, "the capacity for agency—for desiring, for forming intentions, and for acting creatively—is inherent in all humans" though people vary by social location with respect to the degree of control they have over social transformation.

3. Here I use quotation marks around *Jezebel* because I am referring to the person in ancient Thyatira who may have been the historical referent for the woman described in Rev 2:20-23. However, I use this convention sparingly in the balance of this essay to avoid the distractions of cumbersome punctuation.

4. In this essay, I differentiate the words *antitype* and *antetype*. I use the word antitype to refer to images that are opposite of each other while also corresponding to each other with respect to the point of the contrast. This is the relationship between Jezebel, John's symbol of the idolatrous church, and the Sun Woman, the symbol of the faithful church. Though the word antitype may sometimes be used to refer to an object that foreshadows another later-occurring and similar object, herein I use the word antetype to describe such relationships. I contend that the two female figures in Revelation anticipate two varying postures later taken by black female Civil Rights activists in the modern period. Thus I am pressing an etymological difference between *anti*types as opposing figures, and *ante*types as those that temporally precede a given figure.

agency for contemporary female readers. My purpose is to discuss images of feminine efficacy in contemporary black life and how the two female characters in John's apocalyptic vision can serve as antetypes for black female activists. In particular, I put these two images of feminine agency in Revelation in conversation with each other and with a contemporary intergenerational conversation among black female activists. In other words, this essay engages in an interwoman(ist) conversation between Jezebel and the Sun Woman that is analogous to the intergenerational conversation that is evoked by the contemporary T-shirt wearing black female activists who critique and honor their mothers all at the same time.

Characterization in the Apocalypse

The characterization in the Apocalypse is an absorbing subject in its own right and the four iconic female characters in Revelation are endlessly fascinating to contemporary readers. Whereas characters in the gospels are developed through dialogue, the characters in the Apocalypse are developed through description. Details about the characters emerge through their actions but especially by means of their appearance and using comparisons and contrasts to other characters in the narrative. For example, in Rev 1:13–16 Jesus first appears as a towering figure robed as a priest and cloaked in the sun, with white woolly hair, fiery blazing eyes, glowing legs like furnace-burnished pillars, and a voice that sounds like the rushing waters of a waterfall. Jesus's next appearance in the narrative is much more complicated, however, as the prophet first describes him as a majestic conquering lion before the vision shifts through the dream logic of apocalyptic into the form of a slaughtered lamb (5:5–6). Thus we may read the Apocalypse as a drama, alert to the fact that major characters often change costumes and that these costume changes reveal new and critical information about the nature of the underlying character.

Many characters in Revelation represent particular individuals or persons; for example, Jesus is clearly a central character, as is the sovereign God enthroned in heaven. Other characters that are depicted as individuals, however, are better understood as composites that represent whole groups of people. One set of characters that fit this description is encountered early in the work, as each of the angels of the seven churches somehow represents the Christians in the corresponding churches. Jesus addresses each one of the angels of the churches in Rev 2–3 via singular pronouns and verbs while also clearly referring to the collective actions of the Christians in the corresponding church with plural nouns and verbs: for example, "I know your works [οἶδά σου τὰ ἔργα] ... you have a few people [ἔχεις ὀλίγα ὀνόματα] in Sardis who have not soiled their garments [ἐμόλυναν τὰ ἱμάτια αὐτῶν]" (3:1, 4 NASB). Even more slippery are the various costumes of the people of God in Revelation. There are a number of characters that represent the church in Revelation: the martyrs under the altar in 6:9–11, the temple in 11:1–2 (cf. 3:12 and altar imagery in 6:9–11 and 16:7), the innumerable multiethnic crowd of 7:9–10, the 144,000 virgin soldiers of 14:1–4 (cf. 7:4–8), the two prophets in 11:3–12, perhaps the twenty-four elders in the throne room (4:6; 5:6),[5] the Bride in 19:7–8, and the holy city New Jerusalem in 21:10–14. All of these characterizations communicate various aspects of John's particular understanding of the people of God.

Another element that is important to John's narrative characterization that is also relevant for our purposes is his use of contrast in character development. In some ways John's use of contrasting characters stands at the heart of the theology of the Apocalypse as the description of the beast from the sea in Rev 13:1–4—the anti-Christ in rhetorical effect if not by explicit mention—contrasts with and opposes Christ's depiction as the resurrected Lamb who receives power and authority from God. Just as John attributes characteristics of God to Christ (see 1:14; cf. Dan 7:9), he uses a similar strategy to describe the relationship between the dragon and the beast from the sea. He assigns to each the same number of heads and horns, thus assigning the symbolism associated with the number of heads and horns with both characters: seven, a number symbolizing divine perfection, and ten, a number attesting to the cosmic extent of oppressive power (cf. 12:3; 13:1; Beale, 1999, 634). While the Lamb is worthy to take the book of judgment from the hand of the one sitting on the throne and to unleash its terrors in chapters 6 and beyond, John narrates a similar relationship between the beast and the dragon, twice mentioning that the

---

5. Beale (1999, 322) helpfully lists some the various ways that the twenty-four elders have been interpreted: (1) astrologically understood stars; (2) angels; (3) Old Testament saints; (4) heavenly representatives of all saints; (5) patriarchs and apostles who represent the whole people of God; (6) the twenty-four books of the Old Testament. In addition, Bauckham (1993) sees these as political figures and Moore (1995) and Aune (1983) see in the twenty-four elders of Revelation an echo of Domitian's innovation of doubling the twelve lictors in the imperial courts of his predecessors (cf. Dio Cassius, *Hist. rom.* 67.4.3).

dragon gives his authority to the beast (13:2, 4) in what amounts to a condensed summary of the more elaborate empowerment scene in 5:6–14. That we may identify this beast as the anti-Christ, however, is also evident from the parallel that John draws between Christ and the beast as we learn that one of the beast's seven heads has received a mortal wound that has been healed (13:3), a data point that does not quite rise to the level of imitating the remarkable depiction of Christ as the Lamb that *still stands* as if it had once been slaughtered (5:6).

Having established how John uses characterization in the Apocalypse, herein I suggest that the Sun Woman of Rev 12 exhibits agency analogous to other depictions of the people of God in Revelation and that as a symbol of faithful obedience, she is the antitype of Jezebel, who represents the unfaithful church. As a symbol of the people of God, the Sun Woman is one of several composite characters in a complex network of personas that appear in multiple other guises in the narrative. For instance, it is the failure to recognize that the Sun Woman and the Bride *both* represent different aspects of the people of God that comes in tension with Tina Pippin's (1992a) insistence that women are excluded from New Jerusalem, which in her view is only populated by the male virgin-warriors of 19:14 (cf. 7:1–8; 14:3–4).[6] The important point here is that John's ecclesiology emerges from both masculine and feminine images of the church, which connects this multifaceted character to God and Christ in an intimate, participatory connection.

A Lady by Any Other Name: Typecasting the Sun Woman

Though many scholars treat the Bride as a symbol of the church in a continuation of the literary habit of identifying Zion with the people of God,

---

6. Pippin 1992a, 195: "The New Jerusalem is a woman, but women are not included in the utopian city. God's future world excludes women but not before marginalizing them first. Of the four females in the text, Jezebel and the Whore are destroyed, the Woman Clothed with the Sun is left in exile, and the Bride is submissive and controlled." For a concurring view see Schaberg, 1992. Though Pippin's analysis of the gender ideology in Revelation is second to none, I still find the preceding quotation to be a puzzling position with respect to the narrative logic of Revelation on its own terms. How can New Jerusalem be absent women when bride imagery is used to name the heavenly advent of the holy city in 21:2, 9–10? When one recognizes that the Sun Woman *is* the bride in a different historical moment, the idea that women are excluded from New Jerusalem is even more difficult to understand.

there is more debate about the Sun Woman's identity.[7] Yet as the woman who gives birth to the Messiah and who is costumed in dream-symbols that evoke the twelve tribes of Israel in Gen 37:5–11, we can see that she also represents a different aspect of the same entity. Though she is one symbol of the people of God in Revelation, we can see that she is also depicted as a female who "acts like a woman" in an ancient setting, by which I mean that she is seen as both passive and maternal (Selvidge 1992). However, if we understand the role of the church in John's vision in its deep connection to the one seated on the throne and to the Lamb, we will be in a better position to understand how the Sun Woman of Rev 12 reveals John's ecclesiology and to see the nature of her agency.

The Sun Woman is dressed in white in a way that connects her to other depictions of the faithful in Revelation. The symbolism of white garments appears first with respect to the faithful saints in Sardis who have not soiled their clothes. In 3:4–5, Christ promises these Sardinians (and all people in the churches who are overcomers) that perseverance will be rewarded with permission to walk with him dressed in white robes "because they are worthy" (ὅτι ἄξιοί εἰσιν; cf. 4:11; 5:9).[8] The innumerable multitude in 7:9–14 who come out of great tribulation also wears white robes that have been washed in the blood of the Lamb (cf. 19:13); and the armies of heaven in 19:14 are similarly clad. In 14:14, the crowned Jesus figure who reaps the harvest of humanity is dressed in a white robe as are the twenty-four elders in 4:4. The white garment symbolism in Rev 6:11 is similar to that in 7:9–14 and is particularly striking. In this verse, the martyrs under the altar are given white robes as they wait for the number of their slaughtered company to be complete. The imagery of white robes surely symbolizes the purity of the wearer, but this association between white robes and suffering (7:9) and martyrdom (6:11) also suggests that

---

7. See, for example, Huber's (2010, 159) association of the Bride with the traditions in Ezek 16, Hos 1–2, and Isa 61:1; Mounce (1977, 236), who sees ideas in Isa 54:11; 2 Esdr 10:7; see also Gal 4:26 as a background, and similarly Blount (2009, 344), who connects the Bride with the theme of Israel as the bride of the Deity in Isa 1:21; 54:1–8; Jer 2:2; Ezek 16:8–14; Hos 2:5; see also Eph 5:32.

8. The promise to overcomers (ὁ νικῶν) in 3:4–5 is one that is addressed to all the churches and not strictly to those in Sardis, given that the exhortations to *each* of the seven of the churches of Asia in chapters 2–3 are intended to be overhead by all (Rev 2:7, 11, 17, 29; 3:6, 13, 22).

they symbolize actions that imitate the Lamb's own sacrificial and praiseworthy actions (5:9; 7:14; 19:13).

Indeed, this idea of the symbolic purity of the white robe coheres with the interpretation of the bright linen wedding garments of the Bride, which is given in chapter 19. Verse 8 tells us that these (white), bright, pure linen clothes are "the righteous deeds of the saints," but the preceding survey suggests that the white clothing symbolism should be understood as the standard costume of the saints in Revelation. In this light it is no wonder that the crowned Sun Woman of 12:1 who represents the people of God and gives birth to the Messiah is also clothed in the sun, that is, clothed in bright, white-hot garments that resemble the Lord in his own regalia (1:16; cf. 10:1; 14:14). This, then, renders the exhortation in 3:18 all the more vivid, as the tepid Laodiceans whose temperature can no longer be differentiated from the ambient environment are urged to purchase white robes to cover their shameful nakedness. The imagery suggests that the problem in Laodicea is that the church is so like its surrounding culture that it has hopelessly compromised its witness and has so few "righteous deeds" for the making of a garment that they are essentially naked. Thus, the Sun Woman is dressed in righteous deeds that echo Jesus's own sacrificial acts, Jesus who is the Faithful Witness from whom all other faithful witness derives (1:5; 3:14). Further, if the two prophets in chapter 11 may be identified as a symbol for the faithful, prophetic church, then the Sun Woman's garb helps us to see her in this same light and not simply as a passive woman who is acted upon rather than being an agent exercising her own agency. In other words, the Sun Woman symbolically *wears* her righteous agency.

The nature of the connection between God, Jesus, and the people of God is further developed in the imagery in chapter 21 where we meet Jerusalem who, in the fluid symbolic universe of the Apocalypse, is both a bride adorned for a husband and a city. Similar to the way that the Sun Woman wears garments that are reminiscent of the Lord Jesus, Jerusalem is depicted in terms that are reminiscent of the description of God. Jerusalem shares the glory of God and the Lamb who light up the city (21:11, 23), and her radiance is described by appealing to some of the same rare jewels that also appear in the description of God in the throne room scene in chapter 4: jasper, carnelian, emerald, and crystal. From this imported throne-imagery in the vision of Jerusalem thus emerges an eschatological portrait of the perfected bride who descends from heaven looking a bit like God. In other words, the appearances of these two women symbolize the agency associated with their faithful witness and participation in the divine activity of God and the Lamb.

Yet when it comes to a contextualized *contemporary* reading of the female symbols in Revelation, none of them fare well in modern scholarship. Adela Yarbro Collins (1976, 57–100) describes the Sun Woman as someone who flees from the dragon and who fails to stand as the ally of the hero or even to participate in the defeat of the foe. For Tina Pippin (1992a, 203) the ideology of gender in the Apocalypse is linked to the passive and controlled agency permitted to women in a patriarchy: giving birth (i.e., 12:2), eating and drinking (i.e., 2:20; 17:4), fornicating (i.e., 2:20; 17:2), or remaining a virgin (i.e., 19:7):

> The mother in Apocalypse 12 is a prime example of women's reproductive power being controlled by men. The war takes precedence, and the child is taken from her.... In the Apocalypse the Monster/Whore is destroyed and replaced with the controlled and controllable image of the Bride. The Bride is passive and receptive to male authority and power. (201–2)

But even as we found above that the Sun Woman *wears* her agency by being dressed in garments that symbolize her sacrificial righteous deeds that imitate the Lamb, there is more to this woman than meets the eye. I suggest that while a judgment regarding the Sun Woman's passivity is a natural and perhaps an inescapable one from the perspective of contemporary thought, it is possible to uncover the woman's agency from within the narrative world of the text. I contend that we may retrieve the Sun Woman's exercise of agency by a focus on three dimensions of the portrait in chapter 12: the ethics of her survival posture (12:6, 14), her capacity for flight (v. 14), and her part in overthrowing evil (10–11).

The first thing that we note is the fact that the woman survives two concentrated attacks by the dragon. In 12:5, the woman's son escapes attack by being taken to heaven, and she herself escapes the dragon's pursuit by fleeing to the wilderness (12:6, cf. vv. 13–14).[9] In addition, the

---

9. I maintain that the woman flees to the wilderness in 12:6 and that this action is recapitulated in 12:13–14. The scene in chapter 12 unfolds in a three panel triptych in which panels 2 and 3 partially recapitulate the action in the first panel while also adding detail to the story. Panel 1 (12:1–6) introduces the main characters: the Sun Woman in labor, her mortally endangered son, and the dragon. Panel 2 (12:7–12) advances the story by giving us more detail about the defeat of the dragon in heaven

woman survives a flood of water aimed at her from the dragon's mouth—perhaps symbolic of being overwhelmed by a flood of chaotic and deceptive speech (12:15-16). Sometimes interpreters describe these incidents as evidence that highlights the passivity of the Sun Woman: instead of taking action on her own behalf, others have to come to her defense when she is under duress. The Sun Woman is a patriarchal vision of femininity. As Paul Duff writes:

> The issue of gender provides an additional contrast between 2:18-29 and chapter 12. In 2:20, as shown earlier, "Jezebel's" deportment is both active and aggressive. Conversely, John depicts the woman of chapter 12 as a passive feminine figure. Whereas "Jezebel" is the subject of virtually all of the active verbs in 2:20, the woman of chapter 12 stands as the subject only of the verbs connected with birthing and flight. It is perhaps fair to say that she does not act in this text but rather is acted upon. She is threatened by the beast and consequently she has to flee "into the wilderness, to a place which had been prepared for her by God" (12:6); the active roles here belong to the beast and the deity. The next part of the scene again emphasizes the passive nature of the woman: in the wilderness, she is fed and protected by God. Later in the text she is pursued, again by the beast, and again she is saved, this time by the earth (12:13-16). (2001, 93-94)

Such interpreters are right that the Sun Woman seems passive in the story and relies on others to rescue her, a posture that anticipates a racialized gender stereotype for white women that I take up in the next section. But I think it is important to set the Sun Woman's behavior in context. In the Apocalypse, God and the Lamb are the only agents that matter; the various characters that symbolize the saints in the work are all either the beneficiaries of God's action, or they are somehow allied with God in performing action through the participation theme discussed above. Further, there is something slightly distasteful in disparaging this woman for needing help in being extricated from dire harm. Persons on the margins who have diminished agency in a system who receive help from powerful others in the community should not be shamed for accepting this help, even if we would agree that the best solutions are those that increase agency for all while simultaneously eliminating danger. It is true that survival cannot

---

and subsequent eviction to earth, and the last section (12:13-17) tells about the continuing conflict between the woman and the dragon on earth.

or should not be the *sole* end for those on the margins, but the agency of unconstrained self-determination as is celebrated in the American myth of rugged individualism may not be the most desirable end either; indeed, it too may be the product of patriarchy.

More important, a part of the reason that the woman survives attack is that in 12:6 she receives nourishment while she is in the wilderness, and the implication is that somehow she is fed in the wilderness by God or perhaps the angels of God (12:7), something that contributes to the helpless, feckless portrait of the woman that we discussed above. How can the fact that she is fed like a helpless child or infant suggest something about her agency? We can move forward by remembering that eating is a moral choice in the Apocalypse, something that is especially highlighted in the letters to the seven churches. In Pergamum, some members of the church are rebuked for eating food sacrificed to idols, and Christ promises that those in this city who resist eating food sacrificed to idols will eat manna instead, God's special food (2:17). The letter also attributes the teaching that promotes eating food sacrificed to idols to the Nicolaitans (2:14–15), which implies that the eating of idol food had been a problem in the church of Ephesus as well since the Nicolaitans are also mentioned in that letter (2:6). Indeed, the letter to Ephesus likewise offers an opportunity to eat God's food instead of idol food, when Christ gives overcomers permission to eat from the tree of life (2:7). Food sacrificed to idols may be the central issue in Thyatira, especially if the fornication mentioned in 2:20 is simply a way of symbolizing the unfaithfulness of eating food sacrificed to idols mentioned in that same verse (πορνεῦσαι καὶ φαγεῖν εἰδωλόθυτα: to fornicate, that is, to eat food sacrificed to idols). In addition, one might also surmise that the relative poverty of Smyrna and wealth of Laodicea is connected to the degree to which the Christians in these communities were integrated into the socioeconomic fabric of the cities, an integration which might well involve participation in the imperial cult or local trade guilds and thus activities that would likewise involve moral choices about eating (Osborne 2002). Given this emphasis on the morality of eating in Revelation, I suggest that when the Sun Woman *chooses* to put herself in the situation where she has to depend on God for food she is, in John's universe at least, demonstrating morally praiseworthy ethical agency.

The Sun Woman's capacity for flight also represents feminine agency. With eagle's wings she flies to the desert in the midst of her conflict with the dragon (v. 14), and I contend that accounts of the woman's diminished or missing agency are overlooking the woman's flight as direct and positive action. Inasmuch as all virtue, agency, purity, or resistance comes from God in the Apocalypse, the wings of the eagle may serve to depict the woman as bearing aspects of the image of God, as in the way that Jerusalem's appearance connotes something similar. If it is true to any extent that the four living creatures personify aspects of God (e.g., Blount 2009, 93), then it may be true that the woman's wings evoke the imagery in Exod 19:4, which say that God bore the Israelites on eagles' wings in their wilderness sojourn and perhaps also the idea that God has the capacity to be anywhere. Against this understanding of the connection and shared agency between the church, Christ, and the one on the throne, we can suggest that the God-given eagles' wings may not be so much about depicting the Sun Woman as flying *from* conflict and attack. Instead, by noting that with wings the woman could have gone anywhere, we can highlight that she flies *into* the desert.

While many associate wilderness imagery with a time of testing and read the Sun Woman's flight there in light of the exodus motif in which Israel was led and fed in their desert wanderings, we should also note that within the narrative horizon of Revelation John has subtly added the idea that the wilderness is also a place of conflict. In 17:3, Babylon is in the wilderness, and inasmuch as she is the only other character that is placed in that setting aside from the Sun Woman, we should perhaps see the Sun Woman's flight to the desert less as an escape and more as entering an arena of engagement with Babylon. Rather than choosing compromise so as to participate safely in the socioeconomic life of the surrounding culture like "Jezebel" advocates, the Sun Woman flees one kind of conflict with the dragon only to engage in another kind of conflict with Babylon.

The most direct example of the Sun Woman's agency, however, appears in the explicit mention of her part in overthrowing evil in 12:10–11. The hymns in Revelation often function to explain the significance of the symbolic action in the surrounding narrative much like the choruses in a Greek play (Osborne 2002, 473). For instance, the hymns in 4:8–11 declare the utter sovereignty of God as depicted in the throne room scene in that chapter, and the hymns in 5:9, 12 likewise unpack the significance of the Lamb's grasp on the scroll of judgment. In keeping with this pattern then, 12:10–12 provides an interpretation of the Sun Woman's story that is told and twice retold in the surrounding narrative. Revelation 12:10 proclaims that God's kingdom has been inaugurated because Satan, the accuser who accuses "our comrades" day and night, has been overthrown, presumably by Michael's angelic host mentioned in 12:7–9. Despite the angels' work of throwing Satan to earth, 12:11 insists that "they" defeat Satan, most likely referring to the saints in 12:10. But it is important to note that in 12:11 the hymn goes on to declare that the defeat of Satan is accomplished by the coincident action of the blood of the Lamb along with the word of their testimony (διὰ τὸν λόγον τῆς μαρτυρίας αὐτῶν); that is, that they did not love their life (οὐκ ἠγάπησαν τὴν ψυχὴν αὐτῶν) even in the face of death.

I maintain that all of this is relevant for understanding the Sun Woman's agency when we note that the comrades have a single testimony and life in 12:11 in a way that is analogous to the single mouth (cf. 11:3, 5; πῦρ ἐκπορεύεται ἐκ τοῦ στόματος αὐτῶν), testimony (11:7; ὅταν τελέσωσιν τὴν μαρτυρίαν αὐτῶν), and body (11:9a; βλέπουσιν ... τὸ πτῶμα αὐτῶν) of the two witnesses in chapter 11. This singularity points to the fact that the two witnesses are a composite character that symbolizes a whole group, and this same literary device applies to the woman of chapter 12 in a way that links her to the other representations of the people of God in the Apocalypse. Thus in context the hymn in 12:10–11 proclaims the Sun Woman's participation in the defeat of Satan as the symbol of the people of God in this part of the narrative. She and her children participate with Christ in overcoming Babylon through their testimony, fearlessly flying into conflict with Babylon even in the face of death, much like the chapter 11 witnesses engage evil earth-dwellers in the great city "called ... Sodom and Egypt." The prophets and the Sun Woman are the same character in different garb, and both are shown in stories that narrate their participation in the overthrow of evil. The Sun Woman's agency especially appears in her moral choice to enter into direct conflict with Babylon, Satan's proxy.

Antitypes and Stereotypes:
Jezebel, the Sun Woman, and Contemporary Women of Color

In this section, I consider the depictions of the Sun Woman and Jezebel with a particular interest in the way that contemporary gendered and racialized stereotypes of women intersect with the interpretation of these characters. I suggest that just as ancient patriarchal stereotypes and tropes about the proper conduct of women may have given rise to details in the characterizations of the women, so too do contemporary gendered and racialized stereotypes intersect with readings of Revelation and the understanding of feminine capacity for action. By engaging two scholars who have explored ancient tropes that may have influenced the construction of the portraits of Jezebel and the Sun Woman, we will be in a better position to see how these ancient tropes reverberate with stereotypes affecting contemporary women of color. Ultimately, this exploration prepares us for the final section where I show how the two depictions of agency resident in the portraits of Jezebel and the Sun Woman function as antetypes for contemporary interpretations of black women's activity in the public square.

Duff's work explores the fear of the uncontrolled and out of control woman in ancient rhetoric. According to Duff, a woman was considered so susceptible to sexual desires and other urges that she was sometimes likened to a wild beast that needed to be tamed and domesticated (2001, 109). Lack of self-control was especially problematic when it came to behavior in the public sphere and women in the public were thought to pose a real threat to the social order, resulting in particularly severe strictures on women's movements outside of the home. She posed a danger to society if she were not controlled by her husband, brother, or father, and social prejudice might label her as a prostitute or sexual predator in ways that are not dissimilar to the rhetoric John uses in describing Babylon. Thus, in view of the lack of clear evidence that sexual sin was actually a problem in John's churches, Duff suggests that the charge of sexual immorality (πορνεία) was elicited by Jezebel's public persona and openness to the larger pagan society (107).

As Duff points out, John does not explicitly call Jezebel "satanic." Nevertheless, he accomplishes something similar by depicting evil Babylon in ways that help readers think about his earlier portrait of the rival leader in Thyatira whom John strategically dubs "Jezebel":

> First, Ahab's wife [Jezebel] was a queen—of the kingdom of Israel in the ninth century BCE; the regal bearing of "Babylon" in chapter 17 would call the Israelite queen to mind. Second, she was associated with sexual promiscuity in the Hebrew Scriptures as well as in the later Jewish tradition, just as "Babylon" is accused of πορνεία in this text. Third, in addition to the πορνεία she was accused of, Queen Jezebel was also guilty of spilling the blood of the prophets of God (see 1 Kings 18:3–4; 13). In this she corresponds to the bloodthirsty whore of Revelation 17 who is drunk on "the blood of the saints and the blood of the witnesses to Jesus." Fourth, the number of allusions to Elijah in other places in the Apocalypse would also point to the figure of Jezebel in this passage, since in the biblical narratives, Elijah was Queen Jezebel's nemesis. Fifth, the fact that the flesh of "Babylon" is devoured in 17:16 calls to mind the fate of the Israelite queen (1 Kings 21:23–24), whose body was eaten by scavengers.... Consequently, it seems fairly obvious that the text invites

the readers to consider "Jezebel" in connection with "Babylon" in the Apocalypse. (2001, 90)

Thus, John attempts to drive a wedge between this female leader of the church who is recognized as a prophet and teacher in the Christian community by using imagery that brands her as a dangerous and out-of-control interloper. She is depicted as an ethnic Other, a loose woman who spews forth deceptive messages that beguile those under her power. Some scholars suggest that Jezebel of Thyatira may not have been advocating a religious practice regarding eating food sacrificed to idols that was broadly considered out of bounds (cf. 1 Cor 8–10). It may be that Jezebel's offense was that she had a difference of opinion with John and was nonetheless able to remain popular in the community (Rev 2:20–23).

Barbara Rossing is the second scholar who investigates ancient stereotypes through her exploration of the two-woman topos that contrasts a good woman with a bad woman as a way of constraining moral choice:

> This topos furnished a framework for exhorting a choice between any two opposing courses of action or allegiances, one of which is personified as seductive and evil and the other which the author wants to recommend as good.... The two feminine figures provide only a dualistic structure of ethical contrast that can be adapted and filled out with a wide range of topics.... Revelation employs the two-woman topos for the purpose of political critique and exhortation ... by filling out the contrasting feminine figures as two powerful empires—God's empire versus Babylon—the author constructs a comprehensive indictment of the Roman empire and an invitation to citizenship in God's alternative realm. (1999, 14–15)

According to Rossing, there are several basic rhetorical elements that make up the topos, which can then be applied in a wide range of social, economic, political, and religious circumstances: (1) the personification of an either/or moral choice as choosing between an evil woman and a good woman; (2) a description of the women's appearance, especially with respect to contrasts in dress and other physical details; (3) a moral disparity between the women; and (4) an ethical exhortation to embrace the one and reject the other (1999, 18). While Rossing explores the two-woman topos with respect to Jerusalem and Babylon as women and cities, I want to suggest another possible use of the two-woman topos that contrasts "evil" Jezebel and the "good" Sun Woman as opposing images that serve to critique and exemplify John's compromised and faithful churches respectively. In addition, I propose that we read Jezebel and the Sun Woman as presenting contrasting images of Christian agency and difference. Jezebel represents a potent independent influence that has been maligned, while the antitypical Sun Woman depicts a participatory agency that has been embraced.

Though above Duff, Rossing, and I make the case that the Sun Woman represents the people of God as a composite character that John uses to highlight particular aspects of this group, Edgar J. Bruns (1964, 460) proposes that she represents both an individual and a composite character. Though certainty is impossible at this distance, it may be that Jezebel similarly represents both an individual and a composite symbol of a group. She may have been a historical female teaching in Thyatira while also representing a theologically compromised church. While the Sun Woman depicts the faithful people of God from the time of the patriarchs through the messianic age contemporary with John, antitypical Jezebel, both as a historic individual and as a composite construction, represents the ideologically compromised people in the church. Both Jezebel and the Sun Woman are depicted as mothers, but Jezebel engages in illicit sexual activity, whether real or metaphorical, while the Sun Woman's labors in childbirth resulting from an approved sexual activity (Duff 2001, 94). While Jezebel's teaching brings potential harm to her children, the Sun Woman removes her children from attack through dependence on God and by taking flight to the desert. Against the backdrop of the two-woman topos, we can see that all of these contrasts serve to exhort John's churches to emulate the one and reject the other.

Notwithstanding the referents beneath these symbols, however, is the troubling nature of the two-woman topos for contemporary readers. According to Pippin's oft-cited work on the topic, John uses two basic feminine archetypes in constructing female images in the Apocalypse—the Heroine and the Whore:

> Reading for gender in the Apocalypse reveals the ideological commitments of the text. The female figures in the text are marginalized, scapegoated, and silenced. The central scene of this erotic fantasy is in the death of the Whore (the evil city) and the transformation of the Bride into the heavenly city. The pure and faithful males are called to come out of the Whore and enter into the Bride. The themes of death and desire are strong in the Apocalypse; although both men and women die, the social construction of the female body is central. This body is both

adored and destroyed. The Apocalypse is a misogynist male fantasy of the end of time. (Pippin 1992a, 193)

Pippin (1992a, 194) says that "in terms of an ideology of gender, women characters in the narrative and women readers are victimized." Similarly, it is common to describe Jezebel and the Sun Woman as a study in contrasts—the former aggressive and guilty of sexual sin and the latter a passive woman without agency who must rely on others to extricate her from her difficulties (Duff 2001, 93). In modern society, the belief that females are weaker and more emotional than males has been one of the most enduring gender stereotypes (Durik et al. 2006, 430–31). The trope of the helpless white women reveals the residue of values from Greco-Roman culture that are still present in modern European American gender typecasts in which pure, child-like, and passive women are protected by men who are strong and competent (431). In contrast to the image of European American women in terms of Victorian and Greco-Roman ideals, Jezebel imagery has become associated with the *femme fatale* in contemporary American culture at best and as a low-down dirty "ho" at worst. Jezebel is seen as a "contradictory, controlling, carnal foreign woman" who is the "foreign influence that is dangerous and brings destruction" (Pippin 1995, 222–23); she is a woman of "masculine temperament" who is able to sway her husband at will (Gehman 1970, 492).

What becomes clear is that the image of Jezebel and the Virgin are archetypes that are played out in various ways about ethnoracial minorities in modern contexts, as many of these same images become ways of excluding and marginalizing women of color in contradistinction from white women. According to Patricia Hill Collins (2004), black women have historically been conceived in terms of two opposing images, that of the Mammy and the Jezebel, both originating from the dysfunction and rationalizations of slavery. The Mammy "house slave" ideal was one in which black women were conceived of as strong, obese, nurturing, ugly, and overwhelmingly loyal to whites. She was Hattie Daniels's beloved (by white audiences) character in *Gone with the Wind*. Collins sees this figure continuing in contemporary black male comics in drag who portray the African American woman as the ugly, masculinized, overbearing mother figure.

The Jezebel, on the other hand, was the antithesis of the paradoxically neutered Earth Mother Mammy.[10] As the other side of the same coin,

---

10. Collins (2004) uses the images of Mule and the Whore in her exploration

she was a hypersexualized, morally loose man-eater who is, to use class-conscious contemporary slang, a ho (Morton 1991).[11] There has been the suggestion that the Jezebel image may have evolved somewhat from the forced oppression of slavery inasmuch as black women were forced to disrobe in auctions and could not help but expose her limbs when forced to do backbreaking labor in the fields (White 1985). Equally, however, the ideology of casting black female slaves as loose women also served as a rationalization for rape by their white male owners, for both economic reasons—such offspring increased the assets of that owner—and out of sexual desire and power. By labeling the black female slave as a Jezebel, the master's sexual abuse was justified by the reasoning that it is impossible to rape an oversexed promiscuous woman (Morton 1991; White 1985; Collins 2004; Schüssler Fiorenza 1991).

These stereotypes also play out regarding other women of color as well. Asian Pacific Americans "in general are often perceived and/or portrayed as quiet, submissive, good at math, hard-working, and nerdy" (Okazaki 1998, 44). As the "lotus blossom," Asian Pacific women are fetishized[12] as "exotic, hyper-erotic ... [and] desirous of sexual domination ... the ideal ... gratifiers of Western neocolonial libidinal formations." As the "antidote to visions of liberated career women who challenge the objectification of women.... Asian Pacific women ... 'discipline' white women, just as Asian Pacific Americans in general are used against their 'nonmodel' counterparts, African Americans." Thus, when seen through the colonial mindset, Asian Pacific American women project "a compliant and cater-

---

of racialized gendered stereotypes rather than those of Mammy and Jezebel. Despite the slightly different imagery, it is easy to see that she is referring to the same social phenomenon that I am.

11. I find it interesting that in discussing racialized and gendered stereotypes with students in my classes, students invariably identify the higher paid "call girl" as a white woman but the "ho" as a black street walker.

12. In Kim (2011; cf. Said, 1979, 92–103), an investigator conducted internet interviews with nine white men who posted ads "seeking an Asian female." One man responded that he was seeking to diversify his experience in dating women from other ethnic groups. Another suggested that a quid pro quo dynamic prevailed: unattractive white males can win with Asian females because such women are seeking white males because they are "superior ... with more money ... and more power." On the other hand, over three quarters of the respondents referenced the (sexual) submissiveness and exotic beauty of Asian women as the source of their desire to date Asian women exclusively, the classic terms of the geisha/Suzie Wong/Madam Butterfly fetish.

ing Asian feminine nature [that] feeds harassers' belief that Asian Pacific American women will be receptive objects of their advances, make good victims, and will not fight back" (Cho 1997, 166). So then, just as African American stereotypes of women involve both asexual and sexually promiscuous modes, so, too, do Asian Pacific American stereotypes. Indeed, stereotypes of Asian Pacific women in popular culture also include a version of the Mammy. In contrast to the passive lotus blossom and the sexually submissive geisha, another prominent stereotype of Asian Pacific women can be found in the image of the "dragon lady," which is popularized recently in the so-called "Tiger mom," a masculinized version of Asian Pacific women that concedes female agency while simultaneously belittling and marginalizing it.

With respect to Latina/Latino stereotypes, gendered stereotypes for this community center around the masculine ideal of *machismo* wherein men are expected to be authoritative, aggressive, and dominant and the feminine ideal of *marianismo* where women are expected to be loving, asexual, passive, emotional, weak and subservient, and thus vulnerable to mistreatment and abuse (Durik et al.; Espin 1986). Similar to the dichotomy of the Mammy and the Jezebel in the African American community and the Lotus Blossom and Geisha stereotypes among Asian Pacific American women, Hispanic stereotypes of women are likewise divided into the "good woman" (*marianismo*) and the rebellious "Hot Tamale" bad woman (Lopez 2015, 102). The *marianista* perspective sees women as hyperfertile mothers, nurturers, care givers, and servants—the apron wearing housemaid—while the "hot Latina" is exotic, sexually available, and more motivated by physical and sexual pleasure than white women" (101–2; Beltran 2002, 82).

It is not too hard to see that black women, Latinas, and Asian Pacific female stereotypes are of a piece. Each group has an aggressive hypersexualized *femme fatale*, the Jezebel who is embodied in the Ho, the Geisha, and the Hot Tamale, and a neutered asexual version embodied in the Mammy, Lotus Blossom, and Maid. Thus society attempts control over all women of color through images of a marginalized and masculinized version centered on out-of-control sexuality and a neutered feminized version that achieves control through the depiction of a lack of agency. But just as the agency of black women and other women of color are constrained by stereotypes that depict them as strong, hypersexualized, and exotic, so too do white women have to contend with living in prisons of passivity, weakness, and confinement to feminized and thus devalued spaces (Morton 1991,

9).[13] Thus "the discourse on Jezebel is guided through the colonial mind. The image of the Other, the foreign, the dangerous and thereby seductive woman is used against medieval women and slave women" no less than on "Southern women who break with tradition" (Pippin 1995, 230). Notwithstanding the fact that society attempts to control all women through the normalization of patriarchal values about proper and improper behavior, we should not lose sight of the fact that not all women suffer equally under these strictures. Even while there are neutered, asexual feminine stereotypes available to women of color in terms of the behavior expected of them which grant a measure of agency, these stereotypes do not generally extend to them the "benefits" of being the objects of protection by society or individual men. The racialization of poverty as represented by the image of the overweight, out-of-control, and ignorant black "Welfare Queen" can also stand as a measure of the way that all poor women are brutalized by stereotypes that undermine broad commitment to antipoverty programs.

"Jezebel" and the Sun Woman as Antetypes for Contemporary Black Women's Agency

Above, I have contended that both Jezebel and the Sun Woman exercise agency. Admittedly, Jezebel's agency is easier to recover given that John's project partially rests on undermining her by portraying her as an out of control woman exercising shameful activity in public. But by connecting the Sun Woman with other portraits of the people of God and closely examining the context of her story we were also able to discern her initiative in engaging Babylon in the wilderness and her participation in overcoming the dragon, who is evil personified. In terms of positive activity, both women exercise intellectual agency, "Jezebel" by teaching, prophesying, and resisting rebuke and the Sun Woman by choosing the desert experience and the conflict associated with it while also trusting that she would be provided for in it. The Sun Woman is thus credited with participating in the overthrow of evil through her trusting witness. On the other hand, both are also victimized by a combination of cultural stereotyping and political critique: Jezebel is shamed in antiquity by practicing the economics of compromise, which makes her indistinguishable from

---

13. Also see Gwin (1985, 46): "Just as black women were forced to be strong, white southern women often were compelled to appear weak."

ANTITYPES, STEREOTYPES, AND ANTETYPES   133

the surrounding culture, and the Sun Woman is shamed in posterity by accounts of her helpless mien. In addition, both women considered here are victimized by violence in the narrative. The Sun Woman is endangered by the dragon himself, the alpha beast at the top of the unholy triad, and the threats against Jezebel *from within the Christian movement* are among the most violent in the whole work and clearly exceed those delivered against Balaam and the Nicolaitans (Marshall 2010, 27).

Likewise the Civil Rights mothers and the #BlackLivesMatter daughters exercise agency in real, though different ways while they are also being marginalized through a combination of cultural stereotyping and political critique. Like the antetypical Sun Woman, the Civil Rights mothers had to be resourceful in using all of the resources in the environment to survive and to participate in their own rescue. These mothers and their families were daily threatened by the violence of a state that had never found its moral and ethical moorings, and they too explicitly placed their faith in God to provide for their needs. But whatever the politics of respectability they may have engaged, we cannot underestimate the sheer courage it took to enter the wilderness of conflict, march into a face-to-face encounter with blatant racism and unreasoning hate backed by empire, and come out overcoming on the other side.

Somewhat like "Jezebel," the #BlackLivesMatter daughters are openly exercising agency in the public square and are on the receiving end of hostility for their troubles. Just as John rebuked "Jezebel" from within the Christian movement for countenancing compromise with trade guilds and the imperial cult, so too are the #BlackLivesMatter daughters being rebuked by their allies on the US political left who scold them for their forceful, public, and disruptive resistance to ongoing violence and injustice. Due to the romanticized patina through which the Civil Rights movement is now imagined, today these young women are coming under attack for using their mothers' same strategy of nonviolent direct action in their protests. Thus, like "Jezebel" was disciplined by John for actions that were sanctioned by Christian leaders in a by-gone era but are deemed inappropriate in a new temporal horizon, so too are the #BlackLivesMatter daughters maligned for using tactics from their antetypical mothers in the sixties that are normally held up as not only legitimate and perfectly acceptable, but even praiseworthy and morally high-minded. Finally, it is important to note that in Revelation "Jezebel" is threatened with violence on a scale that exceeds that which is directed towards other compromisers in the seven churches in a way that seems analogous to the over-militarized state sanctioned violence that the #BlackLivesMatter daughters face today. The women and men in this contemporary movement protest violence against black and brown people who are routinely, cavalierly, and mortally threatened by racist policing practices that are exacerbated by broken accountability structures in which the same prosecutors who are charged with protecting the people's access to justice are complicit in perpetuating a callous indifference to black and brown lives.[14]

In my view, it is the recognition of the logic that underlies deployment of the Jezebel trope that those 1960s-era mothers of the Civil Rights movement resisted when they carefully adopted the politics of respectability. Even as these mothers engaged in nonviolent protest and unruly civil disobedience, they did so while carefully coiffed and groomed in all of the accoutrements available to them in imitation of demure white womanhood. Caught in the double bind of maneuvering between stereotypes of lawless, out-of-control black predators, on the one hand, and a passive acceptance of the indignities of black life in the Jim Crow regime, on the other, these mothers of the Civil Rights movement steered a careful course by managing the images of the movement as they and others deliberately chose Rosa Parks as the right face of the movement.

Younger black women today appear to have less patience with the compromises made by their mothers in an earlier generation as indicated by the way that they are eschewing respectability in public and willingly embracing labels such as "aggressive" and "disruptive" that are intended to silence and suppress actions that are unseemly to the white gaze and that challenge white authority. The T-shirt that so captured my attention—"This Ain't Yo Mama's Civil Rights Movement"—represents an intergenerational conversation about the nature of black female agency, one that reminds me of the tensions between the female images of the church in John's account—one pictured as faithful and the other as compromised.

---

14. The harrowing account of black life in Ferguson, Missouri, as documented in the Department of Justice report on the local police and criminal justice system, is required reading for anyone interested in getting a detailed description of the contemporary face of racism, including routine violations of the First and Fourth Amendments by police. This report can be accessed online ("Investigation of the Ferguson Police Department" 2015).

Conclusion

By comparing and contrasting two portraits of feminine agency in the Apocalypse and in modern black life, I am not setting up a "cat-fight" by construing one model as an ideal and a second as deficient and therefore excluded as a norm. It is true that the inner church conflict in Revelation can be understood in terms of tension between two women, with Jezebel as a representative of the compromised church, on one hand, and the Sun Woman as representative of the faithful, engaged, and trusting church, on the other. But instead I am suggesting that both of the women in Revelation preserve and pass down their mitochondrial DNA—those genetic markers that are transmitted only through the female line—allowing modern readers of Revelation to detect their connections to ancient feminine portraits of agency. If the ideologies of Revelation are deemed oppressively misogynistic, then it can help to read the text through the analogous experiences of contemporary marginalized women of color who *are* agents and who take up the work of saving their sons, daughters, and themselves using the God-given resources available to them through the public demonstration of the power of their intellect, the strength of their resistance, and the moral force of their choices.

Works Cited

Aune, David E. 1983. "The Influence of Roman Imperial Court Ceremonial on the Apocalypse of John." *Papers of the Chicago Society of Biblical Research* 28:5–26.

Bauckham, Richard. 1993. *The Climax of Prophecy*. Edinburgh: T&T Clark.

Beale, G. K. 1999. *The Book of Revelation: A Commentary on the Greek Text*. NIGTC. Grand Rapids: Eerdmans.

Beltran, M. 2002. "The Hollywood Latina Body as Site of Social Struggle: Media Constructions of Stardom and Jennifer Lopez's 'Crossover Butt.'" *Quarterly Review of Film and Video* 19:71–86.

"Black Lives Matter." n.d. *Wikipedia*. http://tinyurl.com/SBL0688j1.

Blount, Brian K. 2009. *Revelation: A Commentary*. NTL. Louisville: Westminster John Knox.

Bruns, J. Edgar. 1964. "The Contrasted Women of Apocalypse 12 and 17." *CBQ* 26:459–463.

Cho, Sumi K. 1997. "Asian Pacific American Women and Racialized Sexual Harassment." Pages 164–73 in *Making More Waves: New Writ-*

ing by Asian American Women. Edited by Elaine H. Kim and Lilia V. Villanueva. Boston: Beacon.

Collins, Patricia Hill. 2004. *Black Sexual Politics: African Americans, Gender, and The New Racism.* New York: Routledge.

Duff, Paul B. 2001. *Who Rides the Beast? Prophetic Rivalry and the Rhetoric of Crisis in the Churches of the Apocalypse.* Oxford: Oxford University Press.

Durik, Amanda M., Janet Shibley Hyde, Amanda C. Marks, Amanda L. Roy, Debra Anaya, and Gretchen Schultz. 2006. "Ethnicity and Gender Stereotypes of Emotion." *Sex Roles* 54:429–45.

Espin, O. M. 1986. "Cultural and Historical Influences on Sexuality in Hispanic/Latin Women." Pages 272–84 in *All American Women: Lines that Divide, Ties That Bind.* Edited by J. Cole. New York: Free Press.

Gehman, Henry Snyder, ed. 1970. *The New Westminster Dictionary of the Bible.* Philadelphia: Westminster.

Gwin, Minrose C. 1985. *Black and White Women of the Old South: The Peculiar Sisterhood in American Literature.* Knoxville: University of Tennessee Press.

Huber, Lynn R. 2010. "Unveiling the Bride: Revelation 19.1–8 and Roman Social Discourse." Pages 159–79 in *A Feminist Companion to the Apocalypse of John.* Edited by Amy-Jill Levine. FCNTECW 13. London: Bloomsbury, 2010.

"Investigation of the Ferguson Police Department." 2015. US Department of Justice Civil Rights Division. http://tinyurl.com/SBL0688k1.

Kim, Bitna. 2011. "Asian Female and Caucasian Male Couples: Exploring the Attraction." *Pastoral Psychology* 60:233–44.

Lopez, Johana P. 2013. "Speaking with Them or Speaking for Them: A Conversation about the Effect of Stereotypes in the Latina/Hispanic Women's Experiences in the United States." *New Horizons in Adult Education and Human Resource Development* 25:99–106.

Marshall, John W. 2010. "Gender and Empire: Sexualized Violence in John's Anti-imperial Apocalypse." Pages 17–32 in *A Feminist Companion to the Apocalypse of John.* Edited by Amy-Jill Levine. FCNTECW 13. London: Bloomsbury Publishing.

Moore, Stephen D. 1995. "The Beatific Vision as a Posing Exhibition: Revelation's Hypermasculine Deity." *JSNT* 60:27–55.

Morton, Patricia. 1991. *Disfigured Images: The Historical Assault on Afro-American Women.* New York: Greenwood.

Mounce, Robert H. 1977. *The Book of Revelation*. NICNT. Grand Rapids: Eerdmans.

Okazaki, Sumie. 1998. "Teaching Gender Issues in Asian American Psychology: A Pedagogical Framework." *Psychology of Women Quarterly* 22:33–52.

Osborne, Grant R. 2002. *Revelation*. BECNT. Grand Rapids: Baker Academic.

Pippin, Tina. 1992a. "Eros and the End: Reading for Gender in the Apocalypse of John." *Semeia* 59:193–210.

———. 1992b. "The Heroine and the Whore: Fantasy and the Female in the Apocalypse of John." *Semeia* 60:67–82.

———. 1995. "Jezebel Re-vamped." *Semeia* 69–70:221–34.

Rossing, Barbara R. 1999. *The Choice between Two Cities: Whore, Bride, and Empire in the Apocalypse*. Harrisburgh, PA: Trinity Press International.

Said, Edward. 1979. *Orientalism*. New York: Vintage.

Schaberg, Jane. 1992. "Response to Tina Pippin, 'Eros and the End.'" *Semeia* 59:219–25.

Schüssler Fiorenza, Elisabeth. 1991. *Revelation: Vision of a Just World*. Minneapolis: Fortress.

Selvidge, Marla J. 1992. "Powerful and Powerless Women in the Apocalypse." *Neot* 26:157–67.

Sewell, William H., Jr. 1992. "A Theory of Structure: Duality, Agency, and Transformation." *American Journal of Sociology* 98:1–29.

White, Deborah Gray. 1985. *Ain't I a Woman? Female Slaves in the Plantation South*. New York: Norton.

"Who We Are." n.d. #BlackLivesMatter. http://tinyurl.com/SBL0688i1.

Yarbro Collins, Adela. 1976. *The Combat Myth in the Book of Revelation*. Missoula, MT: Scholars Press.

One More Time with Assata on My Mind: A Womanist Rereading of the Escape to Egypt (Matt 2:13–23) in Dialogue with an African American Woman Fugitive Narrative

Shively T. J. Smith

> I was thinking of the African American women who, like I, were hungry for stories about women they could identify with. A good writer knows her audience, their interests, their backgrounds, their idioms, their way of viewing reality. And she makes use of this information as she guides them through theological and exegetical terrain. (Weems 1991a, 30)

Introduction

In 1991, Renita J. Weems, the first African American woman to earn a doctorate degree in Old Testament (1989), penned the quotation above in an article called "Do You See What I See?" In this article Weems described in detail and with great candor her rationale for writing the book *Just a Sister Away* (1988). I would come across her article as a young graduate student wrestling with my own voice and place in the field of biblical studies in which African American female bodies (and the bodies of women of color in general, for that matter) remain few even twenty years after Weems earned her doctorate. I read Weems's book *Just a Sister Away*, however, years earlier as a nineteen-year-old undergraduate at Fisk University. In that setting I learned that African American women had something valuable to say about the meaning and influence of biblical canons on our lives and the lives of the diverse others that we love. As a young woman and budding scholar reading and rereading Weems, I grew certain that biblical language and imagery is *my* language and imagery and not just the discipline and language of others that I have to learn in order to earn a terminal degree in religion.

Weems's work fortified my deep-seated belief that African American women readers of the Bible (be they in the academy, the church, corporate, grassroots community organizations, and/or civic clubs) have a responsibility to our communities, ourselves, and our God to articulate the meaning we ascertain from the resonances and clashes between biblical passages and our manifold realities of struggle, survival, sisterhood, community, family, and so forth (Weems 1991b, 64). As I revisit Weems's work now as a scholar of New Testament, I remain compelled by her assertion that "marginalized readers of the Bible in general, and African American women in particular … use whatever means necessary to recover the voice of the oppressed within biblical texts" by relying "upon their own experience of oppression as their guide" (73). In short, womanist biblical interpretation is a wholly and unapologetically *invested* reading of the bible, which dances between the realities of black womanhood and the ancient biblical world (Weems 2014, 45–46).

Whereas Weems often focuses on interpersonal relationships and behaviors, as exemplified in her studies of the correspondences between biblical accounts of the Hagar-Sarah relationship and African and Caucasian American women's social histories, another kind of relationship to which womanist readings can attend is the changing undercurrents between people and land, both ancient and contemporary (Weems 1988, 1991a, 1991b, 2014). As the relationships between ethnic groups and countries shift, particularly in light of imperial and colonial conflict and control, so can political allegiances and sociocultural practice. The annals of African American women's history, specifically female fugitive narratives of people like Assata Shakur, express some of the challenges and promise accompanying such changes.

By listening to Shakur's account of her transition from life in the United States to life in Cuba, issues related to the reasons for political flight, changing territorial relations, and the challenges of cultural adaptation surface, which calls to question the biblical story of the flight of Jesus's family from Judea to Egypt in Matt 2:13–23. The similarities and differences between the two fugitive stories uncover narrative tension and provide impetus for assessing dominant Western biases against or erasure of Egypt as a flourishing province that could provide legitimate sanctuary in antiquity. In light of such study, a rereading of Matthew's account of the sociopolitical flight of Jesus's family can redefine the literary import and function of Egypt in the story's plot and correct misleading information and attitudes about Egypt's prominence in the Greco-Roman world at large. Moreover, using Shakur's story to read Matt 2 afresh expands the breadth of African American women's experiences and history that womanist biblical readings engage in its interpretative work. It is to the task of correction and expansion the essay now turns.

Rehearsing the Story of Assata Shakur's Flight

The dedication page to the autobiography of Assata Shakur (formerly known as JoAnne Deborah Byron and Joanne Chesimard) records, "Assata Shakur is the FBI's most wanted woman. In 1979 she escaped from prison, was granted asylum in Cuba, and has been a fugitive ever since" (Shakur 1987). At its opening, Shakur's book establishes her personal narrative as the story of a political refugee from the United States of America. She is a person forced to leave all that she knows in order to escape an unjust system that has labeled her a threat to its structure. Whereas Matt 2:13–23 recounts an ancient instance of political escape, Shakur lives in the wake of a modern version cast in an African American female body.

Born in New York on July 16, 1947, Shakur grew up living between her mother, grandparents, and aunt. During the 1960s, in her early twenties, Shakur became involved in political activism and protest as a college student. Her first arrest took place in 1967 with one hundred other students from Borough of Manhattan Community College. The students protested curriculum deficiencies in black studies and a lack of black faculty by chaining and locking the entrance to a college building. In 1970, Shakur graduated from the City College of New York and joined the Black Panther Party, Harlem branch. She focused the bulk of her revolutionary efforts on education in African American neighborhoods, coordinating a local school breakfast program (Shakur 1987, 218–19; Gates and Appiah 1999, 1697–98).

Soon after, however, she left the Black Panther Party for the Black Liberation Army. From 1971 to 1973, Shakur was charged and acquitted of bank robbery, murder of a drug dealer, and attempted murder of a police officer. While waiting for her acquittal, on May 2, 1973, she and two other friends were stopped on the New Jersey Turnpike by New Jersey State troopers for an allegedly broken taillight. A gunfight ensued, and Shakur was shot twice. One of her travel companions along with one of the New

Jersey State troopers involved in the altercation were killed. Shakur was indicted for the trooper's murder.

During the trial, Shakur maintained her innocence. Evidence was presented in the form of medical testimony that "her wounds would have kept her from firing a fatal blow" (Gates and Appiah 1999, 1698). Several journalists covered the trial and reported, along with well-known news outlets like *The New York Times*, that the prosecution could not prove Shakur fired the fatal shot (Robinson 2000, 34). Evidence also revealed Shakur received substandard medical care after the shooting. She was subject to long periods of solitary confinement and beaten. In an essay first published in October 1973 while Shakur was imprisoned in New Jersey and awaiting trial, she penned these words:

> Black people must learn how to struggle by struggling. We must learn much by our mistakes. I want to apologize to you, my black brothers and sisters, for being on the New Jersey Turnpike. I should have known better. The Turnpike is a check point where black people are stopped, searched, harassed, and assaulted. (reproduced in Shakur 1987, 52)

With these words, the only crime Shakur takes responsibility for is being careless and caught off guard as a target of hatred. In her autobiography, she describes the details surrounding the shootout and prolonged instances of police brutality and attack that ensued.

> In the background, I could hear what sounded like gunfire. But I was fading and dreaming. Suddenly, the door flew open and I felt myself being dragged out onto the pavement. Pushed and punched, a foot upside my head, a kick in the stomach. Police were everywhere. One had a gun to my head. (Shakur 1987, 3)

When asked directly by an *Emerge Magazine* journalist who shot the state trooper that night on the New Jersey State Turnpike, Shakur responds: "The gun that shot Werner Foerster [the state trooper] was found under the body of Zayd Malik Shakur [one of her traveling companions], in his hand. Blood was on the trigger. So you can draw your own conclusions" (Robinson 2000, 34).

In 1977, Shakur was convicted and sentenced to life in prison for murdering one trooper and assaulting another despite evidence to the contrary. In 1979, she was "liberated" from the Correctional Facility for Women in

Clinton, New Jersey, state prison, after which she went underground and resurfaced in Cuba in 1987 (Robinson 2000, 35).

Many details of Shakur's story remain unresolved. Yet, her personal account of flight captures some of the cognitive dissonance and cultural misinformation that popular Western scripts about modern Cuba and ancient Egypt share. Current interpretations of Matt 2:13–23 often fail to adequately account for Egypt's esteemed political and cultural position in the ancient world and, in turn, diminish its interpretative value in the gospel as an ideal site of refuge. Blinded by ubiquitous and popular misconceptions and uncomplimentary appraisals, contemporary descriptions make it difficult for modern readers of the Bible to identify with Egypt's prestige, role, and self-sufficiency in the gospel. Likewise, popular sociopolitical narratives from American soil about Cuba have historically diminished, or even demonized, the island. The historic "policy of hostility" and American embargo of Cuba since the Cold War has fueled negative popular perceptions that reflect limited understanding of the changing landscape of US-Cuban political relations as well as the richness of Cuban history and culture (Dominguez 2012a; 2012b; Leogrande 2015).

The continuity between contemporary perceptions of Egypt in Matt 2 and Assata Shakur's accounts of her escape to Cuba offer an angle for wrestling with the historic territorial relations and cultural dynamics that lie just below the literary surface of the gospel account. Such correspondence prompts retrieval of Egypt's literary, historical, and theological significance at the time of the Gospel of Matthew's composition in the latter part of the first-century CE. Moreover, it demands a reassessment of the literary function and impact of Egypt in the gospel story. The first step in connecting the Shakur-Matthew accounts of flight is considering the historic identity of Egypt in the ancient world and why such retrieval is necessary for a comprehensive understanding of the biblical story in the first place.

Greco-Roman and Hellenistic Jewish Perceptions of "Egypt"

The story of the flight to Egypt appears only in Matthew. No other gospel reports it or refers to Egypt at all.[1] Yet, the story's significance should not be underestimated. Matthew 2:13–23 begins by recounting the recent

---

1. Among all the New Testament writings, Egypt is mentioned most in the book of Acts. With the exception of the Pentecost story, references to Egypt in the book of Acts occur primarily in the speeches of Stephen and Paul as they rehearse Israel's his-

departure of the magi from the Bethlehem residence of Joseph, Mary, and the child Jesus. It then shifts to describing Joseph's dream in which "the Lord" appears and demands that his young family "flee to Egypt" (*pheuge eis Aigypton*, Matt 2:13) and remain until the imminent threat of Herod's systematic search, seizure, and execution of all children under the age of two ends (Matt 2:16). Upon returning to Judea, they hear news about the ascent of another Roman threat—namely, Herod's son, Archelaus, who now rules in place of his father in Judea, Samaria, and Idumea (4 BCE–6 CE). Consequently, Joseph opts to live elsewhere, settling in Nazareth of Galilee (Matt 2:22–23). After the story, Egypt fades into the background and is never mentioned again in the Gospel of Matthew.

Like the other gospels, Matthew's account of Jesus's life is set in the world of Roman imperial power, which is characterized by its "diverse ethnicities and cultures" (Carter 2006, 3). Leveraging alliances with local kings and elites, Rome "controlled political, economic, and military structures to benefit themselves at the expense of others" (Carter 2003, 1745–46). Moreover, imperial perceptions of territories and regional peoples contributed to the forms of domination and response Roman agents exercised in specific locales.

By the latter part of the first century CE, during the period of the oral Jesus traditions and the growing circulation of early Christian writings, there was a tenor of both infatuation and disdain for Egypt throughout Greco-Roman writings. The Roman fixation on Egypt was due to popular perceptions as well as historic record. In Herodas's *Mimes* (ca. 270 BCE), Egypt is described as a place where a young woman can lose her lover to the entices of the culture because

> Aphrodite's headquarters are down there. In Egypt they have everything that exists or is made anywhere in the wide world: wealth, sports, power, excellent climate, fame, sights, philosophers, gold, young men, a shrine of the sibling gods, an enlightened king, the Museum, wine—in short, every good thing he might desire. And women! More women, by Hades' Persephone, than the sky boasts stars. And looks! Like the goddesses who once incited Paris to judge their beauty. (1.23–26; cited in Brown 2004, 76–77; Lewis 1986, 10)

---

tory and refer to the patriarch Joseph, the prophet Moses, and the Exodus experience (Acts 2:10; 7:9–12, 15, 17–18, 34, 36, 39–40; 13:17).

Popular Greco-Roman literature depicts Egypt as a paradise of luxury, longing, and excess. It has ample provision for all and is wealthy enough to meet the needs and desires of any that traverse its lands. In contrast to Judea in the first century CE, "the revenue of Egypt contributed to the empire an annual amount equal to Caesar's Gallic conquests and more than twelve times the revenue garnered from the province of Judea (see Velleius Paterculus 2.39; Josephus, *B.J.* 2.386–388)" (Brown 2004, 81).

Politically, Roman Egypt was a military force that participated in securing, maintaining, or overthrowing imperial rulership (Mackay 2004, 214–15). Descriptions of Egypt by Strabo, a Greek geographer living at the turn of the first-century CE, attests to Egypt's military might and relative peace under Roman control (Strabo, *Geogr.* 17.1.52–53; 17.2.4–5; 18.1.12–13). In addition to describing Egypt broadly, Strabo itemizes Alexandria's architectural features. He says, "In short, the city of Alexandria abounds with public and sacred buildings. The most beautiful of the former is the Gymnasium, with porticos exceeding a stadium in extent. In the middle of it are the court of justice and groves" (Strabo, *Geogr.* 17.1.10 [Hamilton and Falconer]). Accordingly, Egypt held distinction as the site of formidable military contingencies and stunning visual landscapes, which those outside the province looked to for support and inspiration.

Nonetheless, Roman imperial views of Egypt were not all positive. While the Romans seemed to have a persistent curiosity of Egypt, its control of the province was hard to maintain, and there was much hostility and mistrust shared between Romans and Egyptians (Nimis 2004, 41; Lewis and Reinhold 1990, 97–103). For example, Tacitus, a Roman historian and senator (56–117 CE), reports that Rome viewed Egypt as a wearisome and volatile province.

> Egypt, with the troops to keep it in order, has been managed from the time of the deified Augustus by Roman knights in place of their former kings. It had seemed wise to keep thus under the direct control of the imperial house a province which is difficult of access, productive of great harvests, but given to civil strife and sudden disturbances because of the fanaticism and superstition of its inhabitants, ignorant as they are of laws and unacquainted with civil magistrates. (Tacitus, *Hist.* 1.11 [Moore and Jackson, LCL])

Tacitus's derogatory tenor and attitude reflect Roman biases toward territories with a penchant to challenge its control. Moreover, his comments allude to Egypt's indigenous forms of religion, strong agricultural economy, relatively safe and strategic position, and strained mixed sociocultural tensions. Such a brief sketch of Roman attitudes does not exhaust the diverse and numerous descriptions of Egypt scattered across Greek and Roman literary sources. One scholar epitomizes the source material by saying it "shows that Egypt played an important *cultural* role in Rome. That is, despite their animosity toward contemporary Egyptians, the Romans were obviously fascinated with Egyptian realia and religion" (Nimis 2004, 43).

Like Greco-Roman literary sources, perceptions of Egypt from Hellenistic Jewish literature vacillate between esteem and contempt. Within the narrative tradition of the Torah, the characterization of Egypt shifts from one story to the next, starting with betrayal and imprisonment of the patriarch Joseph (LXX Gen 37–50) through the stories of Moses and the exodus (LXX Exod 1–24). For instance, the patriarch Joseph's arrival in Egypt as an imprisoned slave (LXX Gen 39:1) introduces the changing dynamics between Egypt and Israel. In this story, Pharaoh—the iconic Egyptian—becomes a hero who saves and restores the innocent when he sets Joseph free and appoints him viceroy (LXX Gen 41:39–46). In the exodus story, Egypt's role changes. Egypt and its king are villains, enslaving God's people and issuing unimaginable persecutions and executions (LXX Exod 1:13–16).

Moreover, Judaism has a long-standing connection to the Egyptian environment in the form of an Egyptian Jewry. Its origins date back to the time of Jeremiah (Let. Aris. 35; Rajak 1984, 107–23). Josephus describes Greek-Egyptian rulership, known as the Ptolemaic dynasty, welcoming Jews to the province and entrusting them to safeguard Egyptian fortresses and territories outside Alexandria (Josephus, *Ag. Ap.* 2.44). By the opening of the first-century, Egyptian Jews and the Roman establishment in Egypt shared a working agreement that afforded the Jewish *politeuma* a certain degree of autonomy as well as investment in the maintenance of Roman Egypt's social-cultural life and political system (Philo, *Flaccus* 55, 45, 62).

Philo of Alexandria, a Jewish philosopher and aristocrat, offers one of the clearest glimpses of some of the popular—albeit more unfortunate—cultural perspectives of "Egypt" dominant among Hellenist Jewish literary circles arising from its province in the early first-century CE. In his two historical treatises, *On the Embassy to Gaius* (*Embassy*) and *Against Flaccus* (*Flaccus*), Philo provides the earliest account of overt anti-Semitic attitudes and violence available by recounting the events surrounding the anti-Jewish pogrom in Alexandria, Egypt in 38 CE. He vilifies the indigenous and Greek Egyptian attackers of Alexandrian Jews, saying, "The greater portion of these men were Egyptians, wicked, worthless men, who had imprinted the venom and evil disposition of their native asps and crocodiles on their own souls, and gave a faithful representation of them there" (Philo, *Embassy* 166 [Yonge]; see also *Flaccus* 19). Philo's anger and apprehension was targeted and twofold (*Flaccus* 41). First, Philo was outraged that the historic legal privileges extended to Alexandrians through the ages was revoked. The ruling Greek Egyptian class demoted Alexandrian Jews to the status of strangers and foreigners and illegally dissolved the rights of their *politeuma* (*politeias anairesin*; *Flaccus* 53–54). Philo's second concern is that modifications to Jews' legal status leave them vulnerable to violent attacks, robbery, and dislocation. By expunging their civic rights, their antagonistic neighbors could physically remove Jews from the land without any legal recourse.

In light of the Jewish genocide that took place in Alexandria, Philo's resentment is understandable. Yet, there is also legitimate resentment on the side of indigenous and Greek Egyptians. Egyptian animosity toward Jewish settlements in their midst was rooted in the inequitable, hegemonic caste system installed by the Greeks and expanded by the Romans. The Roman rulers purposely renewed Jewish privileges and legal standing while repeatedly denying indigenous Alexandrians legal standing and visibility in their own land of origin. One scholar summarizes the state of affairs:

> Generally speaking, the situation of the Egyptian diaspora was complex: the substantial Jewish minority ... was cornered between two more or less hostile elements: the indigenous Egyptians and Greeks, masters of the land since the conquest of Alexander.... The majority of Egyptians were relegated to the bottom of the social scale. The Macedonian Greeks occupied the upper echelons. Judeans, Samaritans, or Syrian immigrants, if they were Greek speaking, came to be counted among the Hellenes. (Hadas-Lebel 2003, 40)

Indigenous and Greek Egyptians regarded Jews as transplants who benefitted and flourished in a land that was not their homeland. Consequently, longstanding resentment festered between the rival communities, rendering the area a volatile space in the first century CE.

Moreover, Alexandrian Jewish communities were notorious for welcoming Jewish emigrants from other parts of the world into their midst. Such practices, however, skewed population numbers and patterns and disrupted Roman control in the regions. For example, Emperor Claudius sent an imperial letter to the region decrying the pogrom and conflict between the Egyptian Greeks and Jews that Philo records. In that correspondence, Claudius also commanded, "I explicitly order the Jews not to agitate for more privileges than they formerly possessed … and not to bring in or admit Jews from Syria or those who sail down from Egypt, a proceeding which will compel me to conceive serious suspicions" (Claudius, *Letter about the Jews in Alexandria*, cited in Cherry 1990, 285–88). Jewish customs involving hospitality and kinship, especially in the diaspora, were perceived as an act of insubordination yet it appears diaspora Jews continued to extend hospitality and asylum to their Jewish kinspeople from elsewhere (Smith 2016).

Conceivably, Philo's acerbic rhetoric and pejorative caricatures of indigenous Egyptians contributes to Western interpretations that dismiss, or at least overlook, the gravitas of Jesus's family retreating to Egypt in Matt 2:13–23. Philo's work enjoys a privileged place in New Testament and Second Temple Jewish studies. These writings serve as a primary source for constructing the historic backgrounds and literary forms of the New Testament writings on both the Greco-Roman and Jewish fronts. This means that Philo's pejorative and one-sided description of "Egypt" distorts modern sensitivities and impedes appreciation for Egypt's affluent reputation, stature, and power in the Greco-Roman world. The privileging of Philo's perspective on the subject of Egypt in New Testament studies potentially forecloses on readers' ability to comprehend and envision Egypt and its indigenous people as anything other than negative. Consequently, historic descriptions of Egypt as a rich, robust, and diverse region is necessary for balancing formidable ancient reports from primary sources like Philo as well as dominant Western interpretations and use of Philo's works as source material for situating the writings of the New Testament in its original Greco-Roman context.

Modern Renderings of "Egypt" and Conventional Interpretations of Matt 2

The assessments and caricatures of Egypt from gentile and Jewish Greco-Roman literature help readers enter the story of Matt 2:13–23 with fresh and more historically grounded eyes. The source material indicates a general Greco-Roman fixation and regard for the region, albeit accompanied by great suspicion and caution. Egypt was not a place of the cursed and impoverished, so much as a region outside territories and powers aspired to become or manage. Egypt carried the air of antiquity, majesty, and prosperity and was traditionally regarded as not only the breadbasket of Rome, supplying grain to the capital city, but also as a steady food source for Judea and other territories during periods of scarcity (Gen 41:57–42:2; Josephus, *Ant.* 20.101).

Standard treatments of Matt 2:13–23 in exegetical commentaries rarely account for Egypt's rich ancient history and its esteemed position of popularity and power in the Greco-Roman world by the close of the first century when the gospel was written and circulating. Indeed, the best of them provide *some* background on Egypt as a Roman-controlled province and the existence of flourishing Jewish communities in the area by the time the family's flight to Egypt would have occurred (Witherington 2006, 69; Brown 2007, 89; Feldman 1993, 184–95; Felder 1991, 128, 137). Most assessments, however, focus on the story's parallels to the patriarch Joseph, the infancy account of Moses, and the events surrounding the exodus and Passover. They typically account for the historicity of Herod's slaughter, reporting that there is no historical evidence that such a massacre occurred and that the ahistorical details represent the gospel writer's attempt to resonate with Moses's infancy story (LXX Exod 4:22–23) (Boring 1995, 146; Hagner 1993, 33–34). The story of Herod's attack on innocent children implies that Jesus is like Moses in that he survives a targeted genocide, which locates Jesus squarely in the Jewish lineage and prophetic tradition.

Beyond that, commentary treatments rarely allow the Egypt reference to sway assessments about its chief interpretative value to Matt 2:13–23. For instance, one commentary says, "Egypt is a Gentile country, but the Christian readers would be primarily thinking that in Israel's history it has always been a refuge for persecuted persons. The extreme brevity makes clear what the narrator's interest is … God's guidance alone saves the child" (Luz 2007, 120). Similarly, another commentary reports, "No novelistic or biographical details of the stay in Egypt are given. In Matthew's theological perspective, the sojourn occurred to fulfill Scripture and to provide another parallel to Moses" (Boring, 146). Still, a third commentary describes Egypt's significance in minimalist terms stating, "Egypt is chosen because it is convenient and removed from Herod's power (and perhaps for the exodus typology it makes possible)" (Hagner 1993, 35–36).

Additionally, commentaries on Matt 2:13–23 often lead or conclude by talking about the passage's literary location in the larger Matthean storyline, highlighting its multiple theophany accounts and prophetic echoes as the real theological gems of the story. The Egypt reference becomes a puzzling and incidental reference that is out of step with the storyline and

Jewish prophetic expectations for the arrival and fulfillment of the Davidic messiah figure. One commentary states: "To modern Christians the application of Hos. 11:1 to Jesus' sojourn in Egypt (v. 15) seems very forced. Surely, it must have been as clear to Matthew as to us that Hosea was here speaking of Israel's exodus from Egypt" (Hare 2009, 15; Harrington 1991, 44). In such readings, Egypt is reduced to a minor detail that is quickly forgotten in the larger literary and theological landscape of the gospel.

Well-known Western artistic renderings of Matt 2:13–23 provide another lens for exploring how Egypt is misunderstood and misrepresented. For instance, Gustave Doré (1832–1883), a French artist and printmaker, depicts Matt 2:13–15 in a black-and-white rendering called, "Joseph and Mary Flee with Jesus to Egypt" (see Lang 2006). The scene depicts Joseph, Mary, and the toddler Jesus leaving Bethlehem. Joseph walks, leading a donkey on its right side while he looks back over his own shoulder with a concerned scowl. Palm trees are the only visible landmarks that a populated Bethlehem is now at a distance. In contrast, Mary and Jesus ride the donkey, and Mary cuddles Jesus on her right side. She faces forward, sporting a worried expression, as she looks slightly heavenward. The land around them is depicted as a barren wasteland with cracked, parched earth underfoot and rolling hills. Behind them lay hints of civilization, foliage, and water and, in turn, resources. Conversely, as they face forward headed toward Egypt, the only guarantee that they will be provided for appears to be the halos above their heads, signaling God is with them. Egypt is portrayed as a primitive region of desolation, isolation, and limited resources.

Likewise, Adam Elsheimer (1578–1610), a German artist who resided in Rome, painted a dark shadowy rendition called "The Flight into Egypt (Matt 2:13–15)" (see Lang 2006). The young family is depicted as huddled in shadows against a forestry cave. A night sky hangs above them filled with stars and a full moon. On the right side of the picture, placed behind the family is a body of water and light. To the left of the picture, in front of the trio, appears an open campfire with two huddled figures and farm animals mulling around. In this painting, Egypt is characterized as dark and wooded. The painting emanates a menacing apprehension.

Unfortunately, such artwork does a better job of reflecting the Western world's appalling legacy of dehistoricizing Egypt rather than accounting for its ancient achievements and advancements (Hegel et al. 1975, 173–74; Howard 1996, 51–53; Thomas 2000, 135; Noel 2009, 61–69). The ancient perceptions and the social-historical standing of Egypt are lost in such classical visual representations of Matt 2:13–23. Observers of such artistic interpretations never realize how important Egypt was to Rome, with its rich cultural heritage and resources and the benefits of its location and its diverse populations. Egypt was the gateway to trade with the East, characterized by its bustling and tolerant multicultural interactions and its status as a major academic center for research and education. It *rivaled Rome* in all aspects (McKenzie 2007, 148–49).

As such, when one reads popular interpretations of Matt 2:13–23 or views classical western visual renderings of it, one becomes less suspicious of the biblical passage and more leery of its interpreters. The ease at which Egypt can be dismissed and labeled as a secondary detail signals there may, indeed, be more to the story than initially considered. Womanist approaches to the Bible, in turn, force contemporary readers of the gospel to grapple with our own misconstructions, misinformation, and biases that are not born in the Jewish and Christian Scriptures but derive from historic Western scripts and valuation (Sadler 2007, 23–30; Evans 2008, 12–19, 38–57).

The challenge, then, for modern readers of Matt 2 is liberating Egypt from an extended interpretative history of oversight and marginality. What is the best approach to reacquainting ourselves to the ancient appreciation of Egypt and reading the passage from that sentiment so that it transforms traditional interpretations? Beyond just rehearsing the historical data (as done above), approaching the passage from a similar modern context supplies a lens through which Egypt is seen as more than simply a foil setting in service to a larger plotline and the gospel's so-called "actual" context. By turning to womanist hermeneutics, which begins with the stories of African American women, modern readers are provided a template for moving from contemporary to ancient contexts in order to appreciate the relational dynamics active in both.

Rereading Matt 2:13–23 in Light of Assata Shakur's Story

Approaching the gospel account of the flight to Egypt with Shakur's story in mind reconfigures its characters, settings, and concerns. Those literary details that mainline interpretations of Matt 2 vilify, or at least ignore, become laudable. Moreover, Shakur's personal account expresses the challenges of political and geographical flight and the cultural adjustments that accompany such extreme measures for securing survival and freedom. Thus, Shakur's transition from the United States to Cuba acts as a window into the exigencies of flight for Jesus's family from Judea to Egypt in the Gospel of Matthew. The correlation between Shakur's Cuba and Matthew's Egypt suggest that the references to "Egypt" in Matt 2:13–23 carry more cultural weight and historical significance than typically acknowledged.

Matthew 2:13–23 juxtaposes two relationships, Jesus to Herod and Judea to Egypt, which are not contrasted so acutely in the other gospels. The Jesus-Herod relationship in Matt 2 conveys the power differentials between local Roman power holders and residents. Yet, rather than portraying local residents at a deficit, the gospel deploys theological discourse and prophetic speech to subvert social-political hierarchies and reverse the flow of power, autonomy, and control. Brandishing a series of prophetic fulfillment formulas from passages like LXX Isa 7:14 and LXX Hos 11:1, Matthew describes the child Jesus as the messianic agent and Son of God destined to "save his people" and one with whom God is present (Matt 1:18, 22–23; 2:15). Consequently, the gospel depicts dominated people in the story as the ones with access to genuine power. While they may not escape Herod's genocidal tactics, they represent the population upon whose behalf God acts with the birth of Jesus as the liberating Christ-figure anticipated by Israelite prophets from the past.

Herod, in contrast, is described as an agent of Rome. The ironic title, "King Herod," in Matt 2:1 signals his client-king status as ruler of Palestine and defender of the Roman system in that region. Shakur's narrative offers insight into the tendency of hegemonic and imperial regimes to protect itself at all cost, which can inform understandings about Herod's actions in the story. Shakur states:

> We [members of the Black Liberation Army] were the number one target of COINTELPRO, the counter-intelligence program that was set up by J. Edgar Hoover and the FBI to "neutralize" political activists. Hoover deemed the Black Panther Party to be the most dangerous organization to the security of the United States. What they did was not only try to kill—actually out and out kill—people like Fred Hampton and Mark Clarke, they set people up on false charges.... They did everything to try and criminalize our movement, and try to destroy our movement. (Robinson 2000, 32)

Shakur's political activism drew the negative attention of political authorities. According to her accounts, she fled America for Cuba to escape legislated discriminatory practices and the unsubstantiated pretenses leading to her imprisonment (Robinson 2000, 34; Shakur 1987, xv–xi, 70, 171–72).

Her characterization of American law enforcement tactics unveils Herod's maneuvering. Whereas Jesus is depicted as an innocent child destined to save other innocent people (Matt 20:28), Herod the Great is depicted as a premeditated mass murderer (Matt 2:7–8, 16), compelled by fear (Matt 2:3), rage (Matt 2:16), and the pressing need to protect the Roman structure. Jesus's birth signaled a threat to Herod's (and in turn Rome's) control rousing Herod to legislate pernicious and systematic deterrents locally.

The second juxtaposition the story establishes is the contrast between dangerous Judea and safe Egypt. As the account unfolds, Herod embodies Roman political intrigue and deception as he extorts information from his Eastern visitors about their journey's purpose and expresses interest in paying homage to the child who fulfills prophetic expectation (Matt 2:6). By Joseph's second dream account (Matt 2:13; cf. 1:20), the gospel renders Judea unsafe for the young, innocent family. The divine imperative to "flee to Egypt" pits Egypt against Judea and establishes geographic boundaries of security, safety, and fairness.

The characterization of Judea as less safe than Egypt in Matthew's account is curious given that Josephus, a first-century Roman-Jewish historian, records Herod traveling freely to Egypt at will. According to Josephus, Herod met Augustus Caesar in Egypt soon after Rome's victory over Mark Antony and Cleopatra. While there, Herod was introduced to Caesar as a "friend" of the empire and was bestowed favor in the form of human captives (namely four hundred of Cleopatra's former Galatian guard) and given more land to govern as a Roman client-king. Having solidified his political friendship, Herod returned to Judea (Josephus, *Ant.* 15.215–218). According to the historical record, Egypt was a province that Herod traversed under the auspices of political friendship to the emperor and representative of Rome, but Matthew portrays Egypt as "safe" from Herod's reach and insists Egypt is the site of political sanctuary for messianic refugees.

Within the LXX, Egypt is frequently depicted as a place of escape and refuge for the political fugitive in need of asylum. For instance, in LXX Jer 33:21–23, a lesser known prophet, Uriah, preaching a similar message of destruction and repentance as the prophets Jeremiah and Micah, fled to Egypt (literally, "enter into Egypt," *isēlthen eis Aigypton*," in LXX Jer 33:21). While Egypt may have provided temporary shelter, Uriah was captured by King Jehoiakim's bounty hunter, Elnathan, and then returned, slaughtered, and buried (LXX Jer 33:22–23). In this case, Egypt is characterized as a compromised refuge that Judah's kings traverse and plunder at will.

In contrast, 1 Kgs 11 depicts Egypt as a secure region that not only extends sanctuary to innocent fugitives but also resources and opportunities. Such hospitality hints at ancient forms of upward mobility. A passage in LXX 1 Kgs 11:17 recounts the childhood escape of Hadad, royal son of the Edomites, who David massacred in large numbers (LXX 2 Sam 8:12–14). Like LXX Jer 33, this passage states that Hadad "entered into Egypt." Unlike the prophet Uriah's plight, Hadad found secure asylum in Egypt as well as resources. The Pharaoh, while supposedly an ally of David's son, Solomon, provided sanctuary to the fugitive Hadad and his companions in spite of his political friendship (LXX 1 Kgs 3:1–2). Pharaoh also extended a generous amount of hospitality providing "a house and arranging bread" for Hadad's group (LXX 1 Kgs 11:18). In fact, Hadad's favor increased, and he was eventually added to the royal Egyptian household through marriage to Pharaoh's sister-in-law (LXX 1 Kgs 11:19). His subsequent son, Ganebath, was reared and educated in the Egyptian royal house as one among the sons of Pharaoh (LXX Kgs 11:20; see Luz 120, n. 22; Witherington 2006, 69).[2]

Another issue Shakur's story raises that casts Matthew's story in a different light is the culture shock accompanying radical and risky relocation. When asked about life in Cuba, Shakur said:

> It's been good. It was hard at the beginning because I had to adjust to another culture and learn another language. I had to adjust to living in a Third World country, which means that things people in the U.S. take for granted like hot running water whenever you turn on the tap are not always available here. But it's been a growing and happy experience for me in many ways. Another thing I've been able to do in Cuba is rest. You live such an intense life in the States. And my life has been more intense than most (laughs). Being in Cuba has allowed me to live in a society that is not at war with itself. There is a sense of community. It's a given in Cuba that, if you fall down, the person next to you is going to help you get up. (White 1997)

---

2. Even, Jeroboam, finds extended sanctuary Egypt once his relationship with Solomon deteriorates to the point his life is threatened (LXX 1 Kgs 11:26–27, 40). Other examples of Egypt serving as a sanctuary for Israel include: "the people" (LXX Jer 48:17; 50:4–7); Onias IV (Josephus, *Ant.* 12.387–388); Jews in the time of Hyrcanus I (Josephus, *Ant.* 14.21); Alexandria in the time of Herod (Josephus, *Ant.* 15.42–49; *B.J.* 7.410).

While the physical distance between Cuba and Florida is only approximately ninety miles, Shakur's description of their economic and social differences puts them worlds apart. Her contrast between the First World status of the United States and the Third World status of Cuba distinguishes their economic and political stability and agendas. Shakur's reflection is particularly striking in light of the aggressive US economic embargo of Cuba first imposed in the 1960s and extended several times since then, which isolated the Cuban government economically and deprived it of US dollars (US Department of the Treasury 2001, 2016). In addition to broadening the economic chasm between the United States and Cuba, the embargo stifled positive and ongoing cultural and social exchange, magnifying the differences between the two countries' particular ways of life, especially from the American perspective.

Yet, Shakur's reflection on these differences is in stark contrast to conventional, post–Cold War American perceptions. She diminishes the significance of Cuba's lower economic ranking (or GDP) compared to the United States and favors, instead, the Cuban lifestyle and attitude—with its communal sensibilities and compassionate neighborly relations—as the luxury item the island provides. Practically speaking, the consequence of such differences is that the rhythm of Shakur's daily life changed. She not only had to acclimate herself to new surroundings, but she had to calibrate her expectations regarding the conveniences and *ethos* of her new residence. She traded US conveniences like reliable, hot, running water for a society that acknowledged and embraced her humanity without antagonism and protest.

Although Matthew does not provide any information about Jesus's childhood stint in Alexandria, the literary and historical data rehearsed above provides a window into some of the similarities and differences one could anticipate (Luz 2007, 20, 120 n. 21; Witherington 2006, 69).[3] Unlike Shakur's situation, Judea and Egypt are not that politically and culturally different, particularly among its Jewish communities. By the first century CE, Jewish communities in both regions were mainstays of the Roman Empire, having been consolidated under Octavian Augustus's rule by 27

---

3. There are traditions about Jesus and his family living in Egypt that include claims he learned magic or worked as a day laborer while there. The bulk of these reports come from Jewish rabbinic literature, which is secondary and tertiary sources to the New Testament. They typically do not carry the same historic value or character as the works of Philo and Josephus (b. Sanh. 107b; b. Šabb. 104b, Origen, *Cels.* 1.28.38).

BCE (Nickle 2001, 47–53). Both held longstanding histories in their areas and the two communities shared strong kinship and resource ties. Under the Ptolemaic dynasty's 125-year control of Judea, Egypt was perceived as an attractive alternative to Judea because of the rulers' willingness to provide work and extend citizenship privileges (Josephus, *Ant.* 12.3–10). Indeed, by the mid-first century CE, the second largest military, political, economic, and cultural city of the Roman Empire would be Alexandria, which also housed the largest and wealthiest Jewish population in the Diaspora (Feldman and Reinhold 1996, 61).

Whereas Shakur underwent a steep cultural metamorphosis and immersion, the gospel's original audience would not have expected Jesus's family to face the same challenge. A trip from Judea to Egypt meant a journey from one Jewish community to another who shared the same ethnoreligious identity (Brown 2004, xii). In fact, the agricultural village of Nazareth, the site to which the family resettled upon returning from Egypt (Matt 2:22–23), was located not far from the Via Maris, the major trade route from Palestine to Egypt, bespeaking the historic mutual exchange of goods, resources, and people prevailing between the two regions (Harrington 1991, 45).

Reconsidering Weems's Approach in Light of the Shakur-Matthew Analogy

Sensitized by Shakur's experiences of systematic and targeted attack, one perceives Judea in Matt 2 as the site of such inhumanity and savagery that even the most innocent populations—namely, toddlers and babies—suffer in its land. In contrast, Egypt becomes the place of benevolence, hospitality, and safety. It is the place of the civilized and the communal. Egypt and Egyptians in Matthew are not the enemy, but the heroic protectors of the innocent. In fact, it is not Egypt's moral compass and leadership that the gospel calls into question, but the powerbrokers and institutions of Judea that force vulnerable bodies to flee with little resources and solace in the first place. By reckoning with Egypt as a real place in the ancient world that has a far-reaching history and strong influence across the ancient Mediterranean Sea, the landscape of the New Testament becomes larger. Consequently, the world of Jesus Christ is portrayed as transnational and transcultural in which the presence of God is portable, accompanying and guiding Jesus's family as they journey (Matt 1:23; 18:20; 28:20).

Given this brief rereading of the flight to Egypt story in Matt 2 in light of Assata Shakur's story of flight to Cuba, three summative remarks about the implications of Weems's womanist approach to reading biblical texts in dialogue with black women's stories is necessary. First, the starting point of womanist interpretation, as conceived by Weems, is the history and experiences of African American women. To embark on its "theological and exegetical terrain" requires seeing African American women's history as an interpretative lens through which the biblical text can make sense. Womanist readings, therefore, draw meaning from the Bible by acknowledging black women's diverse realities. It is also suspicious of conventional biblical interpretations spawned to buttress systemic hierarchies and power differentials, which regularly consign women of color to lower tiers of authority and/or limit their numbers and voices (Day 2012; Douglas 2015; Lightsey 2015; Harris-Perry 2011; Alexander 2012; Riggs 2003).

Womanist interpretation recognizes that biblical writings are products of the winners and have been used as instruments of dominance by enfranchised masses. The Bible, therefore, "cannot be understood as some universal, transcendent, timeless force to which world readers—in the name of being pious and faithful followers—must meekly submit. It must be understood as a politically and socially drenched text invested in ordering relations between people, legitimating some viewpoints, and delegitimizing other viewpoints" (Weems 2014, 47). Consequently, Shakur's story of politically and socially conditioned events, offers a window into seeing how those dynamics were at work in Matt 2.

Secondly, it is important to state that womanist interpretation is not exclusively Christian. Authentic womanist readings interrogate biblical passages in light of the diverse experiences of African American women—whether Christian or non-Christian, youth or elder, straight or lesbian, single or married, wealthy or impoverished, educated or uneducated, free or incarcerated, mother or daughter, childless or motherless. In fact, it may be the minor or foil characters in these biblical narratives—namely, those who are silent or silenced, dismissed or overlooked, underestimated or demeaned, powerless or subordinate—that are comprehended best through the lens of African American women's historic predicaments and successes. Thus, much of the work of womanist interpretation is pluralistic in nature. It is at its best when its theological and exegetical discourses are enriched by the inner social, cultural, and religious diversity of African American women. Weems (2014, 45), however, never apologizes for her interpretative work rising from the lives and concerns of the African American Christian women from whom and to whom she hails. Her position on this matter represents the degree of freedom womanist approaches extend to all. All are able to claim the locations from which and to which they speak.

So, can there be such a thing as womanist biblical interpretation in service to black Muslim women, black Jewish women, black humanist women, black Buddhist women, and so forth? Absolutely. Indeed, in this global twenty-first century, emerging generations of womanist biblical scholars need to be absolutely committed to generating and expanding interpretative discourses and foci so that it reflects the entirety of black women's existence, perspectives, and locations past, present, and future. Though the initial epicenter of womanist approaches to the Bible is African American womanhood, womanist readings should address how it connects to the stories and histories of other female and marginal locations across the world, such as the Indian Dalits, Syrian refugees, victims of the Nigerian schoolgirl abductions, terrorized and targeted Muslim Americans, or immigrant and migrant workers who avoid using community health clinics when ill for fear of discovery and deportation (just to name a few).

The task before the next generations of African American women biblical scholars is building on the work of trailblazers like Weems and Clarice Martin (the first African American woman to earn a doctorate in New Testament in 1985) by appropriating their approaches as tools for addressing compounded forms of oppression (Martin 1991, 206–31; 1998, 203–33; 2015, 19–41). These oppressions affect not only African American women but bodies and communities elsewhere. As Shakur (1987, 267) says, "Any community seriously concerned with its own freedom has to be concerned about other peoples' freedom as well." The task requires expanding and diversifying our repertoire of multicultural sources, concerns, and conversation partners and wielding biblical discourse to speak about trends in global and local disparities, oppressions, calamities, and triumphs. In short, an aim of womanist biblical interpretation is to inspire and foster a chorus of interpretative voices and perspectives, not to limit it to a single voice.

Third, in womanist readings, the Bible is deliberately approached as *a* source of language, imagery, knowledge, and critique engaging black women's experience, rather than serving as *the only* credible material available for meaning making and reflection. Other texts, such as African American women's literature, music, art, biography, activism, and intellectual artifacts are useful—I dare say, even necessary—sources informing authentic womanist biblical interpretation. While exegetical methods undergird readings dedicated to the historical, literary, and textual dimensions of ancient writings, the primary interpretative work of womanist analyses of the Bible is hermeneutical. Ultimately, womanist interpretation embraces the task of naming the text's life-affirming qualities while limiting or even outright rejecting biblical portrayals and imperatives that diminish or dismiss the realities of black womanhood.

Room exists for further consideration of the parallels and distinctions between Matt 2 and Shakur's story, such as the role of language, fostering new kinship bonds elsewhere while maintaining old bonds, managing divided territorial allegiances, and even probing US-Cuba relations as it continues to unfold. To be sure, using Shakur's story as a lens for reading Matt 2:13–23 elevates Egypt's status and function, putting it on par with the ancient region of Judea as well as the capital city of the empire, Rome. The reverse is also true. Using Matthew's story of the flight to Egypt as a lens for recalling Shakur's story counterbalances US perceptions of Cuba as a place of repression. In Shakur's story, America, not Cuba, fits the typology of Judea in Matt 2, with its repressive and hostile measures for ensuring compliance to the status quo while Cuba is characterized as the site of respite and liberation, comparable to Egypt's function in the gospel story. This brief investigation, hopefully, provides a framework for future study and consideration of the parallels between Shakur's story and Matt 2:13–23 as well as an approach to handling other such complementary and disruptive relationships not yet imagined but necessary to the task of womanist hermeneutics.

Works Cited

Alexander, Michelle. 2012. *The New Jim Crow: Mass Incarceration in the Age of Colorblindness*. Rev. Ed. New York: New Press.

Boring, M. Eugene. 1995. "The Gospel of Matthew: Introduction, Commentary, and Reflections." *NIB* 8:89–505.

Brown, Michael Joseph. 2004. *The Lord's Prayer through North American Eyes: A Window into Early Christianity*. New York: Bloomsbury T&T Clark.

———. 2007. "Matthew." Pages 85–120 in *True to Our Native Land: An African American New Testament Commentary*. Edited by Brian K. Blount, Cain Hope Felder, Clarice Jannette Martin, and Emerson B. Powery. Minneapolis: Fortress.

Carter, Warren. 2003. "The Gospel according to Matthew." Pages 1745–47 in *The New Interpreter's Study Bible: New Revised Standard Version with the Apocrypha*. Edited by Walter J. Harrelson. Nashville: Abingdon.

———. 2006. *The Roman Empire and the New Testament: An Essential Guide*. Nashville: Abingdon.

Cherry, David. 2001. *The Roman World: A Sourcebook; Roman World*. Malden, MA: Blackwell.

Day, Keri. 2012. *Unfinished Business: Black Women, the Black Church, and the Struggle to Thrive in America*. Maryknoll, NY: Orbis Books.

Dominguez, Jorge I. 2012a. "Introduction: On the Brink of Change; Cuba's Economy and Society at the Start of the 2010s." Pages 1–18 in *Cuban Economic and Social Development: Policy Reforms and Challenges in the Twenty-First Century*. Edited by Jorge I. Dominiguez. Cambridge: Harvard University Press.

———. 2012b. "Reshaping the Relations between the United States and Cuba." Pages 32–51 in *Debating U.S.-Cuban Relations: Shall We Play Ball?* Edited by Jorge I. Dominguez, Rafael Hernández, and Lorena Barberia. New York: Routledge.

Douglas, Kelly Brown. 2015. *Stand Your Ground: Black Bodies and the Justice of God*. Maryknoll, NY: Orbis Books.

Evans, Curtis J. 2008. *The Burden of Black Religion*. Oxford: Oxford University Press.

Felder, Cain Hope. 1991. "Race, Racism, and the Biblical Narratives." Pages 127–45 in *Stony the Road We Trod: African American Biblical Interpretation*. Edited by Cain Hope Felder. Minneapolis: Fortress.

Feldman, Louis H. 1993. *Jew and Gentile in the Ancient World: Attitudes and Interactions from Alexander to Justinian*. Princeton: Princeton University Press.

Feldman, Louis H., and Meyer Reinhold. 1996. *Jewish Life and Thought among Greeks and Romans: Primary Readings*. Minneapolis: Augsburg.

Gates, Henry Louis, and Anthony Appiah, eds. 1999. "Shakur, Assata." Pages 1697–98 in *Africana: The Encyclopedia of the African and African American Experience*. New York: Basic Books.

Hadas-Lebel, Mireille. 2003. *Philo of Alexandria: A Thinker in the Jewish Diaspora*. Translated by Robyn Frechet. Leiden: Brill.

Hagner, Donald A. 1993. *Matthew 1–13*. WBC 33A. Dallas: Word.

Hare, Douglas R. A. 2009. *Matthew: Interpretation*. Louisville: Westminster John Knox.
Harrington, Daniel J. 1991. *The Gospel of Matthew*. SP 1. Collegeville, MI: Liturgical.
Harris-Perry, Melissa V. 2011. *Sister Citizens: Shame, Stereotypes, and Black Women in America*. New Haven: Yale University Press.
Hegel, Georg Wilhelm Friedrich, Robert F. Brown, and Peter Crafts Hodgson. 1975. *Lectures on the Philosophy of World History*. Cambridge Studies in the History and Theory of Politics. Cambridge: Cambridge University Press.
Howard, Don. 1996. "The History That We Are: Philosophy as Discipline and the Multiculturalism Debate." Pages 43–76 in *Cross-Cultural Conversation: Initiation*. Edited by Anindita Niyogi Balslev. AARCCS 5. Atlanta: Scholars.
Lang, David. 2006. *The Accordance Gallery of Bible Art*. Accordance electronic ed. Altamonte Springs: OakTree Software.
Leogrande, William M. 2015. "Normalizing US-Cuba Relations: Escaping the Shackles of the Past." *International Affairs* 91:473–88.
Lewis, Naphtali. 1986. *Greeks in Ptolemaic Egypt: Case Studies in the Social History of the Hellenistic World*. New York: Oxford University Press.
Lewis, Shelton Naphtali, and Meyer Reinhold, eds. 1990. *Roman Civilization: Selected Readings*. Vol. 1, *The Republic and the August Age*. New York: Columbia University Press.
Lightsey, Pamela R. 2015. *Our Lives Matter: A Womanist Queer Theology*. Eugene, OR: Pickwick.
Luz, Ulrich. 2007. *Matthew 1–7*. Hermeneia. Translated by James E. Crouch. Minneapolis: Fortress.
Mackay, Christopher S. 2004. *Ancient Rome: A Military and Political History*. Cambridge: Cambridge University Press.
Martin, Clarice. 1991. "The Haustfeln (Household Codes) in African American Biblical Interpretation: 'Free Slaves' and 'Subordinate Women.'" Pages 206–31 in *Stony the Road We Trod: African American Biblical Interpretation*. Edited by Cain Hope Felder. Minneapolis: Fortress.
———. 1998. "'Somebody Done Hoodoo'd the Hoodoo Man': Language, Power, Resistance, and the Effective History of Pauline Texts in American Slavery." *Semeia* 83–84:203–33.
———. 2015. "Womanist Interpretations of the New Testament: The Quest for Holistic and Inclusive Translation and Interpretation." Pages 19–41

in *I Found God in Me: A Womanist Biblical Hermeneutics Reader*. Edited by Mitzi J. Smith. Eugene, OR: Cascade.

McKenzie, Judith. 2007. *The Architecture of Alexandria and Egypt, C. 300 B. C. to A. D. 700*. Pelican History of Art 63. New Haven: Yale University Press.

Nickle, Keith F. 2001. *The Synoptic Gospels: An Introduction, Revised and Expanded*. Louisville: Westminster John Knox.

Nimis, Stephen. 2004. "Egypt in Greco-Roman History and Fiction." *Alif: Journal of Comparative Poetics* 24:34–67.

Noel, James Anthony. 2009. *Black Religion and the Imagination of Matter in the Atlantic World*. New York: Palgrave MacMillan.

Philo. 1962. *Legatio ad Gaium or Embassy to Gaius*. Translated by F. H. Colson. LCL. Cambridge: Harvard University Press.

Rajak, Tessa. 1984. "Was There A Roman Charter for the Jews?" *JRS* 74:107–23.

Riggs, Marcia Y. 2003. *Plenty Good Room: Women versus Male Power in the Black Church*. Cleveland: Pilgrim.

Robinson, Lori S. 2000. "A Survivor: Exclusive Assata Shakur in Cuba." *Emerge*, May, 32–35.

Sadler, Rodney S. 2007. "The Place and Role of Africa and African Imagery in the Bible." Pages 23–30 in *True to Our Native Land: An African American New Testament Commentary*. Edited by Brian K. Blount, Cain Hope Felder, Clarice Jannette Martin, and Emerson B. Powery. Minneapolis: Fortress.

Shakur, Assata. 1987. *Assata: An Autobiography*. London: Zed Books.

Smith, Shively T. J. 2016. *Strangers to Family: Diaspora and 1 Peter's Invention of God's Household*. Waco, TX: Baylor University Press.

Strabo. 1854–1857. *The Geography of Strabo: Literally Translated, with Notes*. Translated by H. C. Hamilton and W. Falconer. London: Bohn.

Tacitus. 1925. *Histories: Books 1–3*. Translated by C. H. Moore and J. Jackson. LCL. Cambridge: Harvard University Press.

Thomas, Helen. 2000. *Romanticism and Slave Narratives: Transatlantic Testimonies*. Cambridge: Cambridge University Press.

US Department of the Treasury. 2001. "What You Need to Know about the U. S. Embargo: An Overview of the Cuban Assets Control Regulations." http://tinyurl.com/SBL0688m1.

———. 2016. "Frequently Asked Questions Related to Cuba." http://tinyurl.com/SBL0688l1.

Weems, Renita J. 1991a. "Do You See What I See? Diversity in Interpretation." *Church and Society* 82:28–43.

———. 1991b. "Reading Her Way through the Struggle: African American Women and the Bible." Pages 57–77 in *Stony the Road We Trod: African American Biblical Interpretation*. Edited by Cain Hope Felder. Minneapolis: Fortress.

———. 1988. *Just a Sister Away: A Womanist Vision of Women's Relationships in the Bible*. Philadelphia: Innis.

———. 2014. "Re-reading for Liberation: African American Women and the Bible." Pages 42–55 in *I Found God in Me: A Womanist Biblical Hermeneutics Reader*. Edited by Mitzi J. Smith. Eugene, OR: Cascade.

White, Evelyn C. 1997. "Prisoner in Paradise: An Interview with Assata Shakur." *Essence Magazine* 28. Repr. Assatashakur.org. http://tinyurl.com/SBL0688n1.

Witherington, Ben. 2006. *Matthew*. SHBC. Macon: Smyth & Helwys.

"Battered Love":
Exposing Abuse in the Book of Job

Marlene Underwood

Introduction

In 1995, womanist scholar Renita Weems published *Battered Love: Marriage, Sex, and Violence in the Hebrew Prophets* to grapple with the disturbing use of violence against women as a metaphor depicting the prophets' perception of God's volatile relationship with Israel. As an example, in Weems's treatment of Hos 2:2–23, she asserts that the marriage metaphor in that text illustrates the divine-human relationship; that is, Hosea's relationship with his wife Gomer parallels YHWH's relationship with Israel. In particular, the text employs the marital-harlotry motif to portray rocky relationships between the faithful and the wayward. Hosea deals with Gomer, his "wife of whoredom" (Hos 1:2b), the way YHWH deals with Israel, which has "turn[ed] to other gods" (Hos 3:1b), by using violence.[1] Even though Weems does not center the African American experience in *Battered Love*, her treatment of this issue that transcends race, class, and gender reflects the womanist concern for wholeness for all people. Following her example, I employ the womanist commitment to all people in my reading of Job.

In the book of Job, God allows the antagonist, the satan,[2] to abuse the protagonist Job. Whereas prophetic literature attempts to justify the

---

1. Hosea threatens to strip his wife Gomer naked and publicly expose her as punishment for her infidelity as a metaphor for YHWH's relationship with Israel (2:3; MT 2:5). Unless otherwise stated, all biblical translations follow the NRSV.

2. *Satan*, despite English translations of the book of Job, is not a personal name but rather a title meaning "accuser" or "adversary." The Hebrew text reflects this by attaching a definite article (*ha-*) to the word (*satan*), or *hassatan*.

divine punishment of a supposedly wayward national figure as an unfaithful spouse, the book of Job is careful to clarify that its eponymous character's suffering is unmerited; Job becomes the abused "wife" for no reason other than that the abusive "husband" YHWH possesses the power to abuse. Kenneth Ngwa (2009, 359) points out that, "Job's suffering is not random; rather, it is well thought out, executed, and evaluated." The violence meted out against Job is premeditated. On two occasions (1:8; 2:6), YHWH puts Job in harm's way, permitting the satan to attack Job economically, emotionally, physically, and socially (Brenner 1981, 129). The image that emerges is not simply that Job suffers, but that he does so because of YHWH's abuse.

In what appears to be a reluctant admission, Rodney Sadler opines about Job, "perhaps his story is most troubling because this good man's change of fortunes comes about because of the will of YHWH, the God in whom he has placed his trust. How frightening the first two chapters are, for though they posit that God is in control of human lives, the reasons for the suffering that God apparently allows remain beyond our understanding" (Masenya and Sadler 2010, 241).

Although the reasons for Job's suffering may be incomprehensible, the cycle of abuse that occurs in the text is not. According to feminist psychologist Lenore Walker (2000, 126), domestic violence (now commonly referred to as intimate-partner violence) comprises three phases: (1) tension building, (2) the acute battering incident, and (3) loving-contrition. These phases are evident in the Job narrative.

To treat the pattern of abuse and its ramifications, this literary- and ideologically-critical womanist reading examines the system of retributive justice that Job challenges. This womanist reading requires defining the three phases of domestic violence and demonstrating how Job's story fits into those phases. Finally, this essay shows modes of protest and resistance and examines implications for modern survivors of abuse.

A womanist essay about a rich patriarch[3] may seem surprising for some readers. The nature and focus of my reading of the book of Job enable me the opportunity to demonstrate the breadth of womanist approaches. As Nyasha Junior (2015, 95) points out, there exists no single definition of *womanist biblical interpretation*. This essay, therefore, emanates from

---

3. Even though this essay does treat Job's unnamed wife, its focus is on the violent relationship between Job, a male character, and YHWH, a supposedly male deity.

two key facets of Alice Walker's definition of *womanist:* a commitment to truth telling and the wholeness of all people. My critique stands in solidarity with victims of domestic violence who are required to engage in "outrageous, audacious, courageous or willful behavior" (Walker 1983, xi). This essay exposes a divine abuser, an image that may be problematic, or even extremely troubling, for some. Audre Lorde (1984, 40) insists that "I have come to believe over and over again that what is most important to me must be spoken, made verbal and shared, even at the risk of having it bruised or misunderstood." So at the risk of alienating readers, I must speak about the damage that the deity inflicts on its devotee as demonstrated in the book of Job. I cannot remain silent about this text's perpetrator, divinity notwithstanding. Such truth-telling expresses the essence of womanism.

My critique is further "committed to the survival and wholeness of entire people"—both Job's entire household and, especially, African American readers of Job's narrative—"male *and* female" (A. Walker 1983, xi). Although the text of Job emerges from ancient contexts, the text continues to impact contemporary reading and listening communities (see Weems 1991, 57; Dube 2000, 160). Therefore, exposing a pattern of abuse analogous to the one that continues to rip apart African American families and communities is critical. The battering suffered by poor, uneducated black women is sickeningly systemic (Richie 1995, 398); but thinking of victims of abuse as singularly poor black women plays into unhelpful stereotypes. Intimate-partner violence impacts every demographic in the United States. No class, color, creed, or other category of persons is exempt. Not one. Yes, women with limited access to resources can be prey to domestic violence but so can old-money heirs and new-money professionals occupying the upper rungs of socioeconomic ladders, studious scholars and scholarly students reading (and teaching) the essays in this volume, and tall, strong, strapping men and other souls[4] who do not "look" as if they possibly could be abused. Finally, my womanist commitment "to the survival and wholeness of [all my] people" does not allow me to ignore the pattern of abuse in this text. So, whether abuse occurs between a pious male patrician and his God in an ancient narrative or between poor or rich contemporary intimate partners in real life, abuse is abuse. Abuse in all its forms—physical,

---

4. The sexual binary of *female* and *male* is woefully inadequate. Anyone can be abused, regardless of sexual orientation or gender identification.

emotional, psychological, and so on—is violent. It is damaging, it can be fatal,[5] and it must be named and stopped.

Retributive Justice

In my discussions with church-going Christians and nonchurched persons who have some idea about the story of Job, two key themes stand out: Job tells what happens, to employ an oft-used phrase, "when bad things happen to good people," and the "patience of Job" (Jas 5:11) sustains him through his trials. In a recent conversation with my father about the book of Job, my father vigorously blamed the satan for Job's suffering. However, upon closer examination of the text, what emerged for me even before that conversation is a much more jarring reality: *God* subjects Job to immeasurable pain (1:8; 2:3), even though Job has done nothing to merit it (1:1; 2:3).

For those unfamiliar with the story, the book of Job recounts the routing and restoration of a rich and upstanding patriarch who becomes the target of an otherworldly wager. On the first occasion that the satan and other divine beings (Heb. *bene ha'elohim*; lit. "sons of the gods") present themselves to YHWH (Job 1:6–8), the deity asks whether the satan has noticed the deity's servant[6] Job, and boasts that "there is no one like him on the earth, a blameless and upright man who fears God and turns away from evil" (1:8). When the satan argues that Job's fear of God is the result of YHWH's protection and blessing (1:10), YHWH gives the satan power over Job's possessions. In rapid succession, messengers, each a lone survivor of the tragedy to be told, inform Job that Sabeans have taken away Job's oxen and donkeys and killed his servants (1:13–15), "fire from God" has consumed Job's sheep and more servants (1:16), Chaldeans have carried off Job's camels and killed more servants still (1:17), and a great wind has razed the house of Job's eldest son and killed all ten of Job's children feasting there (1:18–19). Even as Job grieves, the text is quick to point out that he "did not sin or charge God with wrongdoing" (1:22).

The second time that the satan and the divine beings go before YHWH (2:1–2), the deity again asks whether the satan has noticed Job and again boasts about this unique "blameless and upright man" who "persists in his

---

5. Susan Hazen-Hammond (1999, 20) refers to the emotional and/or spiritual destruction of one person by another as "soul murder."
6. In Hebrew, *'ebed* also can mean "slave."

integrity, although [the satan] incited [YHWH] against him, to destroy him for no reason" (2:3). YHWH then succumbs to the satan's "incitement" a second time. When the satan argues that Job would curse YHWH if the deity would "touch [Job's] bone and flesh" (2:5), YHWH gives the satan power over Job's body (2:6). The one thing that YHWH does not permit the satan, though is to take Job's life. Instead, the satan causes Job insufferable pain.

In contrast to the terse exchange between Job and his nameless wife (2:9–10), who suggests an immediate solution to Job's woes—"*barek* God and die" (2:9)[7]—are the poetic point-counterpoint rounds between Job and his friends Eliphaz the Temanite, Bildad the Shuhite, Zophar the Naamathite, and later, Elihu son of Bachel the Buzite, each trying to grasp the reasons for Job's plight, each pleading with Job to admit his sin so his suffering can end (chs. 3–37).

The speeches of Job's friends highlight their adherence to the system of retributive justice, the Deuteronomistic tradition that the good deed a person or nation (i.e., Israel) performs is rewarded, but the evil a person or nation perpetrates is punished, usually in the form of curses. What makes this form of justice retributive is that the deity is justified in meting out punishment for the people's covenant infidelity.[8] Ken Stone (2006, 291) notes that many of the claims maintained by Job's friends mirror orthodox theology. Their perception of retributive justice falls in line with many passages from the Bible, particularly those in Deuteronomy and the Deuteronomistic History.[9]

The prologue of Job alludes to Deut 28, which contains an extensive list of curses that will befall Israel if the nation disobeys YHWH. Verse 35 cites one of the more onerous consequences: "The LORD will strike you on the

---

7. The Hebrew verb *barak* actually means "bless." *Barak* also occurs in Job 1:11 and 2:9, where, again, it is translated as "curse" (NRSV) or "blaspheme" (JPS). Although the use of *barak* is believed to be a euphemism against the blasphemy of cursing God, my reading of the verb as "bless" flips the motive of Job's wife's mandate from contention to mercy; that is, if Job blesses God, maybe the deity will end Job's suffering by ending his life.

8. In the book of Job, it is the patriarch, and not a nation, that bears the brunt of what his friends perceive as some type of covenant infidelity. Perhaps this purports that Job represents a corporate character or that the consequences of sin have shifted from the corporate level to the individual.

9. The Deuteronomistic History is an academic term that refers to the historical narratives in Joshua, Judges, 1 and 2 Samuel, and 1 and 2 Kings.

knees and on the legs with grievous boils of which you cannot be healed, from the sole of your foot to the crown of your head" (see Beal 2003, 69; Stone 2006, 288). Yet this is exactly what occurs to Job: "So Satan went out from the presence of the LORD, and inflicted loathsome sores on Job from the sole of his foot to the crown of his head" (2:7). But whereas the Israelites in Deut 28 risk "grievous boils" if they disobey YHWH, Job contracts "loathsome sores" precisely because he was "blameless and upright, one who feared God and turned away from evil" (1:1; 2:3).

Deuteronomistic blessings and curses also appear in the epilogue of Job. Deuteronomy 30:3 promises that if the people return to YHWH, "then the LORD your God will restore your fortunes and have compassion on you, gathering you from all the peoples among whom the LORD your God has scattered you." Similarly, YHWH restores Job's fortunes, again using words similar to those found in Deuteronomy: "And the LORD restored the fortunes of Job when he had prayed for his friends; and the LORD gave Job twice as much as he had before" (42:10). But whereas in Deuteronomy, YHWH restores the fortunes of a once wayward people who have returned to God, in Job, YHWH restores the fortunes of a man who never left God in the first place. One key difference in the blessings-curses-blessings cycle evident in both Deuteronomy and Job is that "Job renders the logic that elsewhere finds that pattern (do right, get blessed; do wrong, get cursed) at best senseless and at worst (in the hands of his friends) menacing" (Stone 2006, 288).

Between the prologue and the epilogue lie multiple demonstrations that Job's friends have bought into the notion of retributive justice. Convinced that Job's trials are the outcome of his transgressions, they urge the patriarch to admit his guilt in hopes that YHWH would show mercy. However, we must also note that toward the end of Job, YHWH proclaims that Job's friends have not spoken about the deity "what is right, as my servant Job has done" (42:8). Although YHWH does not specify what Job has been right about, this charge seems to convey the idea that the book of Job hardly validates the orthodox theology that Job's friends typify. Instead, the same deity whom the friends attempt to defend ends up rejecting their claims (Stone 2006, 291).

Having been domesticated by their commitment to a tradition steeped in blessings and curses, it is no wonder that Job's friends respond the way they do (Kirk-Duggan 2009, 631). Yet their replies remain ambiguous. Do their harsh words show an utter lack of compassion, or are they attempts to force Job out of his misery by insisting that he confess uncommitted sins? Either way, Job is left mourning and sitting in an ash heap, covered from head to toe in "loathsome sores" (2:7), subjected to worms and filth (7:5), and considered an outcast to his family and his community (19:13–19). "Job, who has lived a life of scrupulous piety and fidelity to God, finds that he is abandoned by God in his hour of need. Job reaches out for help, cries out for answers, and meets only silence from the divine and silencing from his friends" (Chastain 1997, 173).

Even though the system of retributive justice attempts to rationalize divine punishment of the nation through the image of the punishments meted out to an adulterous wife, what makes Job's punishment so heinous is that it has nothing to do with any sin on his part (2:3). Rather, Job is the pawn in a celestial bet that tests his motivation for worshipping God (1:9–10). According to Benjamin Abotchie Ntreh,

> the setting for the predicament is put in the realm of the spirit world—a debate between God and the tester (Satan) about why Job worships God for nothing.... The ground for this contest is something that is beyond the comprehension of both Job and the people of his time. The pathetic thing is that Job is not even aware of what is happening to him. (2004, 144)

Without wanting to justify the abuse of victims on the grounds of their wrongdoing, the case of Job stands outside of the system of retributive justice precisely because of his innocence. This system robs him of any claims to innocence precisely because divine punishments, displayed in the way they are in Job's life, are automatically viewed as just, appropriate, and beyond question.

The book of Job may possibly present a case for questioning the nature of divine justice. Sadler posits that the inhabitants of postexilic Judah questioned the veracity of retributive justice. Having survived the "greatest tragedy in their collective history" (Masenya and Sadler 2010, 241), the Judeans contemplated their supposedly eternal covenant with YHWH, which ended when they were conquered by Babylon and taken into captivity in 587/6 BCE (more about this later). The book of Job with its exposure of the grim truths of retributive justice, then, may represent Judah's dissatisfaction with the simplistic ideas that obedience garners rewards but disobedience conjures curses (Masenya and Sadler 2010, 241). Job's narrative disputes the notion of retributive justice and, by implication, whether God is just.

Exposing the Abuse in the Book of Job

As I argued above, Job's treatment by YHWH approximates to that of a victim of domestic and intimate-partner violence. According to Margi Laird McCue, the Oregon Domestic Violence Council defines domestic violence (i.e., violence between adult partners) as "a pattern of coercive behavior used by one person to control and subordinate another in an intimate relationship. These behaviors include physical, sexual, emotional, and economic abuse. Tactics of coercion, terrorism, degradation, exploitation and violence are used to engender fear in the victim in order to enforce compliance" (2008, 3). Oregon's definition characterizes the violence as a pattern of behaviors (not a single incident), refers to various types of abuse, states the relationship of the victim to the perpetrator, establishes the purpose of control and subordination, and lists the methods (3).

Lenore Walker, a feminist psychologist, educator, and activist, works on the cycle of domestic violence, its effects on battered women and families, and the role public policy can play in assisting survivors. As previously mentioned, Walker demarcates the abuse cycle into three distinct phases: (1) tension building, (2) the acute battering incident, and (3) loving-contrition.

Phase one involves the gradual escalation of tension displayed by discrete acts causing increased friction, such as name-calling, other mean intentional behaviors, and/or physical abuse. The abuser expresses dissatisfaction and hostility but not in an extreme or maximally explosive form. The victim (usually a woman) attempts to placate the batterer, doing what she thinks might please, calm down, or, at least, what will not further aggravate the abuser (usually a man). Exhausted from the constant stress, the victim usually withdraws from the abuser (2000, 126).

Phase two is characterized by the uncontrollable discharge of the tensions that have built up during phase one. The violator typically lets loose a barrage of verbal and physical aggression that can leave the victim severely shaken and injured. The victim does her best to protect herself, often covering parts of her face and body to block some of the blows. This phase ends when the battering stops (2000, 126–27).

During phase three, the batterer may apologize profusely, try to assist the victim, show kindness and remorse, and shower the victim with gifts and/or promises. At this point, the batterer may believe that he will never allow himself to be violent again. Because the victim wants to believe the batter, she may continue to hope in his ability to change (2000, 127). Let us examine how Walker's three-part abuse cycle appears in this story and therefore reveals an abusive aspect of God.

Phase One: Tension Building

In the tension-building phase, unrest develops in the divine council when the satan, functioning as a "prosecutor intent on establishing justice" (Habel 1985, 89), presents itself among the other heavenly beings (1:6–7). For no stated reason, YHWH directs the satan's attention to Job not once but twice: "Have you considered my servant Job? There is no one like him on the earth, a blameless and upright man who fears God and turns away from evil" (1:8; 2:6). When the satan challenges the motivation behind Job's ideal character (1:9–11; 2:4–5), the deity grants the satan access first to Job's possessions (1:12) and then to Job's body (2:6).

The abuse that YHWH permits the satan to wreak on Job is physical (1:7), emotional (ch. 3), and economic (1:14–19). The nature of the abuse illustrates neglect (1:12; 2:6) and exploitation (Job suffers for no reason; 2:3). Strictly speaking, YHWH is not husband, and the violence that Job endures is not spousal abuse. However, the violence done to Job still parallels the marriage metaphor, even though the metaphor describes a husband correcting a presumed wayward wife, but the deity affirms Job's character as "blameless and upright" (1:8; 2:3; see 1:1). Domestic violence experts frequently point out that the victim does not have to have done anything to deserve the abuse. Job lives an exemplary life (1:1) and appeases the deity (1:6) on behalf of his children. Yet despite his piety, Job ends up in the same beleaguered straits as the wife in the prophetic metaphors: the victim of intimate-partner violence. But whether deemed guilty or innocent, neither the wife nor Job deserves to be tortured.

The violence that ensues in the book of Job is intimate abuse. For David R. Blumenthal (1993, 248), abuse from either God or people is unjustified. Furthermore, in pondering what the suffering of an innocent man bespeaks about God, Carol A. Newsom offers:

> Because [Job] suffers without being guilty, Job can only conclude that either some enormous mistake has been made about him or, more disturbingly, that God is not a just god but rather a monstrous tyrant. The book had begun as an inquiry into the motives of human piety. Through the compelling speeches of Job it becomes an examination of the character of God. (1998, 139)

In the discussion between YHWH and the satan, what is especially intriguing are the satan's observations, "But stretch out your hand now, and touch all that he has, and he will *barak* you to your face" (1:11) and "But stretch out your hand now and touch his bone and his flesh, and he will *barak* you to your face" (2:5). In both instances, the satan characterizes YHWH's touch as having deleterious effects. However, as the story unfolds, YHWH is never depicted as the one who touches Job; instead the satan performs these deeds. When the satan touches Job's possessions and then his body, the satan seems to be functioning—with the deity's knowledge and permission—as YHWH's agent. Though Job's pleas to be left alone by YHWH attest to this (see 7:16, 19; 10:20), YHWH blames the satan for inciting the deity to destroy Job "for no reason" (2:3). However, the relationship between YHWH and the satan is intrinsic. Therefore, as Stone observes:

> the satan, then never acts independently of God, who seems in the narrative much less interested in Job's well-being than in winning a wager. Job is caught up in forces of which he is partly unaware and over which he has no control.... God and the satan are ... working together; indeed, God actually acknowledges that the satan "incites" God to do things (2:3). Much later in the book, the narrator will even identify God rather than the satan as the one who brought "all the evil" upon Job (42:11). (2006, 288)

Phase Two: The Acute Battering Incident

During the second phase of abuse, the acute battering incident, the satan destroys Job's wealth in a harrowing progression from livestock (1:14–17), to young male servants (1:15–17), and, finally, to Job's children (1:18–19). When the first round of abuse occurs, Job attempts to placate the batterer—YHWH—in his cry, "The Lord gave, and the Lord has taken away; blessed be the name of the Lord" (1:21). But neither mourning his children (1:20) nor continuing in his integrity (1:22) puts an end to Job's abuse. Rather, after annihilating Job's possessions and progeny, YHWH's agent inflicts "loathsome sores on Job from the sole of his foot to the crown of his head" (2:7).

When Job's friends hear of his distress, they decide "to go to console and comfort him" (2:11). However, the manifestation of Job's emotional and physical wounds is so severe that initially his friends fail to recognize him (2:12). What follows are round after round of Job's friends trying to convince him to confess his sins so that he may be forgiven and restored to his community. Mary Ann Beavis (2002, 107–8) declares that "the tendency of family members, clergy and counselors to deny or minimize the abuse or blame the victim is frequently reported by incest survivors." Even though it does not occur in the context of incest, the rhetoric of Job's friends, which intensifies from Eliphaz's gentle prodding that Job "not despise the discipline of the Almighty" (5:17) to Bildad's harsh insistence that no one is righteous (ch. 25), demonstrates Beavis's observation about the tendency to blame the victim. Some may even surmise that the words of Job's friends escalate the verbal abuse.

Despite their mistaken notions concerning Job's guilt, the friends attempt to offer, if not solace, then a solution to Job's woes. But unlike the friends, the deity remains silent until emerging from the whirlwind (38:1). Newsom (2003, 234) astutely observes that "when God speaks, it tends to bring conversation to an end." When YHWH does finally speak, the deity pummels the patriarch with intimidating questions about creation that he cannot possibly answer (e.g., 39:1) but provides no solutions to Job's immediate problems (see Ntreh 2004, 148). At times, YHWH even proves to be downright sarcastic, mocking the number of years that Job has lived in juxtaposition with the deity (38:21). Moreover, the deity never replies directly to Job's questions. For example, even though Job asks YHWH to let him know about the transgressions he must have committed to merit this type of punishment (e.g., 10:2; 13:23), the deity never states whether Job has committed any sins (Stone 2006, 295).

YHWH's dialogical deflections signal the deity's refusal to acknowledge its abuse of Job, his family, and the community whose working sons have been slaughtered, even if these all take place by proxy. For Kimberly Parsons Chastain:

> God's Dialogue [sic] speeches are oddly reminiscent of an abuser's attempt to defuse accusations by the diffusion of information. The lack of real dialogue, the mounting anger of the community, Job's wavering, and even his eventual submission (if that is what it is) parallel what [has been] described as the "sexual abuse accommodation syndrome."... In a situation where no one wants to believe a victim's claims, the claims themselves will wear thin and seem to waver. (1997, 172)

In line with Chastain's assertion, Job's claims of innocence vanish when he attempts to respond to the deity. What he holds fast to in rows with friends suddenly escape him in his encounter with God. Indeed, Job's answers convey his insignificance (40:3–5), his ignorance (42:3), and his self-loathing and repentance (42:6), a far cry from Job's earlier demands that YHWH answer his charges of injustice (e.g., 9:19–24, 32–33). In the formidable meeting with his divine abuser, Job does what victims often do: he cowers.

Phase Three: Loving Contrition

In the third and final phase, loving-contrition, YHWH exhibits the extravagance typical of a batterer (see L. Walker 2009, 37). YHWH reinstates Job's good standing by admitting that he was right about the deity (42:7), though precisely what Job was right about remains unknown.[10] YHWH goes on to restore Job's wealth "twice as much as he had before" (42:10). Siblings, who comfort Job for "all the evil that the LORD had brought upon him" (42:11) and enrich Job with money and gold rings, are returned; the numbers of Job's sheep, camels, oxen, and donkeys are doubled (42:12); and ten more children (seven sons and three daughters[11]) are born (42:13).[12] Although Job lives an additional one hundred and forty years (42:16), the text does not specify whether YHWH has restored Job's health. In the end, Job dies "old and full of days" (42:17), signaling either a happy ending to this hero's tale, or, more likely, the end of the third phase of a cycle of abuse that is destined to recur.

Ntreh (2004, 148) notes that Job's "restoration did not seem to be the real answer that Job was looking for. It seems that Job was more satisfied that God had come to vindicate him," although the text does not indicate Job's level of satisfaction. Rather, the fact that Job obeys YHWH's command to pray for his friends (42:8) may communicate Job's fear of a deity who has the power to eliminate Job's wealth, health, children, and social standing. Cheryl Kirk-Duggan (2009, 631) agrees that God is cast as a

---

10. In 42:8, YHWH neither admits to nor regrets the abuse perpetrated against Job.

11. In contrast to their nameless mother, the three new daughters are named: Jemimah, Keziah, and Keren-happuch (42:14). Like their ten surprisingly nameless brothers, the daughters surprisingly receive an inheritance from their father (42:15).

12. The story fails to mention whether YHWH has blessed Job with more *ne'ar'im*. If livestock are mentioned, it is puzzling that the "young men" are not, especially if they tend to the affairs of Job's household and are a sign of Job's wealth and returned status.

"tyrant" and an abuser but, in the end, is proclaimed just. She continues that Job

> casts doubt on God's holiness and righteousness.... The sages ... have recast holiness to represent a holy, leprous Gentile who lives in an unholy land with unholy people.... In so doing, the sages implicitly question God's holiness and portray God as a bullying, almost demonic caricature. God bestows holiness, yet it must be pursued by humans.... Ultimately, however, the sages offer no conclusive explanations, and God's ways remain inscrutable. (631)

In contrast to Kirk-Duggan's characterization of the sages' portrait of Job, the aim of this essay is precisely to scrutinize "God's ways." In the book of Job, YHWH's actions fit the pattern of a batterer, and my commitment to the health and well-being of my community will not permit me to redeem this violent divine victimizer.

Protest and Resistance

The book of Job and the aforementioned passages in Hosea portray a deity that appears to be predisposed to abuse and violence. Given the centrality, and often authoritative, position of these narratives in many Jewish and Christian faith traditions, what do we do with these problematic passages? The following scholars have weighed in on this issue.

Gracia Fay Ellwood's stance on troubling texts is guided by her Quaker commitments. The final authority for the Friends is the movement of the Spirit within each person, not the written word. Additionally, Quakers are committed to nonviolence and equality. So according to Ellwood, it is relatively easy for them to learn from the Bible without struggling with its "texts of terror."[13] Ignoring these texts necessitates turning a blind eye to any damaging impact they have (1988, 3).

Dawn Robinson Rose rebuffs difficult passages outright. "Israel no more deserved the Holocaust than women deserved rape.... If God is justice, I cannot find God in this picture" of retribution (2000, 147). Instead, Rose envisions a "new God fashioned out of intervention and action" (148), and she calls on others to assist abused women, insisting that "in

---

13. In *Texts of Terror* (1984), Phyllis Trible explicates four biblical texts that affirm violence against women.

saving other women, some of us save our mothers and sisters as well. In rebellion we find our God and our lives" (150).

Blumenthal (1993, 243) calls the rejection of abusive biblical passages "unsophisticated," because it excludes the unnerving aspects of humanity and divinity. Blumenthal asserts that we cannot comprehend ourselves or God if we extricate what disturbs us or revise what offends us. He recognizes that "the texts on God's abusiveness are there. To censor them out because they are not 'ethical' [referring to Brueggemann's 1985 comment about psalms calling for vengeance] is to limit our understanding of the complexity of human and divine existence" (245). Blumenthal does not espouse bypassing difficult passages, but neither does he advocate uncritically embracing them. Instead, he calls for a theology of protest, "a religiously proper faith stance toward God" (253). Protest necessarily involves questioning God about issues of justice, a response undergirded by biblical precedents. For example, Abraham argues for Sodom (Gen 18), and Moses vigorously defends the people (Exod 5, 32; Num 14); national and personal laments in Jeremiah and the Psalms also are forms of protest (Blumenthal 1993, 251).

Closely aligned to protest is resistance. For Traci C. West (1999, 151), "resistance involves any sign of dissent with the consuming effects of intimate and social violence. When a woman survives, she accomplishes resistance." The same can be said for Job, whose affirmations of innocence (e.g., ch. 16) and cries for justice (e.g., 6:8; 9:19–24, 32–33; 10:2) constitute acts of protest against an abusive deity and whose survival of extreme physical and emotional torment attest to his resistance.

In addition to defining the three phases of abuse evident in domestic violence, Lenore Walker's (2009, 251) work includes educating the public about the types of "institutional remedies" that survivors of abuse need:

- places that provide refuge, including safe houses and shelters (191);
- legal alternatives, including police protection (206), restraining orders (210), temporary financial support (215), regulated child visitation (219), legal assistance for abused persons attempting to divorce their batterers (220) or who have injured or killed their batterers (220);
- medical options, including private doctors and clinics (224) and company-sponsored medical and counseling services (225);
- psychotherapy, including crisis intervention (231) and therapy for individuals (233), groups, and couples (244).

Walker elucidates other societal changes that could help to mitigate domestic violence: changes in family structures to alleviate the stresses imposed on nuclear families (251), methods of disciplining children that exclude hitting (252), parent education classes (253), doing away with "sex-role stereotyping" (253), and addressing generational abuse (254). Walker understands that "programs for battered women should be sensitive to the bilingual and multicultural needs of ethnic and minority women" (185).

Even though the resources Walker names are essential, the sad truth is that not all abuse survivors have access to these networks, so they have to create alternatives. Womanist pastoral theologian Stephanie M. Crumpton (2014, 125) outlines six self-care strategies practiced by African American female survivors of abuse. These "uninstitutionalized experiences" bear repeating in their entirety:

- encounters with other mothers and sisterfriends whose practical support and alternative insights on intimate and cultural violence mirrored their humanity and firmed up their interior experience of self;
- female cultural self-objects, who, through acts of service, civic office, and performance on public platforms offered uplifting visual images and spiritual insight that empowered them to survive, heal, and resist a culture that normalizes violence against them;
- examination of the impact of religious messages that mediate or mitigate cultural violence through misogynistic/patriarchal gender norms in their relationships with God, self, and others;
- reconstructing a spirituality that honors the particularities of their personal experience, integrates non-Christian religious traditions and offers theological language that mirrors back the fullness of their distinctly female humanity (inclusive of their bodies) as a reflection of God's femininity;
- embodied spiritual practices that simultaneously connected them to God while also functioning as a strategy for interrupting unwanted cultural access to their bodies and ethnic identities;
- transforming the position that trauma holds in their lives by using personal experiences and stories of overcoming to help other women who have similarly struggled with intimate violence. (125–26)

Blumenthal (1993, 247–48) concludes that "God is abusive, but not always." During the times that God is abusive, vehement dissent is in order. But how do we protest a God who is portrayed as a divine perpetrator in biblical texts? Moreover, how do we survive flesh-and-blood abusers? Although Blumenthal offers these points in his reconstruction of a "post-holocaust, abuse-sensitive" protest theology, the following steps also can be used in response to an abuser, whether divine or human: (1) we acknowledge that we have been victims of abuse, "unjustified punishment and suffering," and that we are not guilty; (2) we distance ourselves from the perpetrator, guarding that distance "theologically and spiritually, in worship and in study" (266); (3) we name the abuser and tell the whole truth; (4) "we … empower ourselves by acknowledging fully our survival, by building human relationships, by participating in worthy causes, and by working and accomplishing our daily and social tasks" (267); and (5) we affirm our spirituality by "affirm[ing] the miracle of healing and the wonder of life" (267).

Conclusion

The book of Job is a compilation of ancient stories depicting the unjust suffering of innocent heroes. If the final form of Job is a postexilic creation, then it could signify the types of trauma that people(s) sustained at the hands of their imperial overlords (Assyrians, Babylonians, and Persians) both in exile and in colonized Yehud. The story tells readers that even though Job's protests do get YHWH's attention, the wounded, outcast, and shamed patriarch survives by capitulating to the deity. If YHWH is a cipher for the ruling classes, both internal (the Yehudites) and external (the colonizing forces), then the story also cautions readers that the only way they can survive is to collaborate with their captors, who, like the deity, control the reins of life and death. Job's story, then, tries to assuage abused communities that if they cower to their abusers, ultimately, they will be rewarded with or at least maintain their privileges in the form of family, financial resources, and long lives. This is the survival strategy proffered. Job's story also depicts that despite one's efforts to do "right," those in control could, on a capricious whim, turn one's life upside down.

In my experiences with various predominantly African American churches, I have seen many congregants look to the Bible for comfort and for instructions about how to "live right." Although I respect their choice to use the Bible in this way, I realize that they do so because they have been conditioned to overlook difficult passages, those that offend our sense of ethics or our beliefs about how God can and does move in our lives. The characterizations of God as a batterer illustrate that relying on others' descriptions of God, particularly when those descriptions present unhealthy models of the divine-human relationship, does not benefit us. The images of God presented in this essay as derived from the book of Job are loathsome. They show a capricious God who seems to be more concerned with protecting its ego or demonstrating its power than in caring for and nurturing its creation. Perhaps the resulting cognitive dissonance demonstrates that the God of the texts (the ones presented here, anyway) and the God of our experiences do not always align.

Newsom (1998, 131) remarks that "the book of Job is rather like a parable in that it tells its frankly outrageous tale for the purpose of disorienting and reorienting the perspectives of its readers." Perhaps the disorienting occurs when readers are brought face-to-face with a patriarchal God who sanctions violence—including the murder of servants and children—to prove a point. YHWH claims that the satan has incited him to "destroy [Job] for no reason" (2:3), but the veracity of that statement can be challenged, because it is YHWH who focuses the satan's attention on Job in the first place (1:8; 2:3). So, Job's suffering is hardly happenstance. Perhaps the reorienting comes when Job's audience reexamines its responses to the text, the deity in the text, or both, in light of contemporary issues. For example, given what we know about the origin of Job's woes, how do we—if at all—use this text when dealing with battered persons? Other than depicting an abusive deity, does Job offer us anything?

In the epilogue, or the loving-contrition phase of an abuse cycle, of Job, the patriarch's brothers and sisters return (42:11),[14] the numbers of his livestock are doubled (42:12), and he is blessed with ten more children, seven sons and three beautiful daughters (42:13–15), the same number as in the beginning of the narrative (1:2). Rather than seeing this as a happy ending, readers may ask whether *any* amount would have been enough to redress the torture and loss that Job has experienced.

---

14. By abandoning Job in the midst of his distress, Job's family is complicit in his abuse. Perhaps the family has bought into the Deuteronomist's notion that sin leads to curses but obedience to blessings, so they want to remain as far away from Job's supposedly extreme sin as they can. They do not come to comfort Job until YHWH has started to restore him. That Job is absolved proves to the family that their patriarch truly has remained "blameless and upright" (Heb., *tam ve yashar*).

How does a parent recover from the death of one child, let alone ten? Similar to other victims of abuse, can Job ever be secure in his relationship with YHWH, knowing that the deity has the power to ruin his life again?[15] Can YHWH, who initiates Job's suffering, ever justify its actions to anyone's satisfaction? Does YHWH ever learn how *not* to abuse? Simplistic solutions to these, and other, difficult questions never will suffice; and neither will silence or inaction.

The concluding chapter of *Battered Love* contains Weems's (1995, 119) challenge to consider that "rethinking the Bible's representation of marriage will not change the fact that both the Bible's culture and our own culture persistently rationalize violence against women." We ignore the abuse perpetrated on women's and children's bodies because our places of worship continue to espouse androcentrism and biblical patriarchy,[16] and our society states that family bonds are sacred and secret, no matter who gets injured. Along the same vein, we ignore the abuse perpetrated on Job's body, perhaps because our psyches will be troubled by acknowledging a dangerous deity, one who flies in the face of the mantra that "God is good all the time; and all the time, God is good." We also ignore the abuse perpetrated against the other victims in the story, Job's unnamed wife, children, and servants, perhaps because in terms of status, they simply do not matter and are easily replaced. However, if we attend to and extend Weems's challenge, then the book of Job can help us to deliberately consider the impact of violence on various forms of intimate relationships, and to act on behalf of those who cannot.

Works Cited

Beal, Timothy K. 2003. "Facing Job." Pages 65–74 in *Levinas and Biblical Studies*. Edited by Tamara Cohn Eskenazi, Gary A. Phillips, and David Jobling. Atlanta: Society of Biblical Literature.

Beavis, Mary Ann. 2002. "'Making Up Stories': A Feminist Reading of the Parable of the Prodigal Son (Lk. 15.11b–32)." Pages 98–122 in *The Lost*

---

15. Compare Job's abuse to that of Isaac (Gen 22:1–14) and Jephthah's daughter (Judg 11:29–40). Because the lives of Job and Isaac are spared, they have to live with the uncertainty that the same abusers who wreak havoc on their lives once can do so again. Jephthah's daughter, whose father takes her life to fulfill a vow to a deity that fails to stop human sacrifice, does not.

16. See, for example, Gen 2:21–23; Eph 5:22; Col 3:18; 1 Tim 4:7; 1 Pet 3:1.

Coin: Parables of Women, Work and Wisdom. New York: Sheffield Academic.

Blumenthal, David R. 1993. *Facing the Abusing God: A Theology of Protest*. Louisville: Westminster John Knox.

Brenner, Athalya. 1981. "God's Answer to Job." *VT* 31:129–37.

Brueggeman, Walter. 1985. "Theodicy in a Social Dimension." *JSOT* 33:3–25.

Chastain, Kimberly Parsons. 1997. "The Dying Art of Demon-Recognition: Victims, Systems, and the Book of Job." Pages 161–78 in *Power, Powerlessness, and the Divine: New Inquiries in Bible and Theology*. Edited by Cynthia L. Rigby. Atlanta: Scholars Press.

Crumpton, Stephanie M. 2014. *A Womanist Pastoral Theology against Intimate and Cultural Violence*. New York: Palgrave Macmillan.

Dube, Musa W. 2000. "Decolonizing White Western Readings of Matthew 15:21–28." Pages 157–96 in *Postcolonial Feminist Interpretation of the Bible*. St. Louis: Chalice.

Ellwood, Gracia Fay. 1988. *Batter My Heart*. Pamphlet 282. Wallingford, PA: Pendle Hill.

Habel, Norman C. 1985. *The Book of Job: A Commentary*. Philadelphia: Westminster.

Hazen-Hammond, Susan. 1999. *Spider Woman's Web: Traditional Native American Tales about Women's Power*. New York: Perigee.

Junior, Nyasha. 2015. *An Introduction to Womanist Biblical Interpretation*. Louisville: Westminster John Knox.

Kirk-Duggan, Cheryl A. 2009. "Introduction to the Book of Job." Pages 630–31 in *The People's Bible*. Edited by Curtiss Paul DeYoung, Wilda C. Gafney, Leticia A. Guardiola-Sáenz, George "Tink" Tinker, and Frank M. Yamada. Minneapolis: Fortress.

Lorde, Audre. 1984. *Sister Outsider: Essays and Speeches*. Berkeley: Crossing Press.

Masenya, Madipoane, and Rodney Sadler Jr. "Job." 2010. Pages 237–43 in *The Africana Bible: Reading Israel's Scriptures from Africa and the African Diaspora*. Edited by Hugh R. Page Jr. Minneapolis: Fortress.

McCue, Margi Laird. 2008. *Domestic Violence: A Reference Handbook*. 2nd ed. Santa Barbara: ABC-CLIO.

Newsom, Carol A. 1998. "Job." Pages 138–44 in *The Women's Bible Commentary*. Edited by Carol A. Newsom and Sharon H. Ringe. Louisville: Westminster John Knox.

———. 2003. *The Book of Job: A Contest of Moral Imaginations*. Oxford: Oxford University Press.

Ngwa, Kenneth. 2009. "Did Job Suffer for Nothing? The Ethics of Piety, Presumption and the Reception of Disaster in the Prologue of Job." *JSOT* 33:359–80.

Ntreh, Benjamin Abotchie. 2004. "Job." Pages 141–50 in *Global Bible Commentary*. Edited by Daniel Patte. Nashville: Abingdon.

Richie, Beth E. 1995. "Battered Black Women: A Challenge for the Black Community." Pages 398–404 in *Words of Fire: An Anthology of African-American Feminist Thought*. Edited by Beverly Guy Sheftall. New York: New Press.

Rose, Dawn Robinson. 2000. "Insider Out: Unmasking the Abusing God." Pages 143–52 in *Take Back the Word: A Queer Reading of the Bible*. Edited by Robert E. Goss and Mona West. Cleveland: Pilgrim.

Stone, Ken. "Job." 2006. Pages 286–303 in *The Queer Bible Commentary*. Edited by Deryn Guest, Robert E. Goss, Mona West, and Thomas Bohache. London: SCM.

Trible, Phyllis. 1984. *Texts of Terror: Literary-Feminist Readings of Biblical Narratives*. Philadelphia: Fortress.

Walker, Alice. 1983. *In Search of Our Mothers' Gardens*. New York: Harcourt Brace Jovanovich.

Walker, Lenore E. 2000. *The Battered Woman Syndrome*. 2nd ed. New York: Springer Publishing.

———. 2009. *The Battered Woman*. New York: William Morrow Paperbacks, 1980. Repr., New York: HarperCollins.

Weems, Renita J. 1991. "Reading Her Way through the Struggle: African American Women and the Bible." Pages 57–77 in *Stony the Road We Trod: African American Biblical Interpretation*. Edited by Cain Hope Felder. Minneapolis: Fortress.

———. 1995. *Battered Love: Marriage, Sex, and Violence in the Hebrew Prophets*. Minneapolis: Fortress.

West, Traci C. 1999. *Wounds of the Spirit: Black Women, Violence, and Resistance Ethics*. New York: New York University Press.

Part 3
Foregrounding Women on the Margins

Black Collectors and Keepers of Tradition: Resources for a Womanist Biblical Ethic of (Re)Interpretation

Gay L. Byron

Introduction

During the early-twentieth century, the United States witnessed a renaissance of black cultural, social, and artistic expression. Several black bibliophiles took to acquiring personal collections containing thousands of books, artifacts, and manuscripts documenting black literature and culture. Many of these private collections are now available for public access at various institutions. These sources bear witness to the valuable role of black collectors as keepers of tradition and purveyors of Africana history, culture, and knowledge. These collectors include Arthur A. Schomburg (1874–1938), whose personal library became the basis for the special collection at what is now known as the Schomburg Center for Research in Black Culture of the New York Public Library; Jesse Moorland and Arthur Spingarn, whose private collections became the foundation for what is now known as the Moorland-Spingarn Research Center (MSRC) at Howard University;[1] Dr. Charles H. Wright (1918–2002), the founder of the Charles H. Wright Museum of African American History in Detroit, which holds the world's largest exhibit on African American culture (see Rich and Wright 1999); Vivian G. Harsh (1890–1960), whose collection of African American literature and history is housed at the Carter G. Woodson Regional Library of the Chicago Public Library (see Schultz

---

1. Dorothy Porter Wesley (1905–1995), who worked for over forty years at the MSRC, is credited with preserving and developing the materials that make up this vast collection (see Sims-Wood 2014 and Beinecke 2013).

and Hast 2001); and Mayme A. Clayton (1923–2006), whose collection of African American literature, manuscripts, and film was moved from the leaky garage behind Clayton's home and settled into what has become the Mayme A. Clayton Library, Museum and Cultural Center in Los Angeles, California (Copage 2008).[2]

These black "bibliophiles and collectors" (see Sinnette, Coates, and Battle 1990) have amassed a treasure trove of artifacts and manuscripts that provide vital source material for researchers and scholars documenting the historical, cultural, social, religious, and political aspects of the Africana diaspora experience.[3] As a result of research undertaken to explore how the language, literature, and legacy of ancient Ethiopia may be utilized for the study of the New Testament and early Christianity (Byron 2006b, 2007), I learned of another black bibliophile and collector, Dr. André Reynolds Tweed (1914–1993), who amassed during his lifetime one of the largest private collections of Ethiopian sacred artifacts and manuscripts in North America.[4] This important, yet unrecognized, collection of sources known as the André Tweed Collection of Sacred Ethiopian Artifacts and Manuscripts lies nestled away in the northeast quadrant of the nation's capital at the Howard University School of Divinity (HUSD). This material offers a fresh opportunity for exploring questions about biblical traditions, in particular those traditions reflecting the origins of Christianity in northeast Africa (Byron 2009). Moreover, this material challenges biblical interpreters and other scholars of religion to reexamine assumptions and methodologies that have determined how such source material may be engaged in the interpretive process.

In this essay I provide a brief biographical sketch of Tweed, summarize the contents of the Tweed Collection, and discuss the value of using extrabiblical sources, such as a fourteenth/fifteenth-century manuscript

---

2. Other African American collections housed at majority white institutions include James Weldon Johnson's collection at Yale University, the W. E. B. DuBois Institute for Afro-American Research at Harvard University, the John Hope Franklin Research Center at Duke University, and the African American Odyssey Collection of the Library of Congress.

3. For a recent discussion on sources that inform African American theology, see Ware 2016, 51–55. Ware identifies a number of libraries, archives, and other collections that document the "lived" experience of black religion.

4. To my knowledge, no one has written a biography about Tweed or analyzed his contributions as an African American art collector. For a photograph of Tweed by Lester Sloan, see Easter, Cheers, and Brooks 1992.

contained in the Tweed Collection, as a basis for developing and naming a womanist biblical ethic of (re)interpretation. In particular, using ethical insights from womanist ways of reading and interpreting sacred texts, I discuss my own experience in working with the Tweed Collection to demonstrate that womanist biblical hermeneutics is first and foremost grounded in emancipatory recovery and reclamation of source material that sheds light on the history, culture, and worldviews of Africa and the Africana diaspora. In addition, this essay reveals how a womanist hermeneutical framework honors the experiences of black women in the interpretive process, overcomes "structured academic amnesia" (Cannon 2006), and transgresses canonical boundaries.

André Reynolds Tweed and the Tweed Collection

Tweed was born in Harlem, New York on April 16, 1914. Both of his parents were born in Jamaica and immigrated to New York City. Tweed studied at the City College of New York and then went on to the Howard University College of Medicine where he graduated in 1942. In 1950, he became the first board-certified black psychiatrist in California and practiced in Los Angeles, while also teaching as an associate clinical professor of Psychology at Loma Linda University (*André Reynolds Tweed Collection of Ethiopian Sacred Artifacts* n.d.).

Dr. Tweed traveled extensively throughout Africa, Europe, and other parts of the world. His love of Ethiopian art, culture, and sacred literature kept him returning to the country and eventually collecting more than 240 artifacts and 150 manuscripts (Hermesch 1994). The artifacts include icons, crosses, diptychs, triptychs, wall hangings, musical instruments, and more. The manuscripts (one hundred codices and fifty scrolls), written in the ancient Ethiopic language known as Ge'ez, include biblical texts, hymns, liturgical works, theological treatises, calendaric, homiletical, hagiographic, religiomagical works, medical texts, and poetry (Isaac 1990, 9). More specifically, the collection has an Old Testament manuscript containing Job, Proverbs, Ecclesiastes, Song of Solomon, Isaiah, and the minor prophets; a seventeenth-century manuscript of the New Testament without the four gospels; an eighteenth-century Acts of Abuna Gabra Manfas Qeddus; several *Deggwas* (church songs or hymns); and *Mashafa Genzat*, a liturgical work concerning the dead (9).

In addition to these manuscripts, there are scrolls that contain prayers for health and healing, as well as symbols, words, secret names, and phrases unintelligible to the uninitiated. Prayers against the evil eye, demons and spirits that cause illness are very common. Among the diseases often mentioned are headache, colic, chest pain, and rheumatism. Vaginal bleeding, spontaneous abortion and child mortality are of special concern. (16)

These scrolls, often encased in leather purses and worn as necklaces or arm bands, have great value for studying the history of diseases in Ethiopia and may also be useful for medical anthropologists and other researchers seeking to understand the connections between healing and spiritual practices.

The collection also includes sacred artifacts of the Ethiopian Orthodox Church such as musical instruments (*masenqos* and *tsenatsels*), prayer sticks (*mequamia*), incense holders (*tsenas*), and processional crosses. Wall hangings featuring the birth of Jesus, the crucifixion of Jesus, and the patron saint of Ethiopia, Giorgis, are also included in the collection. Although not a part of the original donation made by Tweed, the Tweed Exhibit at HUSD features paintings[5] of the baptism of the Ethiopian eunuch (Acts 8:26–39) and Abuna Tekla Haymanot, the founder of the Debre Libanos monastery in Ethiopia. The latter is commonly depicted as an elderly man with wings on his back and with his right foot severed from his body to symbolize how he used to pray standing for so long on one foot that it eventually fell off. According to Taddesse Tamrat (1975; see also 1972), "most of the monastic communities in Ethiopia derive their origin from him and are collectively known as the House of Tekla-Haymanot."

Tweed donated his collection to HUSD shortly before his death in December 1993 (see Hermesch 1994). According to Cain Hope Felder, Professor of New Testament Language and Literature at HUSD, Tweed, at the encouragement of his colleague and friend Ephraim Isaac, an Ethiopian scholar and former director of the Institute of Semitic Studies in Princeton, New Jersey, decided to give his collection to his alma mater instead of other viable alternatives.[6] He considered HUSD a much more accessible and historically meaningful location for the collection, given its

---

5. In 2010, during the Annual Alumni Convocation, HUSD unveiled two Ethiopian paintings by contemporary artist Meseretu Wondie, which were donated anonymously in honor of the late Louis Gilden, a civil rights lawyer who dedicated himself to serving the legal needs of the oppressed (see "Gallery of Religious Art," n.d.).

6. Tweed considered giving the material to the Hill Museum and Manuscript Library and the Firestone Library of Princeton University. See notes from interview with Cain Hope Felder (Byron 2006a).

mission to promote research pertaining to Africa and the Africana diaspora.

Manuscript Mix-Up: Provenance Matters

Before coming to HUSD, some of the material in the Tweed Collection was on exhibit from December 13, 1990, to May 12, 1991, at the California Afro-American Museum in Los Angeles. It is through a catalogue published to commemorate this exhibit that I first learned of a manuscript referred to as the Acts of Peter (*Ethiopian Sacred Artifacts from the Dr. André Tweed Collection* 1990). Isaac (1990, 9) claims that "perhaps the most important manuscript in the collection is the 15th-century manuscript containing such apocryphal works as the Acts of Peter and other apostles." Although Isaac's introductory essay in the catalogue mentions the Acts of Peter, there is a photograph of a manuscript labeled Acts of St. Paul and Other Apostles in another part of the catalogue (11).

As a result of my previous work on the Acts of Peter analyzing a disturbing depiction of an "Ethiopian woman" in a Greek version of the text,[7] I wanted to examine this Ethiopic version of the Acts of Peter (if, in fact, it was actually the Acts of Peter) in order to assess whether the same narrative appeared in the text. Regrettably, at that time, the Ethiopian artifacts in the Tweed Collection were not catalogued, and there was no scholarly trail to this material beyond the brief nineteen-page exhibit catalogue published in 1990.[8] My curiosity about this text coupled with a fellowship granted by the Luce Foundation set me on a research journey to learn more about the legacy of ancient Ethiopians and Ethiopia for the study of the New Testament and Christian origins (Byron 2006b).

Therefore, I initiated a prolonged series of email communications and phone calls with HUSD's Associate Dean for Academic Affairs at that time, Dr. Henry Ferry.[9] He had become the primary person responsible for organizing the Tweed Collection and setting-up an exhibit to show-

---

7. "A most evil-looking woman, who looked like an Ethiopian, not an Egyptian, but was all black, clothed in filthy rags. She was dancing with an iron collar about her neck and chains on her hands and feet" (Byron 2002, 17).

8. Recently the Ethiopic (Ge'ez) manuscripts at HUSD have been digitized and catalogued through a collaborative effort of Alice Ogden Bellis and Steve Delamarter (see Melaku et al. n.d.).

9. Ferry also served on the faculty of HUSD as Professor of Church History. I

case some of the more representative and important materials contained therein. Ferry was extremely gracious in providing access to the exhibit and even more in providing space for me to examine the manuscript and to take digital images of each page. During this research, I clarified the name of the text referred to in the exhibit catalogue and confirmed that it was actually the Acts (Gädlä) of Paul, not the Acts of Peter. Moreover, upon thorough review of the document, I discovered that there was also another text in this same codex, known as the Acts (Gädlä) of Särabamon (fols. 119a–167a; Byron 2006b, 2015; Amsalu 2013).

A few weeks after my visit to HUSD, I traveled to Collegeville, Minnesota, to meet with Dr. Getatchew Haile, a respected expert and scholar of Ethiopian manuscripts. After sharing with him my photos of the manuscript, he referred me to the microfilm record (Ethiopian Manuscript Microfilm Library [EMML] #6533), which indicates that the document had been filmed by representatives of the Hill Museum and Manuscript Library (HMML) in 1976. According to the microfilm record, the manuscript, which I had reviewed at HUSD, is the property of the Debre Libanos Monastery in the Shewa region of Ethiopia.[10] Apparently, sometime after the Acts of Paul text was microfilmed at Debre Libanos, Tweed acquired it and included it in his collection of Ethiopic material, presumably without regard to questions related to provenance now at the forefront of many professional societies that rely on ancient artifacts for research purposes (ASOR Board of Trustees 2015; Society of Biblical Literature Council 2016).

The year 1970 is considered the international benchmark for understanding how to deal with circulated antiquities. This is when the United Nations Educational, Scientific, and Cultural Organization (UNESCO) finalized the Convention on the Means of Prohibiting and Preventing the Illicit Import, Export, and Transfer of Ownership of Cultural Property. The "1970 Convention," as it is commonly understood, was created in response to the escalating looting of archaeological sites and the dismemberment of historical structures to provide objects for sale on the international art market (Gerstenblith 2013). It creates a framework for

---

remain grateful for all of his support in facilitating my research on the manuscript under discussion and the Tweed Collection as a whole.

10. There are actually two important monasteries called Debre Libanos in Ethiopia, one in Tegray and the other in Shewa. See Prouty and Rosenfeld 1981, 46. The text under review was the property of the monastery of the Shewa region, which is considered one of the most famous monasteries in Ethiopia.

the regulation of the trade in cultural objects by calling on nations to establish a licensing system for the export of cultural objects; to protect cultural objects from looting, theft, and illegal export; and to assist each other in recovering illegally exported cultural objects. However, the date of 1970 by itself bears no legal significance. Rather, each nation determines whether and when to ratify an international convention. (364)

The 1970 Convention is useful for professional societies, museum leaders, educational institutions, and other organizations that deal with ethical questions associated with using foreign antiquities (Cuno 2008). However, legal scholar Patty Gerstenblith (2013, 372) claims that the agreement on the use of the 1970 standard "has begun to erode," and there are no clear answers to questions related to the ownership of rare antiquities.

This may, in part, explain why, as much as Haile and I were both surprised, fascinated, and even stunned by the discrepancy in the ownership records of the document, we focused more on the content of my research as opposed to the larger ethical questions related to the provenance of the document. At that time, my trips to HUSD and to HMML were part of a larger research project concerned with exploring how the history, culture, and religious heritage of ancient Ethiopia may be utilized for the study of the New Testament (Byron 2006b). Thus, given this research agenda and focus, Haile referred me to historical writings and other sources that would inform my understanding of this text and illuminate some of the theoretical and methodological challenges that revolve around the use of Ethiopic manuscripts.

One such challenge is the fact that most of the surviving documents from Ethiopia are from the thirteenth-fourteenth centuries or later, a time frame that is considered too late for the analysis of the early Christian world of the first through sixth centuries. In addition, most Ethiopic documents were destroyed either during fires, wars, or other consequences resulting from the reign of the Islamic ruler Gragn during the sixteenth century.[11] So, although we have a vast array of Ethiopic literature, the most significant being the book of Enoch (which survives in its entirety in the Ethiopic version), this material is usually not included in

---

11. Gragn, also known as Ahmad ibn-Ibrahim al-Ghazi, is the leader of the Islamic forces that defeated Christians during a series of revolts from 1527–1560 (see Prouty and Rosenfeld 1981, 100–102).

surveys of the New Testament in the same way as more traditional Greek and Latin sources.

Coupled with this limitation of the late date of the sources is the overall consensus among scholars of antiquity that most of the extant information about ancient Ethiopians is legendary and thus unreliable for critical historical or exegetical purposes. Thus, the story of the two Syrians Frumentius and Aedesius is cited as the chief text supporting the arrival of Christianity in Axum during the fourth century CE, yet it is usually relegated to the category of *legend* when it comes to assessing its reliability for interpretive purposes (Rufinus, *Hist.* 1.9).

Both of these methodological challenges point to the ideological bias that runs implicit in traditional scholarship dealing with ancient Ethiopia. For example, the editor of a sourcebook on Kush and Axum[12] excludes what he calls the "native literary tradition concerning Axum" because of the "heavy ideological burden" of this material associated with the Solomonic dynasty and the Queen of Sheba (Burstein 2009, 15). Thus, sources such as (1) Axumite royal inscriptions and coins, (2) references to Axum in ancient classical and Christian literature (mostly references by Greek and Latin writers), (3) European travelers' reports, and (4) modern archaeology are included (Burstein 2009, 15), while actual writings from the Ethiopic tradition are ignored in this sourcebook.

In addition to seeking to understand these methodological challenges related to Ethiopic sources, Haile suggested that I consult the English translation of the *Gadla Hawaryat*, or Contendings of the Apostles, which includes the histories, lives, preaching activities, and martyrdoms of the apostles. This volume contains an English translation of the Ethiopic text published by E. A. Wallis Budge (1899, 1901) based on two manuscripts—Oriental 678 (A) and Oriental 683 (B)—that are housed at the British Museum in London.[13] According to Budge (1899, vi), the older manuscript (Oriental 678) was probably written in the fifteenth century, and the later manuscript (Oriental 683) most likely belongs to the first half of the seventeenth century. The British Museum acquired these texts after the British Army removed them from the Church of Madhane Alam in

---

12. Kush and Axum are precursors in ancient writings to what today is known as "Ethiopia."

13. In this volume, Budge includes a translation of the *Gadle Pawlos* or the Acts of Paul, based on the seventeenth-century manuscript—Oriental 683 (1899:436–599; 1901:435–582).

Magdala in 1868 after defeating Ethiopian troops during the reign of King Tewodros II (r. 1855–1868) (Budge 1899, v).

Richard Pankhurst, a prominent Ethiopian historian, describes the British occupation of Magdala as follows:

> The British troops then looted the capital, and carried off from the Church of Madhane Alam, and elsewhere, well over three hundred manuscripts. These were deposited in the British Museum and several other libraries in Britain, and proved of seminal importance to European scholarship on Ethiopia. (1993, 28)

It is a well-documented fact that museums and libraries across Europe and in the United States are filled with manuscripts and other cultural artifacts from African countries, namely, Egypt and Ethiopia (Rodney 1974, C. Williams 1987). Yet, debates are still ensuing among scholars, museum directors, and other leaders dealing with antiquities as to how best to deal with the ethical imperatives associated with researching unprovenanced (Cuno 2008 and 2009) and provenanced material as in the example from Magdala mentioned above.

Although, as far as we can determine, Tweed was not aware of the implications of his acquisitions as it pertains to debates regarding provenance, nor was he on a campaign to loot Ethiopic manuscripts as described in the case of the British Army above, the Acts of Paul and Acts of Serabamon manuscript (now referred to as Tweed MS150) is one example of an item in a United States collection that does not rightfully belong in this country. Thus, given my commitments as a womanist biblical critic (which I discuss more fully in the next section) and the fact that since my initial research with the Tweed Collection I have now relocated to HUSD and serve as the Associate Dean for Academic Affairs, facilitating the return of the manuscript to the Debre Libanos Monastery, its rightful home, became a new administrative and research imperative.

Back in 2006, when I first encountered the Acts of Paul and Acts of Serabamon Ethiopic manuscript, I was enthralled with how such a valuable document and such a full collection of material was tucked away at HUSD, for the most part off the beaten path of scholarly engagement. Indeed, my research outcomes revolved around making these sources *accessible* to scholars, students, and other interested researchers. I likewise emphasized the Axumite Empire of the ancient Ethiopians, which was thriving alongside the Roman Empire, and theorized about how the sources and insights from this empire might be used to expand the geographical and canonical boundaries of early Christianity (2009). With this broader orientation to the ancient world(s) of the early Christians, I was equipped more fully to introduce my students to New Testament writings by including lectures, maps, and source material about the ancient Ethiopians. Indeed, accessing the Tweed Collection opened a brand new interpretive world that had previously eluded my hermeneutical framework.

Yet there is now much more to this story.

A Womanist Biblical Ethic of (Re)Interpretation: Transgressing Canonical Boundaries and Overcoming Academic Amnesia

> A womanist ... is committed to survival and wholeness of entire people, male and female. Not a separatist, except periodically, for health. (Walker 1983, xi)

In what she considers her "prolegomena" or "introductory observations" about womanist theology written in 1987, Delores S. Williams outlines the meaning of womanist and suggests that "many sources—biblical, theological, ecclesiastical, social, anthropological, economic, and material from *other religious traditions* [emphasis mine]—will inform the development of this theology" (180). Williams was one of the first theologians to articulate the principal concerns and elements that inform Christian womanist theological methodology, carefully delineating how it differs from black theology and feminist theology. Other theologians and ethicists, such as Jacquelyn Grant, Katie Cannon, Emilie Townes, and Kelly Brown Douglas continued to develop theoretical frameworks, sources, and methods that give rise to womanist theology and ethics. Overwhelmingly, the focus is on the experiences of black women, and in particular their social, religious, and cultural experience (D. Williams 1987, 180). Thus, female slave narratives, autobiographies, testimonies by black church women, and other literature capturing the everyday-lives of black women (especially those who are impoverished and disenfranchised) are authoritative sources for womanist theologians. As valuable as these sources are for unearthing the marginalized experiences of black women, anthropologist and theologian Linda E. Thomas raises a challenge to this privileging of literary sources among womanist scholars:

> The overwhelming majority of contemporary womanist religious scholars rely primarily on written texts, such as, fiction, biography, and autobiography. I agree with the value of these crucial sources and methodological approaches; however, I urge that we examine further our procedural tools of analysis. Not only should womanist scholars include historical texts and literature in our theological constructs and reconstruction of knowledge, but we should also embrace a research process which engages poor black women who are living human documents. (Thomas 1998–1999, 496)

Thomas argues for an ethnographic methodology that reveals and gives voice to women on the edges of society.

Indeed these "living human documents" are of importance for womanist theologians. However, we would be remiss if we overlook the contributions of black women bibliophiles and collectors, and other women who have been on the forefront of creating political and educational opportunities and institutions. Black women bibliophiles, such as Dorothy Porter Wesley and Mayme Clayton, mentioned at the beginning of this essay have accumulated and curated source documents that facilitate research on different aspects of black women's lives—not just *poor* black women. To borrow a phrase from Cheryl Townsend Gilkes, "if it wasn't for the(se) women," we would not have access to the variegated realities of black women (and men) who represent the vast educational experiences, sociopolitical backgrounds, and economic and class distinctions of blacks in the United States, Caribbean, and other parts of the Africana diaspora. Their activism and commitments to the survival and wholeness of black people included the preservation of black artifacts, literature, and culture for generations to come.

New Testament biblical critic Clarice J. Martin (1999, 656), in her definition of womanist biblical interpretation in the *Dictionary of Biblical Interpretation*, discusses how "the Bible remains for a significant number of African American women and men the primary (though not exclusive) conduit of the community's understanding of God's being and acts—the church's book—and a plumb line for the life and practice of the Christian community."[14] She discusses how "the Bible has functioned as a historic, life-giving, and empowering resource for both African Americans and the larger human community," yet she also notes how African Americans

---

14. Here Martin paraphrases Evans 1992, 33.

"acknowledge the problematics of the Bible as a pervasively androcentric, patriarchal text." Thus womanist biblical scholars, according to Martin, "impart a hermeneutic of suspicion to the interpretative task."[15]

Renita Weems makes a similar observation in her essay "Reading *Her* Way through the Struggle":

> After all, the Bible (rather, its contents) has not been presented to African American women as one of a number of books available to her to read or not read as she pleases. For African American (Protestant) women, the Bible has been the *only* book passed down from her ancestors, and it has been presented to her as *the* medium for experiencing and knowing the will of the Christian God. (1991, 63)

While this is largely true, what would it look like if we privileged the activism of women such as Porter Wesley and Clayton, the oral traditions of poor women, and the living human documents that represent the legacy and traditions of Ethiopians, including Ethiopian women who are mentioned in monastic writings and who are living in monastic communities today? Could these living sources—past and present—expand our canon beyond the sixty-six books of the Protestant Bible?

This emphasis on the women themselves as living sources resonates most with my goal of moving beyond canonical sources for interpreting the sacred texts and cultures that are reflected in the New Testament. This also resonates with scholarship that highlights oral manifestations of the sacred and the notion of "theorizing Scriptures" that is now developing among some biblical critics and scholars of religion (e.g., Wimbush 2008; Love 2012; Darden 2015).

For example, in *Divining the Self: A Study in Yoruba Myth and Human Consciousness*, Velma E. Love (2012) examines the unwritten scriptures, known as the Odu,[16] of the Yoruba tradition. She takes up the challenge of determining what it means for the scholar of religion to study scripture as both text and performance by examining African American engagements with Yoruba scriptures (5). In short, she looks at the performative role of

---

15. For more on this "hermeneutic of suspicion," see Schüssler Fiorenza, 1984.
16. The term *Odu* refers to the entire living scripture, which comprises 256 individual *odu*s, or divinatory signs. Each of the 256 *odu*s is said to have an infinite number of *ese*, i.e., verses, stories, and proverbs that may be drawn upon by the diviner when consulting with a client (Love 2012, 22).

the Odu and uses the term *scriptures* to refer to the active engagement of an oral corpus of material deemed to have a certain authority and relevance for assessing, interpreting, and shaping human behavior and activity (20).

Love's research exposes how important it is to include other sources of authority when it comes to interpreting sacred texts. This is a theoretical framework useful for overcoming the ideological biases mentioned earlier that exclude Ethiopic source material that is deemed late and legendary and thus beyond the acceptable purview for New Testament studies. By shifting the locus of authority, this material would be taken seriously as a source for expanding the early Christian milieu for interpretation. Furthermore, sources in the Tweed Collection, such as some of the healing scrolls, psalms, or theological treatises, would become accessible as source material, not only for biblical interpreters, but also for scholars in other disciplines such as medicine, literature, sacred music, et cetera. In addition, the language itself, Ge'ez, would need to be offered alongside Greek, Hebrew, and Aramaic in theological schools. Clearly, this would open a path for gaining a different understanding of the world of the early Christians, and it would likewise expand the curricular offerings for students living in an ethnically diverse, multireligious, global world (Byron 2012).

Expanding the biblical canon in the Africana experience is not new. However, when it comes to including other (extrabiblical) sources among biblical scholars and in the church, we are only now beginning to embrace this methodological trajectory. Feminist biblical critic Denise Kimber Buell in her essay "Canons Unbound" suggests that

> nonbiblical texts, traditions, and wo/men's experiences [are] to be understood as possible sites for divine revelation, liberating ethics, and wisdom. A few feminist biblical interpreters have called for a transformation of feminist New Testament studies that decenters the status of the New Testament texts by approaching *all* scriptures of the world as sites of potentially liberating knowledge. (2014, 296)

Buell is not alone in this assessment as scholars such as Deirdre Good (2012) and Karen King (2003) have identified important insights that can be gained when extracanonical sources are put in conversation with biblical material. Good (2012, 633–39) identifies women's roles and experiences as ascetics, martyrs, widows, deacons, prophets and scholars, which offers a "different portrait of women's leadership, pastoral capacities, scholarly activities, and endurance of religious persecution."[17] King's (2003, 3) important work on the Gospel of Mary provides "a radical interpretation of Jesus' teachings as a path to inner spiritual knowledge" and "presents the most straightforward and convincing argument in any early Christian writing for the legitimacy of women's leadership." In one section of the text, Mary is in the midst of a postresurrection experience with the Savior and other disciples, and, at the invitation of Peter, she clarifies for the disciples the message they had received:

> Peter said to Mary, "Sister, we know that the Savior loved you more than all other women. Tell us the words of the Savior that you remember, the things which you know that we don't because we haven't heard them." Mary responded, "I will teach you about what is hidden from you." And she began to speak these words to them. (Gos. Mary 6; King 2003, 15)

Overall, it is the exclusion of such stories about women, their writings, and their experiences that lead to what Katie Cannon calls "structured academic amnesia."

Cannon (2006, 19–20) describes this phenomenon while recounting her personal story of physical assault by a white man in a New York City hotel on her way to an ecclesiastical gathering of Presbyterian women of color. She discusses how several years later, while being interviewed for an article dealing with clergywomen, Cannon told a *Wall Street Journal* reporter about the incident. By that time, however, the hotel where the incident took place no longer existed, and the reporter after not being able to fact-check the story sufficiently was told by her boss that Cannon's story was "no longer plausible because there was no evidence in recent memory" to substantiate that the hotel in fact *ever* existed. Cannon summarizes this troubling encounter by saying, "it is as if this true Womanist story never happened" (20–21). Her reflections offer a theoretical lynchpin or hermeneutical wedge for exposing the methodological challenges associated with claims that presuppose "reliable," "objective," or "authentic" sources are the only legitimate material for scholarly interpretation. Thus, sources considered "late," "legendary," "subjective," "ideologically burdened," or

---

17. She examines the Nag-Hammadi Library, in particular the Gospel of Mary, Valentinus and Ptolemy's *Letter to Flora*, the Apocryphal Acts of the Apostles, Philo's *Contemplative Life*, the Martyrdom of Saints Perpetua and Felicitas, etc.

representative of unrecognizable expressions of "scripturalizing" are relegated to the "sea of forgetfulness."

This structured academic amnesia is relentless and has many consequences, which ultimately result in a set of theoretical frameworks that preclude serious engagement of the experiences of black women (especially Ethiopian women in early Christian writings) and the texts and traditions of the vast Africana sacred experiences. Cannon raises questions about the structured and controlled nature of academic discourses that prescribe illusive objectivity as a theoretical norm. Moreover, this academic amnesia also erases the experiences of the interpreters who bring a different set of assumptions and principles informed by the experiences of black women. Cannon takes a bold stand and invites womanist critics and others who cast their lot with us to assess what it might mean to "re-member and re-present in our authentic interest" (21). Indeed, I extend her challenge to include what it might mean to (re)interpret early Christian writings with my own authentic experience in mind.

Manuscript Returned: Provenance [Still] Matters

Within months after arriving at HUSD in 2012 to take on a new administrative role at the school, I became aware of the digital catalogue that was now in the process of being completed.[18] During the digitizing process, Ted Erho, a cataloguer and Research Fellow at HMML, identified a discrepancy in the provenance of one of the manuscripts,[19] which was later labeled Tweed MS150. This is the same document, the Acts of Paul and the Acts of Serabamon, I had previously called to the attention of Haile at HMML and had shared with dozens of audiences in lectures and other discussions disseminating the outcomes of my research (Byron 2006b; 2015). At this point my HUSD colleague Alice Ogden Bellis began to press officials at the university to take action in exploring viable options for returning the text to Ethiopia.

As well-intentioned as her efforts were, many external parties began to encroach upon the process to the point where it was virtually impossible to resolve the best way to move forward. Eventually I intervened, and

---

18. See Melaku et al. n.d. Alice Ogden Bellis of HUSD and Steve Delamarter of George Fox University made digital images of the manuscripts in the Tweed Collection during the summer 2012.

19. Private conversation with Ted Erho, August 2015.

along with the assistance of leaders of the Ethiopian Orthodox Church and other scholars and leaders in the Ethiopian and academic community engaged with the retrieval of Ethiopic manuscripts,[20] we at HUSD were able to sort through the various complexities and work out a plan for the return of the manuscript (Tweed MS150) to the Debre Libanos Monastery.

Throughout this process, which extended for nearly three years, I learned a great deal about the ethics of scholarship that has informed what I can now identify as a womanist biblical ethic of (re)interpretation. As mentioned earlier, this hermeneutical framework transgresses canonical boundaries and exposes structured academic amnesia. Indeed, the seeds that were planted during my early phases of research on the Tweed Collection and Tweed MS150 were coming to fruition in this new evolution of scholarly-leadership.

By January 2016, a small delegation from HUSD returned Tweed MS150 to Ethiopia (see Surratt 2016).[21] Given the fact that there was no legal mandate to return the manuscript, we sought to do so because of the ethical imperative that warrants such a witness of goodwill and relationship-building in the face of "restitutionary injustices" and other legal strongholds that hinder the return of sacred artifacts (Gerstenblith 2013, 372). In our return of the manuscript, we were not only concerned with correcting the provenance discrepancy by getting the document back to its rightful home, but we were also intent on honoring the rich tradition of the Ethiopian Orthodox Church and the enduring legacy of the Debre Libanos Monastery. Moreover, the opportunity to be in partnership with the monks and the wider community of the Debre Libanos Monastery far-exceeded our loss of Tweed MS150 and the tangible act of returning the document. We established a historical bond that will extend in perpetuity through the memory of the elaborate ceremony and the symbolic plaque

---

20. The number of colleagues who contributed to this effort is exhaustive. I am greatly indebted to Memher Zebene Lemma, double alumnus of HUSD and local priest of the Debre Genat Medhane Alem Ethiopian Orthodox (Tawahedo) Church, who worked tirelessly and generously with me and Bellis in this effort. In addition, Dr. Getatchew Haile, Ato Kidane Alemeheyu, and Dr. Steve Delamarter were instrumental in offering letters and other forms of assistance.

21. The School of Divinity delegation included: Alton B. Pollard III (Dean), Gay L. Byron (Associate Dean), Alice Ogden Bellis (Professor of Hebrew Bible/Old Testament), Zebene Lemma (alumnus), and Lawrence R. Rodgers (student); Blain Zerihun (staff) provided administrative support throughout the process and accompanied the delegation to the monastery on January 11, 2016.

that was given to the monks and included in the museum associated with the monastery.

Womanist scholars are committed, following Alice Walker's (1983, xi) teaching, to the "survival and wholeness²² of entire people, male and female. Not a separatist." Thus, my involvement in the return of the manuscript was always focused on this presupposition. In other words, it "took the whole village" to bring about the restitution of this artifact. What looked like a fleeting, serendipitous discovery almost ten years ago has now evolved into a full story that is ready to be told. Indeed, this is a case where this true womanist story *did* happen (Cannon 2016, *pace* Banks 2016).

Conclusion

Black collectors and their collections provide an invaluable trove of source material for biblical interpreters, in general, and womanist biblical interpreters in particular. These extracanonical sources help interpreters recover muted voices and archival information related to the Africana experience. In particular, the Tweed Collection calls attention to an overlooked trajectory of early Christianity. By honoring the tradition of black bibliophiles and collectors, womanist biblical critics have access to a whole new set of resources that illuminate the ethical mandates inherent in the interpretive process.

Beyond the privileging of the Bible and other literary sources (especially those of poor and marginalized black women), this essay demonstrates how womanist biblical critics may also gain valuable source material from women who are political leaders, educators, and even bibliophiles and collectors, such as Dorothy Porter Wesley and Mayme Clayton. In this vein, it is imperative that the experiences of women like Porter Wesley and Clayton and the sources they have assembled become accessible to biblical interpreters—not so much because of their struggles, but rather because of their role and authority as curators and producers of knowledge.

I am indebted to black bibliophiles and collectors like the ones discussed throughout this essay. They have enabled me to develop a womanist

---

22. See St. Clair (2006) for a womanist ethic of wholeness. My understanding of wholeness extends beyond biblical resources and embraces a wide range of sacred texts.

biblical ethic of (re)interpretation that includes living sources, creative collaboration, critical inquiry, and a quest for survival and wholeness of entire people throughout the globe. Their activism, passion, and commitment empowered me to persevere in my own interpretive commitments related to Ethiopic sources, especially those in the Tweed Collection. Womanist biblical critics must claim the ethical priorities and presuppositions that undergird their scholarly endeavors and offer (re)interpretations of sacred texts that transgress canonical boundaries and dismantle structured academic amnesia.

Works Cited

Amsalu Tefera. 2013. "Gädlä Särabamon: The Case of the Ethiopic Version." Paper presented during a workshop, EMML@40: The Life and Legacy of the Ethiopian Manuscript Microfilm Library. Organized by the Hill Museum & Manuscript Library, Saint John's University, Collegeville, MN, July 25–26, 2013. https://alinsuciu.com/2014/01/02/guest-post-amsalu-tefera-sarabamon-of-nikou-in-ethiopian-literature/.

André Reynolds Tweed Collection of Ethiopian Sacred Artifacts. n.d. Tweed Pamphlet. Howard University School of Divinity.

ASOR Board of Trustees. 2015. "Policy on Professional Conduct." ASOR. http://tinyurl.com/SBL0688q1.

Banks, Adelle. 2016. "Howard Divinity School Returns Sacred Ethiopian Manuscript to Orthodox Monastery." Religion News Service. http://tinyurl.com/SBL0688p1.

Beinecke Staff. 2013. *Guide to the Dorothy Porter Wesley Papers.* JWJ MSS 93. Beinecke Rare Book and Manuscript Library, Yale University, New Haven, CT.

Budge, E. A. Wallis. 1899, 1901. *Contendings of the Apostles (Mashafa Gadla Hawaryat).* 2 vols. Amsterdam: APA-Philo Press.

Buell, Denise Kimber. 2014. "Canons Unbound." Pages 293–306 in *Feminist Biblical Studies in the Twentieth Century: Scholarship and Movement.* Edited by Elisabeth Schüssler Fiorenza. Atlanta: Society of Biblical Literature.

Burstein, Stanley, ed. 2009. *Ancient African Civilizations: Kush and Axum.* Princeton: Wiener.

Byron, Gay L. 2002. *Symbolic Blackness and Ethnic Difference in Early Christian Literature.* New York: Routledge.

———. 2006a. "Interview Notes with Dr. Cain Hope Felder." Washington, DC: Howard University School of Divinity.

———. 2006b. "Utilizing the Legacy of Ancient Ethiopians and Ethiopia for the Study of the New Testament and Christian Origins: A Report of Travel, Research, and Collaboration." Report submitted to the Association of Theological Schools. Luce Fellows Program. Pittsburgh, PA.

———. 2006–2007. "Manuscripts, Meanings, and (Re)Membering: Ethiopian Women in Early Christianity." *JRT* 83-99.

———. 2007. "Uncovering the Origins of Christianity in Ancient Ethiopia: A Report of Travel and Research." *The Presbyterian Outlook*:13–14.

———. 2009. "Ancient Ethiopia and the New Testament: Ethnic (Con)texts and Racialized (Sub)texts." Pages 161–19 in *They Were All Gathered Together in One Place: Toward Minority Biblical Criticism*. Edited by Fernando Segovia, Randall Bailey, and Benny Liew. SemeiaSt 57. Atlanta: Society of Biblical Literature, 2009.

———. 2012. "Race, Ethnicity, and the Bible: Pedagogical Challenges and Curricular Opportunities." *TTR* 15:105–24.

———. 2015. "An Ethiopic Version of the Acts of Paul." Paper presented at the Nineteenth International Conference of Ethiopian Studies. Warsaw, Poland. 24–28 August 2015.

Cannon, Katie G. 2006. "Structured Academic Amnesia: As If This True Womanist Story Never Happened." Pages 19–28 in *Deeper Shades of Purple: Womanism in Religion and Society*. Edited by Stacey M. Floyd-Thomas. New York: New York University Press.

Copage, Eric V. February 2008. "The Race to Save Black History." *Ebony Magazine*. 117–22.

Cuno, James, ed. 2008. *Who Owns Antiquity: Museums and the Battle over Our Ancient Heritage*. Princeton: Princeton University Press.

———. 2009. *Whose Culture? The Promise of Museums and the Debate over Antiquities*. Princeton: Princeton University Press.

Darden, Lynne St. Clair. 2015. *Scripturalizing Revelation: An African American-Postcolonial Reading of Empire*. Atlanta: SBL Press.

Easter, Eric, D. Michael Cheers, and Dudley M. Brooks, eds. 1992. *Songs of My People: African Americans, a Self-Portrait*. Introduction by Gordon Parks. Boston: Little, Brown.

Ethiopian Sacred Artifacts from the Dr. André Tweed Collection. 1990. Organized by the California Afro-American Museum; Lizzetta LeFalle-Collins, Curator of Visual Arts. Los Angeles: California Afro-American Museum.

Evans, James H., Jr. 1992. *We Have Been Believers: An African American Systematic Theology.* Minneapolis: Fortress.

"Gallery of Religious Art." n.d. Howard University School of Divinity. http://tinyurl.com/SBL0688t1.

Gerstenblith, Patty. 2013. "The Meaning of 1970 for the Acquisition of Archaeological Objects." *JFA* 38:364–73.

Good, Deirdre. 2012. "Beyond the Canon." Pages 633–39 in *Women's Bible Commentary.* Edited by Carol A. Newsom, Sharon H. Ringe, and Jacqueline E. Lapsley. 3rd ed. Twentieth-Anniversary ed. Louisville: Westminster John Knox.

Haile, Getatchew. 1993. "Ethiopic Literature." Pages 47–56 in *African Zion: The Sacred Art of Ethiopia.* Edited by Roderick Grierson. New Haven: Yale University Press.

Hermesch, Alan. 1994. *Ethiopian Artifacts Donated to Divinity School; Dedication Ceremonies to Be Held.* Tweed Press Release. Howard University. 22 February.

Isaac, Ephraim. 1990. "Sacred Literature and Objects of the Ethiopian Church." Pages 8–18 in *Ethiopian Sacred Artifacts from the André Tweed Collection.* Los Angeles: California Afro-American Museum.

King, Karen L. 2003. *The Gospel of Mary of Magdala: Jesus and the First Woman Apostle.* Santa Rosa, CA: Polebridge.

Love, Velma E. 2012. *Divining the Self: A Study in Yoruba Myth and Human Consciousness.* University Park, PA: Pennsylvania State University Press.

Martin, Clarice J. 1999. "Womanist Biblical Interpretation." *DBI* 2:655–58.

Melaku Terafe, Stephen Delamarter, Jeremy Brown, and Alice Ogden Bellis, eds. n.d. *Ethiopic Manuscript Imaging Project (EMIP).* Catalogue of the André Tweed Collection of Sacred Ethiopian Artifacts and Manuscripts. Howard University School of Divinity, Washington, DC. http://tinyurl.com/SBL0688r1.

Pankhurst, Richard. 1993. "Ethiopia Revealed: Merchants, Travelers, and Scholars." Pages 19–31 in *African Zion: The Sacred Art of Ethiopia.* Edited by Roderick Grierson. Fort Worth: InterCultura.

Prouty, Chris, and Eugene Rosenfeld. 1981. *Historical Dictionary of Ethiopia.* Metuchen: Scarecrow Press.

Rich, Wilbur C., and Roberta Hughes Wright. 1999. *The Wright Man: A Biography of Charles H. Wright, M.D.* Southfield, MI: Charro Books.

Rodney, Walter. 1974. *How Europe Underdeveloped Africa.* Washington, DC: Howard University Press.

Schultz, Rima Lunin, and Adele Hast, eds. 2001. *Women Building Chicago 1790–1990: A Biographical Dictionary*. Bloomington: Indiana University Press.

Schüssler Fiorenza, Elisabeth. 1984. *Bread Not Stone: The Challenge of Feminist Biblical Interpretation*. Boston: Beacon.

Sims-Wood, Janet. 2014. *Dorothy Porter Wesley at Howard University: Building a Legacy of Black History*. Charleston: History Press.

Sinnette, Elinor Des Verney, W. Paul Coates, and Thomas C. Battle, eds. 1990. *Black Bibliophiles and Collectors: Preservers of Black History*. Washington, DC: Howard University Press.

Society of Biblical Literature Council. 2016. "SBL Policy on Scholarly Presentation and Publication of Ancient Artifacts. https://www.sbl-site.org/assets/pdfs/SBL-Artifacts-Policy_20160903.pdf.

St. Clair, Raquel. 2006. "Womanist Biblical Interpretation." Pages 54–62 in *True to Our Native Land: An African American New Testament Commentary*. Edited by Brian K. Blount, Cain Hope Felder, Clarice J. Martin, and Emerson B. Powery. Minneapolis: Fortress.

Surratt, Brittany A. B. 2016. *Howard University School of Divinity Delegation Embarks on Historic Ethiopian Journey to Return Sacred Manuscript*. Tweed Press Release. Howard University. 11 January. http://tinyurl.com/SBL0688s1.

Tamrat, Taddasse. 1972. *Church and State in Ethiopia (1270–1527)*. Oxford: Oxford University Press.

———. 1975. *From the Early Times to the End of the Zagwe Dynasty c. 1270 A.D.* Vol. 1 of *The Dictionary of Ethiopian Biography*. Edited by Belaynesh Michael, S. Chojnacki, and Richard Pankhurst. Addis Ababa: Institute of Ethiopian Studies.

Thomas, Linda E. 1998–1999. "Womanist Theology, Epistemology, and a New Anthropological Paradigm." *Cross Currents* 48:488–99.

Walker, Alice. 1983. *In Search of Our Mothers' Gardens*. New York: Harcourt Brace Jovanovich.

Ware, Frederick L. 2016. *African American Theology: An Introduction*. Louisville: Westminster John Knox.

Weems, Renita J. 1991. "Reading Her Way through the Struggle: African American Women and the Bible." Pages 57–77 in *Stony the Road We Trod: African American Biblical Interpretation*. Edited by Cain Hope Felder. Minneapolis: Fortress.

Williams, Chancellor. 1987. *The Destruction of Black Civilization*. Chicago: Third World Press.

Williams, Delores S. 1987. "Womanist Theology: Black Women's Voices." *Christianity and Crisis* 47:66–70.

Wimbush, Vincent L., ed. 2008. *Theorizing Scriptures: New Critical Orientations to a Cultural Phenomenon*. New Brunswick: Rutgers University Press.

Flowing from Breast to Breast: An Examination of Dis/placed Motherhood in African American and Indian Wet Nurses

Sharon Jacob and Jennifer T. Kaalund

> Pharaoh's daughter said to her, "Take this child and nurse it for me, and I will give you your wages." So the woman took the child and nursed it. (Exod 2:9)

Motherhood disassociated from the womb creates a space for women who perform an unorthodox motherhood and rewrites the script of maternal love through their displaced bodies. In her book *Wet Nursing*, Valerie Fildes (1988, 1) writes: "Social, political, and religious factors played an important role in determining the incidence and extent of professional breastfeeding in different societies throughout history." As the epigraph attests, across space and time, black and brown women's bodies have been employed as wet nurses. In her article "Diasporas Old and New: Women in the Transnational World," Gayatri Chakravorty Spivak (1997, 92) notes that "every rupture is also a repetition. The only significant difference is the use, abuse, participation and role of women." The separation of a mother from her child in order for her to nurse a child that is not her own is a rupture, and this rupture elucidates the ways in which women's bodies have been used and abused in sustaining imperial powers—old and new. Women's bodies played an important role in the nurture of empire in the contexts of African American slavery and the British colonization of India.[1]

---

1. Throughout this essay we will use the term *empire* similar to Michael Hardt and Antonio Negri's (2000, xiv–xv) description of a system that wields "enormous powers of oppression and destruction" that is "characterized by its lack of boundaries." However, we suggest that empire "timeless and omnipresent" contains both older forms of

The colored breasts of wet nurses employed to service the imperial powers of their time fetishized into sacred objects, become sites of desire as well as derision. However, these milk mothers similar in their tasks of sustenance and nurture still differ in their historical time of existence and the power they wield within their imperial contexts, as one is a mother enslaved by the empire, the other is a mother who enslaves herself for the empire. At the same time, these colored breasts servicing the empire and peeking through the textual pages of history not only bears witness to the exploitation of women of color but also exposes moments of subversion that often manage to slip through the powerful grip of the empire.

This essay weaves together stories of women of color; though distinctive in terms of their personal circumstances, historical reality, and social contexts, they reveal a stark and disturbing connection between these milk mothers that one cannot ignore. That is, despite the ways that empire attempts to reduce these women's worth to their ability to produce and reproduce, it is the same life-giving ability contained in these women's bodies that defies portraying them as simply victims of their circumstances. Instead, their narratives expound the ways in which mothers acknowledge their power, assert their autonomy, and resist imperial power. The connection between these milk mothers extends to the sacred texts from our own religious traditions. The woman clothed in the sun in Rev 12 and the Goddess Kali, similar to the African American wet nurse and the *ayah/amah*,[2] are maternal figures whose bodies are life giving and life sustaining as well as threatening. Excess love flowing through the fetishized breasts of wet nurses creates a new way for us to read the mother goddesses in both the Christian and Hindu tradition.

Weaving together the stories of these wet nurses reveal not only their connections, but also the dissonance between them. We highlight that while the stories of both these historical maternal figures are *similar* they

---

imperialisms, as well as newer forms of rule. Systems of oppression, therefore, transcend time and space. The colonized *bodies* of the African American and the Indian wet nurses are territorialized by empires and at the same time are deterritorialized as they represent commoditized bodies of women of color globally.

2. In colonial writings, the term *ayah* or *amah* are often used interchangeably and used to refer to Indian women who served as maternal figures to imperial infants from the British Raj. The category of *ayah/amah* was not only limited to wet nurses but also nannies. For the purpose of this paper, we will be focusing on the relationship between the *ayah/amah* and the colonial infant and the ways in which the bodies and the breasts of these women nurture and nourish the children belonging to the empire.

are not quite *the same* (Bhabha 1994, 122).[3] As such, this essay is not an attempt to essentialize the life experiences of mothers of color. Instead, we present each experience in its historical context as unique allowing them to speak for themselves. As a result, the tension is apparent and purposeful. There are rarely simple, straightforward problems or resolutions, as this essay makes apparent. Our aim is to amplify the voices of these women while at the same time acknowledging that their experiences are distinctive and irreducible. Concomitantly, telling the stories together is synergetic. Collectively the narratives of these milk mothers expose the destructive and persisting ways that imperial powers exploit colored women's bodies and how these mentalities are then inscribed into our religious texts and our cultural imaginations.

Womanist Approaches: Maternal Longings—Past, Present, and Future

This essay began as a conversation between two women. The conversation revolved around mothers, women's bodies, postcolonialism, and imperial powers. As two women who are also mothers—African American and Indian—we shared the stories of African American and Indian wet nurses and our stories, as well. The result is an essay that speaks to the solidarity and the strength of two mothers separated by time and history, yet connected in their oppression, their strength to love excessively, and their resilient ability to survive their exploitation that is embedded deeply in their race and gender. The stories of these mothers etched on their black and brown breasts remind us of our own maternal longings of our forgotten histories.

Examining the history of womanist thought, we are reminded that a womanist is "a woman who loves other women, sexually and/or nonsexually ... appreciates and prefers women's culture, women's emotional flexibility (values tears as natural counterbalance of laughter), and women's strength" (Walker 2005, 11). This definition offered by Alice Walker, the mother of womanism, instructs that womanist work brings women together. Womanist religious thought is not solely concerned with black female identity and the centering of our stories and voices (though this

---

3. We borrow this expression from Bhabha (1994, 122), who writes, "colonial mimicry is the desire for a reformed, recognizable Other. As a subject of difference that is almost the same, but not quite. Which is to say, that the discourse of mimicry is constructed around an ambivalence."

remains an important aspect); it also involves challenging the oppressive forces, such as empire, that oppose the well-being of our community. The African American and Indian wet nurses are part of a global community of women of color, marginalized by gender and race. We tell their stories together to underscore how the hegemonic ruling class seeks to regulate the bodies of women of color. At the same time, by bringing the stories of these women to the fore, we hope to create a community, a sisterhood where colored bodies narrate stories on their terms and stand united in their diversity against their oppressors.

Womanist work facilitates these conversations between women of color, boldly enabling us to transverse boundaries of race, ethnicity, time, and space. That is, a womanist hermeneutics is always already dialogical; it is contextual. It is story telling and truth sharing. Womanist hermeneutics enable us to reaffirm the significance of the lived experiences of African American and Indian wet nurses—a reality that is rooted in both race and gender.[4] The readings of their lives become texts that are read, interpreted, and centered. These texts are didactic, teaching us from spaces of marginalization, while speaking from places of imposed silences.[5] As texts, the lives of the wet nurses, these mothers to others, are then employed as a lens, a hermeneutical key, through which to read mothers in sacred texts.

It is imperative that we learn from the past, particularly as contemporary issues concerning the regulation of women's bodies persist. When interrogated along the lines of race, ethnicity, and geography the treatment of the bodies of women of color can often echo our troubled history. Our common desire to recognize the power of mothers, despite the terms upon which "mother" is defined resulted in this collaboration. Coleman (2013, 23) describes third wave womanist religious thought as "contradictory, ambiguous, multiple, hybrid, personal and political." These terms are descriptive of the hermeneutic employed in this essay. Reading the sacred

---

4. Delores Williams (1993, 185) notes that "womanist words and descriptions must be true to the reality they claim to represent—black women's lived experience in the everyday world." She argues that African American women need to develop their own terms to describe their experiences with oppression. Oppression that not only addresses black men oppressing black women, but white men and white women oppressing black women.

5. In her book *Introducing Womanist Theology*, Stephanie Y. Mitchem (2002, 47) drawing from a woman named Azana writes, "Azana's words are applicable to womanist theology with an imperative to begin with black women's lives as texts, celebrating and validating their own selves."

texts through the lens of the colored breasts highlights an approach that results in acknowledging the complexity of interpreting mothers in imperial contexts. Despite their circumstances, the power and tenacity of these women cannot be denied. Their narratives (historical and sacred) are poignant and worthy of interrogation as the struggle for the autonomy of the bodies of women of color persists.

The Black Breast: Sustaining the Land of the Free

The commodification of black women's bodies elucidates one of the ways in which empire displaces motherhood by using the body of a mother to sustain its existence. During American slavocracy, a black woman's greatest asset was considered to be her fecundity. Producers of life, (re)producing for the empire—black women were faced with the tragic reality that not only were their bodies not their own, but their children also belonged to another. While the separation of enslaved mothers from their children is well attested, African American wet nurses witnessed yet another kind of displacement of motherhood that took place during slavery.[6]

Wet nurses were women who were "chosen" or, more precisely, forced to nourish the babies of the slave owner; that is, they had to perpetuate the same empire that enslaved them, most often at the neglect of their own children. Historian Wilma A. Dunaway's (2003, 140) *The African American Family in Slavery and Emancipation* observes: "wet nursing required slave mothers to transfer to white offspring the nurturing and affection they should have been able to allocate to their own children." Not only was the misappropriation of their milk a travesty, but also the displacement of nurturing and affection created a conundrum for these mothers, whose autonomy over their own bodies was limited.

The work of a wet nurse should not be glamorized. Nursing is indeed work, physical labor, and, within the context of American slavocracy, a demonstration of another way the bodies of black women were used. Supplying the life-giving force necessary for the survival of her future owner, these women were forced to actively participate in the perpetuation of their and their children's enslavement. However, for an enslaved woman to

---

6. Frederick Douglass (1995, 14) recalls being separated from his mother soon after birth. In addition to describing her own grandmother as a cook and wet nurse, Harriett Jacob (2012) recounts numerous examples of mothers and their children being separated in her book, *Incidents in the Life of a Slave Girl*.

fulfill this unfathomable role, she had to be both human enough to supply the milk and yet superhuman in her abilities to continually produce. In her book *Laboring Women: Gender and Reproduction in the New World*, Jennifer Morgan argues:

> As slaveowners contemplated women's reproductive potential with greed and opportunism, they utilized both outrageous images and callously indifferent strategies to ultimately inscribe enslaved women as racially and culturally different while creating an economic and moral environment in which the appropriation of a woman's children as well as her childbearing potential became rational, and indeed, natural. (2004, 7)

Moreover, for a wet nurse, proximity necessitated differentiation. There was a constant need to assert a distinction between black and white, between the enslaved and the free. Forced into a position of surrogacy, wet nurses experienced the violent effects that proximity creates: in the house, embracing a future master, returning his gaze. How close is too close? What happens when one child has two mothers and another child has none?

For slaveholding men, black women were those "whose pain-free reproduction (at least to European men) indicated that they did not descend from Eve and who illustrated their proclivity for hard work through their ability to simultaneously till the soil and birth a child. Such imaginary women suggested an immutable difference between Africans and Europeans, a difference ultimately codified as race" (Morgan 2004, 8). Yet such a difference is undermined by her ability to serve as a nurse. Morgan continues, "the interplay between inherited beliefs about gender, race, and civility coalesced to shape slaveowners' implicit expectations that their wealth and, indeed, that of the entire colonial Empires, deprived from the reproductive potential of African women" (8). Yet, for the wet nurse, this "reproductive potential" is diminished, at least for her own children, as her milk temporarily satiates the empire. However, the empire's desires prove to be insatiable. Slave owners often forced black women to stop breastfeeding their own children early so that they could continue breeding, and slaveholding women were discouraged from breastfeeding for the same reasons, necessitating a certain subset of enslaved women to act as wet nurses. That is, both women needed to produce children. The need for the role of the black woman could be diminished, but it could not be denied. Without her, there could be no empire; her contributions extended beyond bodily reproduction.

To further solidify the distance between slaveholding men and enslaved women, more often than not, the enslaved women were viewed as the property of slaveholding women. The relationship between slaveholding women and enslaved women was particularly complex. Historian Elizabeth Fox-Genovese (1988, 140) observes: "The intimacy of mistress and slave encouraged conflict as well as affection. The lines of class and race gave mistresses a license to interpret any sign of independence as impudence, impertinence, obstinacy. The slaves, we must be sure, saw it differently. The shadow of the slave owner brooded over all." Indeed, the power wielded by slaveholding women was tempered by the power that the slaveholding men wielded over them; "gender ascribed white and black women to a common sphere within the household, even as class and race separated them" (142). Such distinctions were necessary to perpetuate the desire for more children of the empire and children for the empire. Enslaved women, well understanding the limits of the mistress's power, not surprisingly tested it.

Proximity gave way to various forms of resistance. Deborah Gray-White (1999, 79) writes of "a less overt form of resistance," one which "involved the use of poison and this suited women because they officiated as cooks and nurses on the plantation.... In 1769 a special issue of the *South Carolina Gazette* carried the story of an enslaved woman who had poisoned her master's infant child." The empire gave birth to various violent expressions. Gray-White highlights several forms of abuse that these enslaved women endured. She recounts the horrific death of a woman named Aunt Betty. She writes: "She had nursed her master through his infancy, lived to see him become a drunk, and then became his victim when, during one of his drunken rampages, he took his shotgun and killed her" (55). To be sure, in some cases wet nurses developed genuine affection for the children they nursed, and those feelings were at times reciprocated. However, what these violent narratives clearly demonstrate is the volatile nature of surrogate motherhood under this oppressive hegemonic system.

The wet nurse further illuminates the role that class, or socioeconomic status, plays in the displacement of motherhood. The wet nurse was the prized possession for those who could afford to possess one: according to John Vlach (2004, 101), "only 12 percent of slaveholders owned 20 or more slaves," and it is unlikely that those smaller plantations that made up the majority would have had wet nurses. This assertion is underscored by the relationship between wealthy whites and the image of the mammy.

According to Jessie Parkhurst, "many a Confederate soldiers was nursed by the 'mammies.'" She goes on to express:

> There was hardly a person of importance or one who belonged to the old aristocracy of the South who did not come under the influence of one of these slave women, and they were proud of the fact. One of the boasts of the "old gentlemen of the South" was that they were reared by a "Black Mammy," and they attributed certain of their good qualities to this influence. (1938, 369)

This boast demonstrated the arrogance of the wealthy few who viewed the surrogate mother as simply another possession. Although the significance of the role of these nurses could be acknowledged, her breast could nurture, her life could be fully devoted to them, and yet these so-called gentlemen could never come to see her as their equal.

The image of the wet nurse is often subsumed in the popularly portrayed figure of the black mammy. Gray-White (1999, 49) provides an outline of the mammy caricature: "She was a woman completely dedicated to the white family, especially to the children of that family. She served also as friend and advisor. She was, in short, surrogate mistress and mother." A wet nurse was not necessarily a mammy, nor was the mammy necessarily a wet nurse; nonetheless, the mammy was an *imaginary* figure created in the minds of those who most likely had never possessed one. On the one hand, black women were constructed as loose, immoral, and less than human beings (suprahuman), and on the other, they were asexual bastions of morality. The latter characterization was particularly the case when these women had intimate contact with slave owners. The identity of the black woman under American slavery is distorted and fractured. She is both/and and neither/nor at the same time. Class, gender, and race converge and diverge in the re/definition of motherhood in the context of American slavery, and religion directs the undercurrent that flows beneath the surface of it all.

Central to the maternal ideal epitomized in the figure of mammy was the characterization of these women as religious. Gray-White (1999, 59–60) recalls a fictionalized mammy character who is portrayed as "virtuous; her whole life, as the narrator puts it, had been 'a recommendation of the religion of the Bible.' Her conduct was so exemplary that the narrator concludes: 'I wish my chance in Heaven were half as good as hers.'" The whitewashed images of the black mammy construe her as a saint. The paradoxes multiply, once again, and we see that although enslaved women were considered not to be descendants of Eve (her capabilities made her superhuman), their enslavement was at the same time justified because they were considered descendants of the cursed Ham (Canaan). The body of the wet nurse contained life-giving properties and at the same time housed the cursed violent realities of slavery.

Similar to the black breast of the African American wet nurse that is desired and despised by the American Empire during the period of slavery, the brown breast of the Indian *ayah/amah* living under the British Empire is subjected to the same scrutiny. This next section while dealing with the historical reality of the Indian wet nurses living under the British Empire and drawing on the connections between the ambivalences of wet nursing under empires also illustrates the differences in social location, personal experiences, and race relationships within their respective empires.

The Brown Breast: Nourishing Mother India

The white body may have successfully and forcefully colonized, captured, and settled upon the brown and dusty body of India, but taming and controlling this maternal land remained an unattainable task for the British Empire. It comes as no surprise then that the temperamental nature of India affected the weakest and the most vulnerable subjects of the empire, that is, women and children.[7] Women who birthed children in the colonies were vulnerable to a variety of dangers from living in countries perceived to be backward. Indrani Sen illustrates:

> Colonial Constructions of India was that it was "no place for a woman." Indeed, the Anglo-Indian woman did suffer from certain specific problems

---

7. Margaret MacMillan (1988, 90), in her novel *Women of the Raj*, writes, "The fundamental and inescapable fact of life in India was probably the climate. The exiles came to feel that it was typical of the country in its variety and in its immense scale—the oppressive heat, the torrential rains, the clouds of dust. Indian storms were characteristically sudden and violent, blowing off roofs and bowling over those unlucky enough to be caught outside. Guidebooks made much of the dangers: India's weather was an enemy to European complexions, European energies, European habits." Ann Laura Stoler (2002, 73) points out, "Colonial conditions were associated with high infant mortality, such that "the life of a European child was nearly condemned in advance." Illnesses ranging from fragile nerves to debilitating fevers were thought to hit women and children hardest. See also Grall 1998, 65.

by virtue of being a woman in the colony. In addition to problems of colonial existence that she commonly shared with her male counterparts, the Anglo-Indian woman also suffered from specific gendered social stresses. These included physical hardships of the tropical climate, the danger of disease, the absence of meaningful social activities, the inevitable dislocations of the family and last but not the least, the frequent death of infant offspring. (2005, 32)

The precarious nature of the colonies meant that women and children of the British Raj needed protection and preservation, as the future of imperial power was at stake. As a result, the irrepressible maternal body that signified death, and destruction, had to be countered by another maternal figure whose body and breast signified life, one that could be easily tamed.

The *ayah* or the *amah* replenished the weak colonial body with her milk and her care pumping life back into the empire. Michael Hardt and Antonio Negri (2000, 144) write, "Power, or forces of social oppression, function by imposing binary structured and totalizing logics on social subjectivities, repressing their difference. These oppressive structures however, are never total, and differences are always in some way expressed." Slipping through totalizing narratives meant to describe and limit Mother India as the "life taker" and the *amah/ayah* as the "life giver" created space for a new form of motherhood in the colonies. The maternal bond shared between the *amah/ayah* and the colonizer was an ambivalent relationship that was born out of the excess, extravagance, the uncontrollability of India. Slipping through the binaries that sought to separate the colonizer from the colonized constructs a maternal figure that signifies life and death to the empire. Thus, it is in the excess Indian milk, the excess language, and the excess heat of India that the ambivalent love for the Other is signified and where the inability to appropriate this "surplus brownness" threatens to destabilize and dismantle the powers of the British Empire.

The Indian senses that sought to overwhelm the delicate white senses of the imperial British subject signify the excessiveness of India. In her monograph, *Women of the Raj*, Margaret MacMillan describes the first impressions of the British *memsahibs*[8] of India saying: "the first impressions the new arrivals had of India were almost always similar. The noise,

---

8. A *memsahib* is a white foreign woman of high social status living in India, especially the wife of a British official (*Merriam-Webster Dictionary*, "memsahib," s.v.).

the smells, the color—and the people in all their dazzling variety. Women's recollections of the initial encounter also reveal an undercurrent of panic. After the enclosed world of the ships, India was too big, too untidy, too crowded—in fact, too much India" (1988, 17). India was too much to handle, and the inability to control this maternal land caused much anxiety within the British Empire. In particular, the climate of India caused much concern. Ann Laura Stoler (2002, 72) writes, "Real and imagined concern over individual reproduction and racial survival contained and compromised white colonial women in concrete ways. Tropical climates were said to cause low fertility, prolonged amenorrhea, and permanent sterility. Belgian doctors held that 'the woman who goes to live in a tropical climate is often lost for the reproduction of the race.'"[9] The perception in the colonies was that the heat in the tropics caused not only miscarriages but was also responsible for infant mortality. MacMillan (1988, 55) notes, "The Indian climate, it was widely agreed, would damage children permanently if they were exposed to it for too long. A child kept in India, warned an eminent physician in 1872, 'will grow up slight, weedy, and delicate, over-precocious it may be, and with general feebleness.'" Colonial constructions of India were quite schizophrenic: while some physicians believed that the climate in India suited young children a great deal, others strongly encouraged European mothers to protect their young children from the Indian heat that had debilitating and devastating effects.[10]

At the same time, the threat that the Indian climate could affect the racial character of the British subject and corrupt and contaminate young minds was a real one. MacMillan (1988, 155) writes, "Nineteenth-century speculations about the effect of climate and environment on racial character made a profound impression on the British in India. Mothers made their children wear topis[11] lest the Indian sun burn its way into their brains." The danger India posed to the British Empire was twofold. On the one hand, the most obvious risk to imperial life was the extreme heat, exotic diseases, and infant mortality; on the other hand, India threatened to contaminate and corrupt the British Empire with her culture. Louis-Ferdinand Céline writes:

---

9. See also Davin 1997, 73; Knibiehler and Goutalier 1985, 92; Vellut 1982, 100.

10. A Lady Resident (1864, 95) writes, "In many respects, India is a more healthy country for very young children than England. How rarely is there an instance of bronchitis, croup, or any other lung disease."

11. The word *topi* is a Hindi word meaning hat or cap.

> There are two sides to the connection between colonialism and disease. First of all, simply the fact that the indigenous population is disease-ridden is itself a justification for the colonial project: "These niggers are sick! You'll see! They're completely corrupt.... They're degenerates!" Disease is a sign of physical and moral corruption, a sign of a lack of civilization. Colonialism's civilizing project, then, is justified by the hygiene it brings. On the other side of the coin, however, from the European perspective, the primary disease of colonialism is disease—or really contagion. (1983, 145)

The sights, sounds, smells, and tastes of India could possibly redirect the imperial senses creating nostalgia for the Other.[12] The cultural memory of India brings to the surface a longing for the Other, a memory that is untouched, untainted, and uncontrolled by the colonizer.[13] Through excess of India, the excess of smells, sounds, and tastes that the colonizer recollects India, sometimes, however, these recollections were not pleasant. MacMillan (1988, 19) writes, "India was frightening. It still frightens present-day travelers. The country is so big, so old, so confusing. Trying to understand India is like trying to seize hold of the image in a kaleidoscope—India has too many people, too many gods, too much past to be grasped in its entirety. And there is the danger, in getting closer to India, of loosing one's foothold in one's own culture." The fear of being contaminated and corrupted also meant that their own feelings of loyalty and love they feel for their own motherland is now forever tainted. India becomes the land that is both desired and derided by the empire.[14] The complex emotions that the colonizer felt toward

---

12. Stoler (2002, 164) inserts the importance of "cultural memory" and the nostalgia one feels for the colonized subject. She writes, "As an opening question, we ask why colonial studies, despite its obvious commitment to questions of memory, has dealt in such circumscribed ways the nature of remembering and the particular forms that memories of the colonial take. We then turn to the specific recollections of former servants to question how their colonial memories were framed, how concrete and sensory memories of cooking, cleaning, and child care evoke sensibilities that other ways of telling do not."

13. Stoler (ibid., 169) points out: "By Ranajit Guha's account, these "small voices" may counter the weight of official discourse because they remain undomesticated and unsullied by "state-managed historiography" and the monopolizing force of official knowledge" (see also Guha 1996).

14. Reporting on one British woman's experience, MacMillan (1988, 21–22) points out, "Mrs. Fay in the 1770s found Madras (now Chennai) beautiful and exotic,

India made it all the more pertinent that they protect their culture and keep it alive in the colonies.

> The memsahibs struggled to keep Britain alive in the midst of India. The struggle was absurd, but there was a sort of heroism in it. They planted English flowers in their gardens and the heat withered them. They covered their furniture with chintz and the white ants chewed their way through. They got patterns for their clothes from Home but the native tailor somehow altered them subtly. They served English food even though half of it had to come out of tins. (20)

The beauty and the heat of India constantly threatened to destroy, destruct, contaminate, and moreover threatened to resurface in the colonial memory whenever possible. The white *memsahibs* had indeed settled and colonized the land of India but had succumbed to her smells, noises, and tastes.[15] The excess and extravagance of Mother India slipping through the hands of oral and written history embedded deep within the subjectivity of the empire threatened to overturn the tables as the colonizer was now at the risk of becoming the colonized. In short, the British Raj had successfully captured India, but could they protect themselves from being captured by Indian excess that threatened to colonize and conquer their memories of the Other for life?

British children signified the future progeny of the empire and protection and preservation of these young lives was an imperative task. Nupur Chaudhuri (1988, 527–28) writes, "After the birth of a child, the memsahib assumed new responsibilities and experienced added anxieties. She faced childrearing in a land where the mortality rate for Anglo-Indian children was more than twice what it was for children in Britain."[16]

---

with its gleaming white buildings 'covered with a sort of shell-lime which takes a polish like marble, and produces a wonderful effect.' And the inhabitants were worthy of their surroundings." Another *memsahib* Minnie Blane talks about the beauty of India when writing to her mother back in England, saying, "The scenery is getting more beautiful. ... The dates, coconuts and bananas are lovely, and rice has the appearance of corn in the distance, and the tress are lovely today" (1988, 22).

15. Chaudhuri (1988, 520) points to this cultural contamination in her essay: "Each British woman came to the colonial world equipped with her original social and cultural patterns, which then became colored by elements of the new world."

16. See also Fayrer 1873, 8. Fayrer, a physician in the Bengal Medical Services, notes that in the Bengal Presidency between 1860 and 1869, the average death rate for British soldiers' children under the age of five was 148.10 per thousand, while

With the life of the colonial infant being constantly at stake in the colonies, the empire had to take whatever measures possible to shield their children from uncontrollable conditions of the colonies. Stoler (2002, 73) illustrates this point: "Maternal and infant health programs instructed European women bound for the tropics in the use of milk substitutes, wet nurses, and breast-feeding practices in an effort to encourage more women to stay in the colonies and to prepare the many more that came."

As we have already seen in the previous section, motherhood in the colonies was not an easy task and required hiring additional bodies that would help care for and preserve the life of the colonial infant. In other words, the imperial infant was weak, dependent, and needed to survive, as a result other bodies were used to protect, nurture, and nourish it from the dangers both seen and unforeseen of the colonies. Colonial women had two important duties living in India; one was to make sure that they could produce future citizens for the empire, and the second was to ensure that these future citizens are protected in order to survive the dangers of the colonies.[17] It was believed that children born in the colonies were weak and needed extra nourishment and sustenance that would help ward off the exotic diseases of colonial India. Chaudhuri (1988, 529) writes, "British physicians apparently believed that the Indian climate was too debilitating for new mothers to breast-feed their children; because European wet nurses were not available, the doctors advised memsahibs to hire *ammahs* (Indian wet nurses) who were low-caste Hindus or Muslims." The *amah/ayah* mimics the duties of a mother and yet at the same time exceeds her maternal love for the Other as her surplus milk produced in her body for her own child is now redirected into the mouth of another infant.[18] Thus, the *amah/ayah* becomes a maternal figure that *almost but does not quite* belong to India.[19]

---

in England during the same period the mortality rate for the same age group was 67.58.

17. "The perceptions and practice that bound women's domesticity to national welfare and racial purity were not confined to colonial women alone. Childrearing in late nineteenth-century Britain was hailed as a national, imperial, and racial duty" (Stoler 2002, 72).

18. Our reading of this excess milk draws on Spivak's analysis of the wet nurse whose breast she argues becomes a "working breast" that produces milk in excess so it can be appropriated in the market. In her section entitled, "A Literary Representation of the Subaltern," Spivak reads the story by Mahasweta Devi entitled "The Breast Giver." This is a story of Jashoda, a professional wet nurse who is employed to feed her

Although, the *amah/ayah* is considered to be a dependable body, the empire and the *memsahib* were never quite able to trust this maternal figure. Flora Anne Steel and Grace Gardiner (1921, 176) write in their book, *The Complete Indian Housekeeper and Cook:* "Some Anglo-Indians also feared that milk of 'native women' might contaminate an English child's character."[20] The milk produced in the brown breast of the Indian wet nurse was desired by the empire, yet the fear of contamination from this excess liquid life force threatens to dismantle the British Raj. The *amah/ayah* had children of her own, and servicing the British Empire meant that her breast needed to be diverted into the mouth of the colonial infant.[21] The excess milk that was produced by the Indian wet nurses was appropriated by the empire, but controlling this maternal figure still remained a challenge for the imperial subject. The British *memsahibs* often complained that these Indian wet nurses knew their importance in the colonial homes and as a result, exploited them mercilessly. Emma Roberts suggested firsthand wet nurses of India were "most expensive and troublesome appendages to a family. There is no other method in which natives can so rapidly impose upon the European community as that in which these children are concerned" (quoted in Chaudhuri 1988, 529). The excess milk produced in the brown breast of *amah*, a maternal figure

---

master's children and as her milk enters into the market it is appropriated. She writes, "The milk that is produced in one's own body for one's own children is a use-value. When there is a superfluity of use values, exchange values arises" (1998, 342).

19. We borrow this term from Bhabha (1994, 123), who notes, "the excess or slippage produced by the ambivalence of mimicry (almost the same, but not quite) does not merely 'rupture' the discourse, but becomes transformed into an uncertainty which fixes the colonial subject as a 'partial' presence. By 'partial' we mean both 'incomplete' and 'virtual.' It is as if the very emergence of the 'colonial' is dependent for its representation upon some strategic limitation or prohibition within the authoritative discourse itself."

20. The primary function of this book was to give advice to the British *memsahib* living in Colonial India about her domestic responsibilities.

21. "Every amah should be examined by a doctor before engaging her, and care should be taken that her own child is taken away by her friends, or she is apt to nurse it by stealth; she should also be prevented from giving her foster-child milk every hour or so, as they will, if left to their own devices" (A Lady Resident 1864, 97). See also Grossman (2001, 24). In this article, Grossman discusses the fatal results wet nursing brought about in India, where women hired to feed white babies were diverting their breasts to service the empire and meanwhile, their own children were dying out of starvation. See also Suleri 1992.

who services the empire, is indicative of her surplus labor. Spivak (1998, 342–43) writes, "The milk she [referring to Jashoda, the protagonist in Devi's short story entitled, the Breast Giver] produces for her children is presumably through 'necessary labor.' The milk that she produces for the children of her master's family is through 'surplus labor.'"[22] The breast milk, produced in surplus by the *amah/ayah* is harnessed and appropriated by the empire, but the fear of contamination illustrates that this excess milk remains uncontrollable.

The relationship between the colonial infant and their Indian wet nurse was a stark reminder to the empire that memories and longings for the native Other were a reality in the colonial context. Relating the memory of an Indo-Dutch woman who has fond memories of her Javanese nanny, Stoler writes:

> I still remember how heavenly I found that; so entirely "imprisoned" in her *slendang*, in the curve of her arm, flat against her body, rolling with her show rocking gait, with the veil-like material of her kabaja [blouse] gently grazing my cheek and her humming resonates in her breast so that I could feel it with the rise and fall of her voice. It was as if she flowed through me. She would … take me in her lap. The fragrance of her body and her clothes, of her *sarung* especially, I must have intensively inhaled, a sort of preerotic! She caressed me by nestling me against her.… Now still I recollect this fragrance, because smells can remind me of it! (2002, 164)[23]

The smells emanating from the body of the *ayah/amah* invoked a sense of comfort within the minds of the colonial subjects. But sometimes, these memories were accompanied with hate occasionally towards their own

---

22. Discussing this idea further Spivak (1998, 342–43) notes, "I am half-fantasizing, rather, about an area where the product of a woman's body has been historically susceptible to idealization—just as, in the classical Marxian argument, the reason why the free (male) laborer becomes a 'proletarian' under capitalism is not that he has nothing but his body but that, his product, being a value-term is susceptible to idealization."

23. See also Scholte 1974, 43–44. MacMillain (1988, 133) writes, "In adulthood, men and women still kept the memory of a much-loved *ayah*, usually a small, plump women with gleaming, oiled hair, dressed in a white sari, who had sung to them, comforted them, and told them wonderful Indian stories. Nancy Vernede, as a child in Lucknow, always went to sleep with reassuring noises of her *ayah's* soft singing and the faint clash of bangles outside the door."

biological mothers and at times towards India (158).[24] The relationship between the colonized *ayah/amah* and the British child was embedded in fond memories. In almost all the manuals, *ayahs* are described as kind, gentle, and caring women.[25] Yet the fear that the *ayah/amah* could contaminate and corrupt future progeny of the empire was real.

The intimate relationship that the colonial infant shared with her/his *ayah/amah* was a reminder to the empire that it was failing to create stringent boundaries that separated the colonizer from the colonized.[26] The *memsahibs* needed the *ayahs/amahs* to help care for their children, but they were unable to fully let go of their racial prejudice towards them still seeing them through suspicious eyes. The *ayah* or *amah*, as we mentioned before, was considered the most important servant within the colonial household, and yet this desired body was also deeply feared because of its ability to contaminate the colonial child. Sometimes, the danger of contamination was physical leading to diseases, but often the danger of contamination for the empire was of a moral nature (MacMillan 1988).[27] This seemed to be the case with native languages that were seen as corrupting young imperial minds, thus resulting in the encouragement of the imperial language that was thought to help build the character of the empire.

---

24. She writes, "They [British children] went from a world that was rich in color and emotions to one that was cold and cramped. In India, they were spoiled and made much of; in Victorian and Edwardian England, they were thrust into a society where children were seen and not heard. They went to schools where India was to be driven out of their systems and Britain drummed in. Unless their mothers stayed to supervise the process, it was hard for the children not to feel abandoned. Sometimes they reacted by hating their parents, sometimes India; to this day, there are men and women who blame that country for separating them from their parents" (Stoler 2002, 158).

25. A Lady Resident (1864, 95) writes, "Ayahs are, as a rule, very fond of babies, and gentle and patient with them to a degree which would astonish the rough and ready English nursemaids." MacMillan (1988, 153) writes, "From the children's point of view, ayahs were gentler than most nannies."

26. See also the section entitled "Breast, Womb, Empire" in Jacob 2015. This chapter deals with the figure of the *ayah* and the *amah* in Colonial India at length.

27. She writes, "According to Birch's Management, children could not possibly learn the necessary virtues of obedience, self-control, and hard work from them. Stories also circulated about ayahs who wiped their charges' eyes on the edges of their saris and thus gave them opthalmia; or those who gave children opium to keep them quiet; or who fondled the penises of little boys in their care. And Indians spoiled children; they cuddled them more than the parents thought necessary and picked up their toys after them" (1988, 153).

Mothers were advised by British physicians to discourage their children from learning native Indian languages since it was believed that learning languages of the inferior culture would lead to a degenerate empire. A Lady Resident (1864,106) writes, "As far as possible children should be prevented from acquiring native dialects, as with the language they are almost certain to imbibe ideas and knowledge most prejudicial to them in every way." While learning English was seen as benefitting the character of the native Indian subject, learning native languages did not serve any real purpose.[28] Speaking English becomes a sign of the subject and speaking the native language is depicted as a tool to control the native mind. Language as Catherine Belsey (1998, 380) reminds us helps one to become a subject saying, "But it is only with its entry into language that the child becomes a full subject." It is interesting to note that the entry of the white child into the symbolic world takes place in colonial India with speaking the native Indian language (MacMillian 1988, 156). Thus, it was the excess of language, the language that fell beyond and grated ungraciously on European ears that threatens to dismantle the British Raj. The native languages corrupt the mind of the colonial infant, but more importantly, the threat takes place in the formation of the colonial subject, who almost but not quite belongs to the empire. The inability to control the memories that bind the maternal figure of the *ayah/amah* with the colonial infant and the language that flows seamlessly from the mouth of the imperial subject not only signifies the corruption and contamination of the British Raj, but it also illustrates the way in which the colonial infant born in India formed in the excess heat, drinking the surplus milk of the *amah/ayah*, speaking the excess language finally becomes a subject that almost but not quite belongs to the empire (MacMillian 1988, 173). At the same time, no matter how hard the *memsahib* tried to separate the colonized infant from their *ayahs/amahs*, their relationships were formed in a love built on an excess. The lines between the colonizer and the colonized that were meant to separate the races could not contain the love that exceeded these lines and constructed a maternal love for the Other that was ambivalent.

---

28. Rosemary Marangoly George (1993–1994, 111) writes, "In the context of colonialism, the language of imperial control and discipline is primarily the imperial language—namely, English or French. 'Native' language acquisition is represented in popular imperial discourses as motivated by an unpolitical, often purely aesthetic/linguistic interest in an alien culture."

Sacred Texts, Sacred Breasts:
Controlled and Uncontrollable Mother Goddesses

Mothers are revered and honored within African American and Indian societies. In fact, in Hinduism, most of the major goddesses are all maternal figures. One prominent maternal figure within the religious and cultural imagination of India who has a profound effect on Indian society is Kali. There are many representations of Kali within Hinduism; she is known as both Durga and Parvati; however, the connection that unites all these representations is the word *Ma* or mother.[29] Monotheistic and patriarchal Christianity portrays the divine as male and yet in Revelation we encounter a woman that challenges such a depiction. In Rev 12, the woman clothed with the sun, like Kali, is also a mother and a goddess.[30] The Sun Woman gives birth and is associated with life in contrast to all the death and destruction in the apocalyptic text. It is death and destruction, however, that is often associated with the maternal body of Kali. While the sun goddess protects her children as a warrior mother, Kali as the warrior goddess threatens to kill everyone in her path. Within the colonial/imperial imagination, both goddesses who embody either life or death have a power that needs to be contained and controlled. Kali to the western eye was a maternal goddess that did not exemplify aspects of traditional mothering at all (Largen 2014, 18). Separated from her children, the woman clothed in the sun's role as a mother seems limited to her ability to give birth. Though attempts are made to control these textual goddesses they, too, are revered.

The Woman Clothed in the Sun

The book of Revelation is a critique of the Roman Empire. This imperial context emboldens the apocalyptic narrative. In a tale of beasts, war, and judgment, the ways in which women are employed should be analyzed in context. In Rev 12, we behold a woman who appears in the heaven. John,

---

29. The word *Ma* is a Hindi word used to refer not only to mothers in India but also to goddesses in India within the Hindu tradition.

30. It is important to note that similar to the African American and the Indian wet nurses who have some similarities and connections but are different historical maternal figures, the mother goddesses in both the Christian and the Hindu tradition although unique are yet still connected.

the writer, describes her as a great sign (σημεῖον). Almost as suddenly as she appears, she disappears into the wilderness. This ambiguously figured woman who is clothed in the sun flies on eagle's wings after giving birth to a male child.[31] Her son is taken away from her. She and her children are pursued by a dragon who seeks to destroy them. This is her story, succinctly. In this apocalyptic text filled with horror and death, she does what no other character does—she ushers in life. Reading her through the interpretative lens of African American wet nurses in the antebellum United States, we see more dramatically how narratives of displaced motherhood in an imperial context occludes the Sun Woman's autonomy (however limited), her potential for resistance, and her power.

In a book concerned with unveiling, what does her story reveal? The Sun Woman, who is considered a goddess by some, wears a crown of stars and walks on the moon. Her only articulation is a cry from the pain of giving birth. The great red dragon, another sign, seeks to devour her male child from the time of his birth. This son is destined for great things: specifically, he is to rule all the nations with an iron rod. He is taken away from her to God. Fleeing into the wilderness, the place prepared for her by God, she is nourished for 1,260 days. A war breaks out in heaven and the great dragon, now identified as the devil and Satan, is cast to the earth. The great dragon pursues the woman dressed in the sun. It is then that she receives eagle's wings to fly into the wilderness. The dragon spews floodwaters that are intended to drown her, but instead the water is swallowed up by the earth. The earth rescues her. Angry, the dragon goes off to make war on the rest of her children, who are described as the ones who keep the commands of God and have the testimony of Jesus.

Although never officially given the title in the text, the Sun Woman of Rev 12 is a mother, one of the most significant roles in the Apocalypse. In her essay "The Heroine and The Whore," Tina Pippin (1992, 135) observes that in Revelation "females are productive when they are reproductive," and the Sun Woman gives birth to a son. In fact, John uses the bodies of women in Revelation to (re)produce his hegemonic ideas. Women are not only marginalized in the text; they are used and then disposed of, even

---

31. Scholars have identified this woman clothed in a variety of ways. In his commentary, Aune (1998, 680) summarizes the possibilities as: (1) "queen of the cosmos"; (2) the church; (3) the bride, heavenly Jerusalem of Rev 19:7–8; (4) the persecuted people of God from whom the Messiah comes (5); an astrological figure; (6) and Isis, the queen of heaven.

violently destroyed (Jezebel, Whore). Despite this death and destruction the Sun Woman, a mother goddess, delivers life.

The reproductive body of the Sun Mother interrupts the text by giving birth. This act creates a discursive space in which the woman's power cannot be contained. The body speaks. In fact, she cries out. In her book *Maternal Impressions*, Cristina Mazzoni (2002, 190) writes: "Birth, then, becomes the unifying human experience insofar as it proclaims that women and men, who are born and live embodied in sexual difference, all and without exception originate in a woman's body. This common necessity should underline rather than erase the sexed identity of the subject." Birth is the great equalizer. However, as the lives of the wet nurse instructs, proximity necessitates differentiation. It is in the sameness that differentiation becomes paramount. The announcement of the child and the child's gender is emphasized in the text.[32] Though she is nameless and rendered voiceless, Mazzoni explains how even her silence speaks. She states: "In silence the voice is quiet but not the word. By establishing birth as a discursive category, the maternal body, with its silence and its words, its impression and its expression, can become meaningful" (193–94). Mazzoni has advised us well to listen to both the words and the silence, as silence can be powerful and deadly. Like the life-giving sustenance of the wet nurses, the life-producing body of this mother gives John what he needed, a male child. Then she is exiled, sent to the wilderness.

Displacement is a tool often employed by those in power. Empires attempt to put people in their "rightful" places. This is why proximity, as we have seen, is dangerous. John sends the woman to the wilderness after her child is snatched away. Here, where she is nourished for three and a half years, the world is fraught with contradictions. Although portrayed as a place of provision and protection, the wilderness is equally dangerous and destructive for a woman who is alone. Provision is often submission clothed in survival. That is, provision only tells the reader that the woman is alive, nothing more. In fact, it is clear that she is not safe because as soon as the dragon is cast down, he pursues her. This time, John gives her wings to fly into another wilderness. In her article "Jesus as Fantasy Mother," Pippin explores the image of birds in the bible and specifically in the Apocalypse. She writes: "Wings are symbols of power, of destruc-

---

32. The birth announcement in Rev 12:5 states: ἔτεκεν υἱόν ἄρσεν ("She gave birth to a son, a male").

tion, and of supernatural realms intersecting, once again, with the human. These wings stir up trouble" (2009, 157). Flying does not free her from her troubles, however. It is only now that we learn about "the war on the rest of her children." She has been separated from all of her children.

The sun-clothed woman and the black wet nurses share not only their roles as mothers but also the loss and pursuit of their children. A surrogate mother, the Sun Woman gives birth but is not allowed to be a mother. Although provision is made for her, she is not allowed to protect or provide for her children. This mother is neither pampered nor protected, but as a warrior, she seeks the protection and provision of *all* her children. The Sun Woman's wilderness experience echoes that of Hagar, who also endured banishment to the wilderness: "Thus the Hagar-wilderness symbolism held together women's and the community's past history, present situation and intimations of hope for a better future" (Williams 1993, 118). Delores Williams continues to explain how the symbolic use of Hagar in the wilderness helped develop African American conceptual life in two ways:

> First, Hagar, functioning as symbol *and* signal in this development, brought together the sacred and the secular in postbellum African-American thought.... This means, then, that black women should not separate "woman-experience" from their experience in the community's survival and liberation struggles involving black men. Second, the Hagar (and child) content of the wilderness symbolism brings together the spiritual and the political. Thus religious life in the black postbellum Christian community can continue to express itself, simultaneously, in both spiritual and political terms. (120–21)

The Sun Woman's narrative functions to remind of the pain of separation and isolation and also provides hope in the creative power that resides in birth. Birth creates the potential for additional connections written in and on the bodies of these women whose creative power gave birth to a future is also apparent. Birth, as a discursive space, connects all women and our pasts and futures and shared experiences. As such, the wilderness experience of the Sun Woman makes her both a sign and a symbol. If she represents a church, an *ekklesia*, as some scholars suggest, she, too, represents bringing together the experiences of women, particularly women of color who are used and abused by hegemonic systems of power. If she stands in the place of anything (as symbol), as a winged mother-goddess, she recalls all the breasts that nurture their communities. African American women whose outstretched arms create safe spaces that correct and affirm, uplift, and support, though not necessarily having had to physically give birth to take on the responsibility of mothering, affirm the strength, regality, power, and resilience of unorthodox mothers.

Goddess Kali in the Linga Purana

To the Western mind accustomed to one God and one holy book, the concept of Hinduism with its multiple gods, books, castes, and multiple rituals caused quite a stir.[33] The sheer confusion of Hinduism was only made worse with the introduction of Kali. In a world, where women were expected to behave in a modest manner and cover up their bodies, the figure of Kali was often described as being grotesque and frightening. In her images, Kali appeared dancing naked wearing human skulls, her long tongue dripped in blood as she stood upon a corpse (MacMillian 1988, 25). In the colonial imagination, Kali was a goddess that broke all the rules of being a woman in India, given the rituals such as female infanticide and sati, where a widow would immolate herself on her husband's pyre. British *memsahibs* often described Indian women in a poor light, believing that in India the men were treating women quite harshly (58). Yet the British *memsahib* was trapped in her own limitation set up for her by the empire, where women were seen as weak subjects that needed protection and care. Thus, it was in between these totalizing narratives of colonial India that described women, whether Indian or British, as helpless victims that the goddess Kali erupts onto the scene.

Without a doubt, Kali held the British colonial imagination, but she was more frightening than revered. The Western mind that was used to seeing the Indian woman only through the lenses of victimhood and weakness now found itself in a new dilemma. How were they supposed to react to this horribly frightening goddess who actively sought to kill men who threatened her land (Urban 2003, 169)? As a goddess of the colonized, Kali represented the excess of India, her image may have been arrested in a statue,

---

33. One of the British *memsahib*, Helen Mackenzie, notes that the difference between the Hindu and Muslim religion was apparent in their architecture. She writes, "The former [i.e., Muslim] is as majestic as perhaps man in his fallen state is capable of conceiving; the latter [i.e., Hindu] is wholly devoid of this quality, and in spite of the beauty of some minor details, the effect of the whole is grotesque" (MacMillan 1988, 65).

but the spirit she inspired in her devotees was uncontrollable (171). At the same time, the figure of Kali as the deeply sexual and morally reprehensible goddess often merged with colonial depictions of India and its women.

In his book *The Underworld of India*, George Fletcher MacMunn (1933) writes, "Anything and everything that deals with sex, procreation, union, and human passion is worshipped and glorified" (quoted in Urban 2003, 173). One of the reasons for this depiction of India and Indians by the British Empire was that Indians were people who were closer to the nature and therefore their minds were like that of a child, incapable of understanding the intellectual West.[34] For the British Empire, the native was childlike incapable of understanding, and yet at the same time, he was also a manipulative and asexual degenerate. The maternal bodies of the *amah/ayah* and Mother India split into dichotomous categories of that life-giver and life-taker is used not only separating these maternal bodies but also juxtaposing them. It is in the body of a mother that life is signified. Kali is often referred to as a mother; however, this mother represents death and destruction rather than life. The motherhood performed by Kali is uncontrollable, frightening, and threatens to destroy the stability of the cosmos. Similar to the Sun Woman in Rev 12 who is relegated to the desert, the figure of Kali often appears both in literature and in paintings on a battlefield. Contained in a space that symbolizes struggle and death literally or figuratively, the powerful bodies of both these mother goddesses become sacred objects that embody both life and death. Kristen Largen (2014, 19) writes, "Many Hindu myths associate her [Kali] with battle, and she is often found in cremation grounds. She wears emblems of death on her own body." The warrior spirit of both these mothers, while appreciated in these texts, also threaten to destabilize imperial imaginations of female stereotypes and as a result needed to be controlled and domesticated. Often times the domestication of these women as we have seen occurs when their maternal instincts are employed to work against their own bodies.

While Mother India threatens to destroy the colonizer, Kali's maternal body threatens to destroy the world. However, as Mother India's "life

---

34. George (1993–1994, 108–9) discusses the importance of housekeeping in colonial India, noting that this was one of the duties of the *memsahibs*. Within the household there were "doors to be locked; corridors to be periodically dusted, rooms to be fumigated and made free of pests; children (i.e., "natives") to be doctored, educated, clothed, and disciplined."

taking force" is countered by the *amahs/ayahs* brown breast that breathes life back into the colonial infant, the destructive and life taking force of Kali is also countered at her breast. David Kinsley, professor of religious studies, spent most of his life writing and researching the gods and goddesses of the Hindu religion. However, it was Kali whom he focused on the most. Called the father of Kali studies, Kinsley helped his western readers understand, think, and articulate their reflections on Kali in English. He writes:

> In another myth, it is as an infant that Sīva calms Kali and stops her rampage by eliciting motherly emotions from her—Kali again has defeated her enemies on the battlefield and begun to dance out of control, drunk on the blood of those she had slain. To calm her and protect the stability of the world. Sīva appears in the midst of the battlefield as an infant who cries out loudly. Seeing the child's distress, Kālī stops her dancing, picks him up, and kisses him on the head. Then she suckles him at her breasts. (1982, 138–39)[35]

Similar to the Indian *ayah/amah* who turns against her own motherland India, Kali's breasts that symbolize life turn against her own body, signifying death. In this myth Kali's anger is calmed only when her body is converted from life-taker to a life-giver. This is similar to the anger that the maternal body of India feels toward the colonizer; it is calmed down by the *ayah/amah* whose maternal body/breast signifies life. At the same time, the role of a life-giver privileged and attached to the bodies of women of color is naturalized and normalized to colored mothers as their bodies are coerced, seduced, and forced to become maternal figures to imperial infants. Thus, slipping through the binary narratives of life-giver and life-taker, the maternal bodies of India and Indians exceed in their love for the Other constructing a bond that is ambivalent and unrelenting.

Conclusion

The colored breasts of these wet nurses expose the complexity of their roles as mothers particularly in an imperial context. Colored breast ser-

---

35. See also Linga Purana 1.106.20–28. Another myth describes Kali beginning her dance of destruction. The only way to calm her down is for her husband, Sīva (Shiva) to lie down and so that she would recognize him and stop her dance of destruction.

vicing the empire is a site of interracial mothering, a contact zone uniting the colonizer and the colonized, the oppressed and the oppressor, enabling the balance of power to shift. As a result, motherhood is redefined through categories of race, class/caste, gender, religion, and economics. Motherhood, understood in this context, must acknowledge the myriad ways in which women create opportunities for change despite their circumstances and a more nuanced conception of motherhood then should be similarly located in religious expressions.

This redefinition of motherhood facilitates a rereading of sacred texts that deploy the images of mothers. These sacred mothers read ambivalently similarly signify life and death, resistance and accommodation. Employing womanist hermeneutics, the experiences of the wet nurses become a lens through which to read and interrogate the intersectionalities of gender, race, and nation in sacred texts. Kali and the woman clothed in the sun have a power that must be contained challenging the notion of mothers as simply loving nurturers.

The expansion of our understanding of motherhood can also be located in contemporary discourses. Black and brown female bodies remain threatened and threatening. The bodies of women of color continue to nurture imperial powers through the provision of cheap labor. Whether in factories or the home of our oppressors, our bodies continue to be exploited as domestic workers, nannies, or transnational surrogates (that is, performing labor by giving birth to imperial infants). These are all examples of the labors disproportionately provided by women of color. It is no surprise that the industry of domestic workers is at times associated with human trafficking, a modern day form of slavery. Our bodies are harnessed for the goods and services desired and often violently disposed of when our capabilities are no longer desired. Women of color continue to be affected by reproductive and environmental violence. These injustices must be challenged.

As this essay demonstrates, though separated by time, space, and circumstances, when we put diverse contexts into conversation, we not only reveal the tenuous nature of imperial power, but we are also compelled to remember these women and recognize that contemporary expressions of exploitations of women of color have ancient roots. This transnational context elucidates that although different, women of color and the exploitation of their bodies maintain a startling resemblance.

Motherhood disassociated from its biological connection to the womb creates a space for those women who participate in an unorthodox mothering and rewrites the script of maternal love. As psychologist Nancy Chodorow (1978, 11) notes in *The Reproduction of Mothering*: "Being a mother, then, is not only bearing a child—it is being a person who socializes and nurtures." Being a "mother to the other" creates an opportunity to effect change. Motherhood is more than nurturing. Layli Phillips (2006, xii) defines motherhood as "a womanist method of social transformation." As such it is not solely, love for the other, but love for ourselves that can transform our communities into places that are safe for women of color and recreate our world into one that can acknowledge that our worth is not limited to our bodies' ability to produce. Making these historical and textual milk mothers visible in our cultural histories enables us to see how their images are reproduced in our contemporary moment and challenges us to recreate a community of shared motherhood where their resistant and resilient spirits continue to flow from breast to breast.

Works Cited

A Lady Resident. 1864. *The Englishwoman in India*. London: Smith, Elder.
Aune, David E. 1998. *Revelation 6–16*. Dallas: Word Books.
Belsey, Catherine. 1998. "Constructing the Subject: Deconstructing the Text." Pages 378–92 in *Contemporary Literary Criticism*. Edited by Robert Con Davis and Ronald Schleifer. 4th ed. New York: Longman.
Bhabha, Homi K. 1994. *The Location of Culture*. New York: Routledge.
Céline, Louis-Ferdinand. 1983. *Journey to the End of the Night*. Translated by Ralph Manheim. New York: New Directions.
Chaudhuri, Nupur. 1988. "Memsahibs and Motherhood in Nineteenth-Century Colonial India." *Victorian Studies* 31:517–35.
Chodorow, Nancy. 1978. *The Reproduction of Mothering*. Berkeley: University of California Press.
Coleman, Monica, ed. 2013. *Ain't I a Womanist Too? Third-Wave Womanist Religious Thought*. Minneapolis: Fortress.
Davin, Anna. 1997. "Imperialism and Motherhood." Pages 87–132 in *Tensions of Empire: Colonial Cultures in a Bourgeois World*. Edited by Fredric Cooper and Ann Laura Stoler. Berkeley: University of California Press.
Douglass, Frederick. 1995. *Narrative of the Life of Frederick Douglass*. Mineola: Dover Publications.

Dunaway, Wilma A. 2003. *The African-American Family in Slavery and Emancipation*. Cambridge: Cambridge University Press.
Fayrer, J. 1873. *European Child-Life in India*. IOL Tract 820. London: Churchill.
Fildes, Valerie. 1988. *Wet Nursing: A History from Antiquity to the Present*. New York: Blackwell.
Fox-Genovese, Elizabeth. 1988. *Within the Plantation Household: Black and White Women of the Old South*. Chapel Hill: University of North Carolina Press.
George, Rosemary Marangoly. 1993–1994. "Homes in the Empire, Empires in the Home." *Cultural Critique* 26:95–127.
Grall, Charles. 1998. *Hygiène colonial appliquée: Hygiène de l'Indochine*. Paris: Baillière.
Gray-White, Deborah. 1999. *Ar'n't I a Woman? Female Slaves in the Plantation South*. New York: Norton.
Grossman, Joyce. 2001. "Ayahs, Dhayes, and Bearers: Mary Sherwood's Indian Experience and Constructions of Subordinated Others." *South Atlantic Review* 66.2:14–44.
Guha, Ranajit. 1996. "The Small Voice of History." Pages 1–12 in *Subaltern Studies X: Writings on South Asian History and Society*. Edited by Gautam Bhadra, Gyan Prakash, and Susie Tharu. Delhi: Oxford University Press.
Hardt, Michael, and Antonio Negri. 2000. *Empire*. Cambridge, MA: Harvard University Press.
Jacob, Harriett. 2012. *Incidents in the Life of a Slave Girl Written by Herself*. New York: Simon & Brown.
Jacob, Sharon. 2015. *Reading Mary Alongside Indian Surrogate Mothers: Violent Love, Oppressive Liberation, and Infancy Narratives*. New York: Palgrave MacMillan.
Kinsley, David. 1982. "The Motherhood of God as Expressed in the Goddess Kali." *Anima* 8:31–42.
Knibiehler, Yvonne, and Régine Goutalier. 1985. *La femme au temps des colonies*. Paris: Stock.
Largen, Kristen Johnson. 2014. "A Walk on the Dark Side: A Christian Reflection on Kali." *CurTM* 41:17–22.
Louis-Ferdinand, Céline. 1983. *Journey to the End of the Night*. Translated by Ralp Manheim. New York: New Directions.
MacMillan, Margaret. 1988. *Women of the Raj: The Mothers, Wives, and Daughters of the British Empire in India*. New York: Random House.

MacMunn, George Fletcher. 1933. *The Underworld of India*. London: Jarrolds.
Mazzoni, Christy. 2002. *Maternal Impressions: Pregnancy and Childbirth in Literature and Theory*. Ithaca, NY: Cornell University Press.
Mitchem, Stephanie Y. 2002. *Introducing Womanist Theology*. Maryknoll, NY: Orbis Books.
Morgan, Jennifer. 2004. *Laboring Women: Gender and Reproduction in the New World*. Philadelphia: University of Pennsylvania Press.
Parkhurst, Jessie. 1938. "The Role of the Black Mammy in the Plantation Household." *JNH* 23:349–69.
Phillips [Maparyan], Layli, ed. 2006. *The Womanist Reader*. New York: Taylor & Francis.
Pippin, Tina. 1992. "The Heroine and the Whore: Fantasy and the Female in the Apocalypse of John." *Semeia* 60:67–82.
———. 2009. "Jesus as Fantasy Mother." Pages 141–56. in *Mother Goose, Mother Jones, Mommie Dearest: Biblical Mothers and Their Children*. Edited by Cheryl A. Kirk-Duggan and Tina Pippin. Atlanta: Society of Biblical Literature.
Scholte, Lin. 1974. *Bibi Koetis voor Altijid*. Amsterdam: Querido.
Sen, Indrani. 2005. "The Memsahib's Madness: The European Woman's Mental Health in Late Nineteenth Century India." *Social Scientist* 33.5/6: 26–48.
Spivak, Gayatri Chakravorty. 1997. "Diasporas Old and New: Women in the Transnational World." Pages 87–116 in *Class Issues: Pedagogy, Cultural Studies, and the Public Sphere*. Edited by Amitava Kumar. New York: New York University Press.
Spivak, Gayatri Chakravorty. 1998. *In Other Worlds: Essays in Cultural Politics*. New York: Routledge.
Steel, Flora Anne, and Grace Gardiner. 1921. *The Complete Indian Housekeeper and Cook*. Rev. ed. London: n.p.
Stoler, Ann Laura. 2002. *Carnal Knowledge and Imperial Power: Race and the Intimate in Colonial Rule*. Berkeley: University of California Press.
Suleri, Sara. 1992. *The Rhetoric of English India*. Chicago, University of Chicago Press.
Urban, Hugh B. 2003. "India's Darkest Heart: Kali in the Colonial Imagination." Pages 169–95 in *Encountering Kālī: In the Margins, at the Center, in the West*. Edited by Rachel Fell McDermott and Jeffrey J. Kripal. Berkeley: University of California Press.

Vellut, Jean-Luc. 1982. "Matériaux pour une image du blanc dans la société coloniale du Congo Belge." Pages 91–116 in *Stéréotypes nationaux et préjugés raciaux aux XIXe et XXe siècles*. Edited by Jean Pirotte. Leuven: Editions Nauwelaerts.

Vlach, John Michael. 2004. "The Plantation Landscape." Pages 95–112 in *American Architectural History: A Contemporary Reader*. Edited by Keith L. Eggener. New York: Routledge.

Walker, Alice. 2005. "Womanist." Page 11 in *A Feminist Theory: A Reader*. Edited by Wendy K. Kolmar and Frances Bartkowski. 2nd ed. Boston: McGraw Hill.

Williams, Delores. 1993. *Sisters in the Wilderness: The Challenge of Womanist God-Talk*. Maryknoll, NY: Orbis Books.

"WE DON'T GIVE BIRTH TO THUGS": FAMILY VALUES, RESPECTABILITY POLITICS, AND JEPHTHAH'S MOTHER

Vanessa Lovelace

Introduction

The subtitle of this volume is *Expanding the Discourse*, and I hope that this reading of Judg 11 will be a welcome addition to previous feminist (e.g., Bal 1988; Day 1989; Exum 1995) and womanist (Weems 1988; Cooper 2003) interpretations of this text. This essay expands on their interpretations of Judg 11, which analyze the story from the perspective of Jephthah's unnamed daughter, by interpreting it from the viewpoint of Jephthah's unnamed and silenced mother, whose social status has a deleterious effect on how others see her son.

Jephthah is a character that readers might regard as the classic tragic hero. Despite his best intentions, Jephthah's error in judgment leads to a disastrous outcome and ultimately, undermines him. As posited by Aristotle, tragedy is delineated by the characters' actions rather than a tragic or fatal "flaw": "You can't have tragedy without action" (Aristotle 1997, 26). Nevertheless, some commentators have suggested that Jephthah was fated for ruin due to the circumstances of his birth. Jephthah's story begins with the narrator describing him both as a *ḥayil gibbôr*, "mighty warrior," and *ben-'iššâ zônâ*, "son of a prostitute"; the former is a description of his heroic qualities, the latter an evaluation of his character. His bad judgment, typical of the tragic figure,[1] admittedly has ramifications on a

---

1. Exum (1992, 57) argues that Jephthah is not a truly tragic figure because he does not sufficiently wrestle with his fate, regardless of the fact that nothing could be done to reverse it; thus "no significant tragic development occurs within his character."

national and personal level. This does not mean that Jephthah's personal family tragedy should be conflated with contributing to Israel's decline as a nation, as suggested by some commentators (see below).

As a womanist scholar, I am sensitive to commentaries on Judg 11:1–12:7 that explicitly or implicitly read the text through the lens of so-called family values or Judeo-Christian values by blaming Jephthah's circumstances on his mother's status. It is to these commentaries that I am responding in this essay.[2] Too often in the white defined politics and policies of the US black people serve as the target for reform by the family values rhetoric on the basis that they lack traditional family values. In the United States, the so-called deterioration of the traditional family, usually code for the decline in the white Protestant nuclear family, supposedly is leading to the decline of America.

The term *family values* is loosely defined as moral and ethical principles traditionally held and transmitted within the family unit, such as responsibility, honesty, and religious commitment (Newman 2007, 23). Individuals and groups from each end of the political spectrum who advocate for the benefits of the intact two-parent family adopt the use of family values rhetoric. In this essay I am referring to the political rhetoric that links family values with religious beliefs to blame nonconforming family formations for their socioeconomic instability instead of oppositional domestic policy directives (Powell 26–27).

What should be noticed is how racism and sexism often intersect in the debate regarding America's demise allegedly due to declining family values. Black mothers, especially if they are unmarried, are often perceived as lacking traditional family values. Therefore, they cannot pass them on to their children, who then are alleged to contribute to the rise in crime and unemployment in black communities (Perry 1996, 9). As we will see below, this is language that sounds familiar to the characterization of Jephthah and his mother.

The argument that black motherhood, especially single black motherhood, has had an adverse effect on the stability of the black family in

---

2. I identify my scholarship and political commitments as womanist. As such, my work analyzes the multidimensional layers of race/ethnicity, gender, sexuality, class, etc. and power dynamics in the biblical texts to bring attention to the weight of these same interlocking forms of oppression experienced by black women due to US policies and politics, which has a deleterious impact on the black community's ability to thrive.

America goes at least as far back as the release in 1965 of the US government report on the state of the black family in America (*The Negro Family: The Case for National Action*), commonly referred to as the Moynihan report after its author Daniel Patrick Moynihan. In that report, Moynihan asserted that the deleterious impact of black women on the black family is manifested in lower educational attainment, high unemployment, poverty, and crime in black communities.

More recently, black mothers are depicted as giving birth to potential criminals. This sentiment is expressed in an email forwarded by Ferguson, Missouri, court clerk Mary Ann Twitty: "A black woman in New Orleans was admitted into the hospital [for] pregnancy termination. Two weeks later she received a check for $5,000. She phoned the hospital to ask who it was from. The hospital said, 'Crimestoppers'" (Lowery and Kindy 2015). This and other racially inflammatory emails were exposed in a report released by the Department of Justice after their investigation of the Ferguson Police Department, following the shooting death of eighteen-year-old black teenager Michael Brown by a white Ferguson police officer. The Justice Department's review concluded that the Ferguson Police Department and municipal court colluded to increase city revenue by treating black residents as "potential offenders," whose excessive fines paid for minor offenses were used to help close the budget gap (Lowery and Kindy 2015).

Black males in particular are judged as menaces to society regardless what they do. If they happen to find themselves in the public glare for having unwittingly transgressed one of the majority culture's unwritten rules, then they will be branded "thugs."[3] An example is when Seattle Seahawks cornerback Richard Sherman went into celebration-mode following his team's 2014 NFC Championship triumph over rival San Francisco 49ers. Just moments after the victory, female sideline reporter Erin Andrews thrust a microphone into Sherman's face. A loud, animated, adrenaline-pumping, chest-thumping Sherman gave an uproarious postgame interview where he taunted 49er opponent Michael Crabtree, whom he had just bested. Within moments of his thirty-second interview, the Twitter-sphere filled with incendiary remarks about Sherman, including referring to him as the N-word, a gorilla, and an ape. However, the most

---

3. Historically, a *thug* was a devotee of the Hindu goddess Kali, who engaged in violent acts of robbery and assassination. Today a thug is known as a "violent person, especially a criminal" (New Oxford Annotated Dictionary, "Thug," s.v.).

frequent slur hurled at him was "thug." There were 625 tweets calling Sherman a thug.

Some sports announcers commented that Andrews looked "frightened" and "threatened" by Sherman. Her producer at Fox Sports, who cut short her interview, claimed that he did so because the situation was getting "dangerous" (Manfred 2014). Some tweets even juxtaposed the pretty, blonde, white reporter and the six-foot-three black football player with the endangered blonde actress Fay Wray and the gorilla King Kong in the 1933 film by the same name. Andrews does not appear frightened during the interview and confirmed as much in tweets later that evening and in subsequent interviews (Klopsis 2014). Nevertheless, Sherman was branded a thug, even though, in his own words, "I wasn't committing any crime, doing anything illegal" (Botelho 2014). Black males in America, from Richard Sherman and Trayvon Martin to Jordan Davis and Barack Obama, are frequently referred to as thugs—despite their successes, despite the fact that they are not criminals or done anything illegal—on the basis that they are the black sons of single mothers.[4]

A study of black mothers in New York City and Westchester County, New York, found that these women were concerned about their sons' wellbeing. They were emotionally fatigued at having to worry about their sons' safety in the presence of law enforcement and expressed feelings of guilt for making choices that were not in their sons' best interests. But most of all the study found that these mothers loved their sons and were proud of them. In the words of one mother, "We don't give birth to thugs; we give birth to children" (Brown-Manning 2013). These are sentiments that I imagine Jephthah's mother sharing.

As a black woman in America, who is also the mother of two sons, I am aware of how the dominant culture's view of black women as either a "hypersexualized Jezebel," "desexualized Mammy," "emasculating Sapphire," "Welfare Queen," or "Angry Black Woman" can have an adverse impact on

---

4. With the exception of Sherman, whose parents are married, Martin, Davis, and Obama's mothers were divorcées. Although Obama's mother was white, she was racialized black for giving birth to a black son. *Daily Beast* reporter Jamelle Bouie, in response to the controversy around Richard Sherman being called "thug," wrote that the epithet had replaced the N-word as the right wing's way of insulting African Americans. For example, conservative pundits regularly refer to President Obama as a "Chicago thug," and defenders of the men who killed Martin and Jordan called the young men "thugs" (Bouie 2014).

how our sons are treated. It calls to mind the opening lines to Margaret Burroughs's poem, "What Shall I Tell My Children Who Are Black?"

> What shall I tell my children who are black
> Of what it means to be a captive in this dark skin?
> What shall I tell my dear one, fruit of my womb,
> of how beautiful they are when everywhere they turn
> they are faced with abhorrence of everything that is black? (1968, 8)

In this essay, using literary criticism and a sociological approach through a womanist hermeneutic, I examine the biblical figure Jephthah (Judg 11:1–12:7) for how a number of biblical commentators implicitly or explicitly suggest that Jephthah's fate is the expected outcome of his birth to a prostitute. I show how the negative evaluations of Jephthah on account of his mother's status are much like the rhetoric around black male children born to single mothers. Jephthah is assigned epithets such as "terrorist," "outlaw," and "thug," all labels that apply to a criminal element who preys on members of his or her own community that have come to be associated with black males. I argue that by representing Jephthah as a thug, lacking traditional family values and a threat to society because he is the son of an unmarried woman, he along with his mother, is racialized black.[5]

A Brief Survey of Recent Studies

Most of the commentaries on Jephthah have focused either on the figure Jephthah as an epic hero known for his military prowess, negotiating skills, and diplomacy, on one hand, and a lawless, opportunistic, controlling, and impulsive fool, on the other, or on Jephthah and his unnamed daughter, the latter whose sacrifice by her father is considered by some commentators as the most disturbing story in the Bible (Jeter 1992; Logan 2009; McCann 2011). Many of the traditional commentaries on the episode of Jephthah's daughter focus mostly on Jephthah than his daughter, from how Jephthah's triumph turned to tragedy, the irrevocability of the vow once YHWH gave Jephthah the victory over the Ammonites (Boling 1975; Pressler 2002), the futility of the vow since it is offered as an inducement: "Jephthah's vow

---

5. Sociologists Michael Omi and Howard Winant (2015, 13) explain *racialization* as applying racial meaning to a previously racially unclassified "relationship, social practice or group."

should never have been made in the first place since it was, in reality, an illegal bribe" (Janzen 2005, 345), and how his fulfillment of the vow meant the end of his family line since his daughter was both his only child and a virgin when she died (Pressler 2002; Smith 2005).

Feminist scholars, beginning in the early 1980s, focused on either critiquing the androcentrism in the story or interpreting it from the perspective of Jephthah's daughter. Phyllis Trible's (1984, 102) reading was one of the earliest feminist treatments of Jephthah's daughter. She emphasized Jephthah's faithfulness to a rash vow, in contrast to his daughter's faithful response. Esther Fuchs (1989, 35) argued that the ambiguity whether Jephthah's daughter was sacrificed or consigned to perpetual virginity functions as a kind of apology for Jephthah's behavior. Cheryl Exum's (1992, 65–66) translation of Judg 11:36 emphasizes her argument that the story's message to women is to submit to paternal authority whatever the cost, since Jephthah's daughter fails to resist her father's authority: "Do to me according to what has gone forth from your mouth now that Yhwh has granted you vindication against your enemies the Ammonites."

Mieke Bal's interest is in the daughter's virginity. She argues that the Hebrew word *bətûlay*, usually translated "my virginity," in Judg 11:37 should be understood as a "life-phase" of a young woman between adolescence and marriage that she describes as "near-ripeness" (1988, 48). Womanist scholar Renita J. Weems (1988, 60–61) focused on the friends of Jephthah's daughter who accompanied her to bewail her virginity: "we can be grateful that Jephthah's daughter, in her one moment of resolve, found a ministry for women to women: the ministry of weeping with God." Valerie Cooper's (2003, 188) womanist approach compared Jephthah's daughter to contemporary black women who sometimes barter their own lives to preserve the honor of the black men in their lives.

Methodological Approach

In this section I discuss Judg 11:1–12:7 from the perspective of sociology of families, specifically the model referred to as the functional perspective on the family. This perspective emphasizes the significance of the family as an institution for preserving social stability by socializing children, providing a major source for emotional and practical support for its members, policing sexual activity and sexual reproduction, and providing its members with a social identity. The functional perspective promotes the conventional family structure with the male breadwinner/stay-at-home mom nuclear family as the ideal one for securing the family's economic stability and children's needs (Barkan 2010, §11.2).

Functionalists maintain that significant deviation from this family structure will create social instability. For example, mothers who work outside the home, especially single mothers are considered a threat to the survival of the family as an institution because they are viewed as ineffective in the socialization of their children, leading to their children's juvenile delinquency. An example of how race and gender play a role in the functionalist perspective is the above-mentioned report on the black family. The report concluded that black families had rejected the majority (white) male-dominated family structure, which resulted in a "tangle of pathology" from which it would be difficult for black families to recover (Moynihan 1965, 31–32).[6] In attributing the cause of the challenges facing black America to the usurpation by black women of male authority in the home, Moynihan stated:

> In essence, the Negro community has been forced into a matriarchal structure which, because it is so out of line with the rest of the American society, seriously retards the progress of the group as a whole, and imposes a crushing blow on the Negro male and, in consequence, on a great many Negro women as well. (31)

The functional perspective is sustained by a family values rhetoric, which shares perspectives on the role of the traditional family in sustaining the nation. When public policy issues on the causes of poverty and their solutions are debated, family values or "Judeo-Christian values" are often included regarding what reforms should be added or excluded (Powell 2006, 10–11). The term *Judeo-Christian* is a myth that claims that Jews and Christians share a common tradition and common belief (A. Cohen 1969).[7] The phrase *Judeo-Christian values* has gained political currency

---

6. Moynihan appropriated the phrase *tangle of pathology* from psychologist Kenneth Clark to describe the cyclical pattern of high birth rates to younger mothers, which leads to low educational attainment and low-income rates, thus depriving their children of opportunities, who then repeat the cycle (McGrath 2010, 2–3).

7. Theologian Arthur A. Cohen (1969) argued that the phrase *Judeo-Christian tradition* was invented to combat the rising anti-Semitism. However, he finds the term incomprehensible because Jews and Christians have fundamentally opposing religious beliefs: Jews expected a redeemer to come out of Zion and Christians affirm that that redeemer, in the person of Jesus Christ, has already come, a belief that Jews reject.

since the last half of the twentieth century. Although both liberals and conservatives bandy about the phrase, religious and political conservatives usually invoke it to decry the lack of Christian ideas and practices, effectively subsuming the *Judeo* in the phrase under the *Christian* (Hicks 2003, 17). As the rhetoric goes, the lack of Judeo-Christian values is manifested by the growing societal ills, including a rise in crime, high-school dropout rate, poverty, and health disparities (Perry 1996, 345).

Family values rhetoric was elevated in the American political lexicon when former Vice President Dan Quayle, in a May 1992 speech at the Commonwealth Club of California (commonly referred to as the "Murphy Brown Speech"), pronounced that the Los Angeles riots that ensued following the acquittal of the police officers who beat black motorist Rodney King were the result of a "poverty of values" in the black community rather than a response to systemic racism and inequality in the United States (M. Cohen 2015).

Quayle opined that at the heart of this lack of values was the rise in the number of children born to mothers who had never married, especially teen mothers. According to Quayle, the failure of blacks to accept traditional American values, individual responsibility, and social mores has left blacks to contend with an increase in poverty, drug and welfare dependency, poor educational outcomes, and crime.

Quayle concluded his speech with a call for a return to Judeo-Christian (meaning white) values that will empower the poor (meaning blacks) to reclaim their moral values, personal responsibility, and independence. Although Quayle never uttered the words *family values* in this speech, it was understood that the family breakdown was a failure of family values.[8] Nor was it happenstance that Quayle framed his argument on the immorality of poor Americans in terms of Judeo-Christian values. Family values rhetoric is rooted in more conservative biblical religious thought and derives much of its core beliefs—and justification—from select biblical teachings and doctrine (Newman 2007, 27).

Black women in general and single black women in particular are not lacking in "biblically based values," despite the cry by critics that a

---

8. The term *family values* actually appeared in the Republican Party platform in 1976. However, Dan Quayle's use of the term family values in a speech at the Republican National Convention in August 1992 propelled the term into the wider cultural context, where soon after family values appeared in the title of nearly 300 media headlines (Collins 1998, 62).

"traditional family" life would cure their poverty (Powell 2006).⁹ Yet the message that single mothers and their children suffer from a poverty of values was expressed by 2016 Republican presidential candidate Ben Carson when asked by satellite radio show host David Webb how to fix the "pandemic" of single-parent birth rates: "We need to face the fact that when young girls have babies out of wedlock, most of the time their education ends with that first baby. And those babies are four times as likely to grow up in poverty, end up in the penal system or the welfare system" (Carson 2015). Given that both men are black conservatives, it is not a stretch to conclude that they were speaking primarily about single black women. This is an example of the "politics of respectability" or "respectability politics," a term coined by Evelyn Brooks Higginbotham (1994, 187) to describe the push for reform of individual black behavior. The men's conversation was draped in the rhetoric of Judeo-Christian family values but lacked a critique of institutional impediments to improvement. This is the same lens through which Carson and Webb and their supporters might likely view Jephthah's mother, an unmarried woman of lower social status who has given birth outside the patriarchal social norms. Like the Jezebel stereotype often attached to black women, they would label her promiscuous and immoral. Her son Jephthah would be made to bear the stigma of his mother's status, his every move judged (pun intended) on that basis. This is the beginning of how Jephthah and his mother, in being decried as contributing to the downfall of Israel for not conforming to "Judeo-Christian" family norms, are racialized black.

Analysis

Jephthah is one of six so-called major judges in the book of Judges, named for charismatic leaders who brought about the deliverance of the Israelites from oppression by their enemies. A major theme in Judges is YHWH's grace and Israel's continuous rejection of the same. A constant refrain in the book is: "And the sons of Israel did the evil thing in the eyes of YHWH" (Judg 2:11; 3:7, 12; 4:1; 6:1; 10:6; 13:1).¹⁰ Therefore, YHWH gave them into

---

9. A nationwide survey conducted jointly by the *Washington Post* and the Kaiser Family Foundation found that black women represented the most religious group in America (Theola Labbé-DeBose 2012).

10. Translations from the MT of the Hebrew Bible are my own unless otherwise indicated.

the hands of their enemies. Commentaries often regard "the evil thing" as religious apostasy. The accusation that the Israelites did what was evil is sometimes followed by the Hebrew conjunctive *wāw*, "and," along with the subordinate clause, "worshiped the Baals" (Judg 2:11), leading one to conclude that this was the source of their guilt.[11] However, more often the text omits the worship of foreign gods, leaving ambiguous whether the evil thing was something other than religious apostasy. For example, Tammi Schneider (2000, 101, 124) contends that "the bad thing" was intermarriage, which led to the worship of foreign gods.

After serving their enemies a number of years the Israelites would cry out to YHWH, who would send judges to rescue them. There would be a period of rest, followed by the people's relapse, and the cycle would repeat itself. However, rather than a cycle, the worsening behavior of the Israelites leads to a deteriorating downward spiral. The pattern was broken in chapter 10 when the Israelites sinned against YHWH, who allowed them once again to be delivered into the hands of their enemies (Judg 10:7-9). However, this time they confessed and turned back to YHWH, and YHWH took pity on Israel but did not send a deliverer to release them (Judg 10:16). As Jack Sasson (2013, 406) stated, this time "God cannot be mollified." With the imminent Ammonite threat near, the Israelites would have to find a deliverer on their own.

We first meet Jephthah in Judg 11:1, who is described by three brief characteristics: he was a Gileadite, a brave fighter, and the son of a prostitute: *wayiptāḥ haggil'ādî hāyâ gibbôr ḥayil wəhû ben-'iššâ zônâ*. A number of interpreters translate the conjunctive *wāw* prefixed to the pronoun "he" as "and." For example, Susan Niditch translated it as, "And Jephthah the Gileadite was a mighty man of valor, *and* he was the son of a whore woman" (2008, 124, emphasis added). Others, such as Sasson (2013, 416), use a comma instead of a conjunction to separate the clauses: "Jephthah of Gilead was well-born, the son of a harlot." However, a number of interpreters translate the conjunction "but": "Now Jephthah the Gileadite was a mighty warrior, *but* he was the son of a harlot" (Webb 2015, 307, emphasis added), "Jephthah, the Gileadite, was a heroic warrior, *but* he was the son of a prostitute" (Guest 2003, 272, emphasis added). The conjunction can be translated "but"; however, it is frequently rendered "and" in Hebrew

---

[11]. It is the Baals and Asherahs in Judg 3:7 and the Baals and the Astartes in 10:6 who are the problem.

grammar texts. The decision to use "and" implies that Jephthah's parentage does not have any bearing on his character. In contrast, "but" conveys the message that, despite his bravery and skill, he will amount to a moral failure on account of his mother's status.

Albert Soggin (1981, 207) expresses this sentiment in his commentary on Judges. He states that Jephthah's illegitimate birth to a prostitute made him a suspect leader in Israel. This is in line with the functional perspective of the family values arguments mentioned earlier, which asserts that children of single or working mothers behave antisocially. Moreover, the argument goes that Jephthah's mother's occupation and status make her unfit to pass along the proper values to her son (Perry 1996, 352). Lillian Klein (1988, 98) contends that Jephthah, "as the son of a harlot, even though Israelite, has neither father nor community as 'father.'" Deryn Guest (2003, 197) adds that Jephthah's "ignominious portrayal" is on account of his mother's status: "His mother, we are told, was a harlot, and his father is said to be 'Gilead'—a none too subtle comment upon his mother's sexual laxity." Both Soggin and Guest's evaluation of Jephthah's character as a result of his mother's status, perhaps without realizing it, reflect a common perception of black mothers who have children out of wedlock.

Robert G. Boling offers a similar critique: "'Gilead had *sired* Jephthah' explicates the statement that he was 'son of a prostitute,' *father unknown*" (1975, 197, emphasis added).[12] Since Gilead could be a personal name or the name of a geographical region, his implication is that any man of Gilead can be the father of Jephthah, since Jephthah has no patronymic. Unfortunately, the representation of Jephthah's mother by some interpreters as a "loose" woman is similar to the stereotype of single black mothers not knowing the paternity of their children's fathers, referred to pejoratively as "baby daddy": "You are not the father!"[13]

The term *sire* functions to dehumanize Jephthah's mother: to sire is to be the male parent of an animal for breeding. Boling's citation that "Gilead had sired Jephthah" conjures images of enslaved African women forced to have sexual relations against their will in order to increase the slave

---

[12]. In fairness, Tammi Schneider (2000, 162) also mentioned the importance of understanding who "sired Jephthah" in relation to his mother's status as a *zônâ*.

[13]. This is a catchphrase popularized by tabloid talk show host Maury Povitch after paternity test results prove that the male guest accused of being the biological father of the female guest's child is not the father.

population for profit. Enslaved women who were fecund were derogatorily referred to as "breeders."

The term *'iššâ zônâ*, usually translated "prostitute" (NRSV, NIV), "harlot" (KJV), or "whore" (Message), can mean a professional sex-worker (Josh 2) or a woman who has had sexual relations outside of marriage or some other unapproved sexual behavior (Ezek 23:44). Niditch (2008, 124), who noted that the Old Latin uses the phrase "fornicating woman," translated the phrase as "whore woman."

Mercedes Bachman contends that when *'iššâ zônâ* is paired with "house of," it usually refers to the professional occupation (Josh 2:1, 6:22). In contrast, she maintains that when the phrase appears alone, it is a reference to single mothers, such as Jephthah's mother in Judg 11:1 and the two women in 1 Kgs 3:16 (2013, 26). However, the marriage restrictions for priests in the Holiness Code prohibit them from marrying both an *'iššâ zônâ* (Lev 21:7) and a *zônâ* (v. 14). In both these instances, the interpretation can mean a woman who has had sexual relations outside of marriage, consensual or otherwise, or a widow, divorcée, or defiled woman. Moreover, scholars agree that Samson's visit to a *'iššâ zônâ*, with the verb "to go, come" (Heb. *bô'*) in Judg 16:1 was of a sexual nature with a professional sex-worker. Whether Jephthah's mother was a professional sex-worker, engaged in socially proscribed sexual behavior, or was "caught in a web of sexual power relations" (Moss 2009, 106), she is not even given the honorific *'em*, Hebrew for "mother" in the text.

There are those commentators who evaluate Jephthah negatively on account of this judged deviation from the traditional family structure. One such commentator is Michael Smith, who argued that Jephthah's personal family problems had a deleterious impact on the nation of Israel. According to Smith, Jephthah's troubles began at childhood, given that his father had set a bad example for him by having "produced Jephthah as a result of his immoral passion with a harlot" (2005, 286).

This is the functionalist perspective that traditional family structure promotes order and stability in family and society, and nontraditional families lead to the failure of society. I am not saying that Smith has racialized Jephthah and his mother as black. However, it is a regular function of family values' advocates to argue that there has been a breakdown of the traditional family structure, and those usually blamed as largely contributing to this spiral are black families (Powell 2006, 73). Interestingly, Smith does not acknowledge Jephthah's father for bringing up Jephthah with the sons of his father's legal wife (Judg 11:2). Fathers in nonmarital childbearing situations are often accused of not being responsible or involved with their children, especially black fathers. However, according to data from a 2013 Centers for Disease Control and Prevention study, American fathers in general and black fathers in particular, were involved in their children's upbringing (Jones and Mosher 2013).[14] For example, 34 percent of noncoresidential black fathers aged 15–44 had bathed, diapered, or dressed their children, and 25 percent had played with their children. These data are contrary to the functional perspective, which ignores diverse family configurations that do not conform to dominant family paradigms.

Jephthah was likely the firstborn in his family. Jephthah's name means "may (God) open" or "(He) God opens," a praise offered up at the birth of a firstborn (*HALOT* 1:425). The sequence of the narrative also suggests that Jephthah's father's wife bore him sons after Jephthah's birth (11:2). Primogeniture was a common practice in the ancient world, and Jephthah, as the firstborn, should have been the patrilineal successor to his father's inheritance. However, when Jephthah's brothers from his father's legitimate wife grew up, they drove Jephthah out of town to keep Jephthah from inheriting in their father's house: "You shall not inherit anything in our father's house; for you are the son of another woman" (11:2). If there were doubts to the identity of Jephthah's father, his brothers did not have any. Given their knowledge, they must have also been aware of Jephthah's mother's identity. They may have known of Jephthah from town gossip during their upbringing or upon their father's death. Or their father may have been open with them about his other son. In any event, they do not refer to her as a "prostitute" but as another "woman" or "wife."

According to the Deuteronomic Code, Jephthah's brothers had no authority to deprive Jephthah of his inheritance. Deuteronomy 21:15–17 states that a firstborn son is entitled to a double portion of his father's inheritance despite being the son of the disliked wife. Although Jephthah's father was not married to his mother, he was still entitled to an inheritance. Several scholars, including David Marcus, have pointed out that Jephthah's brothers could not have expelled him without the sanction of the elders through a legal process: "The brothers initiated the dis-inheriting proceedings, but it was the elders in their role as a juridical court who pronounced the verdict and ruled against Jephthah" (Marcus 1990, 106).

---

14. The researchers measured a father's involvement with his children as how often he engaged in activities within a four-week period, whether or not he lived with his children (Jones and Mosher 2012).

There is an unfortunate parallel here between Jephthah and young black males who find themselves entrapped in family or criminal court systems due to neglect, crime, or delinquency.

Jephthah fled from his brothers to the land of Tob where he drew "outlaws" (Heb. *ănāšîm rēqîm*; lit. "worthless" or "empty" men) to himself, and they went out with him (Judg 11:3). Here is where Jephthah earned his title as a "mighty warrior." Commentators have referred to Jephthah and the men gathered around him as guerrilla fighters (McCann 2011, 80), mercenaries (Boling 1975, 196; Schneider 2000, 165), military ruffians (Niditch 2008, 131), and even "thugs": "Jephthah's thugs are precisely the reason why he is approached in the first place" (Brensinger 1999, 129). Each of these titles infers a group of men resorting to crime or other disreputable means to earn a living. These are men who had to operate "outside the institutional power base" (Niditch 2008, 131).

Jephthah's need to operate outside the centers of power is a result of his having been forced into exile by his brothers, who were part of the social institution—the *bêt 'āb*, "father's house"—that should have protected and provided for him. Instead, they posed a threat to Jephthah. The verb "to flee" (Heb. *bāraḥ*) suggests that he was in imminent danger from his brothers.

Jephthah's circumstances can certainly be compared to many young black men, who, excluded from social attainment due to lagging educational and skill achievement, incarceration and limited access to the labor force, resort to the underground economy as a source of income (Smith and Joe 1994, 10, 12).[15] Yet, critics like Carson and Webb, who are quick to blame single mothers for raising children whom they argue become an economic burden on society, fail to acknowledge that these young men, like Jephthah, who was stripped of their economic and social stability, nevertheless inculcate a strong work ethic and individual responsibility, virtues promoted by the family values proponents. Moreover, like Jephthah, many of them are also respected for their survival skills in dangerous communities (12). Jephthah's critics are not willing to concede that he played their game—that if one works hard enough they will get ahead, values perhaps passed down by his mother—and won.

---

15. "Underground economy," also referred to as "informal" economy, include activities such as unreported or "under the table" income, such as babysitting, construction, and hustling odd jobs, to illegal activities such as robbery, drug dealing and organized crime (Smith and Joe 1994, 12).

So when the Israelites were in need of a military leader because YHWH did not send a deliverer when the Ammonites rose up against Israel, the elders of Gilead went and retrieved Jephthah from Tob to make him their commander (Judg 11:5–6). The chiefs and elders had previously agreed to offer anyone willing to fight on their behalf the reward of being head over the people of Gilead (10:18). Jephthah responded, "Did you not hate me and drive me out of my father's house? Why have you come to me now that you are in trouble?" (11:7). As mentioned above, the elders had made his eviction by his brothers possible, which is why Jephthah accuses the elders of being responsible.

Brensinger (1999, 129) observes that it was no surprise that the people of Gilead were willing to swallow their pride and turn to Jephthah, since Jephthah's association with the band of fighters is what gave them the confidence that he would be successful. The elders ask Jephthah in essence to "let bygones be bygones" and come and fight the Ammonites on their behalf and they will make him head over them all (Judg 11:8).

Jephthah was likely not aware of this deal, but his suspicion of their attempted rapprochement led them to fear that he would decline their initial proposal, so they offered to make him head of Gilead. They used the language of restoration to appeal to Jephthah. The verb "to turn back" or "to return" (Heb. *šûb*) can also mean "to bring back." The suggestion is that they were willing to include him in the institutional power base.

The elders might have been sincere in their desire to reconcile with Jephthah, or their motives might have been purely self-serving. He responds that if they bring him home and YHWH gives him the victory over the Ammonites then he would be head of the Gileadites (11:9). It is Jephthah, not the elders who introduce the deity into the agreement. Although some scholars doubt the sincerity of Jephthah's attributing the victory to YHWH, he holds the elders to their offer to make him commander and head by speaking all these words before YHWH at Mizpah (11:11), even though the people had already made Jephthah head and commander over them.

A common condemnation of single mothers mentioned above is that they do not possess traditional family values so they do not pass them on to their children. However, one might view Jephthah's reference to the deity at this point as evidence of one who received traditional religious values. Moreover, scholars often mention Jephthah's adept diplomacy in dealing with the Ammonite threat. Not only does he attempt to peacefully negotiate with the Ammonites (12:12), but also when the king rebuffs his overture to resolve this border clash, Jephthah recounts Israel's journey to acquire the land in dispute (Num 21:10–20; 33:5–49) and how YHWH gifted this land to the Israelites (Judg 11:12–24). He concludes by stating that YHWH the Judge would adjudicate between Israel and Ammon (11:27).

Despite the number of commentaries that laud Jephthah for attempting to use diplomacy rather than force with the Ammonites and Jephthah's recitation of Israel's entrance in Palestine, there are some who judge Jephthah as a failure at negotiating, such as Guest, who claimed that Jephthah was a poor negotiator for not having been adequately trained in the ways of YHWH by a proper Israelite mother. On one level, this view is based on the argument that Jephthah gets some of the details wrong.[16] However, on another level, this judgment is on account of Jephthah making the mistake of placing Chemosh on the same level as YHWH, evidence in their eyes that Jephthah's mother had not passed on Israelite values to her son.

If Jephthah is guilty of anything it is being overzealous. Once diplomatic efforts failed military conflict ensued. It is reported that the spirit of YHWH was upon Jephthah, and he "passed over to Gilead and Manasseh, and he passed over to Mizpah of Gilead. And from Mizpah of Gilead he passed over to the sons of Ammon" (11:29). The deity, who had been silent concerning the activities of humans in this whole affair, now shows at least tacit approval of Jephthah as Israel's judge. Jephthah is now the charismatic leader in Israel having been endowed with YHWH's spirit.

The repeated use of the verb *'ābar*, "to pass over, through, or by," in verse 29 (3x) suggests that Jephthah is building momentum with each victory over each town he passed over. Under the influence of the spirit, Jephthah became intoxicated by the euphoria of this experience, and he got caught up. Jephthah was so taken by the experience of YHWH's spirit upon him that in the midst of the battle he makes a rash vow that if YHWH would give the Ammonites into his hand that whoever came forth from his house would be offered as a burnt sacrifice to YHWH (11:30–31).[17] Other scholars have offered different motives for Jephthah's vow: fear, rejection,

---

16. Klein and others mention that Jephthah appears to conflate the kings. However, J. Maxwell Miller (1989, 585) argues that Num 33:10–20 relies on Judg 11:12 and Num 33.

17. Scholars have engaged in much debate whether *hāyâ hayyôṣē'* should be translated "whoever" (Pressler 2002, 202) or "whatever" (Boling 1975, 206) comes out of the doors of my house (Judg 11:31). Either translation is acceptable. However, the

ambition, and so on. Where some have called the vow "impetuous" and rash, Webb (1986, 40) disagrees arguing that "the vow is not impulsive; it is shrewd and calculating—entirely in keeping with Jephthah's character as we have come to know it." Arguably, Jephthah did not need to make the vow since YHWH was already likely to grant his petition for victory.

The text states that Jephthah delivered the Ammonites a decisive defeat, as was expected, given that YHWH's spirit upon him guaranteed a successful outcome (Judg 11:32–33). Therefore, he was obliged to fulfill his vow made to YHWH. The tragic outcome unfolds when he returns home and is greeted with hand drums and dancing by his daughter, his only child (11:34) in celebration of his victory. The reader is not told her name or the name of her mother. The text, though, conveys Jephthah's surprise at seeing his daughter. The Hebrew particle *hinneh* usually translated "lo!" or "behold!" regularly introduces something newly recognized (BDB 243). At that moment, Jephthah realizes the consequence of his ill-fated vow to YHWH.

I agree with commentators who contend that Jephthah should have expected his daughter to be the first to come out the doors of his house. It was a tradition in Israel for women to come out to meet the victors with hand drums and dances, such as Miriam, who took a hand drum and led the women in song and dance after Israel's victory over Pharaoh at the sea of reeds (Exod 15:20). Also the women of Israel joined in antiphonal singing and dancing accompanied by musical instruments to greet Saul with a hero's welcome home from battle (1 Sam 18:6–7).

Nevertheless, the writer insists that Jephthah is caught unaware by her emergence from the house and expresses grief upon the realization that he would have to offer his daughter as a sacrifice. Tearing his clothes he cried, "Alas, my daughter! You have brought me to my knees. You have become (the cause of) my troubles. I have opened my mouth to YHWH, and I cannot turn back" (Judg 11:35).[18] Jephthah, who had been so eloquent in his speech in his negotiations with the elders and the king of Ammon has been less so in his vow to YHWH. His daughter acquiesced saying, "My father, you have opened your mouth to YHWH, do to me according to

---

reader was likely expecting a servant or Jephthah's daughter, leading many commentators to interpret the clause as whoever.

18. I find it disturbing that many of our youth choirs sing an arrangement of these lyrics, "Open My Mouth" by Dexter Walker and Zion Movement: "I open my mouth unto the Lord and I won't turn back. I will go, I shall go to see what the end's gonna be."

what came forth from your mouth, now that YHWH has done for you vengeance against your enemies, against the sons of Ammon" (11:36). Her response is worded in a way that is reminiscent of Jephthah's vow to YHWH, and now he must do to her as he had vowed.

Scholars debate whether or not Jephthah's daughter had to be sacrificed despite the claim by some that the vow was irrevocable. There are those who argue that a substitute animal could have manifested itself, as in the Akedah, "the binding of Isaac" when YHWH asked Abraham to sacrifice Isaac in Gen 22. Jon Levenson (1993, 14) proposed that, as a firstborn daughter, she could have been declared unsuitable to be offered as a burnt offering to YHWH. Sasson (2013, 416) suggested that the people of Gilead could have interceded on her behalf, as the people did for Jonathan and ransomed him when his father Saul was going to kill him in 1 Sam 14. But there is no intercessor for Jephthah's daughter.

Jephthah made an error in judgment that cost him his only child. However, his action is neither the sum total of his character nor a fatal flaw that resulted from being born to parents outside a "suitable" family situation. In the brief account of his daughter's sacrifice, we are shown a father raising his daughter on his own. When she asks for two months to bewail the fact that she will never know a man sexually, he obliges (Judg 11:37), perhaps thinking that this will give him time to figure out how to reverse the circumstances. YHWH's silence, which indicates that "God neither requires nor rejects human sacrifice" (Exum 1992, 60), provides no comfort.

Michael Smith, quoted above as having passed judgment on Jephthah's parentage, states that Jephthah's tale is an example of the failure of the family in Israel's history during the period of the Judges. If Jephthah's parents had modeled for him the traditional family, then his family line would not have come to an end through the sacrifice of his *virgin* daughter: "With Jephthah's daughter's virginity finalized, there was no possibility of any future offspring, in contrast to the secondary judges listed around them," who were more than fruitful (2005, 297).

Lillian Klein describes Jephthah as a "pitiable" figure whose ignorance of YHWH's statutes and ordinances render him an insufficient deliverer. Klein is referring to the prohibition against child sacrifice. Her argument is that the custom of sacrificing the firstborn son as a burnt offering to YHWH was obsolete by Jephthah's time and that if he had been raised properly he would have known, despite YHWH's silence in the matter of Jephthah's daughter. At least she acknowledges that child sacrifice might have been part of the Israelite cultus, in contrast to those who contend that Jephthah had adopted the practices of the Canaanites.[19]

Still, Klein (1988, 98) argues that Jephthah lacks any "historical memory" of the basic tenets of the religion of YHWH because he grew up without a father, the one "responsible for passing on the male bonding, the knowledge of history." According to Klein, as the progeny of his father's sexual indiscretion with a prostitute, it should not come as a surprise when Jephthah brings ruin to Israel: "Whether with foreign women (Gideon's concubine) or not (the harlot-mother of Jephthah), non-familial Israelite proliferation is shown as potentially destructive" (99).

Both Smith and Klein, without coming out and directly blaming Jephthah's mother for his tragedy, sound much like Moynihan, Quayle, and Carson in attributing any moral failures of Jephthah to the lack of strong male leadership in the family because his father stepped outside the traditional family structure to father a child by a woman who was not his wife. As mentioned above Moynihan, who cautioned that black children risked "being caught up in a tangle of pathology" due to being in a non-traditional family structure, blamed the mother. Interestingly, Smith and Klein attribute Jephthah's tragedy to the poor example set for Jephthah by his father. Yet, family values' advocates usually assign the mother responsibility for the socialization of children, which raises the question: why Jephthah's father's sons by his wife are not faulted for lacking moral values?

As I have shown, Judeo-Christian values relating to family and self-reliance have been racially ascribed to whites; blacks are handed epithets such as antisocial, antifamily, and welfare dependent. Family values rhetoric promotes the idealized nuclear family (married, heterosexual couple with the breadwinning father and stay-at-home mother) and marginalizes poor, black, and alternative family arrangements and then blames them for the breakdown of the family. Single black mothers especially are viewed as sexually immoral and therefore incapable of passing traditional family values to their children, who, as some contend, grow up to be juvenile delinquents. Therefore, explicit readings of Jephthah such as Michael Smith's through the lens of family values have the unintentional effect of racializing Jephthah and his mother as black by assigning to them attributes that have been ascribed to black mothers and their children. As such

---

19. According to some scholars, there is no indisputable evidence that the Canaanites practiced child sacrifice (Sasson 2013, 412).

Jephthah, like Trayvon Martin, Jordan Davis, and even President Obama, despite their upbringing and although their mothers did not give birth to thugs, are still seen as such.

Works Cited

Aristotle. 1997. *Poetics*. Translated by George Whalley. Edited by John Baxter and Patrick Atherton. Montreal: McGill-Queen's University Press.
Bachmann, Mercedes Garcia. 2013. *Women at Work in the Deuteronomistic History*. Atlanta: Society of Biblical Literature.
Bal, Mieke. 1988. *Death and Dissymetry: The Politics of Coherence in the Book of Judges*. Chicago: University of Chicago Press.
Barkan, Steven E. "The Family." In *Sociology: Understanding and Changing the Social World*. Brief Edition. Vol. 1.0. http://tinyurl.com/SBL0688u1.
Boling, Robert G. 1975. *Judges*. AB 6A. Garden City, NY: Doubleday.
Botelho, Greg. 2014. "Don't Call Him a 'Thug' and Four Other Things You Should Know about Richard Sherman." CNN. http://tinyurl.com/SBL0688z2.
Bouie, Jamelle. 2014. "Richard Sherman Is Right: Thug Is the New N-Word." *www.thedailybeast.com*. http://tinyurl.com/SBL0688x1.
Brensinger, Terry L. 1999. *Judges*. Believers Church Bible Commentary. Scottdale, PA: Herald Press.
Brown-Manning, Robyn. 2013. "We Don't Give Birth to Thugs; We Give Birth to Children: The Emotional Journeys of African-American Mothers Raising Sons under American Racism." PhD diss., City University of New York.
Burroughs, Margaret. 1968. *What Shall I Tell My Children Who Are Black?* Chicago: M.A.A.H. Press.
Carson, Benjamin. 2015. "Dr. Ben Carson on Traditional Families," interview by David Webb. *David Webb Show*. SiriusXM.
Cohen, Arthur A. 1969. "The Myth of the Judeo-Christian Tradition." *Commentary*. http://tinyurl.com/SBL0688a2.
Cohen, Michael A. 2015. "Vice President Dan Quayle: The 'Murphy Brown Speech.'" Live from the Campaign Trail. http://tinyurl.com/SBL0688b2.
Collins, Patricia Hill. 1998. "It's All in the Family: Intersections of Gender, Race, and Nation." *Hypatia* 13.3:62–82.

Cooper, Valerie C. 2003. "Some Place to Cry: Jephthah's Daughter and the Double Dilemma of Black Women in America." Pages 181–91 in *Pregnant Passion: Gender, Sex, and Violence in the Hebrew Bible*. Edited by Cheryl A. Kirk-Duggan. Atlanta: Society of Biblical Literature.

Day, Peggy. 1989. *Gender and Difference in Ancient Israel*. Minneapolis: Fortress.

Exum, J. Cheryl. 1992. *Tragedy and Biblical Narrative: Arrows of the Almighty*. Cambridge: Cambridge University Press.

———. 1995. "Feminist Criticism: Whose Interests Are Being Served?" Pages 65–90 in *Judges and Methods: New Approaches in Biblical Studies*. Edited by Gale A. Yee. Minneapolis: Fortress.

Fuchs, Esther. 1989. "Marginalization, Ambiguity, Silencing: The Story of Jephthah's Daughter." *JFSR* 5:35–45.

Guest, P. Deryn. 2003. "Judges." Pages 190–207 in *Eerdman's Commentary on the Bible*. Edited by James D. G. Gunn and John William Rogerson. Grand Rapids: Eerdmans.

Hicks, Douglas. 2003. *Religion and the Workplace: Pluralism, Spirituality, Leadership*. Cambridge: Cambridge University Press.

Higginbotham, Evelyn Brooks. 1994. *Righteous Discontent: The Women's Movement in the Black Baptist Church, 1880–1920*. Cambridge: Harvard University Press.

Janzen, David. 2005. "Why the Deuteronomist Told about the Sacrifice of Jephthah's Daughter." *JSOT* 29:339–57.

Jeter, Joseph R., Jr. 2003. *Preaching Judges*. St. Louis: Chalice.

Jones, Jo, and William D. Mosher. 2013. *National Health Statistics Report*. Centers for Disease Control. http://tinyurl.com/SBL0688c2.

Klein, Lillian R. 1988. *Triumph of Irony in the Book of Judges*. JSOTSup 68. Sheffield: Almond Press.

Klopsis, Nick. 2014. "Erin Andrews Wasn't 'Scared' during Richard Sherman Interview." Newsday. http://tinyurl.com/SBL0688y2.

Labbé-DeBose, Theola. 2012. "Black Women Are among Country's Most Religious Groups." *Washington Post*. http://tinyurl.com/SBL0688d2.

Levenson, Jon D. 1993. *The Death and Resurrection of the Beloved Son*. New Haven: Yale University Press.

Logan, Alice. 2009. "Rehabilitating Jephthah." *JBL* 128:665–85.

Lowery, Wesley, and Kimberly Kindy. 2015. "These Are the Racially Charged E-mails That Got Three Ferguson Police and Court Officials Fired." *Washington Post*. http://tinyurl.com/SBL0688e2.

Manfred, Tony. 2014. "Fox Explains Why It Cut Off the Richard Sherman-Erin Andrews Interview." Business Insider. http://tinyurl.com/SBL0688x2.

Marcus, David. 1990. "The Legal Dispute between Jephthah and the Elders." *HAR* 12:105–14.

McCann, Clinton J. 2011. *Judges*. IBC. Louisville: Westminster John Knox Press.

McGrath, Colin. 2010. "Navigating the 'Tangle of Pathology': Community Organization and Family Strength in Watts on the Eve of the 1965 Rebellion." *Northwestern Undergraduate Research Journal* 6:6–10.

Miller, J. Maxwell. 1989. "The Israelite Journey through (around) Moab and Moabite Toponymy." *JBL* 108:577–99.

Moynihan, Daniel Patrick. 1965. *The Negro Family: The Case for National Action*. Washington, DC: United States Government.

Moss, Otis, III. 2009. "Sermon: 'When Thugs Get Saved: Judges 11:1–11.'" Pages 104–14 in *More Power in the Pulpit: How America's Most Effective Black Preachers Prepare Their Sermons*. Edited by Cleophus J. LaRue. Louisville: Westminster John Knox.

Newman, Jay. 2007. *Pious Pro-family Rhetoric: Postures and Paradoxes in Philosophical Perspective*. New York: Lang.

Niditch, Susan. 2008. *Judges: A Commentary*. Louisville: Presbyterian Publishing.

Omi, Michael, and Howard Winant. 2015. "Introduction: Racial Formation in the United States." Pages 1–18 in *Racial Formation in the United States*. Edited by Michael and Howard Winant Omi. 3rd ed. London: Routledge.

Perry, Twila. 1996. "Family Values, Race, Feminism and Public Policy." *Santa Clara Law Review* 36.2:345–74.

Powell, Elizabeth Caroline. 2006. "The Political Use of 'Family Values' Rhetoric." MA Thesis, Georgia State University.

Pressler, Carolyn. 2002. *Joshua, Judges and Ruth*. Louisville: Westminster John Knox.

Sasson, Jack M. 2013. "Jephthah: Chutzpah and Overreach in a Hebrew Judge." Pages 405–20 in *Literature as Politics, Politics as Literature: Essays on the Ancient Near East in Honor of Peter Machinist*. Edited by David S. Vanderhooft and Abraham Winitzer. Winona Lake, IN: Eisenbrauns.

Schneider, Tammi J. 2000. *Judges*. Berit Olam. Edited by David W. Cotter. Collegeville, MN: Liturgical Press.

Smith, Michael J. 2005. "The Failure of the Family in Judges, Part 1: Jephthah." *BSac* 162:279–98.
Smith, Ralph, and Tom Joe. 1994. *World without Work: The Causes and Consequences of Black Male Joblessness*. Washington, DC: Center for the Study of Social Policy; Philadelphia: Philadelphia Children's Network.
Soggin, J. Albert. 1981. *Judges: A Commentary*. OTL. Translated by John Bowden. Philadelphia: Westminster.
Trible, Phyllis. 1984. *Texts of Terror: Literary-Feminist Readings of Biblical Narratives*. Philadelphia: Fortress.
Webb, Barry. 2015. *Judges and Ruth: God in Chaos*. Preaching the Word. Wheaton, IL: Crossway.
Weems, Renita J. 1988. *Just A Sister Away: A Womanist Vision of Women's Relationships in the Bible*. San Diego, CA: LuraMedia.

Part 4
Illuminating Biblical Children/Childhood

Outrageous, Audacious, Courageous, Willful: Reading the Enslaved Girl of Acts 12

Margaret Aymer

> From *womanish* ...
> Usually referring to outrageous, audacious, courageous or willful behavior ...
> Acting grown up. (Walker 2015, 17)

We overlook her, usually. She sits right at the entrance, near the outside. She listens for us knocking on the outer gate, seeking sanctuary. She announces our presence to the gathering of the Way. Luke[1] calls her Rhoda, perhaps more a moniker than a true name. Yet he never allows her to speak in her own words. She runs along the borders of Christian community, unseen, unheard.

Rhoda appears during the penultimate narrative of Simon Peter in Acts.[2] Objectively, she can be read as a bit player. Her entire story is contextualized and told within seven verses. However, womanist biblical hermeneutics requires that African American women's stories matter. These stories have included enslaved girls, girls like Rhoda. Therefore, Rhoda's story must matter. We must take her seriously. To do so, we must "read darkness," the trauma of Rhoda's existence (Wimbush 2003, 21). Further, as womanists teach, we must read darkness intersectionally. Race *and* gender *and* class oppression, taken collectively, cause black women's trauma. To analyze these discreetly is not to tell the whole story. So too it is with this

---

1. For the sake of clarity, I refer to the author of Luke-Acts as "Luke." Like many biblical scholars, I uphold the anonymity of Luke-Acts.

2. That is, the imprisonment and escape of Peter (Acts 12:1–19). Peter appears once more, in verse 7 of the story of the Jerusalem council in Acts 15. Later I argue that "Rhoda" may be a moniker rather than the girl slave's actual name.

enslaved girl. If we are to read her darkness, we must read the trauma of her existence intersectionally. In this essay, I propose such a reading.

This enslaved girl, I argue, serves as an interpretative wedge. Reading her darkness intersectionally helps us hear silenced voices, hers and others'. Hers is a "womanist" voice, by Alice Walker's poetic description. Through her actions, she shows herself to be "acting grown up" (Walker 2015, 17). Despite unsubtle threats from her owners, she speaks. Her refusal to be silenced constitutes womanish, "audacious, courageous … *willful* behavior" (17). The darkness of this girl's life also illuminates the enigmatic early church. We see the Jerusalem church as all too human, a traumatic gathering. In the face of political oppression, they cannot see the oppression they perpetuate. In the face of their own darkness, for one enslaved girl they perpetuate intersectional darkness.

I read Rhoda as what Shanell Smith (2014) would call an "ambi*veil*ant" reader. Smith proposes this womanist hermeneutic in her investigation of Woman Babylon. I read as a black woman conscious of Dubosian double consciousness. Signified upon, racialized into a nonnative culture, I struggle to speak clearly. I so easily allow the imposed veil—African American—to occlude my particularity. Yet, my particularity—Caribbean, naturalized, economic migrant—informs my reading. So too does my privilege—ordained Presbyterian minister, tenured professor. I am a black woman in America. However, unlike Rhoda, my voice bears weight; it is heard. Thus I take seriously Smith's ambi*veil*ant challenge. She warns that complicity and resistance coexist "in every colonized subject" (64). This is true for me and for Luke, Rhoda's narrator. It is true for Luke's church and for my Presbyterian Church (USA).

Listening to Rhoda's silenced challenge of the early church raises questions. How does Rhoda's story challenge the idealized narrative of the early church? How does she subvert the belief that Luke's narratives favor women? How are we, as women of privilege, complicit in her story? What may we learn from this subaltern's silenced cry of liberation? I will attend to these at the end of this essay.

First, however, we must attend to Rhoda. Two contextual conversations begin this process of paying attention. The first conversation more fully explores the hermeneutical context for this essay. Here, "darkness," "womanist," and "ambi*veil*ance" are more fully discussed. The second conversation attends to the sociohistorical context. Slavery during the New Testament era is explored here. Keeping Rhoda in mind, particular attention is given to women, children. Next, we turn to Luke's narrative, reading it exegetically, darkly, ambi*veil*ently. Following this, we attend to some objections to our womanist reading. Finally, we return to the questions, seeking to learn from audacious Rhoda. For in her story, the subaltern tries to speak. Through her actions, the slave girl audaciously cries freedom.

Making Our Differences Strengths

> Those of us who stand outside the circle of this society's definition of acceptable women; those of us who have been forged in the crucibles of difference—those of us who are poor, who are lesbians, who are Black, who are older—know that survival is not an academic skill. It is learning how to take our differences and make them strengths. (Lorde 1984, 112)[3]

In 2003, Vincent Wimbush proposed an interpretative wedge he called "reading darkness."

> Anyone can read darkness.... It is a particular orientation, a sensibility, a way of being in and seeing the world. It is viewing and experiencing the world in emergency mode, as through the individual and collective experience of trauma. (Wimbush 2003, 21)

Reading darkness requires biblical interpreters to attend to contemporary traumas. This attention informs how, even whether, texts are read as Scriptures. When reading darkness, one cannot escape into the fictive past. Contemporary traumas drive one's readings and inform one's interpretative questions. Communities of darkness readers read Daniel and ask "Why not every man?" They read Jesus's crucifixion as a lynching and ask "Were you there?"[4]

Wimbush's challenge intersects importantly with womanist biblical interpretative concerns. Here, *womanist* describes reading a particular kind of darkness: intersectional oppression. Womanists attend to trauma

---

3. This portion of Lorde's famous essay precedes and contextualizes her familiar quotation about "the master's tools." For Lorde, those who cannot use the masters' tools include those who are black, those who are poor, those who are old, and those who are from LGBTQ communities.

4. "Didn't My Lord Deliver Daniel?" and "Were You There When They Crucified My Lord?" are sorrow songs from the days of African and African American enslavement.

based on racism/ethnocentrism *and* sexism *and* classism. Further, womanists privilege the experiences of African American women as interpretative "wedges."[5] These experiences break open new questions to be asked of ancient texts. They raise the question of intersectional darkness in/and the Scriptures. Intersectional darkness is most profoundly experienced by "those of us who stand outside the circle of this society's definition of acceptable women" (Lorde 1984, 112). These know that they will never be integrated into the power structure. Their task: "learning how to take our differences and make them strengths" (112). For, they will never be afforded the master's tools. At any rate, those tools will not dismantle the master's house (112). In the face of trauma, they declare "I'se still climbing" (Hughes 1990, 187). A womanist biblical interpretation must strive to hear these women. It must attend to their trauma and strength as interpretative guides.

To the traditional darknesses of the womanist intersection, let me add two. These are necessary to read Rhoda's darkness. First, age—her youth—presents its own trauma not captured by the unholy triumvirate. Living intersectional trauma as an adult woman is one matter. Living intersectional trauma as a girl is another. Rhoda is a child. Therefore, her darkness must include her youth. Reading with Rhoda must cause us to see enslaved girls. Her vulnerability is heightened; her trauma, intensified.

Second, Rhoda raises questions of forced migration and human trafficking. Womanism emerges from female descendants of forced migrants, enslaved Africans. Yet, displacement and migration rarely figure in womanist interpretation. Rhoda forces us to add forced migration to the traumatic intersection. She makes us attend to Roman exposure of infants. She calls to mind refugee and displaced children. Moreover, Rhoda locates human trafficking and child slavery within the earliest church.

Race, class, gender, age, and forced migration all contour Rhoda's darkness. To read her darkness as a womanist biblical interpretation requires all five. However, if we are to take Smith seriously, it requires still more. Black female biblical interpreters, and other womanists, live a paradoxical existence. We may not experience all of Rhoda's intersectionality. Nevertheless, we face racism and sexism and, sometimes, even classism (Kendzior 2014; Cottom 2014; Cannon 2011, 237–46). Paradoxically, we

---

5. Thus, I use quotations by black women, African American and Caribbean, to frame this discussion.

read ancient languages, history; we wield "the master's tools" (Lorde 1984, 112). Thus we also live at another intersection. Ours is the intersection of privilege and disempowerment, signifier and signified upon.

Smith's (2014, 64) self-critical ambi*veil*ant hermeneutic proposes a way into this paradox. Smith invites us to hold both privilege and trauma in tension. She calls us to acknowledge our own particularities. For, despite the homogenizing function of the veil, we have different stories. In claiming our stories, we refuse to be silenced by imposed racialization. Moreover, our stories serve to expand the discourse, as this volume intends. See, for example, my inclusion of migration and age above. These are not random insights on my part. I was an immigrant child.[6] Thankfully, I have never been trafficked or enslaved. In this way, I have far more privilege than other migrant children. Still, I do have some existential understanding of deracination and displacement. This understanding informs my work, despite the strictures of the veil (Aymer 2014, 2015). I bring my immigrant questions to this discussion also. It is my hope that they intersect with, and expand upon, womanist intersectionality.

Smith further calls us to name our participation in perpetuating darkness. Like Smith, I too must name my privilege. I am, first, a "naturalized" American. I am *from* the Global South, but I vote in the United States. This, despite the racializing veil, marks me with international privilege. I am also an academic. A black female professor, I teach at a predominantly white institution. Unlike three-fourths of the teaching faculty in higher education, I have tenure (American Association of University Professors, n.d.). My denomination of ordination, the PCUSA, is also predominantly white (Presbyterian Mission Agency Research Center, 2011). Through the racializing veil, I am signified as subjugated. Yet, I exercise societal power and am given voice by the powerful. Ambi*veil*ant reading invites this self-conscious positioning of both/andness.

This self-identification serves to guide how we read darkness. We must name trauma as perpetuated in these ancient writings. We must also allow the writings to illuminate our complicity in trauma (S. Smith 2014, 181). In our womanist work, we pause to note the ambi*veil*ence in intersectionality. We unmask and name places of simultaneous oppression and complicity. The Bible is not exempted from this analysis. Neither are we.

---

6. My family immigrated to the United States during the 1970s from Jamaica. To read more about the societal trauma that was Jamaica of that period, consider the fictionalized account *A Brief History of Seven Killings* (James 2015).

"Pangs Excruciating"

> I, young in life, by seeming cruel fate
> Was snatch'd from Afric's fancy'd happy seat:
> What pangs excruciating must molest,
> What sorrows labour in my parent's breast? (Wheatley, 1772)

A commonly held myth contends ancient slavery was benign compared to US slavery. The myth is understandable when one considers the source. Biblical writings have supported slaveholders and recounted horrors inflicted upon slaves (Luke 12:42–48; Col 3:22–25; Eph 6:5–8; 1 Tim 6:1–2; 1 Pet 2:18–25). Abolitionist darkness readers thus faced a dilemma. They needed the Christian Scriptures, the "master's tools," to challenge chattel slavery. Yet, these writings often worsened the problem. The solution sometimes required a protective stance toward the scriptures. Frederick Douglass, the African American abolitionist, demonstrates such protectiveness:

> They have declared that the Bible sanctions slavery. What do we do in such a case? What do you do when you are told by the slaveholders of America that the Bible sanctions slavery? Do you go and throw your Bible in the fire?… Do you declare that a thing is bad because it has been misused, abused, and made a bad use of? Do you throw it away on that account? No! You press it to your bosom all the more closely; you read it all the more diligently; and prove that it is on the side of liberty—and not on the side of slavery. (Douglass 1985, 362–63)

For Douglass, to concede biblical sanctions of slavery was to admit defeat. He could not do so. Neither could later interpreters who read the Bible on behalf of liberation. The myth of benign ancient slavery derives from this kind of protectiveness.

However, the historical facts do not support this common myth. Studies demonstrate that ancient slavery, even among Christians, could be quite brutal (Wiedemann 1981, 106–20; Jo-Ann Shelton 1988, 168–90; Harrill 2006; Glancy 2006; contra Lewis and Reinhold, 1990). Jennifer Glancy's recent work on ancient Christian slaveholding bears this out. Consider Glancy's (2006, 9) description of a metal slave collar inscribed with a cross. This was not some random symbol. The slavemaster was Felix, an archdeacon of the church. The collar's intent was to keep his slave from becoming a fugitive. Glancy argues, convincingly, that the church uncritically participated in slavery's brutality. In reading Acts 12, this has two consequences. First, we may not assume that Mary treats Rhoda well. Luke does not tell us of a collar on Rhoda. Nevertheless, Christian leaders still considered their slaves to be human-footed property.

Second, the church's participation in human slavery necessitated participation in slaveholding ideology. Slaveholding ideology ontologically dehumanized the enslaved, denying the slave body personhood. The enslaved body, instead, became a cipher for the master. As such, slaves bore physical insults intended for their owners. Striking someone's slave was not insulting the person struck. Slaves, having no personhood, could not thus be insulted. Instead, the insult would reverberate upon the enslaved person's owner (Glancy 2006, 12). However, even to the slavemaster, the insult would be limited. After all, that a slave suffered physical injury was unremarkable. Glancy, citing Galen, notes that "a man was not hurt by physical or verbal insults to his slave in the same measure that he would be hurt by similar insults to his wife and children" (12). The implications for our reading of Mary's slave girl are clear. She is not intended to be read, or seen, as a person. Rhoda is a slave, not a person. Thus she gets to be a body double for Mary. She does, and suffers, what Mary never would.

Although slaves had no personhood, they were supposed to have undesirable characteristics. Aristotle proposed that the bodies of slaves naturally displayed a stronger physicality. "Nature must ... have intended to make the bodies of free men and of slaves different ... slaves' bodies strong for the services they have to do, those of free men upright and not much use for that kind of work" (*Pol.* 1.2 [Wiedemann 1981, 19]). Aristotle's musings profoundly influenced Hellenistic physiognomy. In *Physiognomonica*, Pseudo-Aristotle differentiates between the servile and free body. The servile body has "bent body carriage constrained in movement, stiff shoulder blades, thick thighs, oversized forehead" (Harrill 2006, 40, citing *Physiogn.* 3.807b5–12). Other characteristics of remark included even hair color and texture.[7]

Moreover, slaves were considered morally and intellectually inferior to free persons. This was reflected in literature and law. Plato, in *Laws*, warns that "there is no element in the soul of a slave that is healthy. A sensible man should not entrust anything to their care" (6.776e [Wiede-

---

7. The similarity between these proposals and the philosophy of racializing of African enslaved persons on the American continents should not be overlooked.

mann 1981, 83]). Achilles Tatius, the Roman writer, concurs. He relates a story of Sothenes, a slave who becomes paralyzed by fear. Tatius concludes, "Slaves as a class are utterly cowardly whenever there is any cause for fear" (*Leuc. Clit.* 7.10.5 [Wiedemann 1981, 62]). Even Christian moralists would join this chorus. Fifth-century Christian moralist Salvian, in speaking about vices to free persons, argues: "Perhaps one of these rich men will object: 'But we just don't do the sorts of things that our slaves do. Among our slaves there are thieves and runaways; among them there are ones totally dominated by their appetites and by greed'" (*Gub. Dei* 4.3.13 [Wiedemann 1981, 58]). Salvian continues, "Of course, these vices are typical of slaves."[8]

Literary tropes follow along these same lines. The most relevant to Acts 12 is the *servus currens* trope. The *servus currens* or "running slave" was a stock character in theater. J. Albert Harrill describes it in this way:

> A slave hurries onto the stage, breathless from haste and excitement, pretending to push aside invisible persons who crowd the street. He has unexpected, urgent news (good or bad) for another character, usually the master. In a monologue, he declares the extraordinary value of the news and its awesome effects, particularly on the personal interests of both master and slave. (2006, 61)

Harrill asserts the dishonor this trope plays to enslaved persons. It stereotypes them "as infantile adults whose puerile self-absorption and unmanly lack of emotional control invariably retard their own efforts to do even the most straightforward of duties asked of them" (61). Further, the running slave appears irrational, a caricature of a freeborn person (62). Harrill correctly points to this trope as underlying Luke's depiction of Rhoda (59–66). Like every running slave, Rhoda appears infantile and irrational. As we will see, the community's response to her announcement bears this out.

Moreover, Rhoda is a female slave. Like male slaves, female slaves performed hard, dirty, and dangerous tasks. And like their male counterparts, female slaves faced denigration and brutality. Juvenal, of course, exaggerates in his *Satires*. Still, his description of a cruel mistress must derive from lived experience:

---

8. Here, again, one should not miss the clear parallels between ancient moralisms and contemporary racializations of the descendants of enslaved Africans as cowardly, untrustworthy, immoral, and ontologically criminal.

Some women hire a torturer on a yearly salary. He whips, while she puts on her makeup, talks to her friends, and examines the gold thread of an embroidered dress. He lashes, while she looks over the columns of the account book.... Poor Pscecas, whose own hair has been torn out by her mistress, and whose clothing has been ripped from her shoulders and breasts by her mistress, combs and styles her mistress's hair. "Why is this curl so high?" the mistress screams, and at once a whipping punishes Pscecas for this crime of the curling iron and sin of a hairstyle. (*Sat.* 6.475–476, 480–484, 490–493 [Shelton 1988, 177–78])

Female slaves also faced trials specific to their gender. Enslaved women, like domesticated cows, were valued for their fertility and milk production. Women of childbearing age frequently nursed the children of their masters.[9] Further, all slaves, male and female, including children, were sex objects. "Slaveholders," notes Glancy (2006, 1), "had unrestricted sexual access to their slaves" (see also Osiek 2003, 259). This right to rape female slaves had many costs. These included the distrust of the mistress, ritualized in the Matralia. A festival to Mater Matuta, the Matralia was restricted to the freeborn. If slave women entered the temple, they were "ritually beaten." This brutality arose out the matrons' jealousy of slave women who "attracted their husbands" (Saller 1998, 89). One never sees such brutality directed toward Rhoda. Still, although called a girl-slave (παιδίσκη), she could run and speak. She was old enough to respond to the gate of the vestibule. Surely she would have known, or seen, the realities facing her. Indeed, she may well have already experienced some of this brutality. Luke does not tell us, nor are we invited to wonder. But a womanist ambi*veil*ant reading requires that we lift this veil. A womanist darkness reading requires that we read this girl's trauma.

She is a girl, not a woman yet. Luke calls her a παιδίσκη, which many have translated "maid." Yet, in our literature, παιδίσκη does not denote voluntary or paid service. The word points to enslavement, the enslavement of a child. Margaret MacDonald (2015, 64) notes that, "child slaves were among the most vulnerable members of early church communities." Further, Rhoda may have been quite young. For most children, childhood began at age seven (34). However, child slaves were expected to start their service at age five (35). Common wisdom stated that children

---

9. Paul of Tarsus uses this practice as a metaphor for his relationship with the church at Thessaloniki (1 Thess 2:7).

were physically frail (Wiedemann 1989, 17–19). Certainly children in the ancient world were vulnerable to all manner of diseases. K. C. Hanson (2008, 12) estimates the life expectancy of a child under the age of five as twenty years. Should one survive until five, life expectancy jumped to forty years (12). Those numbers would have been worse for enslaved children. Margaret MacDonald (2015, 36) describes a slave girl whose remains were found at Pompeii: "while the infant was adorned with bronze jewels indicating upper-class status, the girl … demonstrated signs of severe malnutrition and prolonged exposure to physical exertion involving heavy lifting—she was likely already exhausted from performing hard labor and entrusted to look after her master's baby."

In addition to the possibility of poor treatment, Acts 12 hides another reality. Just like adult slaves, slave children were sexual objects. Certain child slaves were adopted as *delicia*, favored or pet slaves. This may seem innocuous. However, MacDonald (2015, 44) reports that "these were slave children cultivated for their charm and good looks.… These children (of both sexes) were often used as sexual favorites." MacDonald goes on to note, pointedly, "It would be naïve … to think that the sexual use of slaves disappeared completely from early Christian communities" despite the silence of Christian manuscripts on the subject (45). Such sexual interaction between a master and his *delicium* was not considered adultery (45). Neither his wife, nor the slave child, had any recourse. Once more, I make no assertion that this is Rhoda's experience. However, as a slave girl, this is her context. We can surmise that if a girl like Rhoda is not facing this, she probably knows other slave girls in Jerusalem who are. All of this further deepens the darkness of Rhoda's trauma.

With this slave girl, questions of ethnicity and migration raise greater challenges. First, one cannot say with certainty where she was born. Child slaves were bought and sold in the marketplace. Among girl slaves, some had been exposed as infants by their fathers (Shelton 1988, 168). As Shelton notes, "Girl infants were exposed more often than boy infants because girls were a financial burden; they could not work to support themselves, and they needed dowries" (27–28). These infants would be "rescued" by a slave trader. Human trafficking of this sort was common during the first century. Some Christians found it loathsome (e.g., Rev 18:13). However, first-century Christians were by no means abolitionists with respect to slavery.

Such a possibility raises more questions. For instance, if this girl was bought at auction, is her name really Rhoda? Rhoda was a common slave name during this period (Keener 2012, 1905). The name marks her as servile. So it could have been a name appointed her by Mary.[10] Her name could also be a derivation of Ῥόδος, Rhodes. The island of Rhodes was a known slave-trading port (Harris 2011, 76, 78, 84). As Wiedemann notes, slaves were often named for the place where they were purchased. Marcus Terentius Varro relates that "when three men buy one slave at Ephesus, often one of them will call him Artemas, while another will call him Ion, after Ionia, the district where he bought him, a third Ephesius because he was born at Ephesus" (*Ling.* 8.9.21 [Wiedemann 1981, 34]). This line of reasoning is necessarily speculative. Luke gives us little evidence. Nevertheless, we cannot rule out the possibility that Rhoda was trafficked. If so, she may also be an involuntary migrant. Displaced from her *patria*, she serves as Mary's σῶμα, her body double.

Of course, Rhoda may have been born in Mary's house. Many slaves were home-born. If this is so, her mother was certainly enslaved. Children of slave mothers were automatically slaves themselves. Her father may or may not have been enslaved. Some have argued that "the majority of slave children [were] the biological offspring of their masters" (MacDonald 2015, 38).[11] In these instances, however, the question of origins does not disappear. If Rhoda herself was not trafficked, surely her ancestors were (Glancy 2006, 71–87). Roman conquests had created large numbers of slaves through the Mediterranean.

This possibility has bearing on Rhoda's ethnicity and migrant status. Whether home-born or trafficked, Rhoda is not part of Mary's "people." We cannot assume that she or her people come from Palestine. She may well have been a gentile girl. Further, her story occurs before the Jerusalem council consensus on gentile membership (Acts 15).[12] Thus, we cannot assume that she is a member of the Way (contra Keener 2012, 1939, 1941–42; Reimer 1995, 242–43; Barrett 2002, 184). Indeed, as I argue, her treatment by those gathered suggests otherwise.

---

10. Consider the use of "George" as the appellation for all Pullman Sleeping Car Porters during the heyday of American rail (Illinois Labor History Society, "Are These Men Really All Named George?").

11. That, in turn, raises the question, Which master? In the case of Acts 12, the only male mentioned is John called Mark. Could Rhoda be John Mark's child, from his sexual abuse of a slave woman?

12. Even in Acts 15, the gentile members in question lived in the diaspora, not in Judea.

Reading darkness requires first identifying the trauma that is darkness. This attempt to situate Rhoda historically helps us with that identification. Rhoda, if that is even her name, is an enslaved girl. As a slave, her body is vulnerable to abuse, sexual or otherwise. As an enslaved child, she works without rest. Like other enslaved children, she lives without guarantee of care or food. Further, she is most likely a gentile girl. Indeed, she may well have been trafficked. However, even if house-born, she is likely culturally deracinated. She is, or should be, the invisible, voiceless subaltern.

To the Earl of Dartmouth, African American poet Phillis Wheatley (1772) writes of the "pangs excruciating" that she and her parents faced at her enslavement. Luke is more taciturn with regards to Rhoda's enslavement. Still, she stands at the gate, an enslaved child. For contemporary readers, Rhoda's presence must raise questions. "What pangs excruciating" does this enslaved child face? This excursus traces this trauma, the darkness of Rhoda's existence. In light of this context, we now attend to Luke's narrative. As we do, we listen for the silenced voice of the subaltern. We attend to the caged bird's song.

The Caged Bird Sings of Freedom: Reading Rhoda (Acts 12:11–17)

> The caged bird sings
>   with a fearful trill
> of things unknown
>   but longed for still
> and his tune is heard
>   on the distant hill
> for the caged bird
>   sings of freedom. (Angelou 1983)

A Caged Bird Flies Free

> And Peter, after he came to himself,[13] said, "Now I truly know[14] that the Lord sent out his messenger and delivered[15] me out of the hand of Herod and of every expectation of the Judean people."[16] (Acts 12:11)

---

13. All translations are mine, based on the critical manuscript in NA[28]. ἑαυτοῦ, BDAG, s.v., 1aγ. Egyptian Vaticanus has αὐτῷ, which has the same force.

14. Perfect with present force; lit. "I am in a state of knowing," and this has resultant internal changes. There is no referent implied regarding how Peter comes to know what he knows about God.

The story of Rhoda begins with emancipation. Peter, imprisoned by Herod, has experienced a miraculous escape (Acts 12:1–10). As a result, what he knows about "the Lord"[17] is fundamentally changed. The use of the verb οἶδα here signals this change as stative.[18] That is, the change reflects external action. However, that action should fundamentally affect Peter's way of living.

According to Peter, his new state of knowing involves two truths: "the Lord sent out his messenger," and "the Lord delivered him out Herod's hand." These are both formulaic statements. The combination of ἐξαποστέλλω and ἄγγελος usually refers to royal envoys (see 2 Sam 3:14; Ps 77:49 LXX; Mal 3:1). Peter's "angel" thus serves as the royal envoy of God. κύριος, ἐξαιρέω, and χείρ together signify divine rescue of the oppressed (see 1 Sam 10:18; 12:10–11; Psa 139:5 LXX). This combination first occurs in Exod 18:8–19. Here Moses and Jethro retell the Israelites' emancipation out of Pharaoh's hand. Peter, thus, now knows the Lord as ruler and emancipator. One might expect this new state of knowing to affect Peter's actions.

The House of Mary

> And after realizing [this],[19] he went to the house of Mary, the mother of John (who is called Mark), where many had been gathered together[20] and were praying. (Acts 12:12)

Mary (Mariam) of Jerusalem is a patron of the church (Keener 2012, 1895–1900). She owns a house and hosts gatherings of the Way. This suggests that she has some level of emancipation as a woman (1892–95). She

---

15. Consummative aorist, focus on the completion of the action. Peter is now completely delivered from Herod (Wallace 2006, 559).

16. Genitive of simple apposition; here I use "Judean people" because the setting is in Judea and the person in question is Herod Agrippa I. Luke cannot here mean all Jewish people.

17. The identity of "the Lord" here is unclear. This is reflected in the manuscript traditions. Some smaller manuscript traditions include ὁ θεός or κύριος ὁ θεός in place of the above.

18. Although οἶδα typically has a present force, this does not remove the stative aspect from this verb.

19. Pronoun supplied.

20. Extensive perfect tense participle in periphrastic construction.

may be a widow no longer needing marriage for financial stability. Alternatively, John (Yochanan), as an adult son, might be her protector (Acts 12:25; 15:37). Regardless, the house and its property, animate and inanimate, are hers. This, as we will see, includes the enslaved girl called Rhoda.

Mary's role as patron and benefactor of the church should be noted. She is, after all, a woman. Gendered oppression functions as a kind of darkness. However, womanist theory requires the reading of intersectional oppression. One cannot simply note Mary's gender. One must also note her class. Mary owns property, a house large enough for the faithful to gather (Keener 2012, 1900–1904). She cannot be numbered among the nonelite who comprised the majority population (Carter 2006, 10). Further, one must note her ethnicity. Mary's Semitic name signals a kind of belonging. In Jerusalem, Mary may even have been on natal soil.[21] Mary's belonging points toward stability, not forced migration and deracination. Unlike others, she did not become a refugee after Stephen's death (Acts 8:1). In short, Mary was neither trafficked nor a migrant, forced or voluntary. She lives with the privilege of cultural belonging. Finally, consider Mary's age. Mary is an adult woman, not a child. Indeed, she is the mother of an adult son (Acts 12:25; 15:37). She may have limited authority as a woman, but it is not the subservience of a child. Roman *matronae* had certain powers at their disposal, especially over the household. As the adult head of her household, Mary would have such powers. These would have included powers over her property, inanimate and animate.

Reading Mary through the expanded darkness of womanist theory informs our understanding. Mary probably experiences the darkness, the trauma, of cultural patriarchy. This must not be downplayed. However, she experiences it as a free, wealthy, settled, home-owning adult. Her darkness must be validated. Yet, it pales in comparison to the trauma of her enslaved persons. How much more so for her enslaved children![22] Peter heads to Mary's house when he realizes he has been freed. He goes with a message of realization. The Lord is an emancipator. The contrast between Peter's message and Mary's lifestyle is striking.

---

21. There is nothing to suggest she is a Galilean. She may well be from Jerusalem itself. Regardless, she is likely from Palestine.

22. Rhoda is the only attested slave in Mary's house. No evidence exists to assert that she was Mary's sole slave.

A Slave Girl Called Rhoda

> And, after he knocked on the door of the gateway, an enslaved girl[23] came to answer,[24] named Rhoda. (Acts 12:13)

Peter is stopped by a gateway (πυλών). Readers of darkness should also pause here. For the presence of a gateway underscores Mary's privilege. Mary does not own a humble dwelling place. Mary owns a more elegant home.[25] Indeed, "the choice of diction contributes to the picture of Mary's ... social status" (πυλών, BDAG, s.v.). Thus, the presence of a slave should not cause surprise. Free rich people of the first century CE owned enslaved people. Still, the slave girl answering the door starkly contrasts with her mistress. A brief summation of the work above makes the contrast clear. Both are women. Mary, however, is an adult; Rhoda a child. Mary is settled; Rhoda or her people are trafficked. Mary is free, a householder, and Rhoda's owner. Rhoda is Mary's "human-footed property." Mary's name signals a cultural belonging. Rhoda's name may not even be her own.

As noted above, slaves functioned as body doubles for their owners (Glancy 2006, 9–38). A slave body would endure dangerous conditions inappropriate for a free body. Age, apparently, did not exempt one from that danger. Mary's community was facing danger, according to Luke. At the beginning of Acts 12, Luke writes of a persecution of Christians by Herod Agrippa (Acts 12:1–3). James, the brother of John, has been executed, Peter imprisoned. Given this undesirable attention, all those gathered in Mary's house faced danger. Any knock on the door could signal arrest, imprisonment, even death. Yet the person sent to face that trouble has no real power. She is an enslaved girl, one of the least powerful persons in the house.

---

23. παιδίσκη, BDAG, s.v.

24. ὑπακουω, BDAG, s.v. This verb has overtones of obedience, fitting for a slave. Papyrus 74 suggests ὑπαντησαι instead, a word less directly connected to class.

25. BDAG (πυλών, s.v.) notes that the word is used "at the apparently elegant residence of Mary, the mother of John Mark." Reimer (1995, 241) argues against such a reading, "especially since it is also said that the house of Simon the tanner had a πυλών." However, another possibility presents itself. Simon the tanner could also be a person of wealth and privilege. To be wealthy is not the same as being honorable in the ancient world.

On Butterfly's Wings

> And when she recognized[26] the voice of Peter, because of [her] joy, she did not open the gateway, but running, she announced that Peter was standing[27] before the gateway. (Acts 12:14)

Rhoda recognizes Peter's voice. If Peter has been a frequent guest in Mary's house, this is unsurprising.[28] Neither should her joy at hearing his voice mask her status. As a slave in Mary's house, Rhoda's life is also in danger. Should persecution become widespread, authorities would question (read "torture") household slaves (Pliny the Younger, *Ep. Tra.* 112). Enslaved women and children would not be exempt from this. Peter's emancipation is good news for Rhoda, not just for the gathering.

Rhoda's running also should be understood in cultural context. Here is where Luke uses the conventional comedic trope of the running slave (Harrill 2006, 60). In doing so, Luke introduces comedy into his narrative. This enslaved, trafficked, gentile girl is supposed to make us laugh. We are supposed to find her funny, even foolish. So the narrator occludes her words and mutes her voice. She speaks, but we never hear her. Instead, we see what Luke wants us to see. Perhaps we might have some sympathy for her. We know that joy makes even grown men act foolishly (see Matt 13:34; Luke 24:41). Still, sympathy differs from taking her seriously. We laugh, knowing she is right. We laugh, knowing she will not be believed.

The trope of the comedic slave or working girl persists into (post) modernity. Consider Prissy, an enslaved girl in *Gone with the Wind* (Fleming, Cukor, and Wood 2000).[29] Played by Thelma "Butterfly" McQueen, Prissy is an ingénue. She is too young to know about childbirth. She is still young enough to be afraid of cows. Yet her fears and innocence do not

---

26. Contemporaneous temporal participle. Aorist participles often function contemporaneously to aorist main verbs (Wallace 2006, 624).

27. Perfect active infinitive. Lit., "She announced Peter to have stood and still be standing before the gateway."

28. Reimer (1995, 242) goes too far in asserting that this demonstrates that "[Rhoda] knew him well." Surely a slave within an urban household could be expected to recognize frequent guests.

29. Prissy's story is told in the twentieth-century. However, this character has not disappeared in the twenty-first century. Frequently, it is played by Latinas. Consider Rosario Salazar of *Will and Grace* played by Shelly Morrison and the role of Consuela on *Family Guy* voiced by Mike Henry.

elicit sympathy. Like Rhoda, she is intended to be a comedic figure. Her daydreaming and singing represent the foolish dawdling of a lazy slave. When she experiences a slap across the face, the audience laughs (Watkins 1999, 242). In that laughter, the darkness of both girls becomes occluded. They cease to be enslaved, trafficked girls, deracinated from their cultural heritage. They become clowns, fools worthy of laughter at best, contempt at worst.

The Caged Bird Sings of Freedom

> But, they said to her, "You are out of your mind." Still, she kept insisting[30] that it was so.[31] But they declared,[32] "It is his messenger." (Acts 12:15)

Rhoda, here, clearly stands subordinate to the gathered community. First, Luke occludes her voice with an infinitive (ἔχειν οὕτως). Unlike Prissy, we never truly hear Rhoda speak. Neither, it seems, do those gathered. Both of their responses contradict her message. The first stands as a warning. The verb μαίνομαι never occurs as a friendly rebuke in our canon. Instead, the verb warns outsiders of inappropriate behavior, or dismisses bizarre speech (cf. 4 Macc 8:5; 10:13; Wis 14:28; Jer 32:16 LXX; 36:26 LXX; John 10:20; Acts 26:24–25; and 1 Cor 14:33). Often those who use μαίνομαι exert authority over the one called mad. An enslaved child would have understood this rebuke. But Rhoda persists. Rhoda acts in a womanish way: "outrageous, audacious, courageous ... willful" (Walker 2015, 17). She acts like a free woman, not a subservient, enslaved, trafficked child. Her audacity should not be taken lightly here. Further insubordination could lead to corporal punishment or worse. Yet, out of the darkness of her five-fold trauma, she speaks emancipation. Peter is free. He is standing at the gate. Rhoda sings of freedom. She will not be silenced.

---

30. The iterative imperfect here highlights Rhoda's bravery given her situation. She has already been called insane by the gathering. Yet, she continues to "sing of freedom."

31. The infinitive of indirect discourse.

32. Here, the imperfect is instantaneous. However, the statement is "vivid, emotionally-charged" (Wallace 2006, 542). This makes sense if the community fears that Peter has already died and that his guardian angel has come to bring them that message (ἄγγελος, BDAG, s.v., 2a). Codex Bezae expands this slightly, adding an element of supposition with τυγχάνω (ἔλεγον πρὸς αὐτήν·τύχον κτλ.). By contrast, Vaticanus removes the emotional element, by substituting the aorist for the imperfect here.

When Rhoda keeps insisting, the gathering must find another solution. Peter must be dead. This must be his guardian angel come to inform them. The community never seizes upon the possibility that Rhoda might be right. Nor would that make sense culturally. Slaves were fools and liars, even more so female enslaved children (see Wiedemann 1981, 51–77; Pervo 2009, 306–7). If an enslaved girl speaks of emancipation, could it be other than madness?

Silenced Singer, Forgotten Song

> But Peter kept persisting[33] in knocking. And when they opened, they saw him[34] and they were astonished. And after motioning to them with his hand to be quiet,[35] he related to them how the Lord led him out of the prison. Then he said, "Tell Jacob and the sisters and brothers these things." And, after leaving, he went to another place. (Acts 12:16–17)

The story of Rhoda ends without her. Those gathered in Mary's house see Peter for themselves. They hear his story of liberation. They receive his instructions: "Tell Jacob and the sisters and brothers." Rhoda, the enslaved girl, disappears. She has borne all of the risk in this narrative. She has been proven truthful and sane. Her insubordination has been justified. Yet, she reaps no reward. Indeed, the story proceeds as though she had never existed. Rhoda's disappearance should trouble us even more than her presence. It underscores plainly her role as property. Having fulfilled her task, she is of no more use to Luke. He discards her and all trace of her disappears. We readers, having seen Rhoda, are left with questions. What happens to an enslaved gentile girl who proclaims emancipation? Does she return to the drudgery of chattel slavery unchanged? What will she endure because of her truthful insubordination? Will she ever experience the manumission she proclaims? These questions are of no concern to Luke.

---

33. Iterative imperfect. Rhoda's insistence is matched by Peter's. Contra Mitzi J. Smith (2011, 128), nothing in this text suggests that Peter's knocking is any more calm than Rhoda's running.

34. Codex Bezae reads, "When they opened and saw, they were astonished," changing εἶδαν to its participial form and, in one manuscript, leaving out the καὶ before ἐξέστησαν.

35. The standard critical manuscripts leave Peter outside of the gathering. Codex Bezae specifically adds εἰσῆλθεν.

But for womanist readers of darkness, these unanswered questions linger. They haunt us like the freedom song of a caged bird.

"Sick of Being the ... Bridge for Everybody"

> I've had enough
> I'm sick of seeing and touching
> Both sides of things
> Sick of being the damn bridge for everybody...
> I do more translating
> Than the Gawdamn U.N. (Rushin 1981)

In Luke's narrative, Rhoda functions as a literary bridge. She connects the manumission of Peter with his appearance. As a bridge, she is often quickly dispatched by commentators, if even mentioned (Dunn 1996, 164; Talbert 1997, 120–21; Walasky 1998, 119; Gaventa 2003, 185; Pelikan 2005, 148–50; Clarence 2007, 199; Williams 2007, 232; Kurtz 2013, 196). James D. G. Dunn does not even mention Rhoda's name.[36] Ignoring Rhoda, or dealing with her briefly, follows Luke's agenda. Luke attends to the way God emancipates particular free, chosen men. Following Luke, we can easily ignore the truth-telling enslaved women. We deny the veracity of their testimony, as does Peter (Luke 22:56). We silence them when their truth exposes us (Acts 16:16). When they refuse to be silenced, we call them mad (Acts 12:15).

Womanist methodology does not allow us to follow Luke too closely. We must attend to intersectionality. We are compelled to read the darkness of Rhoda's world. To do so is to read Rhoda on her own terms. She cannot simply be a literary bridge in the story of Peter. She has her own story. To the extent that we can know it, we must tell it. Telling Rhoda's story restores her personhood, if not her name and birthright. She ceases to be a tool, an object to perform a task. Her story becomes an intersection, an intersection between enslavement and freedom. She stands at the crossroads of ideal and real communities of faith. Her role of truth-teller holds us to account. If we accept Peter's emancipatory testimony, what are

---

36. Noteworthy in his abbreviated treatment is Demetrius K. Williams (2007, 232); Williams's treatment of Rhoda is particularly unfortunate, given the nature of the commentary and the darkness of Rhoda's intersectional existence as enslaved and possibly trafficked girl.

the implications for Rhoda? Can we follow a liberating God while enslaving a trafficked gentile girl?

Not every commentator ignores Rhoda, of course (see Pervo 2009, 306–7; Allen 2013, 111). However, some who mention her euphemize her position in the community (Keener 2012, 1903–1942; Reimer 1995, 242). Rhoda's boldness supposedly demonstrates that Mary's house practiced enslavement differently. Rhoda's insistence points to *Mary's* gentleness as a slaveowner.[37] Or, perhaps she belongs to some other household. Surely she could not have been Mary's slave, while acting this way. Reading Rhoda's womanish behavior as a reflection on Mary's magnanimity erases Rhoda. Rhoda as recalcitrant slave, taking a risk for liberation, disappears. μαίνῃ goes unnoticed as a warning to a subordinate that she is out of place. Instead, we read Rhoda as "the happy slave." Her audaciousness signals not her fortitude but the believers' righteousness. Reading Rhoda this way makes her a bridge of a different sort. She bridges the "original church" and the imperfect contemporary church. Crossing that bridge allows reclamation of an illusory utopian beginning. Rhoda's darkness goes unread, and her voice unheard. She translates a simple message of "what we have to get back to." This reading allows us to ignore injustice in the earliest Christian gatherings.

Moreover, reading Rhoda as "the happy slave" short-circuits a necessary critique. Her presence raises hard questions about the compromised emancipatory vision of Luke-Acts. Luke-Acts begins with songs of societal reversals (see, e.g., Luke 1:46–56). Luke's Jesus preaches first about emancipating the oppressed (Luke 4:18). Luke testifies through Peter that even slaves will prophesy (Acts 2:18). Yet, by Acts 12, the oppressed are not freed. By Acts 12, Mary of Jerusalem is a slaveowner. By Acts 12, an enslaved girl crying freedom faces the rebuke (μαίνῃ). Rhoda should cause wonder but not because Peter is free. Rhoda should cause wonder because *she* is not free. Yet, she serves as a bridge. She, a girl enslaved, must translate emancipation to the gathered believers. She, trafficked and displaced, serves as their human-footed bridge to freedom. When we pay attention to her, we realize the illusiveness of utopia. Even the earliest recipients of the liberating word failed. Even they could not understand freedom except by crossing a slave girl's back.

---

37. A noted and welcome exception to this trend is M. Smith 2011, 95–132. Smith agrees with my assessments generally. However, she does not attend either to Rhoda's age or forced migration in her treatment of this passage.

"We Speak"

> We speak
> not to agitate you
> but in spite of your agitation
> because
> we are workers
> peasants
> leaders
> you see
> and we were not born
> to be your vassals (Collins 1992, 55)

Rhoda's insistent, silenced speech agitates those of us who would listen. Many will not. The gatekeepers of biblical studies still privilege philology over emancipation. Luke's agenda still marginalizes those he uses to fulfill it. Still Rhoda speaks. She speaks urgently about emancipation. Her body, her experience, speak urgently about enslavement, trafficking, and childhood. Displacement and dishonor, violence and abuse were practiced by nascent Christianity. This she speaks as clearly as if Luke had recorded her words. Her speech, her person, even her silencing agitates us. For she, like Merle Collins (1992, 55), speaks to us plainly. "[I was] not born to be your vassal." To hear her requires a different kind of reading. She requires of those of us privileged academic voices a womanist disruption.

The womanist disruption stands as an older cousin to the #BlackLivesMatter disruption. #BlackLivesMatter requires a reassessment of police violence against African Americans. It demands this reassessment from a resistant culture. The womanist disruption in biblical studies likewise requires us to reassess. We reassess by reading darkness, trauma, intersectionally. We reassess by expanding the intersectional discourse to include other lived traumas. We read the biblical texts themselves, historically, literarily, exegetically. We read them and begin to outline the darknesses inscribed in them. Then we speak, even when our speech agitates. In order to cry freedom, we risk the ephithet $\mu\alpha\acute{\iota}\nu\eta$. This has been and continues to be the work of womanist epistemology.

Likewise, we who, like Mary of Jerusalem, embody power alongside trauma, speak. We speak because our voices are not as readily silenced. We speak to the institutions, academic and ecclesial, that have empowered us. We look to our own hands, our own lives. We acknowledge that our lifestyles depend on Rhoda's work (Reagon 1985; Ehrenreich 2011).

We unmask our own excuses for abetting global enslavement of our kin. Unlike Mary, we hear, and we believe our sister. And then we speak, even when our speech agitates. In order to cry freedom, we too risk the ephithet μαίνῃ.

Yet even the womanist disruption needs disrupting sometimes. This is the hope and the gift of this volume. For this volume includes voices like mine. I speak with a black immigrant Caribbean American voice. I embody, like most North American blacks, the transatlantic slave trade. However, I also come from persons with no reported memory of segregation.[38] My nearest field-working relatives came from the Indian subcontinent. They were beguiled into cane fields by the wiles of British imperialists (Lai 1993). Panamanian cousins speak Spanish into one ear. British Caribbean ex-colonials, and their English descendants, speak in another. Imperialism and power are never far from my mind. Neither is migration. I too read the tripartite disruption raised by womanism. To it, I add questions informed by my privilege and trauma. Here, I have included questions of migration, deracination, and trafficking. Elsewhere, I have also included matters of empire (Aymer 2012).

All of these are forms of darkness, trauma. Yet the racializing veil occludes them all. They have been occluded for the convenience of white racism. They continue to be occluded in service of political and cultural unity. In attempting to perform an ambi*veil*ant reading, I hope to join Smith in tearing the veil. In so doing, I hope to model a broadening of the womanist disruption. For immigrant black American women and men also read darkness, trauma, intersectionality. We add our own traumas and complicities as we read. Yes, we complicate matters. Our presence can agitate a settled narrative. Yet, in spite of the agitation we might cause, like Rhoda, "we speak."

Works Cited

Allen, Ronald J. 2013. *Acts of the Apostles*. Minneapolis: Fortress.
American Association of University Professors. n.d. "Background Facts on Contingent Faculty." http://tinyurl.com/SBL0688f2.
Angelou, Maya. 1983. "Caged Bird." http://tinyurl.com/SBL0688g2.

---

38. This is not to say that segregation did not take place in Caribbean society. Rather, this is the report on which both of my parents and many of my family members still insist.

Aymer, Margaret. 2012. "Acts of the Apostles." Pages 536–46 in *Women's Bible Commentary*. Edited by Carol A. Newsom, Sharon H. Ringe, and Jacqueline E. Lapsley. 3rd ed. Louisville: Westminster John Knox.

———. 2014. "Rootlessness and Community in Contexts of Diaspora." Pages 47–62 in *Fortress Commentary on the Bible: The New Testament*. Edited by Margaret Aymer, Cynthia Briggs Kittredge, and David Sanchez. Minneapolis: Fortress.

Barrett, C. K. 2002. *Acts: A Shorter Commentary*. London: T&T Clark.

Cannon, Katie Geneva. 2011. "Unearthing Ethical Treasures: The Intrusive Markers of Social Class." Pages 237–46 in *Womanist Theological Ethics: A Reader*. Edited by Katie Geneva Cannon and Angela D. Sims. Louisville: Westminster John Knox.

Carter, Warren. 2006. *The Roman Empire and the New Testament: An Essential Guide*. Nashville: Abingdon.

Clarence, J. Bradley. 2007. *Acts*. Macon, GA: Smyth & Helwys.

Collins, Merle. 1992. "Because the Dawn Breaks." Pages 53–55 in *The Heinemann Book of Caribbean Poetry*. Edited by Stewart Brown and Ian McDonald. Oxford: Heinemann Educational Publishers.

Cottom, Tressie McMillan. 2014. "The New Old Labor Crisis." Slate. http://tinyurl.com/SBL0688h2.

Douglass, Frederick. 1985. "The American Constitution and the Slave." Pages 340–66 in *The Frederick Douglass Papers: 1855-63*. Edited by J. W. Blassingame. Vol. 3 of *The Frederick Douglass Papers: Series 1, Speeches, Debates and Interviews*. New Haven: Yale University Press.

Dunn, James D. G. 1996. *The Acts of the Apostles*. Epworth Commentaries. London: Epworth.

Ehrenreich, Barbara. 2011. *Nickeled and Dimed: On (Not) Getting by in America*. New York: Picador.

Fleming, Victor, George Cukor, and Sam Wood, dirs. 1939. *Gone with the Wind*. Loew's Inc.

Gaventa, Beverly. 2003. *Acts*. Nashville: Abingdon.

Glancy, Jennifer. 2006. *Slavery in the New Testament*. Minneapolis: Fortress.

Hanson, K. C. 2008. *Palestine in the Time of Jesus: Social Structures and Social Conflicts*. 2nd ed. Minneapolis: Fortress.

Harrill, J. Albert. 2006. *Slaves in the New Testament: Literary, Social and Moral Dimensions*. Minneapolis: Augsburg Fortress.

Harris, W. V. 2011. *Rome's Imperial Economy*. New York: Oxford.

Hughes, Langston. 1990. "Mother to Son." *Selected Poems of Langston Hughes*. New York: Vintage Classics.
Illinois Labor History Society. n.d. "Are These Men Really All Named George?" http://tinyurl.com/SBL0688jk.
James, Marlon. 2015. *A Brief History of Seven Killings*. New York: Riverhead Books.
Keener, Craig S. 2012. *Acts: An Exegetical Commentary*. Vol. 2, *3:1–14:28*. Grand Rapids: Baker Academic.
Kendzior, Sarah. 2014. "The Adjunct Crisis Is Everyone's Problem." The Chronicle Vitae. http://tinyurl.com/SBL0688i2.
Kurtz, William. 2013. *Acts of the Apostles*. Grand Rapids: Baker Academic.
Lai, Walton Look. 1993. *Indentured Labor, Caribbean Sugar: Chinese and Indian Migrants to the British West Indies, 1838–1918*. Baltimore: Johns Hopkins University Press.
Lewis, Shelton Naphtali, and Meyer Reinhold. 1990. *Roman Civilization: Selected Readings*. Vol. 2, *The Empire*. New York: Columbia University Press.
Lorde, Audre. 1984. "The Master's Tools Will Never Dismantle the Master's House." Page 110–13 in *Sister Outsider: Essays and Speeches*. Berkeley, CA: Crossing.
MacDonald, Margaret. 2015. *The Power of Children: The Construction of Christian Families in the Greco-Roman World*. Waco: Baylor University Press.
Osiek, Carolyn. 2003. "Female Slaves, *Porneia*, and the Limits of Obedience." Pages 255–76 in *Early Christian Families in Context: An Interdisciplinary Dialogue*. Edited by David Balch and Carolyn Osiek. Grand Rapids: Eerdmans.
Pelikan, Jaroslav. 2005. *Acts*. Grand Rapids: Brazos.
Pervo, Richard I. 2009. *Acts: A Commentary*. Hermeneia. Minneapolis: Fortress.
Presbyterian Mission Agency Research Center. 2011. "The Top 10 Most Frequently Asked Questions about the PC(USA)." http://tinyurl.com/SBL0688hi.
Reagon, Bernice Johnson. 1985. "Are My Hands Clean?" Songtalk.
Reimer, Ivoni Richter. 1995. *Women in the Acts of the Apostles: A Feminist Liberation Perspective*. Translated by Linda M. Maloney. Minneapolis: Fortress.
Rushin, Donna Kate. 1981. "The Bridge Poem." http://tinyurl.com/SBL068812.

Saller, Richard. 1998. "Symbols of Gender and Status Hierarchies in the Roman Household." Pages 85–91 in *Women and Slaves in Greco-Roman Culture*. Edited by Sandra R. Joshel and Sheila Murnaghan. New Ed. London: Routledge.

Shelton, Jo-Ann. 1988. *As the Romans Did: A Sourcebook in Roman Social History*. New York: Oxford.

Smith, Mitzi J. 2011. *The Literary Construction of the Other in the Acts of the Apostles: Charismatics, the Jews and Women*. PTMS 154. Eugene: Pickwick.

Smith, Shanell. 2014. *The Woman Babylon and the Marks of Empire: Reading Revelation with a Postcolonial Womanist Hermeneutics of Ambiveilance*. Minneapolis: Fortress.

Talbert, Charles H. 1997. *Reading Acts: A Literary and Theological Commentary on the Acts of the Apostles*. New York: Crossroad.

Walasky, Paul. 1998. *Acts*. Westminster Bible Commentary. Louisville: Westminster John Knox.

Walker, Alice. 2015. "Womanist." Page 17 in *I Found God in Me: A Womanist Biblical Hermeneutics Reader*. Edited by Mitzi J. Smith. Eugene, OR: Cascade.

Wallace, Daniel B. 2006. *Greek Grammar beyond the Basics: An Exegetical Syntax of the New Testament*. Grand Rapids: Zondervan.

Watkins, Mel. 1999. *On the Real Side: A History of African American Comedy from Slavery to Chris Rock*. 2nd ed. Chicago: Lawrence Hill.

Wheatley, Phillis. 1772. "To the Right Honorable William, Earl of Dartmouth." http://tinyurl.com/SBL0688m2.

Wiedemann, Thomas. 1981. *Greek and Roman Slavery*. New York: Routledge.

———. 1989. *Adults and Children in the Roman Empire*. New Haven: Yale University Press.

Williams, Demetrius K. 2007. "The Acts of the Apostles." Pages 213–48 in *True to Our Native Land: An African American New Testament Commentary*. Edited by Brian K. Blount, Cain Hope Felder, Clarice J. Martin, and Emerson B. Powery. Minneapolis: Fortress.

Wimbush, Vincent L. 2003. *African Americans and the Bible: Sacred Texts and Social Structures*. Edited by Vincent L. Wimbush. New York: Continuum.

"Nobody's Free until Everybody's Free": Exploring Gender and Class Injustice in a Story about Children (Luke 18:15–17)

Bridgett A. Green

Introduction

Few would suspect that the story of Jesus's blessing the children has a liberationist imperative. This story maintains Luke's theme that Jesus came to liberate the oppressed (see 4:18–19) by inverting power from those that society privileges with rank and stature to those often marginalized and disenfranchised (see 1:51–52). After admonishing his disciples' rude and unwelcoming behavior, Jesus elevates the crowd of infants and caretakers and humbles the disciples who tried to prohibit them from experiencing God's kingdom. The disciples' actions reflect the society's status-conscious worldview and social politics that disregard the invisible and most vulnerable members. Jesus's actions do not. In Luke 18:15–17, Jesus continues to teach and work for a different social politic—the kingdom of God. In God's kingdom, the social politics shifts social power dynamics by valuing those considered the least and ensuring their well-being. The kingdom of God is a different political reality that transforms the social landscape where everybody's free.

"Nobody's free until everybody's free" became a major political slogan in the freedom movements of the 1970s. This slogan originated as the title of Fannie Lou Hamer's speech at the founding meeting of the National Women's Political Caucus (NWPC) in 1971. A human rights activist, Hamer was a leader in various campaigns for justice including Voting Rights, Civil Rights, and Poor People's campaign. In her speech, she analyzes the myth of equality as espoused in the US political narrative. She examines the power dynamics that create, maintain, and perpetuate sexism, classism, and racism of all women, people of color, and children in US society and political systems. Hamer uses her analysis to spur action by the powerful and disempowered alike to create change and bring forth justice in their lives. Living and surviving the oppression of Jim and Jane Crow Mississippi as a poor African American woman shaped Hamer's politics, informed her critiques of human injustice, and undergirded her theology of justice. Throughout her life, she fought the political subjugation of white supremacy, economic exploitation of sharecropping, and the social oppression of sexism. Her faith, fight, and activism formed her critical analysis and interpretation of society's power dynamics that allowed her to see and work for different social politics—one that resembles God's politics. Hamer's hermeneutic is built upon the deep conviction that nobody's free until everybody's free.

In this essay I develop a womanist biblical interpretation from Hamer's gender, class, and racial analysis of her context as presented in "Nobody's Free until Everybody's Free."[1] To accomplish this task, I begin by examining her life's experiences and speech in order to understand the liberationist hermeneutic she employs while analyzing US political narrative of the 1960s and 1970s. With Hamer's hermeneutic as a guide, I analyze the dynamics of gender and class in the sociopolitical relationships in the story of Jesus's blessing of the children in Luke 18:15–17. I argue that Luke's version of this story conveys liberationist imperatives that empower the marginalized and admonish the privileged to change the power dynamics and social politics to ensure fairness, equity, and dignity for all people. Because the term womanist was just emerging during Hamer's lifetime, it is crucial to describe womanism and its applicability to her work.

Hamer and Womanist Hermeneutics

Hamer analyzed and criticized the sexism, racism, and classism legitimated, maintained, and perpetuated by the social, political, and economic structures in the United States. Throughout her life, she observed the impact of injustice and discrimination perpetrated on black sharecroppers. She observed that white supremacy and patriarchy not only maintained gender, race, and class inequities, but also endangered lives of

---

1. I am identifying my womanist hermeneutic and in no way ascribing to Hamer a term with which she would have been unfamiliar and by which she may not have identified herself.

many through poverty, hunger, lack of education, and war. Hamer's critical analysis of her context is a precursor of womanism. Womanism is a perspective that centers on the intersectionality of gender, class, and race. In *An Introduction to Womanist Biblical Interpretation*, Nyasha Junior (2015) asserts that the roots of womanism include women's activism in the United States as well as womanist scholarship in religious fields and feminist biblical interpretation. Hamer's cultural criticism of US society as demonstrated in her speech shapes my womanist biblical interpretation of Luke 18:15–17.

Using Hamer's speech as a theoretical framework for my womanist approach continues in a tradition of womanist academic scholarship that centers life experiences of African American women as an epistemology for constructing theological and ethical praxis of life (Townes 1993; Cannon 1985). This chapter incorporates Hamer's activism as a hermeneutic to examine important issues of discipleship and justice. I am particularly interested in Hamer's concern for the well-being of children as part of her work for gender equality, economic equity, and civil rights. Before analyzing the hermeneutic that Hamer engages in her address, we must examine the cultural and political context of her life that informs her interpretive lens.

Hamer and Her Sociopolitical Context

The roots of Hamer's political and theological worldview grew in the cotton fields of rural Mississippi. Born October 6, 1917, to Lou Ella and James Lee Townsend in Montgomery County, Mississippi, Hamer was the youngest of twenty children (Houck and Dixon 2009). As a young child laborer on a plantation, she could describe white landowners economic exploitation of poor blacks. Rhetorical scholars Maegan Parker Brooks and Davis W. Houck note:

> After all this work, she insisted, "We wouldn't have anything: we wouldn't have anything to eat; sometimes we wouldn't have anything but water and bread." The white landowners, on the other hand, "would have very good food" and yet "they wasn't doing anything," she observed. To her child's mind, the solution seemed simple: "to make it you had to be white, and I wanted to be white." (2011, xiv)

Observing that white landowners ate well without doing work, whereas black families like hers did all of the work while having hardly anything to eat, young Hamer associated economic exploitation with white supremacy. In addition to economic suffering, Hamer experienced the weight of racism bearing on her self-esteem. Observing her internalizing racism, her mother instilled pride in being black and female in young Hamer by admonishing her to respect herself as a black woman and sharing that others would do the same. Furthermore, with a Baptist preacher for a father and a mother who was a religious education leader, Hamer learned divine justice in church and at home. Her parents taught divine justice by imparting that white people were not unscathed by the sharecropping system (Brooks and Houck, xiv). Even as a child, Hamer developed critical race and class-consciousness that would eventually empower her political subversion and activism.

In addition to learning about the burdens of racism and classism, Hamer acquired theological and rhetorical education in her home. Because of her parents' church leadership, she was able to connect contemporary issues with the biblical text; she developed a black liberationist hermeneutic that interpreted Christian Scriptures and formed a theology against slavery and racism (xv). Hamer learned that God fights for the oppressed, the poor, and the powerless. This theology and connection with the Christian Scriptures polished her critical lens for understanding the roots of racism and classism in her community and throughout the United States. Her faith and church background gave her the inner strength, confidence, and courage to fight injustice and work for human rights.

Undergirded by faith and confidence instilled in her youth, during the time when Hamer and her family were sharecroppers, she spent her life resisting racial, political, economic, and gender oppression. Her husband worked in the field, and she worked as a timekeeper, recording the workers' harvest. Hamer knew that the landowners exploited workers with rigged scales, therefore she used her own device to weigh the workers' crop fairly when the landowners were not watching (xvii). This subversive act lifted, if only slightly, the weight of economic oppression that kept family and neighbors in perpetual debt and hunger. She, too, suffered from the harsh work and living conditions—the human indignities of hunger and hard labor—forced upon her and her community because she was black, poor, uneducated, and disenfranchised. Hamer knew that the laws were set to maintain power among whites, men, and landowners, and she must help change those laws in order change her life and the lives of others. To change her personal situation, she must change the political situation.

The Voting Rights movement was the first of many that educated and empowered Hamer to seek her God-given rights via the political process. In the summer of 1962, several organizations of the freedom movement worked in Mississippi informing African Americans of their political rights as well as educating them on the voting registration process (xviii).[2] After being fired from the plantation (where she had worked for twenty years) for attempting to register to vote, Hamer was free to advocate for voting rights and to testify to the violent atrocities against citizens (xix). As the white leaders and police sought to suppress Hamer's activism with harassment and beatings, they stoked the fire of her determination and passion for justice. Known to be a gifted orator, Hamer testified at the Democratic National Convention in 1964 on national television about the abuse, the trampling of human rights, and the desecration of the human dignity of blacks in Mississippi.[3] Her testimony gave her national attention and infuriated President Lyndon B. Johnson (xix–xx). Her appearance at the national convention marked the beginning of Hamer's activism on behalf of the poor and contributed to the election of the first African American legislator in Mississippi since Reconstruction (Robert G. Clark Jr.). Later in 1968, Hamer became one of the delegates to the Democratic National Convention in Chicago.

Along with her Civil Rights activism, Hamer worked against hunger and poverty. She founded Freedom Farm Cooperative with her speaking honoraria and fundraising. The collective purchased land, animals, seeds, and farm machinery for food production and access for the poor citizens in Sunflower County. Growing up in the one of the poorest families in Mississippi, Hamer experienced hunger. Later she witnessed the malnutrition of her own children and among the families in her community (xx). A unique feature of Hamer's activism is her concern for the

---

2. Hamer worked for Student Nonviolent Coordinating Committee (SNCC) as one of the oldest full-time voting advocates. She became the target of white terrorism, suffering a massive beating in June of 1963 while jailed in Winona, Mississippi.

3. As a gifted orator, Hamer led workshops and gave speeches throughout the South during her work with SNCC. Plainspoken, she communicated effectively about her experiences, strategies for mobilization, and the need for support in the movement. Like her male counterparts, Hamer's rhetoric included a Baptist preaching aesthetic built on a theological foundation that interpreted Christian Scriptures as a source for liberation, comfort, and empowerment. Despite having only a sixth-grade education, she was an energetic speaker and teacher.

wellbeing of children.[4] Her food program was for all poor families in Sunflower County—black and white.

Although her politics and activism were explicitly rooted in the struggle of racism and poverty, Hamer was also concerned with gender equality. The Civil Rights movement was not without its fair share of women who were equally concerned with gender *and* racial equality. In addition to Hamer were Rosa Parks, Pauli Murray, Shirley Chisholm, Dorothy Height, Diane Nash, Ella Baker, Marian Wright Edelman, and many others. As their political and civic struggle centered on issues of racial discrimination, inequality, and disenfranchisement, they faced sexism both within the movement and in their daily lives. They suffered indignities and inequities that were unique to their experiences as African American women. As Gloria Steinem, leader and spokesperson for the feminist movement of the late 1960s and 1970s, confessed: black women invented the feminist movement (Tisdale 2015).

Hamer's activism developed in the crucible of Jim and Jane Crow Mississippi. Living and surviving in poverty as an African American female sharecropper on land owned by white men, she learned at a young age that the racism, sexism, and classism that she and her family endured were not part of God's plan. Hamer was called to fight for civil rights, economic equity, and gender equality not just for herself, but for all people, including children, oppressed by the white supremacist patriarchal capitalism that kept people disenfranchised and poor. Her activism embodied Alice Walker's (1983, xi) second definition of womanist, "Committed to survival and wholeness of entire people, male *and* female."

Hamer's Protowomanist Hermeneutic

"Nobody's Free until Everybody's Free" is a protowomanist speech that addresses racism, sexism, classism, and advocacy for children. While deconstructing the power dynamics that undergird racial discrimination, gender inequity, and economic disparities in society, Hamer describes and defines human rights as being inclusive of equal and civil rights; children's health and well-being; political and economic empowerment; and poverty

---

4. Although Marian Wright Edelman's activism on the behalf of poor children began in the late 1960s, Hamer brought issues regarding children to the feminist political discourse at the meeting of the NWPC in 1971.

advocacy. In this section, I analyze Hamer's speech to procure her hermeneutics of the text of her life and US political narrative.

Examining the US political narrative of equality and democracy, Hamer addresses various political and economic oppressions imbedded in racism, sexism, and classism. Her quest is to fight for human rights for those dying daily from the effects of a white male political oligarchy that bares no concern for marginalized, disenfranchised, oppressed, and neglected communities. She quips, "And I think about the Constitution of the United States that says, 'with the people, for the people, and by the people.' And every time I hear it now I just double over in laughing because it's not true; it hasn't been true" (Brooks and Houck 2011, 136). Hamer illustrates the irony in the claims of US democracy being "for the people by the people"; it is actually for the few by the few, that is, a small ruling class of white elite men. While confronting societal problems, her speech includes stories and real examples that challenge, encourage, and empower the audience to transform society by using their power to turn the world upside and establish new political reality. Equally instructive, Hamer inspires a critical awareness.

Hamer's advocacy of female solidarity in the fight for equal representation in government grew from the fact that women share similar issues of oppression. She contends that women would govern differently. Their concerns would differ from men as they prioritize the needs of women and children. In addition to fighting for equal rights for women, Hamer asserts that women would use their political power to protect and care for children. In the wake of the Vietnam War, violence against college protesters, killings of innocent children, drug abuse among youth she argues that "if women had more power in this country we wouldn't have the young people dying in Vietnam that we have dying there today. We wouldn't have young people dying in the United States that we have today" (136).[5] In addition to caring for children's physical bodies, Hamer invites the caucus to advocate for children's health and wholeness. She asks the audience to fight against the poor education, malnutrition, and lack of healthcare among the nation's African American as well as poor white children (138). Hamer's gender politics include the power of women to protect their lives and the lives of the society's most vulnerable—the children.

---

5. Hamer brought an African American mother to the convention whose daughter was shot, after commencement while holding her diploma, by local whites in Drew, Mississippi.

While arguing that women's political leadership would bring peace and protection, Hamer acknowledges that race matters would have an effect in their feminist coalition. She explains that all women do not have the same issues. First, Hamer contends that African American women have always known that they were not free, unlike white women. Although white women fought for liberation throughout US history, Hamer offers, "But for so many of them it was a rude awakening, a few years ago when they woke up, and found out that not only were they not free, but that they had a whole lot of problems, not like mine, but similar to mine" (135–36). Her point is that African American women were always aware of their oppression, especially due to race but also due to gender. Second, Hamer recognizes that among the women present at the progressive meeting are those who still advocated for racist policies within feminist concerns. For example, she mentions, "I do know in this audience there must be some people here that talk about not wanting our kids to go to school together" (138). Third, Hamer confesses that she does not want to be liberated from African American men. As she agrees with the caucus that more women need to be in office, she asserts that more African Americans do too. She further argues that black men have suffered much under the weight of white supremacy, even claiming that they have worse problems than she (136).

Although her solidarity with African American men is uncritical of the sexism that some African American women experienced by some African American men, Hamer relates that they struggle together against political disenfranchisement and human indignity of racism. Her speech illustrates an intersectionality of racism and sexism that African American women experience by white society. While foregrounding racial differences and concerns in the women's movement, Hamer declares that these gaps must be bridged to tackle the problems that confront the collective of women and minoritized communities.

While critical, Hamer's speech is encouraging and empowering. Despite the national context of a white supremacist oligarchy, Hamer declares that women and minoritized communities can transform society. She exclaims, "But if you think about hooking up with all these women of all different colors and all the minority hooking on with the majority of women of voting strength in this country, we would become one hell of a majority" (138). She paints a picture of a broad coalition of minoritized and oppressed communities that have the political power to bend the arc of justice. Her speech inspires a hope that change is possible. With each assessment of the gender, racial, and class injustice in society, Hamer offers commentary and examples of how individuals and groups can strategize and achieve equality, equity, and empowerment for themselves and one another. Her vision requires that each person use their power and privilege to create a realm that gives space and voice for everyone. To close her speech, Hamer reveals the source of political imagination and faith in an in-breaking of new sociopolitical reality: her theology. Evoking the story of Esther, she concludes, "So, I'm saying to you today, 'Who knows but that I have cometh to the kingdom for such a time as this'" (139). Hamer's ending reassures the audience that their fight for justice is not theirs alone; it is also God's fight. With God, they will prevail.

"Nobody's Free until Everybody's Free" reveals that Hamer's activism is deeply concerned with issues of gender, class, and race because of her experiences as a poor Southern, African American woman. She analyzes the power dynamics in the sociopolitical relationships in order to deconstruct the issues that perpetuate injustice and construct strategies for every person to participate in transforming society. Illustrating her liberationist imperative to be committed to the wholeness for an entire people, Hamer's aims to raise the awareness that true freedom is dependent upon the freedom of everyone. Her speech "comforts the afflicted and afflicts the comfortable." Luke's story of Jesus blessing the children does the same.

Jesus Blesses the Children

Demonstrating a concern for children as part of her gender analysis as well as classism and racism, Hamer's womanist hermeneutic undergirds my argument that Luke's version of Jesus's blessing of children illustrates liberationist imperatives to transform the social reality so that everybody's free in the kingdom of God. The imperatives empower the marginalized and admonish the privileged to change the power dynamics of social politics to ensure fairness, equity, and dignity. Because the social political dynamics in Luke 18:15–17 are not obvious to most, traditional interpretations focus on explicit theological messages in the story. Their work emphasizes Jesus's message and tries to understand how he connects discipleship to children, humility, hospitality, and the kingdom of God.

Interpreting Jesus's blessing of children as an illustration on humility, traditional scholarship focuses on the characterization of children in the quest to understand Jesus's saying at the end of the story (18:16–17). Jesus exclaims that the kingdom of God belongs to children and those like them. Furthermore, he teaches that those who care to enter the kingdom of God must receive it as a child. John Fitzmyer (1981) and Jerome Kodell (1987), among others, assert that the story is an extension of the preceding teaching of the parable of the Pharisee and the Tax Collector (vv. 9–14). Fitzmyer contends that the children are humble like the tax collector. Kodell adds that Luke describes the children as humble by contrast to the characterizations of the Pharisee (vv. 9–14) and rich ruler (vv. 18–30). His argument is summed up in this analogy: the Pharisee is to the rich ruler as the tax collector is to the children. Referring to this contrast, Kodell (1987, 426) concludes, "Lucan editing has sharpened the theme of lowliness as a mark of discipleship in the story of the children (18:15–17)." For Fitzmyer and Kodell, the kingdom of God belongs to anyone who is humble. On the other hand, Stephen Fowl (1993, 158) asserts that the childlike behavior about which Jesus refers is not about humility but a willingness to drop everything to attach themselves to an object or a person with single-mindedness. To enter God's kingdom, one must be solely dependent on God.

Fitzmyer, Kodell, and Fowl claim that God's kingdom requires humility and openness, as modeled by children. Dependent on the narrative to describe the character of children, their arguments suggest that all or most children are homogeneous models of humility. Further, if their characterizations include infants, their findings propose that infant personalities can be assessed. Their analysis seems to assume that all cultures value and characterize children the same way across time. Although the narrative sequence provides context for reading the text, the cultural context of the narrative fills the gaps that the text assumes the first readers already know. Although their interpretations challenge readers to be meek in character, they do not offer any guidance regarding the social politics of the text. Therefore, with their readings those in power do not have to humble themselves before any person or bear any responsibility to participate in transforming unjust sociopolitical relationships within their communities. As a result, their interpretations could suggest one may continue to induce injustice, inequities, and inferiorization in others while being humble in spirit before God. The narrative offers clues for other interpretations.

Jesus's blessing of the children in verses 15–17 contains a critical departure from its Markan source material. Luke makes a small, and yet significant, revision to this story: he changes Mark's children (παιδία) to infants (βρέφη) (see Mark 10:13–19; Matt 19:13–15).[6] Traditional scholar-

---

6. βρέφη: neuter plural accusative of βρέφος (BDAG, s.v.).

ship seems to overlook this change with their focus on the humility and openness of children. By describing the children as infants, though, Luke deemphasizes their characterization as key to Jesus's point and instead emphasizes their social status. Concurring with Justo González, I argue that the infants' status is crucial. González (2010, 214) asserts, "By changing Mark's 'children' to 'infants', Luke is underscoring their vulnerability. And it is precisely to such that the kingdom of God belongs." The change underscores Luke's message that the kingdom of God transforms power dynamics in sociopolitics in order to free the oppressed (see 4:16–19). Although the infants' status as lowly and powerless is not lost in traditional scholarship, it is not central to their interpretation. Analyzing the power dynamics among the characters becomes critical for interpreting Jesus's message about who enters God's kingdom. As in Hamer's speech, this story illustrates the disciples' discriminatory practices of denying the lower classes access to Jesus and Jesus's work to overturn them. Understanding the status of infants in the Greco-Roman world is helpful in interpreting the story.

Infants and Women: Underestimated

The Greco-Roman world treated children as inferior, powerless dependents with little to no rights. In general, the culture viewed them as a liability, burden, and commodity until they can contribute to the family. This concept of childhood is foreign to US modern readers, and it is absent in most analyses of Luke 18:15–17. Those interpretations utilize popular notions that children, especially infants, are innocent and precious who need adult protection. However, childhood innocence is a relatively recent phenomenon that slowly developed during the Enlightenment period and became fully formed in the US during the mid-nineteenth century. In the US antebellum period, childhood innocence was racialized, being phenotypically identified with white children as epitomized by Little Eve in *Uncle Tom's Cabin* (Bernstein 2011). Therefore, enslaved and nonwhite children were not innocent. Understanding the dynamics and lessons in the story of Jesus's blessing the children is predicated on Roman cultural concepts of children and childhood.

In essence, Roman ideology of children assessed them as inferiors. Describing a child's status in ancient society, Ronald Clark (2002) argues that adults viewed children as equal to slaves; small people with little rights; unprotected by Jewish law; and subject to abuse. He concludes that children were seen along with women as those without rights. Although Clark's research regarding children is rather reductive, children, despite the varied ways in which their families may have regarded them, were a vulnerable class without power and voice. Generally, children of Galilee would be on par with outcasts and the marginalized, having nothing to afford them respect. Therefore, infants would be even more vulnerable than other children in any family situation. While being dependent on family caregivers for protection, safety, and support, they also need them for basic necessities, including feedings, food, healthcare, and mobility. On their own, they are helpless, powerless, and completely defenseless.

By identifying the children as infants, Luke brings women into the conversation. Women were most likely the ones bringing the infants for Jesus to touch. They were probably mothers, sisters, grandmothers, nurses, and other female members of the household.[7] In the kyriarchy, they would have limited status and respect. However, Luke, like Mark obscures the female presence by embedding them in the person and number of the verb προσέφερον, which translates "they were bringing." Modern translators perpetuate this offense when they add "people" as the subject of the verb instead of women.[8] By being ambiguous about who brings the babies, Luke renders the women invisible. Their invisibility in the text contributes to the lack of scholarly consideration of social politics in the story. Not naming the women explicitly, Luke, biblical translators, and interpreters perpetuate the marginalization and invisibility of the women in the story. Although Luke followed his source material regarding the verb, his use of infants illuminates gender dynamics in the story.

Jesus blessing the children does not offer many clues regarding Luke's intent in using infants; however, we are able to see the potential impact. By including infants, the story acknowledges the women along with the children who were in the crowd listening to Jesus. They recognize Jesus's power to bring good news and healing. At this point in Luke, Jesus has a reputation for his power to cure terminal diseases and to resurrect the dead (see 5:13, 6:19; 7:14; 7:39; 8:44–47). Seeking Jesus's touch for their

---

7. One could argue that some men were bringing the infants as well. Yet, those men would be feminized in Rome's kyriarchy as members of the domestic sphere.

8. At best, the KJV and ASV of Luke 18:15–17 render a wooden translation of the story by translating the προσέφερον with simply the third-person plural pronoun "they were bringing." Modern translations, including the NRSV, the NIV, along with the NET and the CET, replace the pronoun with "people were bringing infants."

infants demonstrates the women's desire for preventive and interventionist care for their children's physical and possibly spiritual well-being. Additionally, the women may be in the crowd for their own well being, as they struggle to survive the social and spiritual warfare that surrounds them. By making this story about infants, Luke demonstrates a concern for the most invisible and marginalized members of humanity.

The Disciples and Their Privilege

Luke portrays the disciples negatively in this story. By chastising the women with infants who come to see Jesus, the disciples treat those who are vulnerable, marginal, and invisible with derision (ἐπιτιμάω).[9] Because most scholarship focuses on their interpretations of Jesus's saying regarding how to receive the kingdom of God as children, many critics analyze the disciples' behavior as a catalyst for Jesus's teaching without carefully considering their actual behavior and the power dynamics undergirding it. Instead, they contend that the disciples are simply inhospitable or have the wrong attitude. Despite Jesus's teaching in an earlier encounter with children on the least being the greatest (9:46–48), the disciples are still status-conscious (Kodell 1987; Clark 2002). The disciples' behavior seems to be motivated by their classist and sexist perspectives that undergird their preoccupation with status. As a result, the women and infants become their foil.

The disciples' behavior suggests class-consciousness and discrimination. Many of them are tradesmen, fishermen, and tax collectors from urban areas who probably lived near or at subsistence levels (Friesen 2004). At this point in Luke, Jesus is traveling in the rural areas of Galilee outside of Jerusalem. Rural communities included small farms with large tax burdens and workers on property controlled by the local and Roman elites, which is a form of sharecropping—a lived experience relatable to Hamer's life (Stegemann and Stegemann 1999). The women and children rebuffed by the disciples are from these poor rural communities. In addition to being poor in general, the women and infants suffered a compounded burden as financial dependents of the adult men in their household. By social and economic standards, the women and infants were of low status.

---

9. ἐπιτιμάω: third-person plural imperfect active indicative meaning to speak seriously, warn, rebuke, reprove, and punish (BDAG, s.v.).

Luke's narrative contextualization of Luke 18:15–17 between Jesus's telling of the parable of the Pharisee and the Tax Collector and his encounter with the rich ruler provide further clues about the disciples' class-consciousness. Jesus's introduction to the parable as being for those who regard others with contempt (v. 9) addresses the preoccupation with status among the disciples as well as others in the crowds. In verses 18–30, the disciples do not hesitate to allow the rich ruler, not only to meet, but to talk with Jesus, which is in stark contrast to their reception of the women and infants.[10] The narrative context suggests that the disciples discriminate against the women and infants due to their status, and therefore keeping them from the knowledge and power of Jesus.

Furthermore, the disciples seem to function out of their privilege of being in Jesus's inner circle. They want to control and police who has access to the benefits and resources that Jesus brings even through his touch. In the midst of jockeying for position, the disciples seem to forget that their place of privilege is relative. In the greater society, they, too, are outcasts and lowly. However, their association with Jesus gives them honor and power in relation to the women. Maybe because these women are unknown to Jesus and the disciples, the disciples flex their power and influence as Jesus's companions to marginalize and ostracize them with scolding.

The disciples may have rebuffed the women and infants because of gender. As men, the disciples have the power to function in the public square, to advocate for their needs, to conduct business in order to sustain a livelihood, to assert their autonomy, and to engage in societal affairs. Women's engagement with the public was restricted. The disciples could have reacted to the women and children leaving their homes and engaging a nonkinsman seemingly without male supervision. To the disciples, they may be transgressing social mores regarding a woman's place. Luke's description of the children as infants and the impact of foregrounding the women suggest that the gender power dynamic could have been a catalyst for the disciples' scorn and status consciousness. However, the women and infants' poverty and lack of connection with Jesus's inner circle could also be factors. On the other hand, the intersectionality of various status markers of lowliness could have been a factor of the disciples' behavior.

---

10. As Kodell argues that the theme of humility, specifically, links the three stories, I assert that status consciousness is a broad concern as well.

Because all of the characters are Judeans, racism or ethnic bias does not appear to be an obvious issue within this story (Byron 2002). Hamer's explicit analysis of the power and influence of white supremacy to disenfranchise and discriminate against African Americans do not apply to this text. However, she advocates for the racial solidarity as a key to fighting injustice in order to live in wholeness. The disciples, along with women and infants are colonized and racialized by Rome (Isaac 2004). Because of this shared oppression, one would imagine that the disciples would work in solidarity for the liberation, health, and wholeness of the women and children. Instead, they choose to act in ways that demonstrate their social privileges.

As in the Civil Rights movement, many African American women worked as workshop leaders, organizers, and protesters, and yet mostly men are remembered for their leadership and activism. When African American women continued their activism in the Equal Rights movement, they were cautioned not to betray their race for gender rights. This sentiment continues in black women's liberationist movements today. Yet, African American men were not required to consider issues particular to African American women in the struggle. In the same way, the disciples' behavior suggests that they did not comprehend that considering the least in their communities is a requirement. The intraracial dynamics among the disciples, women, and children illustrate that shared racial oppression does not guarantee solidarity or consideration for shared justice. However, as Hamer's activism foregrounds racial solidarity in the fight for justice, Jesus's response to the disciples may value racial solidarity as well.

Overall, Jesus is not impressed with his disciples. He reverses the impact of their unjust and oppressive behavior by declaring, "Let the children come to me and do not stop them because the kingdom of God belongs to such as these. Truly, I tell you whoever does not receive the kingdom of God as [one receives] a child will never enter it" (vv. 16–17, my translation) (Bauer 2000; Green 1997; Carroll 2012).[11] Jesus's words and deeds upend the disciples' expectations of who gets access to him and, therefore, the kingdom of God. As the disciples exalt themselves, they are humbled by Jesus's response; and the women and infants who are humbled by society's ideologies of class and gender and the disciples' mistreatment

---

11. ὡς is a particle that can designate an ellipsis. Both Green and Carroll offer plausible interpretations of v. 17 when ellipsis is considered.

are exalted by Jesus. Jesus reverses the status of the disciples and the women and children. According to Carroll (2012), this status reversal, especially in light of verse 14, demonstrates that the kingdom of God belongs to those considered lowly and not those who are powerful, privileged, and high status. Indeed, the kingdom of God does belong to the less privileged and powerful. However, Jesus's message does not stop there. By saying that the kingdom of God belongs to those who are like children (infants) does not exclude those whom society privileges from participation or membership. Instead, it indicates that the kingdom belongs especially to those who are considered lowly, to the chagrin of those using worldly standards. Furthermore, to interpret this story as one that is simply meant to teach humility seems to stop short of the text's potential meaning. In addition to divine justice, the story illustrates liberationist imperatives for restorative justice.

The liberationist imperative is in Jesus's example to affirm and empower those oppressed and powerless. By welcoming the women and infants, Jesus affirms the women's determination and decision to come for a blessing. He validates their concerns for their babies and respects their right to seek healing and protection for their families. His response supports their struggles and encourages their transgression of societal norms to acquire the justice, equality, and abundance that God's kingdom brings in their lives. Jesus demonstrates a commitment to the wholeness of everyone in the community. Protecting and caring for infants is important to Jesus's ministry of justice, liberation, and human dignity of God's kingdom.

Another liberationist imperative is Jesus's example to hold those in power accountable. Clark (2002, 243) pronounces, "The Lukan writer uses the children's story to remind the church of its responsibility to social justice for all classes of people. This justice would only work through identifying with the outcasts and humble of society." Although I agree with Clark's first statement, I disagree with the statement that one must "identify with the outcasts and humble." The statement suggests that one must be humble as outcasts to empathize, understand, and fight injustice. This stance may evoke almsgiving and charitable work; however, many with power and privilege do not assume responsibility for contributing to changes in policy and practices that perpetuate injustices. Jesus's blessing the children does more than identify those who are poor, powerless, and underprivileged; it identifies the sociopolitical dynamics that maintain the oppression of the women and children. While illustrating the discriminatory behavior and lived policies of gender and class injustice, the story demonstrates the power of individuals as change agents in God's kingdom. Jesus holds those with power responsible for eradicating injustice as partners in God's transformative work. The work of the disciples, and those in power, is to open the gates of power to include those such as the women and children. Jesus's blessing the children illustrates that the kingdom of God requires the participation of everyone—the powerful and the powerless; the privileged and underprivileged; the low and high in sociopolitical hierarchies.

Therefore, to receive the kingdom of God as (one receives) a child is the third liberationist imperative. Jesus's final statement suggests that the reader has learned from his example in this encounter. Therefore, one is to receive the kingdom of God with a responsibility to share in God's work to change sociopolitical dynamics. Also, the saying suggests that one is to receive the kingdom of God with anticipation of the joys and some trials. Although Greco-Roman children were treated as social inferiors, adults anticipated that they would grow, contributing greatly to their lives and bringing some challenges. Therefore, disciples should anticipate the kingdom's huge impact on their lives. In addition to the joy, the kingdom and its work will bring challenges. Finally, one is to receive God's kingdom without prejudice and pretense. Without regard to status or circumstance, Jesus tends to the women and children without delay or excuses. God expects the disciples to respond to God's kingdom without delay. As the kingdom of God belongs to everyone, everyone is to receive it with responsibility, anticipation, joy, and immediacy.

Summary

Using Hamer's activism as a springboard for a womanist hermeneutic, I argue that Luke 18:15–17 illustrates liberationist imperatives that empower the marginalized and admonishes the privileged to change the power dynamics and social politics to ensure fairness, equity, and dignity of all people. These imperatives become apparent when analyzing the class and gender dynamics among the women, the infants, disciples, and Jesus. When the disciples perpetuate marginalization and injustice in their rebuff of women and their infants, Jesus responds in word and deed. While inviting the women and the children to join him, Jesus informs the crowds that the kingdom of God is a place where the poor receive the good news, the oppressed are free, and those with privilege are partners to make it so. In Hamer's words, it's a place where everybody's free.

Works Cited

Bernstein, Robin. 2011. *Racial Innocence: Performing American Childhood from Slavery to Civil Rights*. New York: New York Press.

Brooks, Maegan Parker, and Davis W. Houck, eds. 2011. *The Speeches of Fannie Lou Hamer: To Tell It Like It Is*. Jackson: University Press of Mississippi.

Byron, Gay L. 2002. *Symbolic Blackness and Ethnic Difference in Early Christian Literature*. New York: Routledge.

Cannon, Katie Geneva. 1985. "The Emergence of Black Feminist Consciousness." Pages 30–40 in *Feminist Interpretation of the Bible*. Edited by Letty M. Russell. Philadelphia: Westminster.

———. 2012. *Luke: A Commentary*. Louisville: Westminster John Knox, 2012.

Clark, Ronald R., Jr. 2002. "Kingdoms, Kids, and Kindness: A New Context for Luke 18:15–17." *Stone-Campbell Journal* 5:235–48.

Fitzmyer, Joseph A. 1981. *The Gospel according to Luke: Introduction, Translation, and Notes*. Garden City, NY: Doubleday.

Fowl, Stephen E. 1993. "Receiving the Kingdom of God as a Child: Children and Riches in Luke 18:15ff." *NTS* 39:153–58.

Friesen, Steven J. 2004. "Poverty in Pauline Studies: Beyond the So-Called New Consensus." *JSNT* 26:323–61.

González, Justo L. 2010. *Luke*. Louisville: Westminster John Knox.

Green, Joel B. 1997. *The Gospel of Luke*. Grand Rapids: Eerdmans.

Houck, Davis W., and David E. Dixon. *Women and the Civil Rights Movement, 1954–1965*. Jackson: University Press of Mississippi, 2009.

Isaac, Benjamin H. 2004. *The Invention of Racism in Classical Antiquity*. Princeton: Princeton University Press.

Junior, Nyasha. 2015. *An Introduction to Womanist Biblical Interpretation*. Louisville: Westminster John Knox.

Kodell, Jerome. 1987. "Luke and the Children: The Beginning and End of the 'Great Interpolation' (Luke 9:46–56, 18:9–23)." *CBQ* 49:415–30.

Stegemann, Ekkehard, and Wolfgang Stegemann. 1999. *The Jesus Movement: A Social History of Its First Century*. Minneapolis: Fortress.

Tisdale, Stacey. 2015. "Gloria Steinem on Black Women: 'They Invented the Feminist Movement.'" http://tinyurl.com/SBL0688n2.

Townes, Emilie Maureen. 1993. *Womanist Justice, Womanist Hope*. Atlanta: Scholars Press.

Walker, Alice. 1983. *In Search of Our Mothers' Gardens: Womanist Prose.* Orlando: Harcourt Brace Jovanovich.

"I WILL MAKE BOYS THEIR PRINCES": A WOMANIST READING OF CHILDREN IN THE BOOK OF ISAIAH

Valerie Bridgeman

On first reading, one might be tempted to believe that the prophetic texts always and only demand protection for children, often railing against those who oppress widows and orphans, for example. In fact, in the first chapter of Isaiah (1:17; 1:23), we are told that justice includes rescuing the oppressed, defending orphans, and pleading for widows. In addition, texts from the Psalms that declare that children are gifts and a heritage from the deity lull us into this thinking (see Ps 127:3). In addition, we are conditioned by our own cultural conceptions of what a child is, how children ought to be treated, and adult—societal and parental—obligations to the safety, care, and wellbeing of children.

But a close reading of the canonical prophetic texts uncovers another understanding of the way children and a metaphorical use of children are described as property, a nuisance, foolish, and in need of constant beating to correct wrong action and insolent attitudes. These characterizations are used to describe a people group—in the book of Isaiah most often ancient Israel, "the children of God." In the last twenty years especially, scholars[1] have begun to more closely attend to the children of the biblical texts—the way they are treated, laws regarding them, and the way they are employed to make points.

This essay adds to the body of literature regarding children in the Hebrew Bible by offering a womanist reading and critique of the way chil-

---

1. See, for a few examples, Bunge, Fretheim, and Gaventa 2008; Faith 2013; Garroway 2014; Angel 2016; Steinberg 2015; Perdue et al. 1997; Baxter 2005; and O'Brien 2008.

dren are portrayed in the first chapters of Isaiah, portrayals that I believe help to set the tone for the collected sayings attributed to the prophet.[2] In this essay, I look at the way these texts denigrate and make children more vulnerable,[3] and at the ways such portrayals explicitly condone child abuse. I have deliberately limited this study to the use of these metaphors and have chosen not to examine the social construction of children and childhood in ancient Israel, either in the biblical texts or in the archeological records.[4]

I consider the implications of these texts in the lives of real children, often the most vulnerable humans among us. Then, as a womanist biblical ethic, I offer an alternative vision to the theological and ideological world of the text that leaves children exposed to brute force and violent beatings in the name of divine correction. I am reading, in the words of Danna Nolan Fewell (2003), "for the sake of our children."[5]

Womanist Interpretation of Prophets

Womanist biblical interpretation is "interested" reading; that is to say, a womanist interpreter reads with goals in mind, and one such goal is for human flourishing unhindered by oppressive systems. As biblical scholar Renita Weems asserts, "womanist biblical hermeneutical reflections do not begin with the Bible. Rather, womanist hermeneutics of liberation

---

2. For a thorough and convincing treatment of Isa 1 and 65–66 as an intentional *inclusio*, see Kim 2011; Franke 2009, 39–40.

3. While Makhosazana K. Nzimande's (2010) essay on "Isaiah" in *The Africana Bible* deals with the patriarchal depiction of women in the book, there is no mention of the way children are depicted, with the notable exception of "the daughters of Zion."

4. There are several resources that do such examinations, including, for example, the volume by Steinberg (2015), which provides foundational work in an effort to answer the question, "what is a child?" and to examine how children might be understood in the social construction of society; Steinberg does not, however, address the way in which prophets use children as polemical language and metaphor in a negative way, the primary work of this essay. I return to her work later, however, when examining the Hebrew words translated "child/children." See also Perdue et al. 1997; Baxter 2005.

5. Danna Nolan Fewell (2003) focuses on stories in the Hebrew Bible that focus on children and ends her book with a prayer based on Isa 11. She does not address the presence or metaphorical use of children in prophetic texts.

begin with African American women's will to survive and thrive as human beings and as the female half of a race of people who live a threatened existence within North American borders" (2003, 24). This will to survive and thrive leads interpreters to think seriously about what constitutes a good life and how that life might be thwarted for the most vulnerable among us. Thus, when reading prophetic texts, a womanist interpreter must ask what vision is put forth by the prophet and whether the prophetic texts have used images that reify danger or denigration of the most vulnerable, which in biblical texts are women, children, and foreigners among ancient Israelite communities. To be sure, laws are laid out to protect all who fit in these categories, and the prophets often rail against leaders for misusing what should be protected persons, for example, the category of "widows and orphans" (Exod 22:22–23; 23:6). That said the prophetic texts themselves often depend on negative assumptions, especially about women and children, in order to make their case.

In my essay for the *Oxford Encyclopedia of the Prophets* (Bridgeman 2016, 483–90), I put forth an argument that womanist interpretations must matter most for the "most vulnerable and furthest from the seat and center of power." By this definition, children in the text deserve our attention. Children, as children, are often used metaphorically in the same way, as are women. Both children and women are often used to "denigrate and berate men in power and to accuse said men of being fickle or erratic" (Bridgeman 2016, 486).

As Weems has noted in her foundational text on the prophetic marriage metaphor, *Battered Love* (1995), metaphors matter and assume a world that listeners—male listeners with power and/or means—would have taken for granted, "that's just the way it is." Since it is true that prophets draw on cultural assumptions, when one reads the prophets it is a fair assessment to say that how the prophet employs language about these protected persons, herein especially children, uncovers presumed common beliefs about children as normative. Or, more specifically, we may judge that the writers believed that their readers and listeners would take their words as normative, necessary, and reasonable. Once we are able to unmask what appear as normative beliefs about children, we may assess how believing such things may have affected the lives of real children. Further, we may assess how our acceptance of the texts' norms affect the way we understand children and how that understanding may affect the way children are affected in our times.

Isaiah's Children

In Isaiah,[6] it is easy to overlook the places where the text is unsafe for and in its portrayal of children. Particularly, by "unsafe," I mean the places where, because they are characterized as rebellious or disobedient, these children are subject to physical punishment, up to and including death, or cultural shaming (cf. Deut 21:18–21). These instances are overlooked because there are other visions of children in Isaiah, to be sure. The vision most familiar to those interested in interpreting the Hebrew Bible as Christian texts is Isa 9, where the child "born to us," bears the weight of the government; a promise of renewal and restoration after the punishment of war and conquering is over. That child is an historic figure, outside the scope of this study. But he is a prophetic sign, born to demonstrate the deity's faithfulness (7:10–17).[7] In fact, Isaiah names three children as "signs," though we often are hard pressed to remember any but Immanuel ("God with us"); the other two are Shear-jashub ("a remnant shall return"; 7:3) and Maher-shalal-hash-baz ("hurry to the spoils"; 8:3). "The three children themselves seem to be quite dispensable, mere vessels for the names that convey God's judgment and promises to Israel" (Lapsley 2008, 84).

In addition, Isa 11, often referred to as the vision of a "peaceable kingdom," depicts a child playing safely over the hole of an asp, a dangerous snake, where the child is not harmed. This depiction portends a world so safe that "natural enemies" do not experience animosity and where the innocence and gullibility of children does not put them in danger. One way to read the text in Isa 11 is to declare that because of the deity's shalom, all creation is at peace. Another, less positive reading, however, is to note that the most vulnerable in the vision (the lamb, the child) are either blissfully unaware of the obvious danger or that the predators have been subdued by

---

6. I am using "Isaiah" as a shortcut for the book itself without making a case for a person named "Isaiah." Neither am I assuming that there are no historical issues about understanding the book of Isaiah, often divided into three sections representing three time periods over which the book is composed. Here I am reading the canonical text as received.

7. Lapsley (2008) argues well that Christian readings of Isaiah as messianic helps us overlook this issue. Lapsley provides a reading of children in Isaiah, focusing first on the naming as sign and on texts regarding orphans. She also examines the metaphors that use children.

the deity, rendering them safe to the vulnerable. In these possible readings, we maintain a consistent way in which children are first introduced to us in the book of Isaiah.

Translating "Child"/"Children" in Isaiah

The book of Isaiah uses several words that are translated "child" or "children" in the NRSV.[8] In some ways, this attempt at inclusive translation obscures the force of the use of children to make points. The suckling or weaning child may be male or female, but it is clear that when speaking of a child that leads the elders or troops, the prophetic text uses the word "young boy," *na'ar*, thus making clear that war games belong in the male sphere. I will return to this notion below. Another term, *'ôlāl* (3:12), often used alongside *yōnēq*, is translated "infant" (as in Ps 8:2[3]).[9] In some places it seems to particularly reflect children vulnerable to the violence of war (e.g., 1 Sam 15:3; Lam 2:11; Jer 44:7). Isaiah 11:8 also uses both "nursing infant," *yōnēq* and "weaned child," *gāmûl*, children in their most vulnerable state.

In the texts regarding the prophet's son, the first word used in Isa 7:16 is *hanna'ar*, "the child," which also may be translated "boy," "lad," "youth" or "servant-boy." The term *na'ar* usually reflects an economic reality of a son (and in its feminine form *na'arâ*, the daughter) who is not in the line of inheritance and may need to seek employment or be given in debt-slavery due to the family's limited resources (Steinberg, 2015, 30–31). This term usually applies to a male young person who is beyond infancy and weaning but before marriage. The term "son," *bēn* (and its feminine equivalent "daughter," *bat*) usually denotes one's kinship relationship to the parent and not a specific age (88–89). Thus, use of these aforementioned terms recognizes economic vulnerability, more so than physical vulnerability as the infant does.

As you can see, these words have a range of meanings and are not to be considered synonymous. Each carries a particular sense. For example, one is always a "son" or "daughter" of one's parent, no matter the age. So an "obedient son" may include the grown son who cares for his household and

---

8. See Steinberg (2015, 26–41), for a treatment of the terms used for children, the number of times they appear in the Hebrew canon, and a more thorough rendering of their range of meanings.

9. The Hebrew versification is given in brackets.

for his elders. Moreover, it is difficult to decide on the age of children in any of the texts. This difficulty is partly due to what makes a child a "child" over against an "adult." Steinberg (2015, 29) argues that a boy or a girl does not cease to be a child until he or she sires or bears children, thereby taking responsibility for a household (29). Childhood is not carefree nor without obligations, she argues. Children, as soon as able, add value to the "house of the father" (64). I now turn my attention to these uses that connote some form of vulnerability in the first four chapters of Isaiah.

Seeing Children, Reading Metaphors

The book of Isaiah introduces us to children as gullible, stubborn, rebellious, and unwilling to listen to sound counsel. Isaiah opens as a vision dated and marked by the reigns of Northern and Southern Kingdom rulers (1:1). In a courtroom scene, the deity brings charges against the ancient Israelite nation-state by asking heaven and earth to take the witness stand to testify against their rebellious nature. As Brittany Kim (2011, 4–5) notes, "Like the parents of the rebellious son in Deut 21:18–21, YHWH brings an accusation against his children before an audience—in this case, before the heavens and the earth, who function as witnesses."[10]

Immediately in 1:2 we are introduced to the people of ancient Israel as children ("sons," Heb. *bānîm*), as the deity declares that the children the deity reared have rebelled against him. They do not know their god as parent. Gene Tucker (2001, 53) rightly notes that this "knowing" is most likely a double entendre reflecting both intimacy or closeness and ignorance. So, these children reject a primary part of the parent-child relationship, that of teacher (Lapsley 2008). These children also are likened to an ox that does not know his owner or a donkey that does not know its master's crib (1:3). The ox and the donkey "know," but Israel "does not know" and does not understand (1:3). These analogies also point toward "dull of understanding" and "stubborn," as donkey and oxen often are considered. In addition, these words alert careful readers to the idea that Israel belongs to YHWH in the same way that the ox and donkey belong to their masters.

Since the people are a possession, the reader also is alerted to the notion that owners may do as they will to their property. Once ownership

---

10. See Darr (1994) for treatment of Israel as the children of God, the household of God, and other social constructions of family comparisons in biblical texts related to ancient Israel.

is established, name-calling soon follows. The people are described as "lacking understanding," "laden with iniquity," "seed that does evil," and "children [Heb. *bānîm*] who deal corruptly" and forsake their God (1:4). The term *seed* reflects the offspring of a people; that is, their dullness and iniquity is inherited and passed on. These negative terms are enjoined to the people as children. While we may not argue that these are epithets, I would maintain that these descriptions, used in conjunction with children reflect what Weems (1995, 15–18) would say is the way metaphors work, in that she notes that prophetic rhetoric reflects some reality to the listener. In Isaiah's case, his audience would recognize this attribute as the way some children are viewed, and thus apt descriptions.

As Patricia Tull (2012, 257) notes, "in calling the people God's rebellious offspring, Isaiah invokes a family code such as Deut 21:18–21." By invoking this code, the reader is prepared for a normalizing of patriarchal power, often enforced by brute violence. After such descriptions, it is no wonder that violence soon follows. What else would the deity (here as the disappointed parent) do except "beat" such children? This beating would be in keeping with Proverbs, for example (19:13; 29:15). When a child is rebellious, that rebellion is an affront and a shame to the child's parent, no less true in Isaiah's rendering of familial relationships. In relationship with the deity, then, rebellion is betrayal, and "in the context of an intimate family relationship, Israel's sin takes on the character of personal betrayal" (Kim 2011, 6).

The text, however, is clear that whatever beatings the people-as-children have received, they "sought" them (1:5): "Why do you seek further beatings?" the text asks, allowing the reader to know that beating is an acceptable form of discipline and that if the child is beaten, he or she "sought" it; or as we might say colloquially in the twenty-first century, "they asked for it," bringing punishment upon themselves.[11] By their deeds the children "made" the deity act in the way the text describes, much like human abusers might say to their victim, "look what you made me do to you." In addition, these children who in Isa 1:4 "despise" their deity and are "estranged," "deserve" whatever happens to them. Even after being beaten, the people, as children, continue in their insolence. On behalf of the deity,

---

11. O'Brien (2008, 80) makes this point: "Isaiah does not criticize the father's beatings but rather the son's willfulness."

the prophet asks: "why do you continue to rebel?" This question seems to infer that the beatings will stop when the rebelling stops.

Chapter 3 continues this negative treatment of children as a metaphor for divine wrath against the people of ancient Israel. The writer begins by naming leaders of the nation-state Judah from every sector of the public arena: "warrior and soldier, judge and prophet, diviner and elder, captain of fifty and dignitary, counselor and skillful magician and expert enchanter" (Isa 3:2–4 NRSV). This list covers governing officials, military officials, respected public elders, and religious leaders. The people have, by their disobedience and idolatry, left the nation bereft of leaders, so much so that the prophet says that God, "will make boys their princes and babes shall rule over them" (3:4). In short, the whole society is under judgment. How does the prophet announce this judgment? He does so by referring to these leaders as "boys" (Heb. nəʿārîm), "babes" (Heb. taʿalûlîm), and "the oppressive (or insolent) youth" (Heb. hannaʿar) (3:5). To refer to men as children (or women) is to shame them by demoting them to the vulnerable status of "child." Here, in this passage, men are told they are no better than boys and thus incapable of wise leadership. This comparison means to shame leaders for rejecting the deity and the prophetic texts find no better way to shame them but to make this comparison. Perhaps the ultimate insult is when the people, as represented by adult free men, are oppressed by children (Heb. məʿôlēl) and ruled over by women at the same time (Isa 3:12). The world is in complete disarray, with the natural order of a loving father displaced.

What readers often remember, however, about Isa 3 is that the prophet demands that leaders "learn to do good; seek justice, rescue the oppressed, defend the orphan, plead for the widow" (3:17). But interpreters must not forget that this commandment comes on the heels of denigrating language about children. Moreover, the full weight of the first four chapters is harsh judgment with grotesque and punitive action on the part of the deity, warranted because a father may punish as he wills his children. Since the deity often is depicted as a father or a man, such depictions may sanction the same behavior among human males or at least may be read as "this is the way a wronged man ought to respond" (O'Brien 2008, 86, passim).

I turn briefly to another child metaphor: the daughter of Zion.[12] In Isaiah, as in other texts, daughter Zion (Heb. bat-ṣiyyôn; 1:8) is most likely

---

12. This section is meant to provide only a brief look at this metaphor in Isaiah.

a personification of the city of Jerusalem. Here the city is "left," with the writer using three examples to intensify the point: left "like a booth in a vineyard," "like a shelter in a cucumber field," and "like a besieged city." As with sons in the earlier text, Daughter Zion's desolation is a result of the rebellion.

The bereft daughter, as the city, has disgraced her father by being whorish (1:21): "How the faithful city has become a whore! She that was full of justice, righteousness lodged in her—but now murderers!" Daughter Zion, then, represents the moral collapse of the people. This language is the language of exile and of lament, in the style of the book of Lamentations.

From Daughter Zion, the prophet turns to "the daughters of Zion," which extends the metaphor of the city as daughter to its inhabitants (3:16–24). The prophet's words lash out at the inhabitants who are women of means, perhaps the daughters or wives of male leaders (cf. Amos 4:1), referring to them as "haughty," dressed in sexually enticing and explicit ways, "glancing wantonly," and wearing ankle jewelry (3:16, 18). Because of their demeanor, they will be afflicted with head sores and stripped naked so that their "secret parts" are exposed (3:17). While "sons" are beaten, "daughters" are subjected to sexualized humiliation, possibly including rape. The "daughters" are unclean, full of "filth," according to 4:4. This filth will be, according to the text, washed away "by a spirit of judgment and by a spirit of burning." To be so depicted means that women are made vulnerable to attacks as expected and normative. Like the son who is beaten, she brings it upon herself by the way she dresses and because she is haughty. This treatment of the daughters symbolically reflects the ways in which cities were overrun in times of war and rape was used as a weapon of war.[13] For Nzimande, Isaiah's depiction of the daughters of Zion exhibits a condescending attitude toward women. The language descriptions reflect a prevailing and denigrating attitude toward women and should be seen as a stereotype and viewed with suspicion, just as with Amos 4:1–3 and Jer 2:23–25, 33 (Nzimande 2010, 139). While it is true that by the end of the canonical book redemption comes for the daughter (62:11), we must not ignore that she is shamed and brutalized first.

There are numerous articles, essays, book chapters, and books on the Daughter of Zion, Daughter Zion, and Daughters of Zion in the Hebrew Bible scholarship (e.g., Dobbs-Allsopp 1993; Floyd 2008; Maier 2008; Boda, Dempsey, and Flesher 2012).

13. For a treatment of rape as a weapon of war, see Camp and Fontaine 1993; and Kelle and Ames 2008.

The first four chapters of Isaiah, then, focus on the depiction of children as children. When those children, however, are attached to their mothers, the language continues to be degrading. In the later canonical sections of Isaiah, they are referred to as "sons [Heb. *bānîm*] of a sorceress," "offspring ["seed"; Heb. *zeraʻ*] of an adulterer and a whore," "children [Heb. *yildê*] of transgression," and "offspring ["seed"; Heb. *zeraʻ*] of deceit" (57:3–4). They mock other children, according to the text. They stick out their tongues like children do and make faces like children do (57:4). These phrases harken back to the beginning of the book where being childish has gotten the people into disfavor with the deity, and this disfavor continues as we are led to believe they are in the moral idolatrous shape they are in because of their parent (here depicted as a woman). Such depictions portray disdain in the prophetic texts toward children and women because, "being the child of a whore, the 'son of a bitch' is and always has been intended to demean and shame" (Bridgeman 2016, 486). Here, it is clear that shaming is at work.[14] Shame, as a category, is used for social control in ancient Israel and its neighboring environs in order to maintain societal "order."

The aforementioned uses of children in the prophetic texts are contained within the family system. Yet, war provides a particular danger to children. They are not spared when hoards of warriors descend on cities. In fact, as the deity "stirs" ancient Israel's enemy, the Medes, against them; the bow and arrow seem to seek out young men (Heb. *naʻārim*) and the "fruit of the womb," which may be understood as the youngest of the young, that is, infants, the most vulnerable. Soldiers do not look with pity because they are children (13:18). War and rumors of it brings about fear, also cloaked in language related to children. The well-used prophetic phrase "like a woman with child" or "like a woman in labor" describes how afraid the people were of God's judgment (cf. Jer 30:6; Mic 4:10). In Isaiah, the birth pangs of fear do not produce; the prophet says of the people, "we writhed, but we gave birth only to wind. We have won no victories on earth" (Isa 26:18). This idea is furthered when the prophet writes in 37:3 that King Hezekiah's time is "a day of distress, of rebuke, and of disgrace" because the woman in labor struggles to the moment of birth and fails because "there is no strength" to birth the child. The use of birthing in this prophetic way

---

14. For a treatment of the "honor and shame" system in the Old Testament/Hebrew Bible, see Stiebert 2002, especially chapter 2 on Isaiah; Matthews 1998; Olyan 1996; Bechtel 1991; Crook 2009.

points to the real danger in the birthing process, where death and birth so intimately meet and a live birth is not a guarantee. This sense of excitement and of foreboding is central to war. Isaiah's war words are not as graphic as some prophets (cf. Jer 13:14; Hos 10:14), but they are no less dangerous.

In Solidarity with Children

I have demonstrated the way in which the prophet uses the life of children, from birth onward, in mostly negative ways to speak about ancient Israel. I have read these texts as the prophet's understanding of children as unruly, dull of understanding, rebellious (unwilling to obey a parent), and the like. I believe this understanding is more than borne out in the texts I have examined. Because these same children have no recourse (they are "owned" like slaves) either in family or clan law, they are particularly vulnerable. This fact, I believe, is why the use of children as a metaphor is so powerful. In the book of Isaiah, these metaphors function to judge the people and to explain the judgment rendered. In this essay, I have focused on these terms related to children beyond their historical context—and sometimes out of their literary context—looking mostly at the way the metaphor is used by the prophetic writer/editor. In so doing, I have tried to highlight these negative inferences of the use of children as metaphor, especially in the first four chapters of the book of Isaiah. For me, this use is problematic, but often overlooked because readers typically are not attuned to this negativity. Earlier interpreters, even when they acknowledge the negativity, often minimize its impact (see, e.g., Tull 2012; Lapsley 2008). These interpreters often do so in an effort to get to the theological point that the metaphor uses (O'Brien 2008 offers a notable difference). To minimize the metaphor, however, is to implicitly condone the abuse and violence contained within it. As a womanist interpreter, who knows the dangers black children encounter in 2016, I cannot afford to dismiss or minimize the overall impact for what the prophetic texts calls.

Much of the language points to the rights of a father to treat his children however he chooses, since they are his property. In the Isaiah texts, the choice when judging the people-as-children is to beat, humiliate, or rape them. Perhaps between people and deity, we must expect such activity. After all, what human may call gods into accountability? In fact, the prophet makes this point by saying that YHWH, "the Holy One of Israel," the "Maker" cannot be questioned, punctuated by this question: "will you question me about my children?" (45:11). The implied and expected answer is "no." But what are we to do with this metaphor if or when it is "translated" between human parent and child as normative and even right in human interactions? If we deem such violence against children unacceptable, is such violence also unacceptable from the deity? I accept Steinberg's (2015 xiii, 121–30) caution that we cannot read these metaphors or texts as if we live in the same culture and times as when they were produced, a helpful reminder that the texts are "other" than current readers and interpreters.

With that caution in mind, I do not believe that womanist interpreters may overlook or minimize this metaphoric use of children in prophetic texts. These texts still "perform" in our times and must be interrogated across the cultural and time divide. Indeed, one of the roles of womanist interpretation is "to look a text squarely in what it actually says and then make ethical decisions about how it may function in a reading community. Or, put another way, sometimes a womanist must point at a text as illustrating what not to do" (Bridgeman 2016, 487). In this way, womanist biblical criticism must become constructive once a text is deemed dangerous to liberation and thriving, goals set forth at the beginning of this essay. Indeed, a womanist biblical criticism "involves empowering readers to judge biblical texts, to not hesitate to read against the grain of the text if needed, and to be ready to take a stand against those texts whose worldview runs counter to one's own vision of God's liberation activity in the world" (Weems 2003, 31).

What are some implications on the lives of children in our times when texts are read as if it were necessary, normal, or right to beat, humiliate, or harm a child as punishment for disobeying or assuming agency in opposition to a parent or other adult? One need only watch the news when a sports figure is supported for beating a four-year-old with a belt until he bleeds.[15] Or when a school-based police officer body slams a young girl and people ask, "what did she do?"[16] Violence against children—like this incident with the girl being yanked from a desk and slung across the

---

15. Minnesota Vikings running back Adrian Peterson was indicted for beating his son with a switch until he bled. A furor ensued between people who were horrified on behalf of the child and those who defended Peterson's right to discipline his child as he chose. There was social media commentary as well as many stories in mainstream media. See Worland 2014.

16. Officer Ben Fields pulled a young teenaged girl from her desk and slammed her against the wall; it was caught on camera. See "Footage Surfaces of South Carolina Police Officer" 2015.

room—is often greeted with words such as, "Well, she or he should have just done what they were told." This sentiment is in Isa 1:5. When do we, as interpreters, argue back from the text and from our own cultural violence that it is not humane or just to beat, humiliate, or shame children, the most vulnerable among us who often are at our mercy? When do we argue that a deity that demands such brutality does not deserve our loyalty? Is it possible to read these metaphors, point out how they cause harm, and then offer a resisting alternative? My argument has no bearing on whether a child has transgressed or not, nor whether a child is "innocent." In other words, just because someone has transgressed does not mean he or she should be brutalized or shamed. In the past few years, this issue has reared its head, in my mind, in the way black people—men, women, boys, and girls—have been demonized when confronted by the paternal law keepers, agents of state or religion. In the United States, studies have documented well that when black children are disciplined, they do not even get the benefit of being treated as "children" and are seen as much older and more dangerous than they are (Goff et al. 2014, 526; and Bernstein 2011).

Conclusion

One benefit in paying close attention to this use of children as metaphor is that it allows us to reflect on who and what we value about human freedom and human flourishing. The prophet puts forth, on one level, a vision of life that is under threat if the deity is crossed. Children represent those who have no say so in how they are treated in society. But do we want to worship God only out of fear? Do we want our children to be in relationship with us with fear as the basis of that relationship? Clearly reflecting the years of exile and distress, the prophetic texts take a turn in which the metaphor moves from angry father to protective and doting mother (66:13). But we must not argue an essentialist claim that fathers are one way and mothers another. Fathers, too, may be protective and nonviolent (as mothers may be violent). Womanist interpreters unmask the patriarchal essentialism and resist it. We must also unmask and resist the notion that children have no agency. We must also affirm that children deserve freedom and flourishing as much as older persons.

Going forward, and for the sake of our children, womanist interpreters must point out the implications of allowing metaphors to stand unchallenged, even when the perpetrator in the text is God. It is not, in my mind, enough to acknowledge that the treatment of children becomes more positive in the latter portion of the canonical Isaiah (Kim 2011). We are called to imagine a world as absurd as the one put forth in Isa 11, where a child may be oblivious of danger because that danger has been subdued by peace. Playing over the entrance of a poisonous snake's hole is risky business. But in the life of God, this vision might serve as a counter voice.

If Weems (2003, 30) is right that people love a story, then womanist biblical work must craft a story worth telling that will make survival and thriving a basic part of children's life among us. We must allow our children to help craft that story, listening to them as they seek to be full members of a just society. When the text offers no counter, ethically we must resist it and imagine an alternative vision where children are safe from cradle to nursing to struggling teenager. As June Jordan says:

> It would be something fine if we could learn how to bless the lives of children. They are the people of new life. Children are the only people nobody can blame. They are the only ones always willing to make a start; they have no choice. Children are the ways the world begins again and again. (Jordan and Bush 1970, 93)

Works Cited

Angel, Hayyim. 2016. "Rebuke Your Mother: But Who Is She? The Identity of the 'Mother' and 'Children' in Hosea 2:4–7." *JBQ* 44:13–20.

Baxter, Jane. 2005. *The Archeology of Childhood: Children, Gender, and Material Culture*. Gender and Archeology 10. Walnut Creek, CA: AltaMira Press.

Bechtel, Lyn M. 1991. "Shame as a Sanction of Social Control in Biblical Israel: Judicial, Political, and Social Shaming." *JSOT* 16:47–76.

Bernstein, Robin. 2011. *Racial Innocence: Performing American Childhood and Race from Slavery to Civil Rights*. New York: New York University Press.

Boda, Mark J., Carol J. Dempsey, and LeAnn Snow Flesher. 2012. *Daughter Zion: Her Portrait, Her Response*. AIL 13. Atlanta: Society of Biblical Literature.

Bridgeman, Valerie. 2016. "Womanist Approaches to the Prophets." Pages 483–90 in *The Oxford Handbook of the Prophets*. Edited by Carolyn J. Sharp. Oxford: Oxford University Press.

Bunge, Marcia J., Terence E. Fretheim, and Beverly Roberts Gaventa. 2008. *The Child in the Bible*. Grand Rapids: Eerdmans.

Camp, Claudia V., and Carole R. Fontaine. 1993. *Women, War, and Metaphor: Language and Society in the Study of the Hebrew Bible. Semeia* 61.
Crook, Zeba. 2009. "Honor, Shame, and Social Status Revisited." *JBL* 128:591–611.
Darr, Katheryn Pfisterer. 1994. *Isaiah's Vision and the Family of God*. Louisville: Westminster John Knox.
Dobbs-Allsopp, Frederick William. 1993. *Weep, O Daughter of Zion: A Study of the City-Lament Genre in the Hebrew Bible*. Rome: Pontifical Biblical Institute.
Faith, Julia. 2013. *Valuable and Vulnerable: Children in the Hebrew Bible, Especially the Elisha Cycle*. BJS 355. Providence, RI: Brown Judaic Studies.
Fewell, Danna Nolan. 2003. *The Children of Israel: Reading the Bible for the Sake of our Children*. Nashville: Abingdon.
Floyd, Michael H. 2008. "Welcome Back, Daughter of Zion!" *CBQ* 70:484–504.
"Footage Surfaces of South Carolina Police Officer Slamming, Dragging Teen Girl in Classroom." 2015. NewsOne. http://tinyurl.com/SBL068802.
Franke, Chris A. 2009. "'Like a Mother I Have Comforted You': The Function of Figurative Language in Isaiah 1:7–26 and 66:7–14." Pages 35–55 in *The Desert Will Bloom: Poetic Visions in Isaiah*. Edited by A. Joseph Everson and Hyun Chul Paul Kim. AIL 4. Atlanta: Society of Biblical Literature.
Garroway, Kristine Henriksen. 2014. "Neither Slave Nor Free: Children Living on the Edge of Social Status." Pages 121–37 in *Windows to the Ancient World of the Hebrew Bible: Essays in Honor of Samuel Greengus*. Edited by John H. Walton, Nancy L. Erickson, and Bill T. Arnold. Winona Lake, IN: Eisenbrauns.
Goff, Phillip Atiba, Matthew Christian Jackson, Brooke Allison, Lewis Di Leone, Carmen Marie Culotta, and Natalie Ann DiTomasso. 2014. "The Essence of Innocence: Consequences of Dehumanizing Black Children." *Journal of Personality and Social Psychology* 106:526–45.
Jordan, June, and Terri Bush. 1970. *The Voice of the Children (Poetry by Children)*. New York: Holt, Rinehart & Winston.
Kelle, Brad, and Frank Ritchel Ames. 2008. *Writing and Reading War: Rhetoric, Gender, and Ethics in Biblical and Modern contexts*. SymS 42. Atlanta: Society of Biblical Literature.

Kim, Brittany. 2011. "From Defiant Children to Contented Babes: An Exploration of Relational Metaphors for Israel in the Frame of Isaiah (Chs. 1 and 65–66)." Paper presented at the Annual Meeting of the Society of Biblical Literature Annual Meeting. San Francisco, CA. 18 November.

Lapsley, Jacqueline E. 2008. "'Look! The Children and I Are as Signs and Portents in Israel': Children in Isaiah." In *The Child in the Bible*. Edited by Marcia J. Bunge, Terence E. Fretheim, and Beverley Roberts Gaventa. Kindle Ed. Grand Rapids: Eerdmans.

Maier, Christl M. 2008. *Daughter Zion, Mother Zion: Gender, Space, and the Sacred in Ancient Israel*. Minneapolis: Fortress.

Matthews, Victor H. 1998. "Honor and Shame in Gender-Related Legal Situations in the Hebrew Bible." Pages 97–112 in *Gender and Law in the Hebrew Bible and the Ancient Near East*. Edited by Victor H. Matthews, Bernard M. Levinson, and Tikva Frymer-Kensky. JSOTSup 262. Sheffield: Sheffield Academic.

Nzimande, Makhosazana K. 2010. "Isaiah." Pages 136–46 in *The Africana Bible: Reading Israel's Scriptures from Africa and the African Diaspora*. Edited by Hugh R. Page Jr. Minneapolis: Fortress.

O'Brien, Julia M. 2008. *Challenging Prophetic Metaphor: Theology and Ideology in the Prophets*. Louisville: Westminster John Knox.

Olyan, Saul M. 1996. "Honor, Shame, and Covenant Relations in Ancient Israel and its Environment." *JBL* 115:201–18.

Perdue, Leo G., Joseph Blenkinsopp, John J. Collins, and Carol Meyers, eds. 1997. *Families in Ancient Israel*. Louisville: Westminster John Knox.

Steinberg, Naomi. 2015. *The World of the Child in the Hebrew Bible*. Edited by David J. A. Clines and Cheryl Exum. HBM 51. Sheffield: Sheffield Phoenix.

Stiebert, Johanna. 2002. *The Construction of Shame in the Hebrew Bible: The Prophetic Contribution*. Londong: Sheffield Academic.

Tucker, Gene M. 2001. "The Book of Isaiah 1–39." *NIB* 6:25–306.

Tull, Patricia K. 2012. "Isaiah." Pages 255–66 in *Women's Bible Commentary*. Edited by Carol A. Newsom, Sharon H. Ringe, and Jacqueline E. Lapsley. 3rd ed. Louisville: Westminster John Knox.

Weems, Renita J. 1995. *Battered Love: Marriage, Sex, and Violence in the Hebrew Prophets*. Minneapolis: Fortress.

———. 2003. "Re-reading for Liberation: African American Women and the Bible." Pages 19–32 in *Feminist Interpretation of the Bible and the Hermeneutics of Liberation*. Edited by Silvia Schroer and Sophia Bietenhard. JSOTSup 374. New York: Sheffield Academic.

Worland, Justin. 2014. "Adrian Peterson Promises Never to Beat His Kid with a Tree Branch Again." Time. http://tinyurl.com/SBL0688q2.

Part 5
In Response

Miracles and Gifts: A Womanist Reading of John 14:12–14 and Ephesians 4:11–16

Layli Maparyan

Introduction

I was raised in the Bahá'í Faith. Thus, my pathway to Christianity, Christ, and the Bible was nonlinear. In fact, I would say it occurred in three phases. As a child, I first learned about Christ and Christianity in Bahá'í Sunday School, where we were taught that God had sent divine Messengers to humanity many times so that everybody could get the message no matter where on earth (or when in history) they lived. We were taught that there was only one true religion—God's religion—and that each Messenger told the same story in different ways so that different people around the world and throughout time could understand it and receive it. We were taught that humanity was maturing and that, each time, each Messenger updated the message just a little so that it would make sense to the people of those times and help humanity grow a little more until the next Messenger came. We were taught that this process would never end and that our Messenger, Bahá'u'lláh, was the most recent in this unbroken chain of communication from God. Thus, I loved and accepted Christ and Christianity from an early age, even though I self-defined as a Bahá'í. I lived the first twenty-four years of my life as an active and committed Bahá'í, in line with the way I had been raised by my parents.

As a young adult, I decided to take a break from religion and to explore nonreligiosity. I like to joke that I was agnostic for one year, but it did not suit me! Even though that year of agnosticism ended with a profound personal affirmation of my indissoluble connection to the Divine, I did not just go back to religious "business as usual." That departure, in fact, inaugurated a twenty-three-year journey of exploration that took me through diverse dimensions of identity, multiple arenas of political activism, and a deep dive into mysticism, metaphysics, and esotericism. Everything I saw and did changed me and how I viewed religion, whether Christianity or the Bahá'í Faith, to which I ultimately returned at the ripe middle age of forty-seven.

Womanism was crucial to that phase of my journey because it provided an organizing principle for my identities, my politics, and my spiritual explorations. As a womanist, I could put myself as a black woman at the center and be the organizing principle of my own life, living a life of curiosity, drawing life force from my passion for the Divine, acknowledging its infinity and exploring its many forms, and voicing my commitment to liberationist politics, spiritually inflected, on the earth plane. Womanism provided a logic that I did not find elsewhere, and writing on womanism as an academic provided me with a welcome vehicle for integrating not only the personal and the professional, not only the scholarly and the activist, but also my intellectual work with the spiritual insights my journey was yielding. It was, at times, a laborious process, not without challenges, realized risks, and, at times, reversals. However, everything came together with the writing of my second book, *The Womanist Idea* (2012), because I finally gave myself permission to speak what I know and to break with the traditions of my discipline. This decision was not without consequences, positive and negative, but it stands as one of the best decisions I ever made.

Like many other womanists, I found that my spiritual and religious orientation was served and enlivened by many traditions. The Bahá'í Faith and Christianity were only two of them. Over time, I studied and gained a great deal from Buddhism and Hinduism, Judaism and Kabbalah, Islam and Sufism, many African and African-derived traditions, including Yoruba, Ifa, Dogon, Bantu-Kongo, Vodoun, Candomblé, and others, and a number of Western esoteric and initiatic traditions. Collectively, my studies and experimentations with diverse practices left me with some profound takeaways and tools. For example, my engagement with diverse meditation practices left me with a confirmed awareness that there are realms beyond the material that are accessible to us as ordinary humans if we simply open the door and walk through it. As with any exercise, practice makes perfect, and the deeper and more consistent the practice, the greater the insights and the deeper the illumination. My exposure to diverse forms of mysticism left me with concrete awareness that this so-called unseeable realm is not only accessible, but it is also lawful and predictable in ways that are worth knowing. Our tendency to refer to this realm as beyond our understanding does a disservice to our power as human beings, not only to know the so-called unknowable, but also to do the so-called undoable.

Through both study and personal experience, I learned that humans are capable of much more than we typically say or think that we are—and definitely more than we are told that we are. We limit ourselves because we have at times failed to explore—collectively or individually—what lies just beyond the boundaries of our accepted discourse about the possible. Messages about what is (or is not) possible not only emanate from the systems of oppression that ensnare us, but also from those who love us but whose viewpoints about human possibility are limited. Because of all of this and more, we grossly underdetermine our own power or genius, and we rob the world of valuable tools for change—for creating the world we would like to see or be in—by failing to push these boundaries and explore them further. But one of the things I love about Jesus Christ that I have received from his teachings and example is his messaging about what is possible and what we are capable of.

In the remainder of this essay, I focus on two of my favorite passages from the Bible, John 14:12–14, in which Jesus speaks, and Eph 4:11–16, in which Paul speaks. I call these passages "miracles" and "gifts," respectively. I was inspired to write on these passages by the title of this series, *Semeia Studies*, which is the biblical Greek word for signs and miracles. Both passages invite us to dialogue about miracles and gifts. I offer a womanist reading—and invite a womanist application—of these passages as both my contribution to and my affirmation of the essays in this volume.

Miracles

> Most assuredly, I say to you, he who believes in Me, the works that I do he will do also; and greater works than these he will do, because I go to My Father. And whatever you ask in My name, that I will do, that the Father may be glorified in the Son. If you ask anything in My name, I will do it. (John 14:12–14, NKJV)

John 14:12 is one of my favorite verses in the Bible because it affirms that we can do miracles. It is not Jesus alone who can do miracles, but also us. He is effectively telling us, "You are like Me. In fact, this stuff that I am doing is just the beginning. Even though I am greater than you, the stuff you can do is even greater than what I have shown you. Because of God, you are so great, and I have come here to show you that. So, get up and do it!!" This is how I read John 14:12.

That being said, I have had many arguments with Christians who insist on believing that we cannot do greater things than Jesus. Yet, Jesus has said that we can. I often feel like this statement in the Bible goes unnoticed or that its meaning is willfully downgraded from what it actually says. Why do we choose not to be miracle workers when it says that we can be? The world is in need of miracles, and we are the ones available to perform them.

My viewpoint on "ordinary" humans and miracle working was deeply influenced by my encounter with mystical, metaphysical, and esoteric teachings from diverse wisdom traditions from around the world, during the portion of my journey where I focused on that. What I discovered is that there is virtually no spiritual tradition that does not teach how to do miracles if you go deep enough into the teachings. Effectively, there is a single and unified science of doing miracles, spoken of with great similarity across traditions, and it is there to learn for anyone who is willing to gain the education. As with any other field of self-development, from athletics to academics, it requires study, practice, concentration, dedication, and levels of physical, mental, emotional, social, and environmental refinement that go beyond the ordinary. But it—the doing of miracles—is not out of reach. The fact is, we have not normalized the learning of these things, but we could, and, arguably, we should. We could decide to operationalize Jesus's statement in John 14:12 and make it so.

In *The Womanist Idea*, I talk about the "Ladder of Learning," from information to knowledge to wisdom to illumination. Present day typical education embraces the first two rungs on the ladder—information and knowledge. Womanism validates the third rung, wisdom, which comes from extracting insight from lived experience rather than book knowledge alone. The world's mystical, metaphysical, and mystery traditions document and elucidate pathways to illumination, which occurs when what we know extends beyond the bounds of everyday, material reality, into the unseen realms that surround, infuse, and produce material reality. Of course, womanists also validate this form of knowing, and, in particular, the many ways that black women and other women rooted in their ancestral traditions engage and propagate it—but it is certainly not something that is validated in what we call formal schooling or higher education, particularly in the West or the hegemonic world. One can get a PhD or any other terminal degree without having acquired wisdom or experienced illumination, even for the moment. Thus, the way we language "higher" education and "terminal" degree limits our seeing and obscures the roles of wisdom and illumination, not only in lifelong learning, but also in manifesting the full capacity of our humanness.

Womanists affirm the divine power of every being, human and nonhuman. Furthermore, womanists as liberationists democratize the invitation to power and illumination for all human beings, regardless of former, perceived, or real relationships to structures of oppression or dehumanization. Womanism invites us to walk into the ontological reality of our own (and each other's) power and greatness, to live there and remake the world from there. From my perspective, this is exactly what Jesus is inviting us to do in John 14:12. In case we feel shaky about it, Jesus is reminding us (in John 14:13–14) that God is powering us all up from the place of infinity, and, thus, if we align with that, we cannot go wrong. Jesus is actually speaking science in this passage, based on my reading of other teachings on the performance in miracles—a science that, I might add, many have argued that Jesus studied with others during his early, formative years. Without questioning Jesus's divine identity, in fact, his identity with God, one still can deduce that he is speaking to ordinary humans about what we can do in the mundane world, once we fully embrace the Divine.

Gifts

> And He Himself gave some to be apostles, some prophets, some evangelists, and some pastors and teachers, for the equipping of the saints for the work of ministry, for the edifying of the body of Christ, till we all come to the unity of the faith and of the knowledge of the Son of God, to a perfect man, to the measure of the stature of the fullness of Christ; that we should no longer be children, tossed to and fro and carried about with every wind of doctrine, by the trickery of men, in the cunning craftiness of deceitful plotting, but, speaking the truth in love, may grow up in all things into Him who is the head—Christ—from whom the whole body, joined and knit together by what every joint supplies, according to the effective working by which every part does its share, causes growth of the body for the edifying of itself in love. (Eph 4:11–16, NKJV)

I love this passage in Ephesians because it talks about the diversity of ways that the Divine plants effectiveness in us as humans, giving each of us some kind of talent and thus some kind of responsibility towards the realization of our collective purpose and wellbeing. The passage adds to the message of John 14:12 by letting us know that we are each invested with different kinds of greatness, all towards the end of a shared self-realization. Apostles are people sent out with a special message or on a special commission. A prophet is a person who delivers messages from God to humanity, who mediates communication between God and humans, and who may serve as an inspired teacher based on what is received from God. An evangelist is someone who talks about something with great enthusiasm, someone who wants to tell the good news, who seeks to transform or convert others through their inspired feeling about the Divine. A pastor is one who guides others along the path, a helper, a minister to a group of people. A teacher is literally one who teaches, one who shares information and helps people to understand it.

The collective purpose here is to become saints, people who are sanctified, that is, purified and holy—people who are clean, healthy, and whole, people who have learned to distinguish between the baser and more noble aspects of life on earth and who can now choose the good, that which affirms our divinity, with intentionality and precision. The collective purpose is also for the body of Christ—humanity—to become edified, that is, educated and improved, which relates to the process of becoming saints, not only individually, but together with each other. Our goals and mandates are clearly outlined and given great dimensionality in the next section of the passage—we are called to unity of faith, knowledge of Christ, and human perfection following the model of Christ. We are being invited to become Christ-like or Christed ourselves. No small order! But it is implied that we can do it and should.

Furthermore, we are advised to mature collectively—"we should no longer be children." What does this mean? We are told: we should no longer shift our thinking with every new faddish doctrine; we should no longer be trickable and dupable or subject to deceit by those who would seek to use our divine energy for their own nefarious (or simply selfish) ends. In other words, we should know—of our own knowledge, not just by received knowledge—what is true and good, and we should stick to it, as the true and good is what will transform us into saints. Does this not sound like Alice Walker's (1984) womanist—"Responsible. In charge. Serious.... Always wanting to know more and in greater depth than is considered 'good' for one"? Ephesians 4:11–16 is tacitly inviting us to rise above the nonsense of systems of oppression and dehumanization that try to talk us out of our deepest self-knowledge and knowledge of the universe, and it is reminding us of the many gifts we have to work with.

Womanists know inherently that we are to speak truth in love and grow up into (i.e., become) our head, Christ, who is both literally our leader (as an embodiment of God) and figuratively the exemplar of the Christing of which we are all inherently capable (despite messaging to the contrary). In my reading, Paul speaks of these things clearly to the churches at Ephesus because he was illumined on the road to Damascus, and from that point forward he had a vision that he had lacked previously. He was an ordinary man, even a bad man, who became Christed and sanctified, although, arguably, imperfectly (we need only examine his gender politics, outlined, for example, just a bit later in Eph 5:22–24, which is a subject for another time). Because he "saw the Light," Paul is an example to us, even if we can still critique him for ongoing human imperfections.[1]

The African principle of Ubuntu, ultimate human collectivity—"I am because we are, and because we are, therefore, I am" (Menkiti 1984)—reverberates in the passage's conclusion, illuminating the reality that the whole body is "knit together by what every joint supplies," a body in which each part does its share, causing growth (maturation) of the body and "the edifying of itself in love." These recursive passages emphasize the power of love ("Jesus is Love") as a vitalizing force, a unifying force, a purifying force, and an illuminating force, that transports us from one state (unrefined, unconscious, ignoble, and unwhole) to another (refined, conscious, noble, and whole), individually and collectively. Love is the invitation issued to us by Jesus, who stands, Christed, waiting for us to arrive to the place of illumination and sanctification with him, but, at the same time, as the Ephesian text alludes, love is also the highway that gets us there.

Womanism affirms the way that human diversity can be harmonized and coordinated for the promotion of human wellbeing, and Eph 4:11 describes human diversity in terms of gifts given to us by Christ, by God, to collectively promote our well-being and advancement along the path of growth. Which gift is yours? Which gift is mine? Which gift is the gift of that person we would like to think is not "of us"? How do we all harmonize and coordinate? How will we link our gifts back to the performing of miracles, of which we are all capable and to which we are all called? A womanist would encourage us to take up this charge, to trust ourselves, to do the work, and to share our bounty. That is what I, too, am calling for.

---

1. Editors' Note: The use of "Paul" in this section is the respondent's understanding of the author of Ephesians and does not reflect the general consensus among scholars that a later author wrote the letter in Paul's name.

Summary

The essays in this volume invite us to a deeper engagement with the Bible. What they have in common is a commitment to liberation, healing, and wholeness—hallmarks of womanist thought and praxis. From questioning the normalization of abuse (of children or adults) in the Bible, to deconstructing how ancient biblical narratives have supported the perpetuation of oppressive or violent beliefs or practices today, to making invisible people visible, to rewriting the stories of defamed biblical women and girls so that their worth and genius is acknowledged, each author, in turn, has given us permission to read the Bible from the wisdom of the soul, rather than from within the often oppressive strictures of received knowledge or tradition. In so doing, each author has reminded us that our souls are alive—*capable*, to use Walker's word—and that the word of God itself is also alive and always ready to engage us. Each author, through this act of *soul* reading, has engaged with the Spirit of the text, that is, with the Divine itself, the source of our being, to the benefit of all of us. My goal in this brief commentary has been to push the boundaries of this consideration about who we are and what we are capable by presenting my own womanist reading of some biblical texts that affirms these aspirations.

Works Cited

Maparyan, Layli. 2012. *The Womanist Idea*. New York: Routledge.
Menkiti, Ifeanyi. 1984. "Person and Community in African Traditional Thought." Pages 171–82 in *African Philosophy: An Introduction*. Edited by Richard Wright. Lanham, MD: University Press of America.
Walker, Alice. 1983. *In Search of Our Mothers' Gardens: Womanist Prose*. San Diego: Harcourt Brace Jovanovich.

Looking Forward from the Horizon: A Response in Africana Sisterhood and Solidarity

Althea Spencer-Miller

How exciting to be able to respond to the frontier expanding essays in this collection. In this eclectic and rich collection are frontiers of hermeneutics, research resources, and cultural imaginations. Not only do the contributors advance the scope within the United States of what it means to do womanist biblical scholarship, they also widen it to include Africana collections, ideas, and interfaces. There is an implicit invitation to engage womanist scholarship with an Africana diasporic accent, effecting a womanist Africana conversation. An Africana diasporic accent invokes ideas of diasporic relations that increase the field of experience, intellectual traditions, histories, and cultures that encounter each other in the United States. My response seeks to be an Africana response to womanist issues in biblical interpretation. I respond to each essay in its own terms. At times, my probes and comments derive from Africana experiences, and these interlaces will extend and develop the global cast already present in this conversation. I organize the essays into thematic groups. The arrangement effects a programmatic response that allows a certain progression and a conversation among these thinkers. The first group is the Africana cluster, continuing after with the second group of mothers, children, and a father, followed by the third, gender relations. The last group, the seasoners, add piquancy by advocating nonacquiescence and heralding the arrival of diasporic *heteroglossia*, a peculiar polylinguality.

The Africana Cluster

Colonialism and its legacy conjoined with the United States' perdurance as an imperial force globally haunts the relationship between African Americans and the rest of the diaspora. Certainly, that reality means that African Americans remain, in significant numbers, the mediators of Africanisms to popular society, social media, and to the professional guild of biblical scholars in the US and biblical scholars outside the United States who are of African descent rarely find their work cited or alluded to in ways that reflect Africana realities beyond the United States. The pressure to remain in communication, translatable, and pertinent to US scholarship often means a restriction of sources, modification of issues and approaches to issues, and a tailoring of concepts, vocabulary, and references such as to remain accessible to scholars whose breadth of reading, cultural experiences, and questions raised do not include the panoramic scope of Africana realities.

This is the breach into which Gay L. Byron's "Black Collectors and Keepers of Tradition: Resources for a Womanist Biblical Ethic of (Re) Interpretation" leaps. Byron's essay decolonizes, reconnects, and reframes conversations within biblical studies. An Africana orientation is itself an act of existential resistance. By introducing the resources of African American collectors and bibliophiles whose collections and works focalize Ethiopia and indeed Africana connections, as in Dr. André Reynolds Tweed of Jamaican parentage and African American heritage, Byron easily enters into Africana hermeneutics, historical relevance, and reclamation. Beyond resistance, Byron as a descendant of colonized and enslaved peoples decolonizes that history. Her essay is an appropriate *Sanaa ya upinzani*[1] and it attains to the frontlines of resistance as anticolonialism.[2]

Shively T. J. Smith's essay emphasizes reconnection in multiple voices. Her astute hermeneutical strategy of using Assata Shakur's fugitive narrative to uncover the importance of Egypt in the Matthean birth narrative opens doors to multiple contemplations including issues of connectivity among the marginalized in imperial times. It is only possible to highlight a few of the major research themes that arise in this essay. I focus on the potentially fecund intersectionalities between Africana and

---

1. Translation: "Art of resistance," in transliterated Kiswahili. See www.omniglot.com. I use Kiswahili for Africana effect and as an Africana act of resistance against the deference usually given to the colonizers' languages.

2. Both terms, *decolonization* and *anticolonialism*, are used with reference to formal and populist forms for dismantling imperial relationships. The sequence in which I use them here is therefore contestable and certainly not discrete.

womanist hermeneutics. Smith underscores, throughout the essay, not only the current connectedness of the African diaspora but the historical connectedness of disparate stigmatized peoples throughout history. Even as she specifies the uninterestedness of Eurocentric scholars in the seemingly miniscule role of Egypt in the birth narrative, she simultaneously highlights, through Shakur's narrative, the conditions of migrants and nomads when quagmired in the discursive and rhetorical webs of various imperial interests. The shifting valences of Egypt was contingent on political circumstances. But what was Egypt at any time in its own historical experience? Once we could only view Egypt through the written legacies of Josephus and Philo, the library at Alexandria, sundry biblical narratives, or the legacy of artists. It seems that is still the case for most biblical scholars. However, Smith invokes the legacies of Cain Hope Felder, Clarice Martin, Renita Weems, and Vincent Wimbush who have asserted the importance of reassessing Africa and therefore Egypt in the Bible.

The question of source credibility that Smith raises highlights a discussion that is not overt but tacit in Byron. Without presuming to resolve questions of source and credibility in a traditional way, I raise the following questions. Resistance to implicit credibility based on ethnic considerations has been a decolonizing strategy. How would womanists and, indeed, Africana scholars negotiate this thorny issue when multiculturalism, globalized relationships, hegemonic coercions, among other offshoots of global power relationships, peer over our shoulders as we sift through all the newness that enters our hermeneutical, exegetical spaces? Perhaps in the womanist spirit of community liberation we will have our conversations for the sake of the children. We may be able to help them know that biblical history and culture are closer to African cultures than to the elitism that enshrines Euromasculine scholarship.

Mothers, Children, and a Father

Sharon Jacob and Jennifer Kaalund epitomize the spirit of connection and the multiplicity of resources that have already been evoked. Their essay exposes the colonial strategy of displaced maternity as a site of ideological contestation and cultural engineering. Maternity is also their lens for interpreting Rev 12 and the Hindu Kali mother narrative. Should one set aside the overreaching heterosexuality of the colonial master's breast voyeurism, there might yet be room to express a lesbian yearning for the breasts of Yahweh[3] or his consort Asherah. Indeed, where scholars explore the meanings of Yahweh and his consort Asherah, the question as to whether Asherah was another disappearing mother is well grounded. As Ronald S. Ecker (1995) says, "We know that Yahweh supplanted the Canaanite God El." He then impishly asks, "But did Yahweh take El's woman too?" By taking Asherah as Yahweh's own and later usurping her feminine does Yahweh make motherhood disappear?

The sexuality of Yahweh as one who opens wombs, closes wombs, and impregnates and of Jesus who wants to be like a mother hen suckling her children is certainly pertinent to this essay. The semen of Yahweh cropped up in a diasporic spread that has growth and presence in just about every part of the globe. Christian missionaries facilitated the penetration of Yahweh in collusion with the hyper-masculinity of Europe's imperial seminality. In Jacob and Kaalund, two colonial histories converge under the auspices of Yahweh's semen only to uncover breasts in their nonconnubial, seductive, seepages. But somehow, the milk goes slightly sour, hypermasculinity's nightmare. While Jacob and Kaalund place these mother figures under the male gaze in both the written form (the case of Revelation) and oral transmission (the case of Kali), they rescue them from that gaze through flight and the goriness of a bloody Kali. These are displaced and replaced mothers whose relatedness in this essay and with the historical background seem to revel in ambiguity as much as hybridity. It is clear in the case of the woman of Rev 12 that her narrative depiction is held together by the male gaze. Is her flight then escape, or is it the spell of doom for her children? What mother dare be saved while leaving her children to be saved … by whom? Kali, on the other hand, is restored to mothering, at least in the Shiva narrative. The bloody gore of her displaced motherhood seems restored by the apparition of Shiva. How actual it is that the ideology of motherhood can make malleable and tractable the reality of motherhood! The bond forged between these two cultures, a conversation elaborated and recorded, exposes the nefariousness of gender, sexuality, and reproduction where mothering is ideologized as critical to the maintenance of a preferred order. The contrastive relationship between Kali and the woman of heaven reveals the singularity of purpose in the control of

---

3. This association relies on the Hebrew masculine noun שד (*shad*) in Song 1:13. The feminine version שדה (*shiddah*) occurs in Eccl 2:8. The translation of the feminine form is uncertain. The masculine noun form has etymological and semantic associations that mean demon, destroyer, and source of food for babies or breast.

women's bodies and our nurturing potential and practices: a helpful analysis for understanding today's battles over reproductive rights.

Bridgett A. Green uses Fannie Lou Hamer's activism as a hermeneutic. As such, it allows her to paint Jesus's welcome of the children in Luke 18:15–17 as counterpoint to the disciples' inhospitality. Thus she characterizes the kingdom of God as an egalitarian, almost utopic ideal and a rejection of the disciples' classism. Yet, her case is built largely on a lexical change in the Lukan version of the passage. Clearly a synoptic contrast is warranted, yet the case that Green raises here might be overstated. It is only in verse 15 that Luke uses βρέφη. In verses 16 and 17, he retains παιδία.[4] Does the author see the difference as negligible? Or does the variation in terms serve to further underscore the vulnerability of children at every stage? By highlighting the vulnerability of the children and the disciples' "hostility," Green reminds us of the precariousness of children and their susceptibility to social forces that surround them.

The extreme contrast between Jesus and the disciples encourages efforts to understand the dialectics that contextualize children's lives. Green's speculation about the unknown bearers of the children reveals some assumptions about the familial roles of men among the rural and urban poor. If the children are socially outcast, then it is a reasonable assumption that those who had time to bring them to Jesus are probably marginal also. We may need to know more about employment and gender among the lower classes in Galilee before closing on the possibility of uncles, brothers, older sisters, and aunts bringing children to Jesus. Note that the disciples seem to reject the persons who brought the children as well as the children. Jesus openly welcomes the children, but should we assume the welcome of those who brought them? Jesus is quite specific about allowing the παιδία to come to him and to identify the kingdom with such. The dynamic is intriguing and raises questions about the level of nuancing that this passage might require in order to produce a more penetrative liberatory interpretation. What, then, are the egalitarian terms of the kingdom in the Lucan version?

Valerie Bridgeman's essay also examines the vulnerability of children and the rhetoric of abuse, focusing on Isaiah. However, children there are more often rhetorical than historical. Bridgeman does not eschew the

---

4. In Peter's denial of Jesus (Luke 22:54–62), the author does a similar age/class shift. In v. 55, he refers to the woman who accosts Jesus as young girl or servant girl. In his protest in v. 57, Peter calls her a woman. This may be a peculiar Lucan word swap.

connection between the two, particularly when the rhetoric is historicized within interpreting traditions and the abuse actualized therein. Assuredly, child abuse spans the United States and the Caribbean. In Jamaica's early postcolonial years, severe punishment was intertwined with ideas of family pride, social advancement, and survival. Self-declaration: I am neither a defender or practitioner of corporal punishment. I find it repulsive, unimaginative, and an easy resort in many instances. I condemn abuse in any form. Yet, I am aware, from that Jamaican experience, of a segment of people for whom severe punishment was connected to survival. Damaged food, clothing, and possessions were not easily replaced. There were no ready second chances for disobedience and waywardness. Any of these lapses could risk permanent disadvantage for social capital, opportunities, and survival. Severe punishment related to the realities of trauma and beleaguerment. The people of Israel were traumatized and beleaguered in exile. Despite my solidarity with Bridgeman's condemnation of abuse and the rhetoric of abuse, I must pose the question: How does this rhetoric of deity abusiveness in a context of subjugation and exile help us to understand the dynamics of power and oppression as they play out on the bodies and psyches of Africana children?

Vanessa Lovelace also tackles issues of class, race, and ideologies of motherhood in her essay. In this instance, a father raised by a single/stigmatized mother and rejected by the family of legal legitimacy rises to become the leader who makes a flawed decision. Yet though flawed and criticized by the tacit and overt advocates of "family values," he remains a man of his painful word. His moral fiber, if integrity rather than expedience be the arbiter, puts his critics to shame—many of whom were probably raised in heterosexual homes of some kind. Searingly, Lovelace exposes the fraudulence of thuggery as it exists in the heart and mouths of those who racialize single mothers. Jephthah may be an imperfect hero, but his stigmatized mother produced a noble, tragic, hero. In commentary and in narrative, as Lovelace indicates, the system that produced him exculpates itself while still indicting his mother as scapegoat. There is much here to reflect on for social values, systemic repressions and coercions, even laws and the criminalization of the innocent, especially black male bodies. Yet the story of the man who rose above it all should be told not only for inspiration but more so for analysis and critique of the family systems that we legitimate and protect. In Sudan, Brazil, the Democratic Republic of the Congo, Israel, Jamaica, Puerto Rico, Rwanda, and other diaspora countries where single motherhood also bears the stains of civil wars, civil strife, and sex trafficking, biblical stories can serve as mechanisms of social mirroring and critical reflection.

Gender Relations

The essays in this group continue a practice already evident in the prior groups. They clearly articulate womanist hermeneutical principles and deploy them for sample interpretations of specific texts. Of course, various black women's experiences, current and historical, contextualize ethnogender stereotyping, disparities, ideologies, and relationships to the dominant society. Yet there are interesting variations among the essays as these thinkers combine their histories and experiences with different methods and disciplines. Simultaneously, in various ways they continue the Africana thematics of connection and expansion as a survey of their work will demonstrate. Cheryl B. Anderson tackles a long standing health issue but in a nontraditional way. She points to the prevalence of HIV/AIDS among African Americans as a generally under-addressed issue in those communities. Her solution is to introduce African American Christians to alternative biblical gender paradigms. Anderson demonstrates how the Song of Songs can generate complex and nuanced discussions of gender and sexuality. In a similar vein, Love L. Sechrest denudes Jezebel and the Sun Woman in Revelation of their ancient stereotypical passivity as she searches for their transmissible textual agency. Sechrest recognizes that the relationship between the two women has controversial contradictions. Yet even these are useful because the two are iconoclastic and dialogical. Black women's current agency seen in the #BlackLivesMatter movement can connect to ancient female agency or use their experiences to address issues of biblical female agency. Both Anderson and Sechrest are ideological iconoclasts.

Marlene Underwood overlays the stages of abuse in intimate relationships on to Yahweh's relationship with Job. She utilizes psychological theory to frame her approach. In her scheme, the deity is not exonerated of abuse. She offers no theodicy. Again, a scriptural work is offered not for emulation but for contemplation and sociocultural reflection. Wil Gafney's essay complexifies the challenge by Underwood. Gafney not only departs from traditional biblical exegetical methodologies, she adopts midrashic commentary from Jewish practices. In her midrashic aggadah, her outlining of the Samson narratives as *agitatsiya* (agitation) propaganda allows her to use the women in Samson's life as a foil for contemplating Delilah. Delilah is a nonaligned woman. She is the one who plays da playa as one unencumbered by conventions. The textual author/s cannot redomesticate her. Disappearance in this instance is victory. She walks a line with which African American women are familiar, and she exits on her own terms. Gafney intentionally adopts the posture of reading from the underside, and so she reads against the ideological grain of the author. This differs from ideological exposure. It is a definitive refusal to play the game the accustomed way. The outcome: a positive evaluation of the wiliness that unequal relationships often require for survival and thriving.

Stacey Davis, on the other hand, selects a text in which she has no game. She interprets as one with whom the text has no familiarity. She is a single woman. She identifies as a feminist. Thus she raises a tetchy question of the relationship between womanists and black feminists. Davis's text choice points to an important development where womanist biblical scholars undertake to interpret passages that are neither biographically nor ethnographically assonant. She leads me to ask: how would a womanist interpret the Farewell Discourses in John or Paul's struggle with the fate and purpose of Jews in Romans 9–11? If these essays are any indication, and I believe they are, then womanism has come of age in a way that can meet these challenges. In many of the essays covered by this response, womanists are demonstrating a leading edge that is characterized by ideological and theological iconoclasm and an Africana panoptic. An Africana panoptic includes various kinds of womanisms and black feminisms and developing nuances in strategies and methodologies. The diversity of approaches indicates daring exploration beyond class, gender, and race. Within biblical studies womanism is chomping at its own box. It will not be contained.

The Seasoners

No, womanist biblical criticism will neither be contained nor constrained by its own past and moorings. This is the inference from Mitzi J. Smith's and Margaret Aymer's essays. They are seasoners because, as good cooks, they add the exclamation mark to this group of essays. Delilah's treacherous and risky dalliance with Samson, as Gafney shows, articulates the dalliance with law enforcers and the rawness of fear that Smith in her essay associates with the Syrophoenician woman. She dares the "lion's[5] den" so

---

5. Lion imagery borrowed from Rev 5:5, where Jesus is referred to as the "Lion of Judah."

to speak and transforms his snarl into a truculent meow as her request is fulfilled. That is the effect of sassiness. Sass is the pizazz of womanist's *heteroglossia*. Is this akin to Aymer's self-description? Hers is the *heteroglossolalia* of multicultural individuality accruing another layer by dint of skin color. Espousing Shanell Smith's ambi*veil*ance, Aymer opens a tapestry upon the social body of Rhoda the slave girl. Upon that tapestry rests the trauma of slave memories that are in the DNA of cultural transmissions across millennia, centuries, and landscapes. Reading darkness brings into view our common ancestors, shared histories of trauma, and a multifaceted hermeneutical constellation. When African Americans speak of their complex ancestry and it resonates with Aymer's, we know we are equipped to understand each other.

In the iconoclastic, revolutionary complectedness of these essays, I quip, revolution means let the sass begin! What does sass mean for biblical studies? Within the Africana group, there are multiple issues of history. How strongly should we who are of African ancestry agree with the truism that there is an insurmountable temporal and geographical gap between our cultures and ancient Mediterranean cultures? What terms do we bring to modify that truism? What kinds of historical and cultural knowledge do we need to have in order to meaningfully interpret ancient texts? What were the major ethnic routes along which the faith traveled? Must they all go through Europe's politics, intellectual history, and elitist mores? What would we effect if our starting points were in Egypt, Ethiopia, or Sudan? The children and parenting theme resonated across each grouping. How do remembered and experienced traumas affect our decision-making processes and impact our modes of discipline? We understand that undoing ideological biblical rhetoric and symbolisms is a multigenerational task.

Works Cited

Clifton, Lucille. 1999. "I Am Accused of Tending to the Past." Poem Hunter. http://tinyurl.com/SBL0688r2.

Ecker, Ron. S. 1995. "Yahweh." In *Adam and Eve Knew: A Dictionary of Sex in the Bible*. Online Ed. Palatka, FL: Hodge & Braddock. http://tinyurl.com/SBL0688s2.

Challenged and Changed

Katharine Doob Sakenfeld

It is an honor that I as a white feminist should be asked to respond to this remarkable collection of womanist essays. I have been challenged and changed by these essays, not just intellectually, but also emotionally, personally. I have been humbled to realize ever more deeply all that I do not know about African American culture and African American women's particular history and experience. The interweaving of the contemporary and the biblical is remarkable throughout, and at some points the contemporary material has left me feeling rather like a beginning student in an introductory course, holding on by my fingernails, realizing how much more there is to know. I am grateful to each of the authors for opening my horizons in various ways.

In some essays, the connections made between the Bible and contemporary issues in the African American community are relatively direct. Other essays offer more indirect threads of connection to the biblical text or are proportionately more focused on themes from African American life and history. But in every case, the effort to trace the writers' hermeneutical paths has been worthwhile, more than I can express in the following brief comments about what mattered most to me in each essay.

In her recent book, Nyasha Junior (2015) suggests that it is difficult to define womanist biblical interpretation for two primary reasons: first, the body of scholarship that self-identifies in this way is still quite small, so that generalization about its range of subject matter is difficult; and second, the question is still debated whether womanist scholarship must be based in personally lived experience and thus can be done only by African American women. Junior points out that feminist biblical scholarship and disability biblical scholarship are not being done only by women or by those with disabilities and also that African American scholars do not all consider themselves womanists; indeed, some write both "womanist" and "traditional" scholarly works. The present volume provides no answer to these issues. This book, though, moves the discussion forward, however, as it expands the body of womanist biblical scholarship and as the authors (all African American women, with one Indian woman coauthor) explicitly state their own understandings of womanist (biblical) scholarship. These theoretical statements are an important contribution of this collection. The articles are a bold testing of the waters, appropriate to the "experimental" genre prized in the Semeia Studies series.

Given the great diversity of approaches and themes in these articles, I have chosen to express my responses seriatim, while keeping a running catalog of the various ways in which "womanism/womanist" is used, a distillation that I hope may help others to grasp the landscape of the book. Each essay foregrounds present and/or historical experience of African American women, but the selection and use (or not) of intersectional approaches varies considerably among the authors. No essay can be properly summarized in just a few sentences, so I select highlights that particularly caught my attention.

Stacy Davis describes herself as a (black) feminist, not a womanist, who nonetheless works intersectionally with womanism (defined as foregrounding black women's lived experience), masculinity, and queer theory. She argues that the personal experience of the author is significant for womanist method but that it need not be revealed in every detail. Her essay helpfully traces the complexity of the relationship between feminism and womanism. Textually, Davis begins with Num 30 and its legal statements about women's vows; the biblical text, however, functions primarily as a springboard for her important observation that single (never married) women are not even in the purview of the biblical regulations and that the Hebrew Bible as a whole scarcely imagines the existence of never married women. Here she opened a new horizon for me, as my own work had focused solely on the economic implications of this text. Given Davis's interest in the single (never married) women, the text requires only brief attention, and she devotes the bulk of her work to cultural, social, economic, religious, and white-prejudicial aspects of the experience of single black women in American society. The weaving together of these themes is especially helpful, as she engages a wide range of literature from social science, popular media, and church perspectives. Her conclusion that "there is no one size fits all model for sexuality and identity" places her focal discussion compellingly into the larger context of gender identity, poverty, and faith.

Wil Gafney's study of Delilah draws me into a text I have almost deliberately avoided in the past. Gafney describes her approach to Delilah as "womanish," drawing particularly on themes in Alice Walker's definition that open the possibility of "not hesitat[ing] to talk back to the Bible or its God." This attitude would seem to be in common with many feminist readings, so I find the womanist focus of the essay more in its steady interweaving of biblical and contemporary womanist practices, such as the importance of naming, as women unnamed in the text are introduced and given names, and Samson's story is traced through their eyes, or the description of Delilah as "grown" in Walker's sense of the term—sexually and emotionally mature and financially independent, a woman without a communal safety net who must hustle to survive. Reading Delilah in this way, and setting her actions in conversation with themes from contemporary African American music, upends the traditional story. She disappears from the story but "appears to be the rare woman who has escaped biblical patriarchy with her body weight in bling." Gafney argues that Delilah and Samson were not married and that Delilah may have been Israelite. Perhaps one could imagine Delilah as one of the single woman never imagined in Num 30.

How can the Song of Songs relate to the AIDS crisis? Cheryl B. Anderson replays Phyllis Trible's classic work on Song in a new key. Anderson introduces readers to the shocking and sadly disproportionate number of HIV/AIDS infections among African Americans. Recognizing the importance of biblical teaching among African American Christians, she presents the Song's commendation of mutual erotic love apart from marriage or procreation as a resource for the black church in reshaping its approach to HIV/AIDS. If Song can also allow for homoerotic relationships (by way of focusing on mutuality rather than hierarchy), then new avenues for conversation about HIV/AIDS may open. This step in her argument moves the hermeneutical possibilities for Song in a fresh and challenging direction. Although Anderson does not theorize her use of "womanist," focus on concerns of the African American community and particularly on its women is central to her project.

Somewhat like Gafney's treatment of Delilah, Mitzi J. Smith's study of the Syro-Phoenecian woman in Mark presents a woman talking back. Picturing Mark's woman alongside Sandra Bland as a "black woman who embodies sass" gave me a fresh perspective on both women. The stark contempt with which the white Texas trooper and Jesus treated the women before them came into sharp focus, as did the dignity of the two women who refused to be cowed, refused to stay silent in the face of mistreatment. The intersectionality of race/ethnicity and gender in both stories exacerbates the danger of sass. Like other authors in this collection, Smith turns to Walker's definition of "womanist," focusing on behaving "outrageously, audaciously, courageously or willfully." When such behavior challenges what is "deleterious and deadly," not just to oneself but to humanity in general, that is sass. Too often, sass is silenced, Smith notes, not just in society, but also in church and academy. I join in her call to celebrate sass.

Love L. Sechrest studies stereotypical negative and positive female characters in the book of Revelation. She considers the Sun Woman and Jezebel through the lenses of the 1960s Civil Rights movement and the 2015 #BlackLivesMatter movement. Womanism appears in the ways Sechrest connects the figures of Revelation to perceptions of black women. In contrast to much current scholarship, including feminist treatments, she first recovers agency for the Sun Woman. Once this is established exegetically, she can point to a difference in style and evaluation of agency between the two characters: "Jezebel represents a potent independent influence that has been maligned, while the antitypical Sun Woman depicts a participatory agency that has been embraced." This contrast is analogous to the contrast Sechrest perceives between the movements of the 1960s and 2015: 1960s civil rights women focused on respectability, while today's younger black women are more comfortable being aggressive and disruptive. The generational conversation about who is faithful and who is compromised in their choices of strategy to confront oppression will no doubt continue. While I imagine there may have been some disruptive black women even in the 1960s movement, Sechrest's analysis challenges me as an older white woman to reassess my own presumably left wing responses in the 1960s and today. Have I placed too much value on the politics of respectability even as I participated in demonstrations?

Shively T. J. Smith draws her perspective on womanist biblical interpretation from the work of Renita Weems, moving between the "realities of black womanhood and the ancient biblical world." Her case study is Assata Shakur's (formerly Joanne Chesimard's) flight to Cuba intersecting with the Matthean account of Jesus's family's flight to Egypt. Having heard of Shakur only negatively for years in my home state New Jersey press (where she was imprisoned before her escape), and having had the opportunity some years ago to visit Cuba on a church visa, I was particularly struck by the connection Smith develops. The heart of her argument, however, relates to places as much as people, as she makes a case for a much more positive view of Egypt as compared to Judea, both historically in the New Testament period and through the lens of the FBI's persecution of Shakur in America compared to Herod's persecution in Judea for fear of Jesus. As in so many of these essays, I am reminded that both in Scripture and in life, what I see first is often a far distance from what may be really there. Smith's essay concludes with constructive proposals for the future of womanist interpretation—it should embrace black women of any religious tradition; it should think globally about women's oppression; it should embrace literature beyond the Bible and even be ready to reject parts of the Bible that diminish black womanhood. Each of these features appears in at least one of the subsequent articles in the volume.

Like Shively Smith, Marlene Underwood takes her womanist cue from the work of Weems, moving out from Weems's treatment of divine abuse of Israel in the prophetic literature to consider divine abuse of Job. Job's case is more extreme, Underwood proposes, because Job is declared innocent as a premise of the book, whereas the prophets at least claim that Israel is at fault. Underwood sees her work as womanist in its solidarity with victims of domestic abuse, solidarity that requires the behavioral characteristics in Walker's classic statement. Focusing primarily on the prologue, whirlwind appearance, and epilogue, Underwood proposes that the three classic stages of domestic abuse (tension building, explosion of violence, and loving remorse) can be traced in the story of Job. She is clear that she cannot accept these "loathsome" images of God and calls on the church not to rationalize violence against women but to act on behalf of victims. The efforts of Job's so-called friends who try to show that his plight is his own fault are likewise deemed reprehensible. Here is an essay that in effect does what Shively Smith proposed—it is prepared to reject a biblical text (or the images in the text). I had a college roommate who never darkened the door of a church for twenty years after we were assigned to read the book of Job. I ask myself whether there is a way to continue wrestling with such a "text of terror"? Is Trible's classic strategy usable even when the abuser is God—to see in the text a mirror of our own human brokenness that creates such an unworthy deity? Is it important to retain such mirrors in our repertoire of sacred texts?

Gay L. Byron draws on Weems and Clarice Martin to underscore the potential harmfulness of some biblical texts and/or interpreters, and she follows Velma Love and others in looking beyond the traditional Christian canon to a broader range of authoritative texts. Byron also argues that womanist hermeneutics can be strengthened by recovering fresh source material, whether written or oral, about black women's lives from many eras. Here she emphasizes the unfortunate tendency of scholars to dismiss ancient sources deemed "late" or "legendary," noting that even living testimony by black women is often discounted as "not objective" or, worse, as "never happened." Byron's particular interest in recovery of Ethiopic traditions of the early church has led to a marvelous detective story with a moving ending in which a precious manuscript is returned home with ceremony to its rightful owners in an Ethiopian Orthodox monastery. The number of people, range of geography, and level of cooperation required to bring the project to fruition is amazing. The growth from chasing down a seemingly small inconsistency in a technical citation to arranging for an international ceremonial event demonstrates not only the quirks of scholarship but the integrity of the scholars who found themselves caught up in this remarkable story. In an era where provenance is no longer just an academic and dollar issue but also a matter of ethics, the world should rejoice that a manuscript has gone home to Ethiopia. My heart is personally warmed because Abune Paulos, the late patriarch of the world-wide Ethiopian Orthodox communion, was a student and friend of mine.

Sharon Jacob and Jennifer Kaalund make a distinctive contribution by presenting parallel examples of the role of "unorthodox mothers": wet nurses in American slavocracy and in the empire context of British colonial India. The lives of these wet nurses are understood as human texts that reveal their structured abuse; their stories provide the lens for interpreting both Christian and Hindu texts and for thinking about other unorthodox mothers, such as "mothers of the church" in African American tradition. Here we see the global aspect of womanist interpretation focusing on the "all people" of Alice Walker's definition, expanding from African Americans to women of color more broadly. Responding to recent discussion, the authors choose not to separate their womanist identity from their womanist scholarship; I note (particularly in reference to the question of who can do womanist work) that one of these two self-identified womanists is Indian, not African American.

Kaalund describes well the intersecting racial, gender, and economic dimensions of forced wet nursing among slaveholding families: the tragedy of black women forced to abandon their own children, the myth of the black mammy that allowed black breasts to suckle white children while still holding to a theory of immutable racial difference, the expressions of affection and also resistance by black wet nurses. Through this lens Kaalund approaches the Sun Woman of Rev 12 with a different perspective from

Sechrest. Here we see the woman as mother who, driven into the wilderness, is forced like a wet nurse to abandon her child; yet this same woman, in her transformation (with eagle's wings), represents the potential of all oppressed women for transcendence and freedom and thus for hope. Again a resistant reading opens a new avenue for reclaiming a difficult biblical text.

Jacob introduces us to the harsh realities of women's life in colonial India, both the sad efforts of the white wives to maintain a British lifestyle in a foreign climate and culture and the painfully complex role of the *amah* (Indian wet nurse). We learn as well of the racialized medical theories of British physicians who suggested both the physical necessity of the wet nurse (to protect the strength of the new mother in the Indian climate) and the fear of the result (that the *amah*'s milk would contaminate the moral fiber of the child). In complicated parallels, the Indian goddess Kali represents both a threat to life and at the same time gives life through her breast.

While I experience the connections drawn to the Sun Woman and to Kali as somewhat indirect, it is important for me to remember that other textual intersections that seem obvious to me now were not so clear to me earlier in my personal feminist history. I am always grateful to writers who propose new connections that may become part of our everyday womanist and feminist textual treasure.

How could I not even have thought about Jephthah's mother before? Perhaps because as white feminist I lacked the lens offered by Vanessa Lovelace. Her study of Jephthah's unnamed mother treats a character thus far mostly ignored by traditional and feminist scholarship. Womanist analysis is not explicitly theorized, but it clearly involves attention to the lived experience of African American women. Lovelace opens an excellent horizon for reflection on family values generally and particularly on current sociocultural and supposedly social-scientific views of single black motherhood in America. White America all too easily refers to black males, especially if born to single mothers, as "thugs," inclined toward violence and criminality. Indeed, *thug* is to be understood as the new N-word, even used for persons such as President Obama. Lovelace considers and criticizes the "functional" sociological perspective on the family structure that promotes the conventional nuclear family as the prime source of social stability. Her review of commentaries shows that scholars frequently denigrate Jephthah's single mother and even implicitly blame her for her son's trajectory in life, all without any textual evidence. Lovelace draws a compelling parallel to white culture's expectation that boys born to single black women will become thugs, and her counter-exegesis of the text is powerful and welcome.

"I will never read Acts 12 the same way again," I said to a friend as I completed reading Margaret Aymer's study of the enslaved girl Rhoda. This essay demonstrates Rhoda's "outrageous, audacious, courageous," that is, womanish, behavior. Aymer's womanist strategy is to "read darkness," Rhoda's trauma at the intersection of race, gender, and class oppression. Rhoda's almost invisible or seemingly only comic character takes on full (and painful) personhood when considered in the context of the Roman slavery system and literary tropes underlying the brief story of Peter's appearance at the door of Mary's home. Indeed, the contrast between Peter's emancipation and Rhoda's unremarked enslavement now takes my breath away. What was her story? Was she an exposed girl infant "rescued" by a trader, a trafficked girl, imported from the island of Rhodes as an involuntary migrant? A gentile? A sexual pet? She is a girl-child (not a grown woman), the silenced subaltern, the caged bird. Attending to Rhoda is like attending to #BlackLivesMatter. All of which leads Aymer to rethink Rhoda's mistress, Mary, embedded in a patriarchal structure but nonetheless a free, wealthy head of household able to exercise some power. Aymer sees herself as more like Mary, called to recognize what privilege she does have, to speak out for the Rhodas of our own world. Aymer's work challenges me to focus more on the least ones who too easily remain unnoticed in my own neighborhood.

Lovelace focused on Jephthah's mother and Aymer focused on Rhoda, characters either ignored or badly represented in traditional exegesis. Bridgett A. Green calls attention to characters who must surely have been present but receive no mention at all in the biblical text, the women in the familiar story of the children brought to Jesus over the disciples' objection. Surely, Green observes, it would have been women who brought these children, especially since in Luke's version those who are brought are actually infants, rather than the "children" of Mark's version. Green's womanist interpretive strategy reads Luke through the work of Fannie Lou Hamer's liberationist hermeneutic, and readers are given an excellent introduction to this pioneering advocate for race/gender/economic justice. Hamer explicitly addressed differences between black and white women's realities and perspectives and had a special concern for children. Viewing Luke's text through the lens of Hamer's work, Green shows us the disciples as class-conscious as well as sexist, not wanting women with their infants from poor rural villages to have any access to Jesus. To receive the kingdom of God in this story is more than to be responsible for all classes of people; it is also to share in God's work to change sociopolitical dynamics. Here as in so many of the essays of this volume, readers are offered an unexpected biblical resource in advocacy for change in power dynamics and social policies.

Valerie Bridgeman draws our attention to children in the book of Isaiah; she considers some negative metaphorical portrayals of Israel as "children of God" (e.g., 1:2, 4) who are brought under condemnation in the prophetic poems and will be subjected to severe punishment. Following Weems, she begins with the experience of African American women and children and then focuses on the ancient cultural assumptions about women and children that allow their misbehavior to be punished in abusive ways. Among further examples, adult males are humiliated by a judgment that allows children to rule over them (3:4); Daughter Zion is denigrated as a whore; and the daughters of Zion are subjected to sexual humiliation that the text blames on their filthy and haughty behavior (3:16–24). Bridgeman recognizes that these are metaphors, but like Underwood, she is more attuned than many commentators to the danger of condoning even metaphorical divine patriarchal abuse and violence. She sees the level of violence against children in our own culture and asks whether we can offer a "resisting alternative" to these harmful biblical metaphors. Her essay has called me to expand my awareness of abusive imagery for the deity beyond marriage metaphors and to reflect afresh on whether the dangers of these metaphors render them theologically unusable.

In conclusion, I express my gratitude for the opportunity to share in this womanist project. Based on my own experience reading these essays, I consider this collection must reading—for white feminists, for black male liberationists, for all women of color, and yes, especially for those who think they do not need to know about this womanist world of advocacy and scholarship. Read and be changed!

Work Cited

Junior, Nyasha. 2015. *An Introduction to Womanist Biblical Interpretation*. Louisville: Westminster John Knox.

The Road We Are Traveling

Emilie M. Townes

Let me be clear about the context out of which I began reading the essays in this volume. There are many claims on the term *womanist*. From Alice Walker's early definition in her landmark book of essays, *In Search of Our Mothers' Gardens: Womanist Prose* in 1983, to contemporary third-wave womanism, the term womanist has been used by many scholars and by those who stand within the Jewish and Christian traditions; clergy and laity, to talk about the ideas and experiences of black women in the United States and in some cases, beyond its national borders.

Many US black women in the theological disciplines have gravitated to the use of Walker's term womanist as both challenge to and a confessional statement for their own work. Walker's four-part definition that contains the elements of tradition, community, self, and critique of white feminist thought provides a fertile ground for religious reflection and practical application. The challenge, which is an interstructured analysis that begins with class, gender, race, sex, and sexuality, provides for a dynamic tension in womanist thought for all of the theological disciplines. Such an analysis is not only descriptive but prescriptive as well. Womanist religious reflections provide descriptive foundations that lead to analytical constructs for the eradication of oppression in the lives of African Americans and, by extension, the rest of humanity and creation.

The confessional element of womanist means that it is a term that cannot be imposed but must be claimed by the black woman who is engaged in the eradication of oppression from her own faith perspective and academic discipline. Hence, the use of the term womanist to describe a theorist or practitioner's work is one of avowal rather than denotation. This confessional stance is crucial as the womanist engaged in theological reflection is also holding in tension her own identity as a black woman with the vicissitudes of the theological discipline or ministry in which she is engaged. This provides an organic undertaking of constant self-reflection in the context of the "doing" of one's vocation and avocation. Also, the womanist is not free to name others as womanist if this is not a term they claim for themselves. For example, it is inaccurate to describe black women from the nineteenth century as womanists. Although many like Ida B. Wells-Barnett, Sojourner Truth, and Anna Julia Cooper employed an interstructured social analysis in their activism, none of these women claimed the term womanist for herself. At best, and most faithfully, these women embody nascent womanism that provides a rich framework for womanists of this era to flesh out.

Moving to the field of religious and theological studies, it is clear that there is no one voice in womanist religious thought but a symphony that at times may be a cacophony. I have come to believe that rather than a discipline, womanist thought is a methodology. I have found no convincing or encompassing definition for womanism because, I think, the interdisciplinary nature of womanist religious thought both within the areas of theological studies (theology, ethics, pastoral care, biblical studies, pastoral studies, practical theology, church history, liturgics, religious education) and with disciplinary partners (history, literary criticism, the social sciences, decolonial studies, critical race theory, gender and sexuality studies, philosophy, anthropology) make it difficult and unwise to try to narrow such a bubbling cauldron of creativity down to a disciplinary stew.

Methodology fits womanist thought better. Proceeding from the simplest understanding of methodology as a particular procedure or set of procedures, womanist thought proposes the interstructured analysis I named above to explore the theological and moral implications of the worlds in which it sits through the lens of the various disciplines that a scholar has been trained in. Hence, this volume represents the authors' insights, questions, outrage, celebration, and more of what each sees through the disciplinary lens of biblical hermeneutics as they use the variety of approaches (literary criticism, social scientific, postcolonial, critical race theory, gender and sexuality studies) within biblical studies to interpret and understand the text and the impact of the text in human lives in creation.

From this context, I was initially intrigued with where the authors, with some coaxing by the editors' choice of subheading and arrangement of the essays, intended to take me. As a sometimes grumpy Christian social ethicist who tries to treat the Bible with respect rather than as a rule book of "dos" and "don'ts" that tempts me to practice the kind of blind obedience that treats sacred texts as a domineering authority rather than as an authoritative resource that demands that I work at understanding its implications for life and human responsibility in today's world; I approached reading these essays with my own discipline as my refracted interpretive lens.

Each of the essays in this volume puts the biblical world in *conversation* with our contemporary world. My emphasis on conversation is intentional and strategic. Rather than demote Scripture to a set of moral laws, the essays appreciate the variety of ways the Bible tells us (commands, stories, parables, legal codes, prophecies, poetry) and shows us who we have been, who we are, and what we are called to become in our current times. But this takes work and diligence as well as faith, belief, and imagination to translate an ancient biblical world into modern times. The writers demonstrate the importance of encouraging engaged readings of the text that appreciate the importance of asking questions, not only of ourselves but also of God, as we approach the Bible as guide and prod.

It is a complex thing we do when we read Scripture and recognize that we are engaging in acts of sometimes dangerous interpretation that questions and expands biblical scholarship while offering entre to voices and experiences that have not been considered by scholars, clergy, and laity. Each of the authors points out the thick is-ness of being a darker-skinned woman engaging texts that have a history of being mined from a white patriarchal hegemonic norm. But I am heartened by the fact that they do and do so with clear scholarly voices.

I found that many of the essays provided new insights for me and each left me with a lingering question or conversation starter. I focus on those questions for the remainder of my response, as this is where I could enter the volume with some sense of equal footing as a Christian social ethicist engaging the biblical world for contemporary societal moral and ethical guides.

Stacy Davis's essay focuses on Num 30 and the vows made by women points out that these vows are controlled by men. With her historian's eye, she asks us to consider what impact ancient invisibility signifies in our modern Christian context as she develops a Christian womanist ethic of singleness that resists hypervisibility and invisibility while "affirming sexual expression and not simply the absence of sexual activity." From the hegemonic masculinity that Davis points to that infuses this chapter in Numbers (and in countless other places in the Hebrew Bible and New Testament), I wondered why singleness is seen as the Other in US society? I do not think it is because we "are made for each other," but rather because we have a notion of purity that is formed by a type of deep asceticism in Christianity that keeps us from embracing our bodies, our creatureliness as good. Instead we see our bodies, our impulses, our desires as suspect so they must be controlled, rather ineptly in modern notions of marriage which themselves are beginning to fray and tear.

Wil Gafney points out in her discussion of Delilah in the book of Judges, that an independent woman is a scary woman, a dangerous woman, who must be either a sex-worker or a promiscuous woman—either of which equals whore. There is no indication in the text itself that Delilah was either. Gafney's hip-hop informed reading of Delilah's story challenges every sermon I have ever heard preached about her. She is one of the few women in the Bible who is a named woman, who survives violence, who is loved, who has her own resources. She is dangerous to us because we do not know what to do with a powerful single woman who has her own strong moral compass that is pointed to survival. Gafney prompted me to wonder what are we teaching in our contemporary churches and seminary classrooms about love if one of the most replicated models is that "agency and subjectivity of love is gendered and unidirectional"? Not only do we treat singleness as suspect; we also undercut genuine community and partnership when we do this.

Given the corners we back ourselves into, it is small wonder that Cheryl B. Anderson's essay on the Song of Songs and HIV/AIDS prevention prompts me to ask why are some forms of sexual expression taboo topics for black churches and not others; or if they are problematic (David, Samson) they are skipped over to laud strong hegemonic male power? The heterosexism and homophobia in black churches (as well as other variously hued churches) is killing us. We need a #SayTheirName movement in our churches and religious gathering places for black LGBT folk. Our "don't ask and don't tell" policy is not working as folks slip away from us because we have not yet had the courage to stand up to the fact that all of who we are as moral, believing creatures is of sacred worth and the kind of mind/spirit/body apartheid we have built theological moats around is not adequate for our times. It is, to my mind, creating suspect hierarchies concerning sex and sexuality (along with other forms of social existence) that begets irresponsible Christianity and suspect scholarship.

Mitzi J. Smith's essay on the Syro-Phoenician woman and sass took me back to M. Shawn Copeland's essay from the 1990s, "Wading through Many Sorrows," where near the end of her essay she discusses the importance of language as a form of resistance. Like Smith who follows her, Copeland (1993, 121) points to that fact that enslaved women intent on freedom sass to "guard, regain, and secure self-esteem; to obtain and hold psychological distance, to speak truth; to challenge 'the atmosphere of moral ambiguity that surrounds them,' and, sometimes, to protect against sexual assault." Smith brings this to bear to our contemporary scene through the death of Sandra Bland while in police custody who was arrested because she sassed a police officer during a traffic stop for suspect reasons. Why is it, I wonder, that so many black, Latino/a, Native American, queer, transgender, and other dispossessed folk are killed because of police actions and no one is to blame or the victims must bear the responsibility for their own executions? Smith reminds us of the power of sass to carve out spaces for our humanity and agency—but we must do so carefully and strategically in the context of a dominating white patriarchal hegemony.

Love L. Sechrest made we wonder about the nature of women's agency—will there come a time when women will not have to combat biblically-based negative stereotypes that are stamped as sacred, natural, normal when they are really little more than the patriarchal longings of men and women in cultures that do not remember women's names? Her look at Jezebel and the Sun Woman in Revelation illuminates the ways in which darker-skinned women's agency is trumped by the stereotype of aggressive hypersexuality while white women are consigned to passivity and weakness. The masculine wins and the rest of us should stay at home. However, the young women who harken to Smith's sass and Delilah's survival strategies will not let the rest of us stay there.

Shively T. J. Smith's pairing of the female fugitive narrative of Assata Shakur with the flight of Jesus's family from Judea to Egypt made me wonder how one establishes "home" when you have been forced to flee from your land? It is no small thing to move from one place to another—it is one of the most stressful things we can do as human beings. But to flee because of threat adds another layer of complexity or disruption where relationships may be difficult to establish and one lives in permanent outsider status and in some cases in fear of arrest, deportation, unethical employers, and death.

Marlene Underwood explores unmerited suffering in the book of Job as mirroring the abused wife in domestic violence. Not content to fall into the common tropes of blaming Satan, rationalizing Yahweh's actions, or unmerited suffering makes us better and stronger; Underwood cuts to the heart of the matter—this is a story of abuse and its ramifications. This prompts me to ask, if Job's friends were really wrong if we place them in the narrative as faithful adherents to a god who has a mean streak or can be capricious with human lives? I am left with this troubling question that stops me in my tracks. If God is an omni-god that is both transcendent and immanent, then there are no limits to what God can and will do to us in creation.

Gay L. Byron's essay that focuses on the use of extrabiblical sources as a basis for developing and naming a womanist biblical ethic of (re)interpretation prompted me to think about Katie Cannon's (2006) note about "structured academic amnesia" that Byron cites in her essay. Byron names a key feature of the essays of this volume—the authors transgress canonical boundaries. They do so not as a matter of pure scholarly interest, but because there is a larger hermeneutical story that must be told if we are to fully engage the challenges found in biblical hermeneutics. Repeatedly plowing through the same interpretative strategies does not give contemporary readers the foundations we need to engage the biblical world on its terms in today's world. We merely read back into the text our triumphs and tribulations without pausing to examine our motives or the studied amnesia we practice as we "forget" that Egypt is in Africa, Jesus was not a white European male, or that ancient Ethiopia is a rich resource for research. Why, I wonder, do we content ourselves with partial scholarship and narrow methodologies that often center on the objective as if it is absolute proof of how various peoples experience their lives or tell their stories? As an ethicist, one of the early lessons I learned is how to argue all sides of an argument, event, idea, situation with as much precision as possible. Objectivity was not high on the list but a persuasive language game was (and is). Controlling what counts as believable, what is remembered, and what is forgotten is a tool of domination and subordination.

Sharon Jacob and Jennifer Kaalund's essay on black and Indian wet nurses and the resonances one finds in the book of Revelation (the Sun Woman appears again) offers the reader a transhistorical look that engages race, ethnicity, and geography. Combining the power of mothers with the commodification of women's breast milk to nourish the babies of the slave owner or the *ayah* or *amah* who replenished the weak colonial body with her milk and care, Jacob and Kaalund point with clarity to the ways in which (mis)appropriation, physical labor, forced surrogacy, denial, property, class, colonialism, ethnicity, caste, and resistance all combined for enslaved black and brown women who were forced into the role of wet nurse. What does it mean when your mother's milk is not your own and you cannot feed your own children? In a world where bodies are as much property and commodity as markers of our ontology, I was sobered by the ways our use of women's bodies is obscene and shifted to the image of the two mossy teeth boys who raped and stole Sethe's milk while Schoolteacher watched and wrote it up in Toni Morrison's (1987) novel, *Beloved*.

Vanessa Lovelace leads the reader through a critique of the traditional "family values" or "Judeo-Christian values" lenses used to read Judg 11:1–12:7. The question that struck me forcefully as I was reading her essay was what are the linkages between homogenized images of the nuclear family and the images of welfare queens, Jezebels, Mammy, Sapphire, the Angry Black Woman, and thugs when it comes to those of us who are darker-skinned in this country and how are these images transmitted and consumed globally? Drawing the connections between the negative images of Jephthah's mother as prostitute, or at best an unmarried woman, as they are transferred to his character, Lovelace makes the connections between this biblical mother and her son with black mothers and their sons as both are seen as threats—with Jephthah and black males cast as lacking traditional family values, thugs, and threats to society because they are sons of an unmarried woman.

Using the disbelieved, silenced enslaved girl Rhoda of Acts 12 as an interpretive wedge, Margaret Aymer points to her subversion of idealized narratives of the early church and the ways in which we can learn today from her silenced cry of liberation as women of some privilege and complicity. Rhoda appears, announces, is not believed, is dismissed, and disappears—like any slave, she is *used*. In this case, it is to fulfill the agenda of the writer of the text. I found myself wondering what are the insights, tools, methods we need to employ to listen to and respond to those who have been silenced by us, but who are speaking and acting despite our lack of awareness and perhaps our disdain? This intentional introspection must be done by all of us—color, gender, physical ability, race, sexuality, and so on do not guarantee that we will not commit the very inhumanities we decry.

Bridgett A. Green uses black freedom fighter Fannie Lou Hamer's class, gender, and racial analysis as a hermeneutical guide for developing a womanist biblical interpretation of Jesus's blessing the children in Luke 18. Using the slogan most identified with Hamer, "nobody's free until everybody's free," Green analyzes the dynamics of gender and class in the sociopolitical relationships in the blessing of the children. Pointing to the liberationist imperatives in the story, Green argues that these imperatives empower the marginalized and admonish the privileged to "change the power dynamics of social politics to ensure fairness, equity, and dignity." As I read along, the nagging question of why is it that we can forget so quickly what it is like to have less than or be judged inferior to once we have gained some measure of security or status? Green's essay left me shaking my head because of our failed humanity.

Valerie Bridgeman looks at the ways in which the first chapters of Isaiah denigrate children and make them more vulnerable and leave them open to child abuse. She moves into our contemporary times to how we carry this child abuse forward and urges us to craft an alternative vision of this onslaught on young lives that eschews them as property solely or worthy of harm and humiliation by paying attention to the metaphoric use of children in texts and in life. Bridgeman prompts me to ask what do we gain by abusing the most vulnerable and helpless in our society? To face the ways in which we too often treat children as afterthoughts in religious communities and society at large may give us a window into the violence that forms our society such that we now see it as inevitable to the human condition rather than as a stumbling block to achieving the common good.

This collection no longer allows me to read or hear the Bible in the ways I have grown accustomed to. It challenges me/us to think more deeply and materially about the implications of how we interpret and what we interpret to others in relation to sacred texts. The book has become a probing conversation partner for me as a Christian social ethicist as I try to integrate deep biblical reflection on texts that settle and unsettle my imagination and my beliefs. Like a true womanist tome, there are common themes but many voices that encourage a lively interdisciplinary conversation that allows those of us who are not biblical scholars to enter the biblical worlds in these essays, examine them on their own terms, and then look at the implications, warnings, and encouragements that they can provide for us today. Ultimately, I am left with one last question: Where do we go from here?

Works Cited

Cannon, Katie G. 2006. "Structured Academic Amnesia: As If This True Womanist Story Never Happened." Pages 19–28 in *Deeper Shades of Purple: Womanism in Religion and Society*. Edited by Stacey M. Floyd-Thomas. New York: New York University Press.

Copeland, M. Shawn. 1993. "'Wading Through Many Sorrows': Toward a Theology of Suffering in Womanist Perspective." Pages 109–29 in *A Troubling in My Soul: Womanist Perspectives on Evil and Suffering*. Edited by Emilie M. Townes. Maryknoll, NY: Orbis Books.

Morrison, Toni. 1987. *Beloved*. New York: Doubleday.

Contributors

Cheryl B. Anderson is Professor of Old Testament at Garrett-Evangelical Theological Seminary in Evanston, Illinois, and she is an ordained elder in the United Methodist Church (Baltimore-Washington Conference). Her current research interests involve contextual and liberationist readings of Scripture in the age of HIV and AIDS. Her publications include *Women, Ideology, and Violence: Critical Theory and the Construction of Gender in the Book of the Covenant and the Deuteronomic Law* (T&T Clark, 2004), and *Ancient Laws and Contemporary Controversies: The Need for Inclusive Biblical Interpretation* (Oxford University Press, 2009).

Margaret Aymer is Associate Professor of New Testament at Austin Presbyterian Theological Seminary in Austin, Texas. Her recent publications include *James: Diaspora Rhetorics of a Friend of God* (Sheffield Phoenix) and the coedited volumes *Islands, Islanders, and the Bible: RumInations* (SBL Press, 2015), and the *Fortress Commentary on the Bible: The New Testament* (Fortress, 2014). Her research interests include ideological criticisms of the New Testament and the use of cross-cultural psychology as an interpretative wedge. Aymer is a Caribbean-born migrant of African, Indian (migrant not indigenous), and Latino descent. She is grateful for the invitation to participate in this volume as a black migrant racialized into the African American discourse.

Valerie Bridgeman is Associate Professor of Homiletics and Hebrew Bible at the Methodist Theological School in Ohio and the Founding President and CEO of WomanPreach! Inc. She is the author of "Womanist Criticism" in the *Oxford Encyclopedia of the Bible and Gender Studies* (Oxford, 2014) and "Womanist Approaches to the Prophets" in *The Oxford Handbook of the Prophets* (Oxford, forthcoming). Valerie has commentaries on Jonah and Nahum in the *Africana Bible* (Fortress, 2010), as well as "Introduction to the Prophets" with Cheryl Kirk-Duggan.

Gay L. Byron is Professor of New Testament and Associate Dean of Academic Affairs at Howard University School of Divinity in Washington, DC. Her publications include *Symbolic Blackness and Ethnic Difference in Early Christian Literature* (Routledge, 2002) and commentaries on the book of James in *True to Our Native Land: An African American New Testament Commentary* (Fortress, 2007) and the twentieth anniversary edition of the *Women's Bible Commentary* (Westminster John Knox, 2012). She has written articles and essays such as "Race, Ethnicity, and the Bible: Pedagogical Challenges and Curricular Opportunities" (*TTR*, 2012) and "Ancient Ethiopia and the New Testament: Ethnic (Con)texts and Racialized (Sub)texts," in *They Were All Together in One Place? Toward Minority Biblical Criticism* (Society of Biblical Literature, 2009). Byron's research interests include the intersection of gender, race, and ethnic identity in the New Testament and early Christianity, with special emphasis on the Axumite Empire.

Stacy Davis is Associate Professor of Religious Studies and past chair of the Gender and Women's Studies department at Saint Mary's College, Notre Dame, Indiana. She is the author of *This Strange Story: Jewish and Christian Interpretation of the Curse of Canaan from Antiquity to 1865* (University Press of America, 2008) and *Haggai and Malachi* in the Wisdom Commentary series (Liturgical Press, 2015). She also has commentaries on "Sirach," "Tobit," "Susanna," "1 Esdras," and "Haggai and Malachi" in *The Africana Bible* (Fortress, 2010), *The Peoples' Bible* (Fortress, 2009), and the *Fortress Commentary on the Bible: Old Testament and Apocrypha* (Fortress, 2014), as well as a response in *Re-presenting Texts: Jewish and Black Biblical Interpretation* (Gorgias, 2013). Davis writes from a feminist critical perspective.

Wil Gafney is Associate Professor of Hebrew Bible at Brite Divinity School in Fort Worth, Texas. She is the author of the *Womanist Midrash: A Reintroduction to the Women of the Torah and the Throne* (Westminster John Knox, forthcoming), *Daughters of Miriam: Women Prophets in Ancient Israel* (Fortress, 2007), and one of the coeditors of *The Peoples' Bible* (Fortress, 2009) and *The Peoples' Companion to the Bible* (Fortress, 2010). She also has contributed essays and commentaries to *The Africana Bible* (Fortress, 2010), *Leviticus and Numbers* in the Texts @ Contexts series (Fortress, 2013), and the books of Nahum, Habakkuk, and Zephaniah in the Wisdom Commentary series (Liturgical Press, forthcoming). Among her research interests are feminist biblical studies, rabbinic studies, and issues in translation.

Bridgett A. Green is a doctoral candidate of New Testament and early Christianity at Vanderbilt University in Nashville, Tennessee. Focused on the narratives in the Gospel of Luke, her research analyzes the transformation of social dynamics in the gospel's polyvalent visions of the kingdom of God. Her methodological approaches include narrative, postcolonial, womanist, and feminist biblical criticisms. She has published articles in the Mark volume of the Feasting on the Gospels series (Westminster John Knox, 2014). She is a teaching elder in the Presbyterian Church (U.S.A.).

Sharon Jacob is Assistant Professor of New Testament at Philips Theological Seminary in Tulsa, Oklahoma. Sharon recently published her book entitled: *Reading Mary Alongside Indian Surrogate Mothers: Violent Love, Oppressive Liberation, and Infancy Narratives* (MacMillan, 2015). In this book Sharon takes a hard look at the growing industry of surrogacy in India and uses the stories of these real life mothers as a lens to reread the biblical figure of Mary in the infancy narratives with the hope that a more complex and nuanced interpretation of her motherhood can begin to emerge within the globalized context. In addition to teaching, Sharon regularly contributes essays to the Feminist Studies of Religion Blog. Her research interests include gender and sexuality studies, feminist theory, race and whiteness theory, and postcolonial theory.

Jennifer T. Kaalund is Assistant Professor of Religious Studies at Iona College in New Rochelle, New York. Her dissertation, "Dis/locating Diaspora: Reading Hebrews and 1 Peter with the African American Great Migration," explores the constructed and contested Christian-Jewish identities in Hebrews and 1 Peter through the lens of the "New Negro," a similarly vulnerable diasporic identity formed during the Great Migration in the early twentieth century. Her research interests include the Pauline corpus and the study of early Christianity in its Roman imperial context with a focus on womanist hermeneutics, postcolonial and cultural studies.

Vanessa Lovelace is Associate Professor of Hebrew Bible at the Interdenominational Theological Center in Atlanta, Georgia. Her publications include "This Woman's Son Shall Not Inherit with My Son: Towards a Womanist Politics of Belonging in the Sarah-Hagar Narratives" (*Journal* *of the Interdenominational Theological Center*, 2015), "Religious Leaders: Hebrew Bible" in *The [Oxford] Encyclopedia of the Bible and Gender Studies* (Oxford, 2014) and "Engaging Christian Identity, Chosenness (Oxford, 2014), and "Violence in a Predominately African American Theological Context" in *Reading in These Times* ([tentative]; Semeia Studies, forthcoming). Her research interests include womanist hermeneutics, feminist theory of gender and nation, and intersectional analysis of race/ethnicity, sexuality, gender and class.

Layli Maparyan is the Katherine Stone Kaufmann '67 Executive Director of the Wellesley Center for Women and holds a faculty appointment in Wellesley College's Department of Africana Studies in Wellesley, Massachusetts. She is the author of *The Womanist Reader* (Routledge , 2006) and *The Womanist Idea* (Routledge, 2012).

Katharine Doob Sakenfeld is the William Albright Eisenberger Professor of Old Testament Literature and Exegesis at Princeton Theological Seminary in Princeton, New Jersey, and former president of the Society of Biblical Literature. Her research focuses on biblical narratives concerning the premonarchical period and on feminist biblical hermeneutics. She served as a member of the NRSV translation committee and as a coeditor of the *Oxford Study Bible* and *Reading the Bible as Women: Perspectives from Africa, Asia, and Latin America* (Scholar's Press, 1997).

Love L. Sechrest is Associate Professor of New Testament at Fuller Theological Seminary in Pasadena, California. She is the author of *A Former Jew: Paul and the Dialectics of Race* (T&T Clark, 2009) and is currently working on a number of book projects. As cochair of the African American Biblical Hermeneutics section in the Society of Biblical Literature, she is a contributor and coeditor of a forthcoming volume on the hermeneutics of Martin Luther King, Jr. In addition, she is working on a monograph entitled *Negotiating Privilege: Race Relations and the New Testament* (Eerdmans, forthcoming), as well as an introduction to First Corinthians in the Phoenix Guides to the New Testament series (Sheffield Phoenix, forthcoming).

Mitzi J. Smith is Professor of New Testament and Early Christian Studies at Ashland Theological Seminary in Detroit, Michigan. She edited *I Found God in Me: A Womanist Biblical Hermeneutics Reader* (Cascade, 2015), and co-edited *Teaching All Nations: Interrogating the Matthean Great Commission* (Fortress, 2014). She also has contributed essays in edited volumes including *Onesimus Our Brother: Reading Religion, Race, and Slavery* (Fortress, 2012) and commentaries on the books of Ephesians and Philemon in *True to Our Native Land: An African American New Testament Commentary* (Fortress, 2007) and the twentieth anniversary edition of the *Women's Bible Commentary* (Westminster John Knox, 2012). Her research interests are womanist, African American, and postcolonial criticisms.

Shively T. J. Smith is Assistant Professor of New Testament at Wesley Theological Seminary in Washington, DC. In addition to her book, *Strangers to Family: Diaspora and 1 Peter's Invention of God's Household* (Baylor University Press, 2016), Smith has contributed to multiple writing projects and series, including the Feasting on the Gospels series (Westminster John Knox) and the Foundations for Learning series text *Writing Theologically* (Fortress). She is a regular contributor to various online commentary endeavors, including the Working Preacher Lectionary and the Odyssey Network's "On Scripture" project. Her research interests include: ancient Jewish-Christian concepts of diaspora and diversity, New Testament studies on Peter and the Synoptic Gospels, and African American and womanist biblical hermeneutics.

Althea Spencer-Miller is Assistant Professor of New Testament at Drew University in Madison, New Jersey. Her publications include coediting *Feminist New Testament Studies: Global and Future Perspectives* (Palgrave Macmillan, 2005), "Women and Christianity in the Caribbean: Living Past the Legacy" in *Women and Christianity* (ABC-CLIO, 2010), "Rethinking Orality for Biblical Studies" in *Postcolonialism and the Hebrew Bible* (Society of Biblical Literature, 2013), and "Creolizing Hermeneutics: A Caribbean Invitation" in *Islands, Islanders, and the Bible: RumInations* (SBL Press, 2015).

Emilie M. Townes is Dean of the Divinity School of Vanderbilt University in Nashville, Tennessee, and E. Rhodes and Leona B. Carpenter Professor of Womanist Ethics and Society, and is immediate past president of the Society for the Study of Black Religion. Her broad areas of expertise include Christian ethics, cultural theory and studies, postmodernism, and social postmodernism. Her publications include *Womanist Ethics and the Cultural Production of Evil* (Palgrave Macmillan, 2006), *Breaking the Fine Rain of Death: African American Health Care and A Womanist Ethic of*

Care (Continuum, 1998), and *In a Blaze of Glory: Womanist Spirituality as Social Witness* (Abingdon, 1995).

Marlene Underwood is an independent scholar who has studied at Drew University and the Interdenominational Theological Center. Her areas of interest include the interplay of empire, exile, economics, and ethnicity in Hebrew Bible texts and, in particular, the roles that women inhabit and negotiate in these arenas. Underwood's studies encompass female biblical characters from the Torah (Rebekah in Gen 24), the Prophets (the girls of Jabesh-Gilead and Shiloh in Judg 21), and the Kethuvim (Ruth in the book of Ruth). Moreover, she reads these characters' stories in light of the prohibitions against marrying foreign women in Ezra-Nehemiah, interrogating the anxieties that those prohibitions seem to be signifying about the overreach of empire, the trauma of exile/deportation, the control of (scarce?) resources, and the permeable boundaries of ethnicity and identity.

Index of Ancient Sources

Old Testament

Genesis
1:26–27	86
1:31	86
2–3	74–76, 78, 88, 89
2:7	75
2:16–17	76
2:22	75
2:23	75
3:16	5
3:24	76
16:6	67
18	178
22	256
24:67	63 n. 24
29:30	63 n. 24
29:32	63 n. 24
34:2	67 n. 34
34:3	63 n. 24
34:26	28
37–50 LXX	146
37:5–11	119
39:1 LXX	146
41:39–40 LXX	146
41:57–42:2	149

Exodus
1–3	54
1–24 LXX	146
1:11	67
1:13–14 LXX	146
2:9	209
4:22 LXX	149
5	198
15:20	255
18:8–9	277
19:4	124
22:22–23	313
23:6	313
32	178

Leviticus
18:18	80
21:7	230

Numbers
14	178
21:10–20	254
30	9, 21–47, 350, 351, 361
30:3–5	27
30:8	27
30:9	27
30:11–15	27
30:16	27
33	254 n. 16
33:5–49	254
33:10–20	254 n. 16

Deuteronomy
6:5	86
21:15–17	251
21:18–21	314, 317
23:3	64 n. 27
23:13–21	26–27 n. 8
24:1–3	28 n. 12
24:2	27 n. 12
28	169
28:35	169
30:3	170

ANCIENT SOURCES INDEX

Deuteronomy (cont.)
33:1	55 n. 14

Joshua
2	n. 169
2:1	28, 250
6:22	250
14:6	55 n. 14

Judges
1:11–12:7	365
2:11	247, 248
3:1–6	63
3:7	247 n. 247
3:12	247
4:1	247
5:23	52 n. 9
6:1	247
8:28	52
9:22	52 n. 10
10:6	247
10:7–9	248
10:16	248
10:18	253
11	239
11:1	240, 243, 248
11:1–12:7	244
11:2	250, 251
11:3	252
11:5–6	253
11:7	253
11:8	253
11:9	253
11:11	253
11:12	254 n. 16
11:12–24	254
11:27	254
11:29	254
11:30–31	254
11:31	254 n. 17
11:32–35	255
11:34	255
11:35	255
11:36	244, 256
11:37	244, 256
12:7	240, 243
12:9	52
12:12	253
13–16	50 n. 7
13:1	247
13:3	54
13:10	54
13:22–23	55
14:1	58
14:3	58
14:4	61
14:5	58
14:7	58
14:8	58
14:15	59
14:17	59
14:18	60
16:1	61, 71, 250
16:4	49
16:4–31	50 n. 7
16:5	67, 69
16:7	68, 69
16:8	69
16:9	69
16:11	69
16:13–16	69
16:17	70
16:19	70
16:21	70
16:21–30	70
17:6	53
18:1	53
19	52
19:1	53
20:5	67 n. 34
20:48	52
21:10–14	52
21:20–13	52
21:23	53

1 Samuel
1:5	63 n. 24
2:27	55 n. 14
10:18	227
12:11	277

ANCIENT SOURCES INDEX

14	256	Nehemiah	
15:30	315	12:24	55 n. 14
18:3	63 n. 24	12:36	55 n. 14
18:6–7	255		
18:17–19:17	60 n. 20	Esther	
20:17	63 n. 24	2:17	63 n. 24
25:44	60 n. 20	Job	
		1:1	166, 168, 173
2 Samuel		1:2	180
1:26	63 n. 24	1:6	173
3:13–16	60 n. 20	1:6–7	173
13:1	63 n. 24	1:7	173
13:14	67 n. 34	1:8	166, 168, 173, 180
13:20	88	1:9–10	171
8:12–14 LXX	154	1:9–11	173
		1:10	168
1 Kings		1:11	169, 169 n. 7, 174
3:12 LXX	154	1:12	173
3:16	250	1:13–15	168
11	154	1:14–17	174
11:1	63 n. 24	1:14–19	173
11:17 LXX	154	1:15–17	174
11:18 LXX	154	1:16	168
11:19 LXX	154	1:17	168
11:20 LXX	154	1:18–19	174
11:26–27 LXX	154 n. 2	1:18–22	168
11:40 LXX	154 n. 2	1:20	174
12:22	55 n. 14	1:21	174
13:1	55 n. 14	2:1–2	168
18:3–4	126	2:3	169, 170–71, 173–74, 180
18:13	126	2:4–5	173
21:23–24	126	2:5	169, 174
		2:6	166, 169, 173
2 Kings	169 n. 9	2:7	170, 171, 174
		2:9	169, 169 n. 7
1 Chronicles		2:9–10	169
4:3	53	2:11	174
		2:12	174
2 Chronicles		3	173
11:21	63 n. 24	3–37	169
		5:17	175
Ezra		6:8	178
3:2	55 n. 14	7:5	171
		7:16	174

Job (cont.)		2:8–17	78
7:19	174	2:10–13	76
9:19–24	176, 178	2:16	80
9:32–33	176, 178	3	79
10:2	175, 178	3:1–4	73
10:20	174	3:1–5	78, 79
13:23	175	3:4	79
16	178	4:10	85
19:13–19	171	5:1	85
25	175	5:2–6	85
31:10	65 n. 31	5:6–7	79
38:1	175	6:3	80
38:21	175	8:2	85
39:1	175		
40:3–4	175	Isaiah	
42:3	175	1	312 n. 2
42:6	176	1:1	316
42:7	176	1:2	316, 356
42:8	170, 176, 176 n. 10	1:3	316
42:10	170	1:4	317, 356
42:11	174, 176, 180	1:5	317, 323
42:12	176, 180	1:8	319
42:13	176	1:17	311
42:13–15	180	1:21	119 n. 7, 319
42:14	176 n. 11	1:23	311
42:15	176 n. 11	3	318
42:16	176	3:2–4	318
42:17	176	3:4	318, 356
		3:5	318
Psalms		3:12	315, 318
8:2	313	3:16–24	319
127:3	311	7:3	314
139:5 LXX	277	7:10–17	314
		7:16	315
Proverbs		8:3	314
7	78	11	312 n. 5
19:13	317	11:8	315
29:15	317	54:1–8	119 n. 7
		54:11	119 n. 7
Ecclesiastes		61:1	119 n. 7
2:8	342 n. 3	65–66	312 n. 2
Song of Songs		Jeremiah	
1:2	85	2:23–25	320
1:13	342 n. 3	2:33	320

13:10	320	1:20	153
13:14	321	1:22–32	152
30:6	320	1:23	156
32:16 LXX	281	2	141, 148, 151, 152, 156, 157, 159
33 LXX	154	2:1	152
33:21 LXX	153	2:3	153
33:21–23 LXX	153	2:6	153
33:22–23 LXX	153	2:7–8	153
35:4	55 n. 14	2:13	143, 153
36:26 LXX	281	2:13–15	150
44:7	320	2:13–23	139, 140, 141, 143, 144, 150, 151, 152, 159
48:17 LXX	154 n. 2		
50:4–7 LXX	154 n. 2	2:15	150, 152
		2:16	143, 153
Lamentations		2:22–23	156
2:11	313	15:21–28	95, 98
		18:20	156
Ezekiel		19:9	38
16	119 n. 7	20:28	153
16:8–14	119 n. 7	28:20	156
23:44	250		
		Mark	
Hosea		1:21–28	107
1–2	119 n. 7	1:24	102
1:2	165	1:34	107
2:2–23	165	1:40–41	102
2:3 (MT 2:5)	165 n. 1, 168	2:5	106
2:5	119 n. 7, 165	3:7–8	100
3:1	165	3:15	107
11:1	150	3:19–20	102
		3:21	102
Amos		3:21–28	107
4:1–13	319	3:22	107
4:1	319	3:23	102, 107
		3:26	102
Micah		3:30	102
4:10	320	5:7	102
		5:39	106
Malachi		6:13	107
3:1	277	7:1–23	101
		7:14–23	101
New Testament		7:24	100
		7:25–30	95, 98
Matthew		7:27	103, 106
1:18	152	7:28	103

Mark (cont.)		John	
7:29	107	2:3–5	109
9:14–29	102	10:20	281
9:17–18	107	14:12	333, 334, 335, 336
9:25	107	14:12–14	331, 333
9:36–37	106	14:13–14	335
9:38–41	107		
10–24	106	Acts	
10:13–16	106	1:7	265
10:28	106	2:10	143–44 n. 1
12:18–21	106	2:18	284
13:12	106	7:9–12	144 n. 1
15:21–28	95, 98	7:15	144 n. 1
		7:17–18	144 n. 1
Luke		7:34	144 n. 1
1:46–56	284	7:36	144 n. 1
1:51–52	291	7:39–40	144 n. 1
4:16–19	301	8:1	278
4:18	284	8:26–39	190
4:18–19	291	10:28	101
5:13	302	12	256, 275 n. 11, 279, 284, 356, 363
6:19	302	12:1–3	279
7:14	302	12:1–10	277
7:39	302	12:1–19	265 n. 2
8:44–47	302	12:11–17	276
9:49–50	107	12:12	277
12:42–48	270	12:13	279
18	363	12:14	280
18:9	303	12:15	281, 283
18:9–14	299	12:16–17	283
18:14	306	12:23	278
18:15	343	13:17	144 n. 1
18:15–17	291, 291, 293, 300–301, 302 n. 8, 304, 307, 343	15	n. 256, 275, 275 n. 12
		15:7	265 n. 2
18:16	343	15:37	278
18:16–17	299, 305	16:1	100
18:17	305 n. 11, 343	16:16	283
18:18–30	299, 304	26:24–25	281
22:54–62	343 n. 4		
22:55	343 n. 4	Romans	
22:56	283	1:26–27	80
22:57	343 n. 4		
24:41	280	1 Corinthians	
		8	127
		14:34	77

Galatians		3:1	117
4:26	119 n. 7	3:4	117
		3:4–5	119, 119 n. 8
Ephesians		3:6	119 n. 8
4:11	337	3:12	117
4:11–16	331, 333, 335–36	3:13	119 n. 8, 120
5:22–24	337	3:18	120
5:32	119 n. 7	3:22	119 n. 8
6:5–8	270	4	120
		4:4	119
Philippians		4:6	117
3:14	59 n. 19	4:8–11	124
		4:11	119
Colossians		5:5	340
3:22–25	270	5:5–6	116
		5:6	117, 118
1 Thessalonians		5:6–14	118
2:7	273	5:9	119, 120, 124
		5:12	124
1 Timothy		6	117
2:9–15	41	6:9–11	117
6:1–2	270	6:11	119
		7:4–8	117
James		7:9	119
5:11	168	7:9–10	117
		7:9–14	119
1 Peter		7:14	120
2:18–25	270	7:18	118
		10:1	120
Revelation		11	125
1:5	120	11:1–2	117
1:13–16	116	11:3	125
1:16	120	11:3–12	117
2	115	11:7	125
2–3	116, 119 n. 8	11:9	125
2:1	120	12	115, 118–19, 121, 121 n. 9, 122, 125, 210, 227–29, 341–42, 354
2:6	123		
2:7	119 n. 8, 123	12:1–6	121 n. 9
2:11	119 n. 8	12:2	121
2:14–15	123	12:3	117, 125
2:17	119 n. 8, 123	12:5	121, n. 229
2:18–29	122	12:6	121, 121 n. 9, n. 122–23
2:20	121, 122, 123	12:7	123
2:20–23	115, 127	12:7–9	124
2:29	119 n. 8	12:7–12	121 n. 9

Revelation (cont.)

12:10	124, 125
12:10–11	121, 124, 125
12:10–12	124
12:11	124
12:13–14	121, 121 n. 9
12:13–16	122
12:13–17	122 n. 9
12:14	121
12:14–15	123
12:15–16	122
13:1	117
13:2	118
13:3	118
13:14	117
14:1–4	117
14:3–4	118
14:4	120
14:14	119
16:7	117
17	126
17:2	121
17:3	124
17:4	121
17:16	126
18:13	274
19	120
19:4	118
19:7	121
19:7–8	228 n. 31
19:7–9	117
19:8	120
19:13	120
19:14	119
21	120
21:2	118 n. 6
21:9–10	118 n. 6
21:11	120
21:23	120

Deuterocanonical Works

Wisdom of Solomon

14:28	281

4 Maccabees

8:5	281
16:73	281

2 Esdras

10:7	119 n. 7

Ancient Jewish Writers

Philo, *Embassy*

166	147

Philo, *Flaccus*

19	147
41	147
53–54	147

Philo, *On the Contemplative Life*

17	200 n.

Josephus, *Bellum judaicum*

7.410	154 n. 2

Josephus, *Jewish Antiquities*

12.3–10	156
12.387–388	154 n. 2
14.21	154 n. 2
15.42–49	154 n. 2
20.101	149

Rabbinic Literature

b. Baba Batra

91a	55, 56 n. 15

b. Berakot

61a, b	56 n. 17

b. 'Eruvin

18b	56 n. 17

b. Nazir

4a	64

ANCIENT SOURCES INDEX

b. Šabbat
    104b   155 n. 3

b. Sanhedrin
    107b   155 n. 3

Genesis Rabbah
    45:7   56 n. 17

Numbers Rabbah
    10:5   55

New Testament Apocrypha and Pseudepigrapha

Acts of Paul   191, 192, 194 n. 13, 195

Acts of Peter   191, 192

Gospel of Mary   200 n. 17

Classical and Ancient Christian Writings

Achilles Tatius, *Leucippe et Clitophon*
    7.10.4   272

Dio Cassius, *Historiae romanae*
    67.4.3   117 n. 5

Juvenal, *Satires*   272
    6.475–476   273
    6.480–484   273
    6.490–493   273

Origen, *Contra Celsum*
    1.28.38   155 n. 3

Pliny the Younger, *Epistulae ad Trajanum*
    112   280

Pseudo-Aristotle, *Physiognomonica*
    3.80b 5–12   271

Rufinus, *Eusebii Historia ecclesiastica a Rufino translata et continuata*
    1.9   194

Salvian, *The Governance of God*
    4.3.13   272

Strabo, *Geographica*
    17.1.10   145
    17.1.52–53   145
    17.2.4–5   145
    18.1.12–13   145

Varro, *De lingua latina*
    8.9.21   275

Other Sacred Sources

Acts of Abuna Gabra Manfas Qeddus   189

Gadla Hawaryat   194

Gadla Serabamon   192, 195

Linga Purana
    1.106.20–28   223

Mashafa Genzat   89

Tweed MS150   195, 201, 202

Odu   198 n. 16, 199

Zohar
    A7a   56 n. 17

Subject Index

abuse, 14, 77, 81, 109, 131, 167 n. 4, 172, 181 n. 14, 285, 321, 353, 366
   child, 301, 344
   cycle of, 12, 166, 172
   divine, 166, 175, 176, 176 n. 10, 177
   generational, 179
   intimate, 173
   sexual, 130, 275 n. 11, 276
   survivors of, 166, 178, 179
   victims of, 167, 171, 180, 182
activism, 96, 158, 197
   nineteenth-century black women, 198, 293, 296 n. 4, 305, 360
   political, 9 141, 152, 332
   social, 3 n. 2, 9
advocacy, 10, 297, 357
   child, children, 296
   HIV and AIDS, 74
African American church, 10, 88, 180. *See also* black church
agency, 53, 59, 63, 96, 121, 122, 131, 133, 362
   black women's, 96, 97, 114–15 n. 2, 345
   children's lack of, 322, 323
   feminine, 115, 123, 135
   Jezebel's, 128, 129, 132
   Job's, 12
   Sun Woman's, 118–21, 124, 125, 128–29, 132
   women's, 110, 114
Anderson, Tanisha, 109
androcentric, 38, 50, 198
Angelou, Maya, 96, 98, 276
autonomy, 33, 152, 210, 213, 228, 304

Barnett, Ida B. Wells, 35, 109, 360
Beyoncé, 9, 35
bias(es), 106, 109, 140, 151, 191, 199
   gender, 29, 100
   male, 103
   racial/ethnic, 100, 305
Bible, 29, 38, 68, 74, 197, 198, 203, 271, 338, 360, 361
   African American women's relationship to, 3 n. 2, 4, 9, 140, 151, 157–59, 197, 312, 353
biblical criticism, 4, 5, 7 n. 8, 322, 346
bibliophile(s), 187, 188, 197, 203
black church(es), 42, 73–75, 77, 80, 81, 196, 351, 362. *See also* African American church
black liberationist hermeneutic, 294
Black Lives Matter, 11, 103
   founders of, 11 n. 9, 114 n. 1
   hashtag, 9, 10, 11, 55, 99, 114, 133–134, 285, 345, 352, 356
   Martin, Trayvon, 10, 98, 114 n. 1, 242, 242 n. 4, 258
   movement, 9, 10, 11, 55, 114, 345, 352
Bland, Sandra, 11, 95, 99, 109, 110, 113, 351, 363
Boyd, Rekia, 109
Brennan, Maeve, 36
Carey, Miriam, 109
Cannon, Katie G., 3, 3 n. 2, 23–24, 42, 196, 200–201, 268, 293
   structured academic amnesia, 189, 200–201, 203, 364
Chapman, Kindra, 109, 110

SUBJECT INDEX

Charleston massacre, 113
Chisholm, Shirley, 96, 296
civil rights, 25, 26 n. 7, 133, 296
   activists, 115 n. 4
   movement, 113–14, 133–34, 296, 305
   protest, 113
Clark, Septima, 109
Clayton, Mayme, 13, 188, 197, 198, 203
Coates, Ta-Nehisi, 96, 107
colonialism, 220, 226 n. 28, 364
colonization, colonized, 13, 57, 101–4, 106, 209, 210 n. 1, 217–18, 221, 225–26, 234, 266, 305
darkness, 14, 99, 278, 281, 286
   intersectional, 265–66, 268, 283 n. 36
   reading, 99, 267, 273, 276, 285, 347
   Wimbush, Vincent, 99, 265, 267
Davis, Angela, 96
Debre Libanos Monastery, 190, 192, 195, 202
Delille, Henriette, 37, 38
diasporic communities, 147, 344
   Africana, 188–89, 191, 197, 339
   black, 5
   Jewish, 148, 156
disenfranchisement, 96–97, 296, 298
Douglas, Kelly Brown, 3, 74, 77, 79, 81, 86–87, 157, 196
empire, 209–10, 210–211 n. 1, 213, 217
   Axumite, 195
   British, 218–19, 223, 227, 232
   Roman, 127, 155–56, 195
Ethiopia, Ethiopic, 13, 188–89, 190–94, 194 n. 12, 195
ethnic/ethnicity, 8, 15, 179, 212, 341, 352
family values, 13, 85, 240, 246, 246 n. 8, 257. *See also* Judeo-Christian values
   traditional, 240, 243, 253, 257, 365
Fanon, Frantz, 96, 102, 103
feminist, 2, 6 n. 7, 12, 25–26 n. 6, 79, 141, 244, 296
   biblical criticism, 4, 7 n. 8
   black, 2, 8, 25
   theological discourse, 3
Gay, Roxane, 24 n. 5, 41

gender, 22 n. 2, 26 n. 7, 27, 49–50, 74, 273, 294
   construction(s) of, 78–89, 278, 304
   inequities, 79, 88
Gilkes, Cheryl Townsend, ix, 3, 197
Grant, Jacquelyn, 3, 3 n. 2, 196
Gray, Freddie, 110, 113
Hamer, Fannie Lou, 9, 11, 109, 291, 294, 295, 295 n. 2, 295 n. 3, 297–299
heteronormativity, 22, 25, 33
heterosexual, 26 n. 8, 30, 33–34, 73–74, 77, 79, 81, 84, 86, 257
Hill, Lauryn, 53
hip-hop, 49, 50, 50 n. 6, 53, 65, 65 n. 29, 67 n. 35
Holiday, Billie, 36
homophobic, 50 n. 6
hooks, bell, 96, 97, 106
hypermasculine, 49
hypersexualized, 68, 130–31, 242, 363
immigrant, 147, 158, 286. *See also* migrant
injustice, 15, 96, 133, 176, 202, 234, 292, 300, 306–7
   gender, 97, 306
   class, 298, 306
interdisciplinary, 7, 15, 360, 366
intersectionality, 37, 268, 293, 298, 352. *See also* oppression
   definition of, 21–22, 22 n. 2
   gender, class, race, 3, 265, 292–93
   gender, race, class, sexuality, 21–22, 240 n. 2, 359
   gender, race, ethnicity, 370
   gender, race, nation, 234
   race and religion, 36
Jay-Z, 53, 65 n. 32
Jeantel, Rachel, 98
Judeo-Christian values, 240, 245, 245 n. 7, 246. *See also* family values
King, Martin Luther, Jr., 114
Knowles, Solange, 42
Latifah, Queen, 53
Lee, Jarena, 3 n. 2
LGBTQ, 33, 80, 83, 267 n. 3

Lorde, Audre, 25–26 n. 6, 87, 89, 96, 108, 167, 267, 267 n. 3, 268, 269
Lyte, MC, 53
mammy, mammies, 115, 129, 129–30 n. 1, 131, 215–16, 242, 354, 365
marginalized, 9, 14, 103, 131, 133, 135, 212, 257
Martin, Clarice J., ix, 1, 3 n. 3–6, 158, 197–98, 341, 353
masculine, masculinity, 34, 88
    gay men, 34
    identity, 34
    studies, 10, 21
masculinized, 129, 131
McKenna, Natasha, 99, 99 n. 2, 109
midrash, 61 n. 22
migrant, migration 158, 268, 269, 275, 278, 284 n. 37, 341
Minaj, Nicki, 49, 50 n. 4, 53
misogynist, 50 n. 6, 128, 135, 179
motherhood, 13, 216, 234
    ideologies of, 216, 234, 302, 344
    single black mothers, 32, 34, 240, 242, 246, 355, 365
    surrogate, 13, 215–16, 230
oppression, 100, 104, 130, 140, 158, 209–10 n. 1, 211, 212 n. 4, 265–66. *See also* intersectionality
    interlocking 8, 97, 101, 240 n. 2
    microaggressions, 8
Other, the, 132, 218, 220–22, 226, 233, 235, 361
patriarchal, 26 n. 7, 317, 323, 357
    norms, 81, 361
    society, 63, 98, 105
    systems, 50, 97
    values, 83, 132
police, 142
    Ferguson, 114, 134 n. 14, 241
    practices, 241, 322
    protests against, 114
    stops, 95, 363
    talking back to, 95
    violence against African Americans, 99 n. 2, 110, 113, 285, 322

politics of respectability, respectability politics, 11, 41, 114, 133, 134, 247
postmodern theory, 37
power dynamics, 8, 15, 240 n. 2, 291, 292, 296, 299, 301, 303
privilege, 35, 198, 268, 285, 291–92
    celibacy, 41
    heterosexual, 81
    male, 77
    white, 29, 41
procreation, 74, 76, 82–86, 88–89
queer theory, 10, 21, 83, 363
racialized, 8, 98, 103, 122, 130 n. 11, 242 n. 4, 243, 301, 305, 344
rape(d), 52, 53, 365
resistance, 11, 37, 95, 97–98, 102, 105, 133, 178, 266, 340, 340 n. 1, 341
retributive justice, 12, 169, 171
Rice, Tamir, 110, 113
Rihanna, 9, 70
sass, 11, 95, 97, 98, 108. *See also* police: talking back to
    politics of, 103
Schomburg, Arthur, 13, 187
Scott, Walter, 113
sexism, 3, 26 n. 7, 29, 96–97, 100–101, 240, 296, 298
sexual, 22 n. 3, 31 n. 20
    expression, 22, 80, 85, 88–89
    independence, 9
    orientation, 11, 81, 86, 167 n. 4,
sexuality, 22, 39–41, 86
sisterhood, 140, 212
Shakur, Assata, 9, 12 n. 10, 140, 141, 143, 352
Shakur, Tupac, 53
Shange, Ntozake, 65
silence(d), 23, 77, 96, 106, 108, 229, 285, 352
slavery, 38, 96, 217
    ancient, 270, 274, 356
    antebellum, 13, 97, 209, 213, 216, 270
    child, 268
    New Testament, 266
Smalls, Biggie, 53

SUBJECT INDEX

Smith, Yvette, 109
social justice, 10, 15, 306
sources, 9, 23, 158, 196
    canonical, 12, 198
    extrabiblical, 16, 188, 199, 364
sources (cont.)
    living, 13, 198, 204
socioeconomic, 13, 41, 123–24, 167, 215
spirituality, 34, 86, 179, 180
stereotypes, 33, 37, 272
    Asia Pacific American women, 115, 131
    black women, 22, 42, 79, 167
    gender, 122, 125, 129, 129–30 n. 10, 232, 249
    hyper-sexual, 26, 363
    Latina/Latino women, 115, 131
    racist, 79
    sexual, 37
Stewart, Maria, 3 n. 2
subaltern, 222 n. 18, 267, 276
subordination, 172, 364
    female, 76–78
subversion, subversive, 50, 95, 98, 105, 210, 365
survival, survive, 2, 26, 96, 99, 108, 178–80, 196, 211, 213, 219, 222, 230, 267, 296
Townes, Emilie M., 4 n. 5, 293
trafficked, trafficking, 268, 274–75, 278–79, 281
trauma, 14, 179–80, 265, 267–69, 269 n. 6, 276, 278, 285–86, 347
Truth, Sojourner, 3 n. 2, 96, 103, 360
Tubman, Harriet, 96
Tweed, André Reynolds, 13, 188, 188 n. 4, 189, 190 n. 6, 192, 195, 340.
violence, 97, 99–100, 178, 317
    against blacks, 11, 134
    against women, 59, 71, 77, 165, 182, 353
    cultural, 179, 323
    domestic, 166–67, 17–73, 178–79
    gender-based, 77
    intimate partner 77, 167,

voice, 3, 107, 140, 158, 203, 211, 266, 269, 276, 285, 360, 361
Walker, Alice, 1–2, 2 n. 1, 23, 24, 51, 96, 167, 203, 211, 266, 296, 336, 351, 359
Weems, Renita J., ix, 1, 4, 4 n. 4, 5, 140, 157–58, 165, 167, 182, 198, 239, 244, 312–13, 317, 322, 324
Wesley, Dorothy Porter, 13, 187 n. 1, 197, 198, 203
West, Traci C., 8, 25, 178
wet nurse(s), 209, 209–10 n. 1, 210, 210 n. 2, 213, 215, 216, 222 n. 18, 230, 233–34, 354
white supremacist, supremacy, 79, 86, 294, 296, 298
Williams, Delores, 3, 3 n. 2, 196, 212 n. 4, 230
Williams, Serena, 37 n. 28
womanish, 2, 51, 51 n. 8, 96, 265–66, 281, 351
womanism, 2 n. 1, 8, 21, 23, 96, 110, 360
womanist, 1, 3, 6, 352, 359
    biblical hermeneutics, 5, 10, 189, 212, 234, 265, 312
    biblical interpretation, 4–5, 7, 51, 140, 158, 166, 312, 349
    definitions of, 2, 51 n. 8, 196, 211, 265
    interpretation, 157, 159, 313, 322, 353–54
    theory, method, 23, 37, 41, 196, 235, 278
women of color, 5, 35, 101, 131
    exclusion from feminist inquiry and analysis, 25, 35
    exclusion from full entitlements, 29–30
Yo-Yo, 53

www.ingramcontent.com/pod-product-compliance
Lightning Source LLC
Chambersburg PA
CBHW031542300426
44111CB00006BA/142